LOVE AGAINST SUBSTITUTION

Cultural Memory
in
the
Present

Hent de Vries, Editor

LOVE AGAINST SUBSTITUTION

*Seventeenth-Century English Literature
and the Meaning of Marriage*

Eric B. Song

STANFORD UNIVERSITY PRESS
STANFORD, CALIFORNIA

STANFORD UNIVERSITY PRESS
Stanford, California

©2022 Eric B. Song. All rights reserved.

No part of this book may be reproduced or transmitted in any form or by any means, electronic or mechanical, including photocopying and recording, or in any information storage or retrieval system without the prior written permission of Stanford University Press.

Printed in the United States of America on acid-free, archival-quality paper

Library of Congress Cataloging-in-Publication Data
ISBN 9781503630444 (cloth)
ISBN 9781503631403 (paper)
ISBN 9781503631410 (ebook)
Library of Congress Control Number 2021038420
CIP data available upon request

Cover art: from Jan van Eyck, *The Arnolfini Portrait*, 1434. Wikimedia Commons
Cover design: Rob Ehle
Typeset by Newgen North America in 11/13.5 Adobe Garamond Pro

These be the Christian husbands.

—SHYLOCK,
The Merchant of Venice

Contents

Acknowledgments	ix
Introduction	1
1 Beguiling Love in the *Amoretti* and the 1590 *Faerie Queene*	27
2 Jealousy against Substitution in *Othello* and *The Winter's Tale*	61
3 *Gondibert* and the Biopolitics of Marriage	97
4 Love against Succession in *Paradise Lost*	136
5 Lucy Hutchinson and the Imperfection of Christian Marriage	178
6 From Remarriage to Tragic Fungibility: Behn's *The Forc'd Marriage* and *Oroonoko*	220
Epilogue	256
Notes	267
Index	311

Acknowledgments

Yes, I got married in the middle of working on this book about marriage. This would be embarrassing except that I married someone unreceptive to the mystifications of marriage that I describe in this book. I feel free to begin by expressing my unflinching gratitude to Sara Bryant.

I have accrued many intellectual debts within the community of early modern scholars. I want to thank Brooke Conti, Alice Dailey, John Garrison, Matthew Kozusko, Seth Lobis, Nichole Miller, Shannon Miller, Marissa Nicosia, Kristen Poole, Katherine Rowe, and Lauren Shohet. I express special gratitude to two early modernists. I have known Andrea Stevens since our days in graduate school; I was first hired as an assistant professor alongside Andrea Walkden. Both have read portions of this book and, more importantly, have remained supportive friends. I also want to thank two medievalist friends, Jamie Taylor and Elly Truitt. Early portions of my work on this book were circulated at the Early Modern Workshop at the University of Illinois, at the Northeast Milton Seminar, and at the Medieval-Renaissance seminar at the University of Pennsylvania. I am grateful to Feisal Mohamed, David Quint, John Rogers, Zachary Lesser, Melissa Sanchez, and all the participants who offered valuable suggestions at these different venues. In 2013 I participated in a seminar led by Sarah Beckwith called Versions of *The Winter's Tale*, as part of the National Humanities Center Summer Institute on Literary Studies. Portions of this work, especially the epilogue, bear the imprints of that experience.

At Swarthmore College, my home institution, two Lang Faculty Fellowships have allowed me to finish this book sooner rather than later. My department has been a site of collegiality and camaraderie. I thank Nat Anderson, Betsy Bolton, Anthony Foy, Nora Johnson, Gina Patnaik, Peter Schmidt, and Craig Williamson. I am especially grateful to Rachel Buurma, Lara Cohen, and Bakirathi Mani for their friendship and frequent exchanges of ideas. I am also very thankful for the continued friendship of Amy Wan, my former colleague from Queens College, CUNY.

It has been a genuine pleasure working with Erica Wetter, Faith Wilson Stein, and Susan Karani at Stanford University Press. I thank them for supporting my project and guiding it to completion. Jennifer Rappaport copyedited the manuscript with great care; the errors that remain are my own. Devin Singh, whom I have known since we were undergraduates at Pomona College, encouraged me to submit my book to the Cultural Memory in the Present series. I thank the series editor Hent de Vries for supporting my work.

Earlier versions of material found in chapters 4 and 6 were published as an article in *ELH* 82, no. 3 (Fall 2013): 681–714, titled "Love against Substitution: John Milton, Aphra Behn, and the Political Theology of Conjugal Narratives," © 2013 Johns Hopkins University Press. An earlier version of material found in chapter 2 was published as an article in *English Literary Renaissance* 51, no. 1 (Winter 2021): 96–120, titled "Othello and the Political Theology of Jealousy," © 2021 University of Chicago Press. I thank both journals for their permission to reprint these materials.

Finally, I express my gratitude to my parents, Allan Hwa Sik and Kwang Ok Song.

Introduction

Even after being ordained in the Church of England in 1615, John Donne was uneasy with the existence of multiple Christian denominations. His *Holy Sonnet* 18 begins with a request: "Show me deare Christ, thy Spouse, so bright and cleare."[1] This opening line relies on a familiar biblical metaphor, and Donne's readers would have immediately understood that Christ's spouse is the church. Yet confusion arises in the poem because the speaker does not know where, exactly, the true church should be found—in Catholic Rome, in Protestant Germany, or somewhere else. In the course of the sonnet, the speaker's bafflement about the divisions within Christianity turns into the basis of a surprising, even scandalous, conclusion. The poem ends by proposing to Christ that his wife

> is most trew, and pleasing to thee, then
> When She'is embrac'd and open to most Men.[2]

The final couplet asks Christ to take pleasure in his wife's promiscuity. In expressing a longing for Christian inclusivity, Donne makes exclusively monogamous marriage feel incompatible with the higher meaning of Christ's love.

The conclusion of Donne's sonnet might be surprising, but it manipulates a confusion that already exists in the New Testament. In the Epistle to the Ephesians, Paul redefines biblical marriage around Christ's love. Yet he eventually resorts to the language of mystery to acknowledge the unresolved problems within his redefinition:

> Wives, submit yourselves unto your own husbands, as unto the Lord. For the husband is the head of the wife, even as Christ is the head of the church: and he is the saviour of the body. Therefore as the church is subject

unto Christ, so let the wives be to their own husbands in every thing. Husbands, love your wives, even as Christ also loved the church, and gave himself for it; that he might sanctify and cleanse it with the washing of water by the word, that he might present it to himself a glorious church, not having spot, or wrinkle, or any such thing; but that it should be holy and without blemish. So ought men to love their wives as their own bodies. He that loveth his wife loveth himself. For no man ever yet hated his own flesh; but nourisheth and cherisheth it, even as the Lord the church: for we are members of his body, of his flesh, and of his bones. For this cause shall a man leave his father and mother, and shall be joined unto his wife, and they two shall be one flesh. This is a great mystery: but I speak concerning Christ and the church. (Eph. 5:22–32)[3]

Paul bases the meaning of Christian marriage on an unstable simile. Wives are instructed to revere their imperfect husbands as if they were like Christ. Gender is supposed to be the decisive factor that dictates which spouse should be regarded as Christlike. Yet if Paul teaches clear-cut gender hierarchy within individual marriages, he crisscrosses gender identifications when he makes marriage the sign of a higher, collective truth. Husbands and wives alike take part in Christ's corporate body. The same husbands who are supposed to be regarded as Christlike by their wives should also understand themselves to be members of Christ's bride. This confusion may seem like the coincidental effect of a metaphor.[4] Yet as scholars such as Melissa Sanchez and Will Stockton have recently shown, the instability of Pauline teaching about marriage has a wide-ranging effect on early modern understandings of love and desire.[5]

In this book, I show that seventeenth-century English writings test the tenability of Pauline teaching by elevating a love that remains stubbornly fixed between two individuals. This kind of love threatens to short-circuit the dynamism between personal experience and corporate truth that Paul describes as a central feature of Christian marriage. Gender asymmetry matters for all the writings that I consider. Yet they do not straightforwardly describe male subjects seeking affirmation from female objects, or husbands being revered as Christlike by their wives. Instead, these writings describe husbands and wives (or would-be husbands and would-be wives) who mutually deem each other to be unique, to the point of being irreplaceable. This book proposes that a recognizably heteronormative pattern of individuality, gender asymmetry, and exclusivity takes hold in the literary imagination partly as a response to the incoherence of biblical teaching. A fixation on the personal register of love might seem to be entirely opposed to the longing expressed in *Holy Sonnet* 18. Donne questions whether fidelity within marriage is appropriate as an expression of Christ's inclusive love. Yet at the same time, the scandalous suggestion at the end of the sonnet restricts gender identification more narrowly than Paul does in redefining biblical marriage. The poem opens with a generically male speaker's desiring to see Christ's implicitly female spouse; it ends with the proposition that Christ's wife should be available to all men. This conclusion does make an erotically charged identification between Christ and Christian men possible by inviting Christ to take pleasure in being a cuckold. Yet this identification is triangulated through a heterosexual embrace at the metaphorical register.[6] Even while unsettling the norm of monogamy, Donne straightens crisscrossed patterns of gender identification. The speaker never has to identify himself as a member of Christ's wife but, instead, identifies himself as one of the men who seek to embrace her within Christ's view.

When it comes to the lived reality of marriage, Donne's biography and religious poetry make clear that a deeply personal love can be both a vehicle for and an obstacle to Christian devotion. By all accounts, Donne deemed his own wife to be singular in his affections. His insistence on marrying Anne More secretly in 1601 (which cost him his preferment and even led to brief imprisonment) is a key part of the biographical lore of Donne's transformation from a philanderer to a divine. This lore includes Izaak Walton's report that Donne, after his wife's death in 1617, vowed to their children never to remarry.[7] Whatever the exact nature of this vow might have been, Donne would never replace his late wife in remarriage. Yet in his religious poetry, he grapples with the way that fixed husbandly devotion can be incompatible with Christian devotion. He writes openly about the way that the intensity of his love for his wife, even after her death, competes with his love for God.

Donne struggles with problems that might be familiar to us in some form even if we do not share his religious outlook. Throughout this book, I take it as axiomatic that love requires some degree of belief—however impressionistic or nebulous—in a beloved person's singularity. Individual uniqueness is an enabling fiction of love. I also take it as axiomatic that we are replaceable. If this were not true, no human institution would outlast a single generation. We might find ourselves being replaced in the workplace, in the classroom, or in our families and other intimate relationships. In some of these roles or offices, being replaced can be a straightforward matter; in others, the notion of our replaceability is difficult to accept or even unbearable. Being loved saves us from feeling that we are simply or entirely replaceable. This book focuses specifically on the alignment of Christian marriage and the loving affirmation of individuality. This alignment is historically contingent, and—for reasons that I describe in the next section—it becomes increasingly prominent in seventeenth-century English writings.

The alignment of love, unique personhood, and Christian marriage generates friction rather than coherence. This book turns to seventeenth-century writings about marriage to study the affective clash between individual love and the idea that one person can take the place of another. I use the term *substitution* to refer to the idea of human replaceability and different forms of replacement. These forms are disparate in nature, but marriage is called on to accommodate them within a tenable experience of love. One form of substitution is reproductive and intergenerational. In the Epistle to the Ephesians, Paul cites the rationale for marriage originally found in Genesis: "And Adam said, This is now bone of my bones, and flesh of my flesh: she shall be called Woman, because she was taken out of Man. Therefore shall a man leave his father and his mother, and shall cleave unto his wife: and they shall be one flesh" (Gen. 2:23–24). Marriage is defined by its capacity to motivate a transfer of attachments across generations. Biblical commentators often note the oddity of Adam speaking about the experience of leaving a father and mother behind. Martin Luther, for example, interprets Adam's utterance as "in the nature of a prophecy" because "[t]here were no fathers and mothers yet, and no children."[8] If the original definition of marriage looks beyond the specific context of Adam and Eve's union in Eden, then the task of intergenerational replacement comes into even clearer focus. After the Fall, marriage does not only foster new, intimate bonds, from one generation to the next. Marriage is a vehicle for replacing mortal people and regulates the reproduction of children who should, if they survive, expect to replace their parents upon their deaths.

When Paul imposes a new meaning on marriage, he replaces an intergenerational rationale of substitution with a sacrificial one. The passage from the Epistle to the Ephesians offers no explicit Christian rationale for reproduction—no statement of a spiritual analogue to the imperative, found in Genesis, to populate the earth. The historical development of Christianity reveals how important this silence is. In the second century, Marcion taught that marriage and reproduction belong to a Hebraic past that is entirely negated as the expression of a deity who differs from the Christian God. In this view, Christians have no need to marry or to bear children. Their proper orientation is to reject the corruption of the physical world. Marcion was rejected by the Church Fathers as a heretic. Yet as Judith Lieu observes in a reconsideration of Marcion's importance, when it comes to the rejection of marriage and reproduction, the "rhetorical antithesis between the heretics and the Church is absolute, but it is evident that the social reality remains less so."[9] The question of whether a Christian needs to have children would continue to matter in seventeenth-century England, even for Protestants who should (according to clear-cut understandings of sectarian differences) reject the value of clerical celibacy. We know, to mention an example that recurs later in this book, that John Milton seriously considered a life of celibacy before eventually marrying. Scholars intrigued by this biographical fact tend to focus on the mythic power of virginity in Milton's imagination.[10] Yet Milton's consideration of lifelong celibacy contains the tacit assumption that there is no strict requirement for a Christian to reproduce. When Milton would later emerge as a proponent of companionate marriage, he would explicitly privilege the spiritual bond between a husband and wife over the practical realities of reproduction and childrearing. The prevailing view in seventeenth-century England was that Christians should marry and reproduce. Yet upholding this view required an oscillation between the definitions of marriage found in the Old Testament and in the New Testament.

Paul's redefinition of marriage sidesteps the practical matter of intergenerational replacement and teaches that the higher meaning of marriage has been revealed through Christ's self-sacrificing care for his bride. Yet the question of how, exactly, Christ "gave himself for" the church, so "that he might sanctify and cleanse it," is one of the fundamental problems of Christian theology. In the late eleventh-century *Why God Became Man* (*Cur deus homo*), Anselm of Canterbury offers an influential account of the atonement. "By what rationale does God forgive the sins of men?" Anselm asks.[11] He theorizes that sin is a debt of honor that all creation owes to God. Christ fulfills this obligation on behalf of humanity through a life of perfect obedience. He confers on his church a goodness it could not achieve on its own. Most relevant to my book is the way that much of Protestant theology, starting with Luther, would go on to adapt Anselm's soteriology to formulate a penal doctrine of atonement. This doctrine promotes a more overtly substitutionary logic of sacrifice. Christ does not just fulfill a debt on behalf of others but takes upon himself a displaced form of punishment.[12] Christ suffers corporal and capital punishment as an innocent substitute. All the writings studied in this book negotiate an affective problem generated by Pauline teaching, especially when it is interpreted through a doctrine of substitutionary atonement: what it means for the affection between two spouses to be defined by the sacrifice of an innocent Son taking on a displaced form of punishment. The penal theory of atonement might have been a widespread teaching in seventeenth-century England, but even some ardently Protestant writers, like Milton, can express misgivings about this teaching and its implications. This book considers how writers from a range of doctrinal convictions imagine a form of intensely personal love that resists easy assimilation to biblical teaching in general and to substitutionary atonement in particular. These writers tend to make it harder rather than easier to feel the supposedly higher truth of Christian marriage.

The mystery of Pauline marriage also generates more straightforwardly practical problems. Paul leaves it unclear why any Christian husband would love a specific wife. This question is resolved neither by the story of Adam's loving Eve (who is created from his flesh and bones) nor of Christ's loving his corporate bride as his own body. Pauline teaching makes it even less clear why any wife would revere her particular husband or would-be husband as Christlike. Christian wives are instructed to live under a form of gender hierarchy that is based on an inexact simile. This burden of untruth placed on women features prominently in the debates over gender published in early seventeenth-century England. In the 1617 treatise *Muzzle for Melastomus*, Rachel Speght rebuts her misogynistic interlocutor by presenting her case that biblical marriage calls for loving union rather than inflexible hierarchy.[13] When interpreting Genesis, she concludes that God granted Adam and Eve joint authority over all the other creatures of the earth.[14] When turning to the Christian redefinition of marriage, she embraces one aspect of Paul's exhortation: "for men ought to love their wives as themselves, because hee that loves his wife, loves himselfe."[15] Yet she qualifies Paul's alignment of Christ and husband. She does admit that the husband's place at the head of a marriage is "a truth ungainesayable."[16] Before making this concession, however, she reminds the reader that "the benefites of [Christ's] death and resurrection, are as availeable, by beleefe, for women as for men; for hee indifferently died for the one sex as well as the other."[17] A husband and a wife are "indifferently" alike insofar as both are imperfect but redeemed.

We can find clear admissions that the alignment of husbands with Christ is not grounded in stable truth in William Gouge's 1622 treatise *Of Domesticall Duties*, a work that reaffirms gender hierarchy even while registering the spiritual benefits of companionate marriage. Gouge grounds his case for male-centered marriage in an extended reading of Paul's Epistle to the Ephesians. When it comes to the Christlike status of the husband, he remarks, "The note of comparison (**Even as*) requireth no *equality*, as if it were possible for an Husband in that *measure* to loue his wife, as Christ loued his Church; (for as Christ in excellency and greatnesse exceedeth man, so in loue and tendernesse)."[18] Gouge acknowledges that Pauline teaching promotes an imperfect simile. Yet his goal is to have wives accept this simile nonetheless. Relying on Pauline precedent, he warns the reader to "conceive no carnall, no earthly thing" concerning the meaning of marriage, "because it is a mysterie."[19] He devotes considerable effort to turning the distinction between the divine meaning of marriage and its imperfect earthly expression to the advantage of men. Much later, he returns to the question of a husband's imputed Christlikeness. Gouge insists that between an imperfect husband and Christ "there may be similitude, resemblance, and fellowship: inequality is no hinderance to these."[20] He needs to be defensive for much of his treatise because the husband's claim to Christlike superiority has proven to be vulnerable as a normative fiction.

My opening example of Donne's *Holy Sonnet* 18 suggests how the misalignment of individual marriage and Christ's love for the church could threaten not only sexist norms but also the compatibility between familiar experience and higher truth claims. Donne's rationale for putting Christian marriage to the test involves another important dimension of Paul's teaching in the Epistle to the Ephesians: the realities of exclusion that frame the dynamism between individual and corporate experience. The context of the Epistle to the Ephesians reveals how Paul attempts a balance between incorporation and exclusion. In the second chapter, Paul reminds his Gentile readers that they were once "without Christ, being aliens from the commonwealth of Israel, and strangers from the covenants of promise, having no hope, and without God in the world" (Eph. 2:12). Paul seeks to address the tensions between the Jewish and Hellenic Christians within the church at Ephesus. He does not fully renounce the distinctive privilege of Jewish believers, who were not previously aliens from Israel. Yet Paul relies on the typological transition from the literal to the spiritual Israel to underscore a new spirit of inclusivity—at least among all those who have accepted Christian teaching. By the time Paul redefines marriage in the fifth chapter, he does not mention the distinction between Jewish and Gentile members of Christ's corporate body, which is also his wife.

In *Holy Sonnet* 18, Donne articulates a desire for a Christian inclusivity that does not seem to exist anywhere in his world. To challenge the impulse toward sectarian exclusivity, he pits Pauline teaching against monogamy itself. For an example of the kind of exclusionary impulse that Donne seeks to subvert, we can turn to John Calvin's remarks about the second commandment. In that commandment, Yahweh forbids Israel from the worship of idols by declaring himself a jealous God. Calvin (to quote from a 1561 English translation) likens God's "feruently burnyng ialousie" to the anger of a husband "yf he see his wiues minde encline to a strang louer."[21] For Calvin, Christians should not simply consider divine jealousy to be relegated to a supposedly outdated Hebraic past. Instead, they should apply the feeling of jealousy toward an affirmation of God's narrow covenant with an elect church. Donne's sonnet, by contrast, surprises the reader into asking why a communal and supposedly universal truth should be expressed in a form that privileges exclusive fidelity.

Crises of Substitution

When I study seventeenth-century English writers who elevate a love that affirms uniqueness, I do not mean to suggest that they invent an entirely new way of writing about marriage. Celebrations of unique love leading to marriage existed long before the seventeenth century.[22] One key precedent for affirming the stubborn fixity of desire lies in comedy—more specifically, in the New Comedy of ancient Greece and its Roman adaptations.[23] Another precedent lies in romance, a genre full of dangerous proxies and doubles that threaten quests for individuation. Ludovico Ariosto's sixteenth-century *Orlando furioso* was influential in showing that a conjugal celebration might achieve a recognizably Virgilian form of closure even at the end of a sprawling romance narrative. Yet in seventeenth-century England, the promotion of a love that rejects all substitutes becomes ascendant across genres, and in a way that would alter cultural history. The sense that loving marriage might permanently affirm the uniqueness of individuals, who may be neither noble in birth nor heroic in battle, begins to register not just as a generic device of closure but also as a desirable and potentially viable mode of domestic life—just barely viable, and in a disruptive or transgressive fashion.

In early modern England, marriage was increasingly promoted as a spiritual bond between a husband and a wife even as it continued to function as a contractual and disciplinary instrument. Frances Dolan offers a summary of the major historical factors involved in the rise of companionate marriage: "the Reformation promoted a direct relationship between the individual and God, as well as increased introspection and self-documentation; political change promoted an increased awareness of individual rights and responsibilities; urbanization ruptured ties to the extended family and local community; and capitalism promoted a sense of the individual as the proprietor of himself and his capacities."[24] These large-scale developments have offered historians and historically minded scholars much to reexamine and to debate. Debates recur about when, exactly, religious and demographic shifts led to changed behaviors and outlooks, and for which segments of the population.[25] In this book, I pursue questions that are less directly about the lives of seventeenth-century English people but focus more on literary history: why and to what end did writers increasingly identify marriage with a love between two individuals who deem each other to be irreplaceable? The answers to these questions are historical in nature, but not simply because literary writings passively reflect shifting attitudes about marriage and personhood. All the writings that I study respond to religious and political upheavals by revisiting the meaning of marriage, and by imagining possible modes of feeling that can arise out of the contradictions in Christian teaching.

The chapters in this book consider writings about marriage by six authors: Edmund Spenser (1552?–99), William Shakespeare (1564–1616), William Davenant (1606–68), John Milton (1608–74), Lucy Hutchinson (1620–81), and Aphra Behn (1640–89). These authors write from different religious viewpoints (from Protestant to likely Roman Catholic, devout to disillusioned), and from opposed political convictions (royalist to republican). Yet they all contribute to a vocabulary that sets the feeling of conjugal love against the notion of substitution. This vocabulary serves as a resource for testing not just the viability of marriage as Paul defines it but also the link between Pauline marriage and hereditary succession. The relationship between marriage and succession needed to be reexamined repeatedly during the numerous upheavals of the seventeenth century. My book begins in the final decade of the sixteenth century, when the unmarried and heirless status of Queen Elizabeth I heightened anxieties about national stability. In 1603 James VI of Scotland ascended to the English throne already married and the father of heirs. The establishment of the new Stuart dynasty in England was certainly not uncontroversial, but the practical function of royal marriage seemed to be restored at last. Yet the middle of this century would be defined by the civil wars that resulted in the public execution of King Charles I in January 1649. This shocking event was followed by an eleven-year experiment in nonmonarchical governance. (Despite the starting point of the book's chapters, I refer to the seventeenth century in the title to refer to the centrality of these events for my argument.) The English republic proved incapable of securing a viable alternative to hereditary succession at the highest level of authority; the Stuart monarchy was restored in 1660. Toward the end of the seventeenth century, the Glorious Revolution of 1688 disrupted the patterns of the Stuart dynasty once again—not by executing King James II but instead by replacing him with his daughter and foreign son-in-law. Across all these crises, fundamental matters of belief and authority were being contested: how one ruler should be replaced by another, whether monarchy is compatible with Christ's kingship, whether God calls his believers to submit to human rulers or to appoint and even replace them. According to Christopher Hill's formulation, this was a period in which not just kingship but even "God was on trial."[26]

This book shows that, in seventeenth-century English writings, Christian marriage had to be put on trial as well.[27] At stake is marriage's capacity to function as an instrument for legitimizing hereditary heirs and, simultaneously, as a religious form that directs intimate experience toward communal belonging. I have already suggested that a stubbornly individual love unsettles the balance of the personal and the corporate that Pauline marriage demands. At the same time, an insistence on individual singularity underscores the absence of a reproductive rationale for marriage within

Pauline theology. A vocabulary defining love against substitution undercuts the prestige of marriage's practical role in producing heirs who should seamlessly replace their parents upon death. In this book, I detail how writers from opposed political positions turned to this shared vocabulary as a way to respond to different moments of turmoil in the seventeenth century. My first two chapters on Spenser and Shakespeare, respectively, describe how a literary vocabulary defining conjugal love against replaceability takes hold across the genres of the Petrarchan sonnet, romance, epic, tragedy, and tragicomedy. The subsequent chapters consider how this vocabulary serves as the basis of more overtly partisan thinking. Royalist writers lament how Christian marriage cannot achieve a balance between the individual and the communal in the absence of a stable hierarchy, with royal marriage setting the precedent for others to follow. Republican writers, by contrast, decry the demands of hereditary succession as being inimical to the genuine love between a husband and a wife. As this book goes on to show, royalist and republican writers reshape, for their own perceived ends, the kernel of untruth within Pauline marriage and the appeal of a personal love that seeks to reject or rise above the realities of replacement.

My work in this book is historically minded, but I believe that the writings I study offer forward-looking lessons about the ongoing negotiation of personal experience with shared truth claims, an intimate feeling of love with communal belonging. Under the pressures of seventeenth-century English history, writers start to imagine the Pauline definition of marriage giving way to impassioned affirmations of the individual. When I look back to these earlier writings, I do so from a vantage point in which individual uniqueness has become entrenched as an enabling fiction, not just for the idea of loving marriage but also for an entire liberal form of life. The role of marriage in balancing individual personhood with corporate belonging does not merely persist now as a quaintly outmoded tradition.[28] We can observe how, across many countries, norms concerning love shape immigration policies that determine when marriage should and should not offer a pathway to naturalized citizenship. In these negotiations, the adjudication of genuine affection can play a decisive role in determining when marriage should be a vehicle of national incorporation and when marriages can be discredited as mere unions of convenience. Feminist legal scholars have detailed the harm that can arise out of policies ostensibly seeking to affirm a liberal and equitable view of marriage.[29]

For a specific example, we can refer to the "attachment requirement" that was in effect in Denmark from 2000 to 2018, as part of the Danish Aliens Act, to restrict the conditions of spousal and familial reunification. Certain marriages could be deemed insufficient as grounds for admission to Denmark for the sake of reunification. In response to this requirement, sociologists have relied on the Foucauldian theory of governmentality to describe marriage and love being deployed as state instruments.[30] This recent example makes it clear that restrictions on naturalization and the perceived illegitimacy of certain marriages are thoroughly bound up with the desire to limit civic acceptance according to views of religious and racial differences. There are certainly valid reasons to safeguard marriage from illiberal arrangements such as forced marriages or child marriages. At the same time, the attempt to defend love, family, and nation from perceived illiberal threats can function as a pretext for excluding immigrants from various African, Asian, and Middle Eastern populations. In 2016 the European Court of Human Rights found, albeit with serious reservations expressed, that parts of the Danish attachment requirement were discriminatory and violated articles of the European Convention on Human Rights.[31] This is just one instance in which marriage continues—even in nominally secular contexts—to regulate who can be affirmed within communal belonging (in this case, the Western liberal nation rather than Christ's body) and which populations might be excluded from the pattern of individuality and incorporation.

Given my desire to balance a historicist outlook with forward-looking concerns, I have found it important to conclude my study of seventeenth-century conjugal narratives with a reading of Aphra Behn's prose fiction *Oroonoko* (1688). Behn locates her conjugal tragedy within the transatlantic slave trade. My chapter does not read *Oroonoko* as expressing any abolitionist sentiment on the author's part. Instead, I describe how *Oroonoko*, published months before the Glorious Revolution, expresses the author's royalist views and decries the imminent ouster of King James II. By fictionalizing the realities of slavery, Behn describes how noble and faithful love meets a tragic end when royal marriage cannot rise above the most starkly literal form of human substitution—the outright commodification of people. When I use the language of fungibility in this last chapter, I rely on the work of scholars who have detailed the racist logics of human fungibility in the histories of American slavery and its long aftermath.[32] My reading of *Oroonoko* discusses how Behn revisits the precedent of *Othello*, a work studied at length in chapter 2. These two readings form the portions of my book that consider a specifically racial understanding of replaceability. In both *Othello* and *Oroonoko*, the demand for personal singularity within loving marriage is framed by the awareness that Black lives are more susceptible to being stripped of personhood—with personal singularity being a tenuous, even marvelous exception.[33] Between the time of *Othello*'s composition in 1603 and that of *Oroonoko*'s, this awareness intensifies owing to England's heightened and more systematic activity in the enslavement of African people. When Othello recounts an earlier experience of being enslaved, it remains unclear by whom and under what pretext he had been enslaved and then freed.[34] In *Oroonoko*, by contrast, the underhanded dealings of English slave traders and colonial administrators form a key basis of Behn's lament—not about the slave trade in the 1660s, necessarily, but about the perceived debasement in English politics in 1688.

In other portions of my book, the form of exclusion that shapes the dynamism between individuality and belonging concerns Jews within the Christian typological imagination. My chapters on Davenant and Hutchinson in particular consider how Jews function as a convenient foil or scapegoat when the project to affirm individual love within Christian marriage runs into incoherence. Since my book studies seventeenth-century English writings about marriage, the realities of transatlantic slavery and more modern forms of antisemitism can only come into partial view. Yet my book as a whole aims to show how a literary form of marriage shapes collective impressions about individual worth and communal belonging within a framework of exclusivity. Seventeenth-century English writings offer us an opportunity to examine how the affirmation of uniqueness develops out of a religious teaching that calls on personal love to point to a shared truth. Within biblical teaching, Christian typology shapes a sense of who is included in the collective experience of a new truth and who remains on the outside. In the writings that I study in this book, we witness one form of overt mystification (the great mystery of Pauline marriage) just starting to give way to another—a nascent liberal form, in which the worth of individuals might be universally affirmed, but only of certain individuals who have the privilege of belonging. This literary reimagining of Christian marriage would exert a long influence in shaping perceptions about the necessity of exclusion—religious, racial, civic, and otherwise—in achieving some elusive balance between the feeling of personal singularity and of communal participation.

Political Theology Is Dead! Long Live Affect Theory!

To study seventeenth-century writings while also looking ahead, this book engages with scholarship that falls under the heading of political theology. Marriage has been a politico-theological form that mediates between practical realities and mythic appeals. As the vehicle for producing legitimate heirs, marriage plays a key role in reconciling what Ernst Kantorowicz labels "the *K*ing's sempiternity and the *k*ing's temporariness."[35] Christian marriage also accommodates a mythology of undying kingship by conferring religious sanction on what is a regulated cycle of intergenerational succession. When the newly crowned James I addressed the English Parliament in 1603, he did not merely appeal to his literal status as a husband and father but reshaped the higher meaning of Christian marriage to suit his purposes: "'What God hath conjoined then, let no man separate.' I am the husband, and all the whole island is my lawful wife."[36] Kantorowicz quotes James to observe that he adapts the *corpus mysticum*, the holy union between Christ and the church. James's reliance on marriage as an expression of Christlike kingship is innovative insofar as this metaphor had been "all but non-existent" in medieval theories of monarchy.[37] Yet this image of the Christlike English king would actually reach its zenith later in the century—and apart from the metaphor of marriage—when James's son Charles I was depicted as a Christlike martyr awaiting his execution, in isolation from his exiled wife.

Kantorowicz's *The King's Two Bodies* (1957) is one of the foundational texts of political theology, but it has an uneasy relationship with a genealogical project of discerning the prehistories of modern politics. In the preface, Kantorowicz articulates his unease with a forward-looking orientation. He admits that his study of medieval political theology "may be taken" as an attempt to understand the medieval origins of a "political theology which *mutatis mutandis* was to remain valid until the twentieth century."[38] Speaking of himself in the third person, however, he cautions, "It would go much too far, however, to assume that the author felt tempted to investigate the emergence of some of the idols of modern political religions merely on account of the horrifying experience of our own time."[39] Despite this hedging, *The King's Two Bodies* would have a lasting significance partly because of its role in genealogical accounts of modern sovereignty—and, specifically, in Michel Foucault's *Discipline and Punish*.[40]

Yet scholars seeking to uncover links between a religious past and modern politics often cite Carl Schmitt's work as the more powerful precedent. When Graham Hammill and Julia Reinhard Lupton attempt to clarify the term *political theology*, they remark, "The norms and forms of religious life are . . . not exactly what concerns political theology, which finds its questions rather in the moment where religion is no longer working—but neither are the secular solutions designed to replace it."[41] Within this provisional definition, Schmitt's widely circulated dictum, "All significant concepts of the modern theory of the state are secularized theological concepts," can function as a rationale and inducement for politico-theological inquiry.[42] Hammill and Lupton observe that political theology is "associated above all" with Schmitt, whose work shows that "the modern age redefines and rebinds politics and theology in an attempt to manage its deepest tendencies toward chaos and dissolution."[43] Other scholars taxonomize political theology into "stronger" and "weaker" modes: the so-called stronger mode is affiliated with Schmitt and licenses seemingly anachronistic connections between a religious past and modernity, whereas the weaker mode is affiliated with Kantorowicz and is more narrowly historicist in its focus.[44]

When early modern scholars work under the shadow of Schmitt, the onetime Nazi jurist and longtime proponent of fascism, they need to qualify the way he legitimizes authoritarianism by appealing to earlier theories of absolutism. Schmitt legitimizes forms of sovereignty that respond to the perceived threats of chaos. Politics are defined around the perception of enmity; sovereignty is defined by the power to decide when to suspend the normal rule of law. The recuperation of Schmitt's reputation in the latter half of the twentieth century would eventually make it common practice to describe him as singularly incisive.[45] My dissatisfaction with these tendencies has intensified alongside the developments that have taken place since I initially began writing this book. In 2016 Donald Trump was elected president of the United States. In the following year, emboldened by Trump's racist nationalism, an assemblage of neo-Nazis, Klansmen, and right-wing militias gathered in Charlottesville, Virginia, ostensibly to protest the proposed removal of a statue of Robert E. Lee. The affiliation between Nazism and American White nationalism was on display, not only in the form of Nazi paraphernalia but also in the collective chant "Jews will not replace us."[46] The resurgence of racist fascism has made it clear that the late twentieth-century scholarly recuperation of Schmitt has gone too far.[47] Even without it, gestures to Schmitt's thinking would likely have circulated in right-wing circles that aim to give a sheen of credibility to jingoism and xenophobia. Yet it strikes me as unacceptable to continue participating in a mode of scholarship that venerates Schmitt as uniquely brilliant. Being honest about the contradictions of liberal democracy should not serve as an alibi to the legitimization of fascist politics.

When I adapt the slogan "The King is dead!" to declare that political theology is dead, I signal my awareness that this mode of thinking will not remain dead but will persist in some revitalized form. In the chapters that follow, I engage selectively with both Kantorowicz and Schmitt, as well as with more recent work in political theology. By examining a literary vocabulary of marriage that mediates between large-scale political and religious matters and intimate experiences, I seek to take up a proposition that Eric Santner offers. Santner suggests that "there is more political theology in everyday life than we might have ever thought."[48] He makes this claim while tracing how the theory of the king's two bodies gives way to a modern understanding of the body politic as bifurcated. He describes the people, in whom power should reside through political representation, as having two bodies. The people are defined both by subjecthood and by bodily forms of life (which he labels as the flesh) that remain irreducible to political representation. By pairing an early modern understanding of the king's two bodies with the fate of the flesh in the modern state, he addresses some fundamental questions: "(1) the relation of parts to whole within a social formation; (2) the way in which the functionality, vitality, or flourishing of the formation is conceived; (3) the successful survival of the formation as self-identical across time, its organization of temporal *succession*; and (4) the sources of legitimacy of the formation: what justifies its existence, makes it more than utterly contingent?"[49] My book turns to seventeenth-century marriage as a form in which all these questions are being renegotiated at once. The writings that I examine test the capacity of marriage to harmonize political and religious mythologies, to balance individual experience with corporate belonging, and to legitimize succession as a valid instrument of stability. What links early modern marriage to modernity is a divided sensibility concerning the allure of personal uniqueness and the realities of replacement. The clash between love and the premise of substitution has politico-theological significance in seventeenth-century writings, and that clash continues to operate in forms of feeling that are at once quotidian and politically charged. In this book, I do not advance the facile claim that pitting love against substitution offers the solution of elevating the personal over the political. Instead, this book traces how the form of marriage is a problem that requires affectively binding solutions that political power can neither provide nor secure for its purposes.

When I continue with "Long live affect theory!" I signal my belief about the viable scholarly successor to political theology. I have suggested that my book focuses on the affective clash produced by a literary definition of marriage as a love between unique individuals. Yet pairing early modern scholarship with affect theory is not a simple matter. The most illuminating analyses within the scholarly turn to affect appeal to shared forms of feeling available within a capitalist social mode. This is true even when affect theory turns to previous centuries. When, for example, Sianne Ngai revisits Herman Melville's 1857 *The Confidence-Man*, she shows why that novel should have proven so alienating to contemporary and future readers (in a way that "Bartleby the Scrivener" has not). Ngai reads the novel as unrelentingly aware of the economic ploy of circulating fake feelings; this ruse is central not just to the marketing of literary fictions but also to market capitalism in general. She is able to make Melville's story newly comprehensible by describing a pattern of affective and monetary circulation that we still recognize because we inhabit a later outgrowth of capitalist society.[50] My book, by contrast, attends to what is still an overtly religious form of feeling about personhood and corporate belonging. If my book is to mediate effectively between a study of political theology and a study of affect, it will do so by mounting a case for a sensibility that emerges out of a theological worldview but would eventually become intertwined with a capitalist, liberal mode of life.

Was This Face the Face?

I close this introduction by offering a concrete example of the thinking that this book offers. I propose one specific occasion for pairing an early modern mystification of marriage, love, and political substitution with a modern confusion concerning heterosexual norms and their relationship to politics. I do this, first, by revisiting what Kantorowicz ignores in Shakespeare's *Richard II* (1595), despite devoting the first chapter of *The King's Two Bodies* to a reading of the play. It is striking that Kantorowicz ignores the female characters in this play and the function of marriage in the unfolding tragedy. Both as a vehicle of reproduction and as a Christian metaphor, marriage is crucial to the play's dramatization of the theory of the king's two bodies. On his way to the Tower in the play's final act, a defeated Richard utters,

> Doubly divorc'd! Bad men, you violate
> A twofold marriage—'twixt my crown and me,
> And then betwixt me and my married wife.—
> Let me unkiss the oath 'twixt thee and me;
> And yet not so, for with a kiss 'twas made. (5.1.71–75)

Richard claims that his literal and metaphorical marriages have been forced into a double divorce. This claim shapes the impression that he emerges as a martyr in defeat. To cast Richard as a bereft and loving husband, Shakespeare's play reimagines the historical Isabella of Valois (nine years old at the time of Richard's death) as an adult queen with whom the king can share a protracted farewell. This scene may be maudlin, but its pathos might work against all the evidence offered previously that Richard has been a bad husband—both to his wife and to his kingdom. The play is now showing or even abetting Richard in an act of political mythmaking through appeals to love. This appeal, in turn, helps to establish the grounds for presenting Richard as a specifically Christlike martyr in defeat. The language of kissing reinforces Richard's multiple outbursts that he has been betrayed by Judases.

Yet *Richard II* reveals how the mythology of Christlike kingship not only functions alongside the reality of marriage but also discredits the roles of women caught within the demands of hereditary succession. The play makes it clear that the tragedy of the king's two bodies is, at the same time, a tragicomedy of noble and royal women. In the second scene of the play, the Duchess of Gloucester serves as a confidant for John of Gaunt, her brother-in-law. The widowed duchess implores John of Gaunt to seek just vengeance on behalf of her late husband. To appeal to John of Gaunt's brotherly duty, the duchess describes all of Edward III's sons as

> seven vials of his sacred blood,
> Or seven fair branches springing from one root. (1.2.12–13)

These metaphors of male kinship entirely efface the reality of mothers. The duchess does go on to acknowledge that Gloucester did not only share a father with John of Gaunt but was also born from

> [t]hat bed, that womb,
> That mettle, that self mould, that fashioned

his brother (1.2.22–23). Yet the duchess continues to elide the full person of the mother through a synecdoche ("that bed") and a chain of metaphors that liken the womb to inanimate vessels. By subordinating real motherhood to patriarchal filiation, her speech accommodates a pervasive metaphor in the play—the earth itself as a common mother to Englishmen. The duchess's fate confirms the impression that she has neither a place nor a role of her own. The next time we hear of her, she has died for no other reason than grief over her late husband.

In the final act, however, the Duchess of York emerges as a character who insists on motherhood's importance, even if it means being a disobedient wife. When the Duke of York plans to expose his son Aumerle as a traitor against the newly crowned Henry, the duchess pleads,

> Wilt thou not hide the trespass of thine own?
> Have we more sons? or are we like to have? (5.2.89–90)

Again, *Richard II* distorts history for the sake of family drama. The historical Aumerle was not the son of the duke's second wife. In Shakespeare's adaptation, the mother clings to her son by deeming him biologically irreplaceable. The duchess's intervention on behalf of her son brings to the play a series of late correctives. She rejects the demands of male kinship insofar as they deny the role of women. In her defiance toward her husband, she resists the effort to make married love a basis of political mythmaking. These recalibrations, in turn, offer Henry Bolingbroke an alternate way to gain adoration as a new king—a political myth that sidesteps both the reality and the metaphor of marriage. The Duchess of York pleads with Henry for clemency on behalf of her son. The scene lapses into farce through punning on the "pardon" that the duchess seeks for Aumerle and the "*pardonne moy*" that she does not want to hear from Henry's lips before he politely condemns her son (5.3.114–31). Yet Henry does pardon Aumerle, and the duchess responds by proclaiming, "A god on earth thou art" (5.3.136). This salute momentarily blurs the line between hyperbole and reverence. If the duchess manages to cut through this scene's farcical nature, she does so through an intensity of maternal care that leads her to deify the king who has exhibited grace toward her son.

At the same time, the questions of gender, reproduction, and marriage that underlie Richard II's tragedy remain disconnected from Henry's provisional triumph. The scene of the duchess securing Aumerle's pardon is followed by Richard's soliloquy in the dungeon at Pomfret Castle. Richard clings to a fantasy of being able to populate his own world in miniature:

> My brain I'll prove the female to my soul,
> My soul the father, and these two beget
> A generation of still-breeding thoughts. (5.5.6–8)

Earlier in the play, after returning from Ireland, he salutes the English earth with a maternal metaphor:

> As a long-parted mother with her child
> Plays fondly with her tears and smiles in meeting,
> So weeping, smiling, greet I thee, my earth. (3.2.8–10)

In contrast to the patriotic appeals to the earth as a common mother that recur in the play, he imagines himself as a mother to emphasize his intrinsic bond to his kingdom. At the end of the play, despite having recognized the fragility of kingship, he cannot fully let go of the fantasy of generating subjects on his own. When, by contrast, King Henry extends grace to the Duchess of York, he finds a way to receive adoration while avoiding any direct entanglements with maternal care or conjugal love.

If we return to Kantorowicz's reading of *Richard II*, we can discern some of the reasons why he might have neglected the topic of marriage. The play's presentation of marriage and of maternal care shows that the tragedy of the king's two bodies can (or even needs to) coexist with tragicomic and farcical rhythms. In Henry Bolingbroke's story, the late swerve into farce confirms that a political mythology of godlike kingship can function even if it has been evacuated of any clear purchase on belief. Only by ignoring such complications can Kantorowicz straightforwardly present *Richard II* as the tragedy of the king's two bodies. Even if Richard temporarily plays the fool in Kantorowicz's account, the tragedy is still a solemn, even hierophantic one that confirms the significance of the politico-theological concept.

To look ahead beyond early modern England, I want to pair *Richard II*'s orchestration of marriage, maternal care, and political mythmaking with a moment in twentieth-century psychoanalytic thinking. I have in mind a section of Sigmund Freud's 1914 "On Narcissism," a signal work in the transformation of the myth of Narcissus into the modern condition of narcissism. This seems like a great leap. Yet I justify it in part by recalling that *Richard II* contains the most explicit display of what we would call wounded narcissism in all of Shakespearean drama. The play replaces the historical reports of Richard signing his own deposition with a mirror scene. In Shakespeare's adaptation, Richard demands a mirror so that he can look at his face as he is stripped of kingship. He asks,

> Was this face the face
> That every day under his household roof
> Did keep ten thousand men? Was this the face
> That like the sun, did make beholders wink? (4.1.281–84).

Shakespeare's engagement with the myth of Narcissus generates a particular form of self-reflexivity and self-misunderstanding. In this scene of shattered narcissism, Henry Bolingbroke corrects the error that persists in Richard's thinking. When Richard declares that breaking the mirror before him amounts to breaking his face, Henry remarks,

> The shadow of your sorrow hath destroy'd
> The shadow of your face. (4.1.292–93)

Richard is willing to accept even this cruelly pointed lesson about mediation, simulacrum, and misrecognition. He concedes that he has continued to mistake his reflected shadow for his being. Yet in contrast both to the

Ovidian myth of Narcissus and to the modern theory of narcissism, Richard's difficult lessons about self-recognition and error exist at a remove from gender difference, erotic desire, and reproduction. As we have seen, Richard's demystified view of himself as king manages to coexist with his confusion about gender and reproduction to the very end. The wounding of Richard's narcissism is religious and political in nature, but he proves incapable of directly confronting related questions about motherhood.

In Freud's 1914 essay, we can witness a modern understanding of narcissism generating a different pattern of confusion. Gender difference, intergenerational substitution, and self-misrecognition are some of the dynamics being explicitly theorized, but their purchase on politics tends to remain obscured. Freud's essay begins with the provocation that narcissism should not merely be associated with the supposed pathologies of autoeroticism and homoeroticism. Freud proposes that narcissism plays a key function in heterosexual subject formation. In this essay, the name of Narcissus begins to merge with Freud's emergent theory of the ego ideal. Yet when Freud seeks to explain how, exactly, narcissism can foster heterosexual attachments by promoting the right kinds of ego ideals, he confronts basic contradictions. If all objects of desire are substitutes for the maternal body, as Freud claims, it is unclear why women would normatively desire men. Freud reverts to the existing association of narcissism with "perverts and homosexuals" to explain that "they have taken as a model not their mother but their own selves."[51] He makes the search for a mother substitute the basis of a heterosexual norm, with male desire typically exhibiting "[c]omplete object-love" whereas women typically remain narcissistic.[52] Freud then offers "a short summary" of the account of heterosexuality he has provided:

A person may love:—

(1) According to the narcissistic type:
    (a) what he himself is (i.e., himself),
    (b) what he himself was,
    (c) what he himself would like to be,
    (d) someone who was once part of himself.
(2) According to the anaclitic (attachment) type:
    (a) the woman who feeds him,
    (b) the man who protects him,
    and the succession of substitutes who take their place.[53]

Under the label of summary, Freud introduces ideas he has not previously discussed. For the first time in this essay, he proposes that the narcissistic sense of self can be split across time—filtered through nostalgia for a past self and a proleptic longing for a future self. This is a crucial distinction because it accommodates the relationship between the ego and the ego ideal being pursued. Yet he introduces it here in slipshod fashion, as part of a post hoc attempt to render heterosexuality coherent. In the foregoing section of the essay, he does discuss a narcissistic desire for "someone who was once part of himself"—but only as part of the claim that motherhood provides an outlet for a woman's tendencies toward narcissism.[54] In the so-called summary, he adds the new idea that attachments can seek a substitute not just for a missing mother but also for "the man who protects." The suggestion that an object attachment can be based on a protective father figure is only a placeholder explanation. It papers over the recurring problem of why any woman would seek a male object to replace a maternal object of attachment.

I have turned to Freud's essay on narcissism at the end of my introduction for reasons that pertain to this book as a whole. Freud offers a highly influential twentieth-century account of the relationship between love and substitution. In this account, all outward-oriented desire is a quest for a substitute for an elusive lost object. My concern in this book is to trace how the contradictions within the Pauline definition of Christian marriage shape a literary vocabulary pitting love against the premise of substitution. Pauline marriage shares some important conceptual elements with Freud's theory of heterosexuality: a dynamism of the self, identification that promises to reshape the self, and confusion concerning the gendered patterns of desire and identification. Paul exhorts all husbands to adopt Christ as their ego ideal (with wives affirming that identification) while, at the same time, understanding themselves as members (along with their wives) of Christ's corporate bride. Even though Freud is obviously elaborating a different theory of heterosexual norms, his terminology helps to clarify why self-love cannot function as the stable form of a love that rejects substitutes. If the singularity of the self is to become a tenable fiction, it must be stabilized through the love of another—while, at the same time, the asymptotic movement toward the self's idealized version is affirmed. This is true both in Pauline marriage (in which husbands and wives define each other with respect to Christ) and in Freud's unstable account of heterosexuality.

Freud's 1914 essay only begins to grapple with the political implications of the dynamic constitution of the self through desire. The narrowly political significance of his account of heterosexuality and narcissism initially seems to be little more than the basis of a small joke. After offering the deceptive summary in the second section of "On Narcissism," Freud elaborates on the way reproduction functions as an inducement for heterosexual union. In contrast to his earlier claim about typically narcissistic women, he now describes babies as fostering in fathers and mothers alike a narcissistic sense of satisfaction. He notes that this is why parents regard their child as "'His Majesty the Baby.'"[55] This phrase is, curiously, in English in the original essay. The notion of a royal baby offers him the grounds for a passing quip about the narcissistic satisfaction to be found in parenting. His developmental narrative of heterosexuality may be confusing insofar as it describes both men and women seeking substitutes for missing maternal objects. Yet the gendered confusion within the rationale for reproduction does not seem in any genuine way linked to the political utility of succession—a concept that is quaint in its outdatedness and also cast as foreign-sounding.

For most of "On Narcissism," Freud remains silent on the modern political implications of his theoretical claims. Yet in the final paragraph, he adds, "The ego ideal opens up an important avenue for the understanding of group psychology. In addition to its individual side, this ideal has a social side; it is also the common ideal of a family, a class, or a nation. It binds not only a person's narcissistic libido, but also a considerable amount of his homosexual libido, which is in this way turned back to the ego."[56] He ends by suggesting the positive dimensions of the way identification and idealization underlie communal formations, including the nation. This optimism is premised on a notion that his essay had tried to overcome in the name of a normative heterosexuality. He believes that the pursuit of one's own ego ideal is fundamentally homosexual because it is a libidinous attachment to some version of oneself.[57] The sense that self-love and self-development are essentially homosexual in nature (because they are directed at a version of the self) recurs at the end of the essay so that he can propose that narcissism can be useful in motivating communal forms such as national belonging.

As I complete this introduction in 2021, I feel compelled to remember that Freud would go on to confront the irrational and murderous forms of nationalism energized by libidinal misidentifications and idealization. If I had completed this book several years earlier, I might have sided more thoroughly with Victoria Kahn's conclusions about political theology in *The Future of Illusion*, published in 2014. When it comes to the beliefs that underlie political fantasies, Kahn argues for a break with religion in the name of a secular *poiesis*. She turns to Freud as a thinker who, up to the brink of World War II, relied on psychoanalysis to diagnose the intractable forms of illusion, including religious faith, at play in nationalism. Fantasy and illusion remain indispensable, but in her account, art proves to be a more beneficial form of *poiesis* when it breaks away from politico-theological legacies. Psychoanalysis and art proved too weak to counteract twentieth-century fascism and genocide, and yet art remains the mode of making that "interprets our fantasies in a form that liberates rather than constrains."[58] I write at a moment characterized by a resurgence of racist nationalisms and an impulse toward authoritarianism. It is easier than ever to psychoanalyze the narcissism, the misrecognitions, the libidinal attachments, and the workings of the death drive that underlie ethno-nationalism.[59] Yet it is also less clear than ever what purchase psychoanalysis and constructive *poiesis* might have in repudiating twenty-first century fascism and in redirecting us toward liberating forms of collective belonging. It is also unclear how viable a decisive break from the politico-theological legacies of the past might be when Christian zeal continues to prove capable of forging alliances with irreligious forms of reactionary politics. A book studying seventeenth-century writings about marriage can offer no direct political prescriptions. Yet I have written in the hope that accounting for how we have inherited ways of feelings about love—in a form that mediates between inclusion and exclusion, between singular lives and ones deemed negotiable in value—might help us understand why irrational forms of exclusion and hatred can circulate effectively in the name of cohesion and personal belonging.

Beguiling Love in the *Amoretti* and the 1590 *Faerie Queene*

In 1591 John Harington's English translation of Ludovico Ariosto's *Orlando furioso* appeared in print. After each canto, Harington adds brief commentaries under the headings of moral, history (or story), allegory, and allusion. Traditionally, the last component of the fourfold method of interpretation would have been the anagogical mode, which draws lessons about the afterlife. Harington replaces anagogy with allusion. By doing so, he suggests that the lessons of *Orlando furioso* do not necessarily point to a spiritual hereafter but instead toward a literary future. From the viewpoints both of moral allegory and of literary history, marriage is the appropriate culmination of the sprawling narrative. After the final canto, Harington summarizes "*the conclusion of* [Ariosto's] *whole worke, that* Rogero *immediatly upon his marriage to Bradamant, killeth* Rodomont." Rodomonte allegorically represents "*the unbridled heat and courage of youth . . . yet after that holy state of matrimonie is entred into, all youthfull wildnes of all kinds, must be cast away.*"[1] By providing this ending, Ariosto shows himself to be "*a perfect imitator of Virgil*," who had concluded the *Aeneid* "*with the death of* Turnus."[2] Yet Virgil's epic famously stops short of celebrating Aeneas's marriage to Lavinia. Fully reconciling valor with love, Mars with Venus, would become one of the high ambitions of Renaissance poetry. Harington praises Ariosto for having fulfilled it.

Marriage shuttles us from an allegorical interpretation to the real world in a more literal way as well. By writing of Bradamante and Ruggiero's marriage, Ariosto celebrates the legendary ancestry of his patron, Ippolito d'Este. Ariosto had a personal investment in celebrating a marriage that supposedly links a literary past to the House of Este. Harington had a different stake in completing his translation of *Orlando furioso*. Queen Elizabeth I was Harington's godmother, but she banished him from her court—at least according to widespread lore—after discovering some unsavory fragments of his literary works. Harington's dedication of his *Orlando* to Elizabeth describes how the queen's bright rays "shall soone disperse all hurtful mistes" from the garden of his literary endeavors; he then declares, "What soever I am or can, is your Maiesties."[3] The bid to regain the queen's favor was apparently successful, at least long enough for Harington to compose other controversial works and then to take part in the Earl of Essex's disastrous 1599 military campaign in Ireland.

In the year that Harington's *Orlando furioso* was first published, Edmund Spenser received from Elizabeth a life pension of fifty pounds for the first installment of *The Faerie Queene*, which had been published in 1590. Like Ariosto, Spenser presents himself as a latter-day Virgil by declaring his intention to sing of both "[f]ierce warres and faithfull loues."[4] At the same time, Spenser offers his poem as an allegorical mirror in which Queen Elizabeth might behold herself, her virtues, and her glory. By the early 1590s, the queen was approaching the age of sixty and the cult surrounding her perpetual virginity had been established. Spenser's epic might aim toward a conjugal conclusion, but his celebration of an unmarried queen licenses a narrative without a decisive happily ever after. Instead, the poem offers a number of deferred and partial unions, beginning with the interrupted betrothal of Redcrosse and Una at the end of book 1. Even before this union of England's patron saint and Christian truth begins to be solemnized, the reader already learns of the future death of Arthur, the composite hero of the entire epic. Arthur seeks the hand of Gloriana, the Queen of Faeryland and the poetic image of Elizabeth as sovereign. Because *The Faerie Queene* never arrives at its conclusion, whether or not Arthur marries Gloriana before his death remains an article of faith rather than of certainty.

In this chapter, I examine the 1590 installment of *The Faerie Queene* alongside Spenser's sonnet sequence, the *Amoretti*, published in 1595 to celebrate the poet's own marriage. This chapter details Spenser's poetic definition of conjugal love as the love between two individuals who define each other's unique personhood. Around this definition, Spenser's lyric and epic projects form a chiastic pattern. As a sonneteer celebrating his love, Spenser labors against the way Petrarchan convention undermines singular identity even while it obsesses over an object of desire. Petrarchan desire threatens to make love generic. The allegorical nature of *The Faerie Queene*, on the other hand, would seem to make love between two concrete individuals partially beside the point. Spenser's characters are not just representations of persons but personifications of meanings. Yet if marriage is an endpoint for both the narrative and the allegory, the drive toward a conjugal conclusion expresses itself through characters seeking the forms of fixity that love both demands and promises. Spenser's epic exists in a state of suspension between characters seeking to stabilize their personhood through marriage but also becoming less individuated as they fulfill their allegorical meanings.

In the *Amoretti*, Spenser interrupts the composition of his epic to celebrate his own marriage. The trajectory of Spenser's later career—"his turn from the world of court to a more private, even bourgeois, identity"—is familiar to us.[5] My reading aims to clarify the poetic, political, and religious meanings of this turn as it hinges around the meanings of marriage. Whereas the poet can claim that his marriage binds together the higher truth of Christ's love with the earthly experience of erotic love, this mediation unravels when marriage is called on to perpetuate a dynasty and to relate the monarchy to divinity. Marriage remains the way out of a poetic terrain and into history, but more perfectly for the poet rather than for his queen. This chapter begins by defining the poetic terms through which the *Amoretti* negotiates individual love within a Christian understanding of marriage. Some of the keywords in this poetic vocabulary include "beguile" and "goodwill"—both capturing the complications of agency in the asymmetrical but supposedly mutual love that Spenser celebrates. I also pay close attention to the way Spenser appeals to the Ovidian myths of Narcissus and of Actaeon in order to transform Petrarchan desire into a more dynamic exchange between the poetic subject and his object of desire. After defining this literary vocabulary, I bring it to bear retrospectively on the first three books of *The Faerie Queene*. Spenser's epic celebrates a queen who maintains "virginal, erotic, and maternal" claims on her subjects all at once.[6] Yet Spenser fragments the queen's persona into a series of substitutes who serve as the subjects and objects of the desire that advances the narrative. Reading the *Amoretti* and *The Faerie Queene* together shows us how defining Christian marriage against substitution promotes a poetic myth of individual love above and beyond the political claims of authority and the regulation of reproduction.

Love between Narcissus and Actaeon

In the *Amoretti*, Spenser's beloved must emerge as a unique object of desire who can, in turn, confer on the speaker the fixed identity of her future husband. Spenser has to work not only within but also against Petrarchan convention, which proves surprisingly unfit for describing the love between two real rather than generic individuals. The question of whether Petrarch's Laura truly existed or whether she was just a pretext for love poetry arose even during the fourteenth-century composition of the *Canzoniere*.[7] Even if the name Laura designates a historical person, Petrarch's sequence ends by renouncing the poet's love for her and redirecting it toward the Virgin Mary. Petrarch requests Mary's mediation as the queen of heaven, and he goes on to describe how Mary has "gathered into [herself] three sweet names: mother, daughter, and bride . . . Lady of that King."[8] Mary promises to fulfill each of these affective claims at once. She replaces Laura as Petrarch's idol and is even addressed as "our goddess (if it is permitted and fitting to say it)" (366.98–99).[9]

As a Protestant sonneteer, Spenser replaces what he deems to be sinful Mariolatry with erotic love sanctioned by Christian marriage. In contrast to Petrarch, he works to differentiate the identities of his queen, his mother, and his future wife. In *Amoretti* 74, he celebrates the fact that the three main women in his life share the "happy name" of Elizabeth.[10] "Ye three Elizabeths for ever live," the conclusion of the poem declares, yet the previous lines make it clear that the third Elizabeth—the speaker's future wife—will be the decisively important one. Mother and queen are verbally linked: the former gave the speaker his being "by kind" whereas the latter has proven "most kind" in conferring honor and wealth (74.5–7). The shifting meanings of "kind" convey how natural kinship gives way to political favor. Yet through the third Elizabeth, Elizabeth Boyle, the speaker's "spirit out of dust was raysed" (74.10). Love that culminates in marriage will allow the Spenserian speaker to be born again like a second Adam. Throughout the sequence, however, the speaker grapples with the knowledge that he is an unworthy suitor. Spenser repeatedly refers to his own meanness, suggesting not only his moral shortcomings but also his lower class station relative to his future wife. Christian marriage promises to mend both of these deficits. *Amoretti* 66, a sonnet aligned with Good Friday, prepares the reader for the triumphant Easter celebration in sonnet 68. By turning Christ's injunction to love one another into an appeal for mutual love leading to marriage, the conclusion of this Easter sequence conflates eros and agape to the speaker's advantage.[11] The alignment between Christ's love and the speaker's plea for reciprocated desire, however, requires some delicate negotiation. When the speaker declares in *Amoretti* 66 that his beloved

> [c]ould not on earth have found one fit for mate,
> Ne but in heaven matchable to none,

he implies that Christ would be the only potential husband who could fully merit her love (6–7). It is fortunate for the speaker that Christ confers merit on the unworthy.

In *Amoretti* 68 Spenser downplays the class anxieties surrounding his marriage through a provisional understanding of Christian redemption. The sonnet anchors conjugal love in Christ's death and resurrection, and it offers a palimpsest of soteriological notions. The first quatrain revolves around the motif—so prominent in medieval art and literature—of Christ's harrowing hell. In Protestant theology, Christ's descent remained an important but shifting item of belief, with Calvin going further than Luther in insisting on Christ's subjective experience of despair rather than a literal entry into hell.[12] Spenser's sonnet does not necessarily dwell on these points, but the second quatrain hews closer to Protestant doctrines of justification. Any possible incompatibilities between the first two quatrains tend to dissolve into the logic of the third, which articulates a formula of Christian love based on measurable merit:

> And that thy love we weighing worthily,
> May likewise love thee for the same againe:
> And for thy sake that all lyke deare didst buy,
> With love may one another entertayne. (68.9–12)

The notion of purchasing intrinsic to redemption brings together accounts of Christ's heroic ransom and Protestant doctrines of imputed righteousness. The opening "[a]nd" of line 11 does not clarify the relationship between the worth of Christ's love (which we should weigh properly) and the price that he had to pay to redeem us. Yet the implication is that these values are commensurate: Christ's all-encompassing love can be measured by the price he paid to redeem us wholesale. As sinners, our collective value is in proportion to Christ's loving sacrifice, and our worth as individuals (richer or poorer) may remain interchangeable. According to the pun on "lyke deare"—which registers clearly after the hunting motif of the previous sonnet—a redeemed individual may have as much value as just one creature in a herd. By balancing these ideas concerning salvation and personal versus collective worth, Spenser reaches toward a happy conclusion regarding Christ, his beloved, and his mean self:

> So let us love, deare love, lyke as we ought,
> Love is the lesson which the Lord us taught. (68.13–14)

Spenser has effaced both his moral and socioeconomic deficiencies through an appeal to salvation imagined as purchasing power. Christ sanctions the speaker and his beloved to "entertayne" one another—to enjoy a mutual possession.

Yet for a Protestant poet promoting erotic love as a proper reflection of Christ's redemptive love, some difficult questions may begin to take shape: What form of love is expressed when the Father punishes his innocent Son in the place of sinful humanity? What is the relationship between this displaced wrath and the experience of conjugal love? To complete a sonnet sequence that aligns a personal love with its higher meaning, Spenser deflects such complicated questions. One solution is somewhat predictable: to emphasize mercy rather than displaced vengeance. "Cho[o]se rather to be praysd for doing good," the final couplet of *Amoretti* 38 advises, "Then to be blamed for spilling guiltless blood" (13–14). Here, the problem of erotic love being perfected by the spilling of Christ's guiltless blood seems irrelevant. This seems merely like Spenser's reiteration of a Petrarchan appeal to a cruel woman. Yet this is a triumph rather than a deficiency of Spenser's project. Christ, as the New Testament teaches, has rendered sacrificial bloodshed obsolete. Spenser shapes this typological supersession of spilling guiltless blood into a generic appeal for loving mercy rather than a deeper investigation of the mystery of the atonement as it relates to human love.

Christian belief does not, however, explain why this particular poet should love that particular woman, or why she should choose to love him. To promote the love between two individuals who affirm each other as singular, Spenser revisits the Ovidian myths that had been embedded within Petrarchism from the start. More specifically, Spenser relies on the myths of Actaeon and of Narcissus. In these linked stories recounted in book 3 of the *Metamorphoses*, erotically charged viewing experiences occasion dangerous subject/object reversals. Actaeon's and Narcissus's respective fates raise questions about human freedom and divine fairness. Actaeon suffers a violent death after accidentally stumbling on Diana bathing. This episode begins with the poet's asking what crime might be attributed to mere error; it concludes with the unresolved question of Diana's fairness or excessive wrath. Narcissus's demise, by contrast, exists at a partial remove from the wrath of Juno. The goddess had lashed out against Tiresias by blinding him when he had testified that women enjoy sex more than men; Jove had compensated for his blindness with prophetic knowledge. Narcissus's fate serves as the first demonstration of Tiresias's prophetic abilities. Tiresias issues Narcissus's mother a conditional: the boy will live a long life "si se non noverit" (if he should not know himself).[13] This if-statement does not simply affirm the sustained possibility of Narcissus's blissful self-ignorance but instead constrains it. If Tiresias's prophetic skill is to be confirmed decisively, then Narcissus will have to be doomed just as the seer predicted. In the myths of Actaeon and Narcissus, the dangers of erotic desire point to shifting questions about human freedom and divine fairness; these myths furnish Spenser with a resource for situating an asymmetrical but mutual form of love within his Protestant understanding of providential oversight.

When it comes to the surprise of reciprocated desire, the turning point of the *Amoretti* lies exactly in between the Good Friday and Easter sonnets, *Amoretti* 66 and 68. The speaker wins the favor of his "deare" in *Amoretti* 67, and this sonnet culminates the project of rendering Petrarchism fit to celebrate the love between two individuals. Petrarch had directly accused Laura of being like Narcissus. *Canzoniere* 45 bemoans her use of a mirror to admire herself; this mirror is described as the poet's rival. This sonnet concludes by warning her of Narcissus's fate. In the very next sonnet, her narcissism turns lethal not just for herself but also for the speaker. When Petrarch decries "i micidiali specchi" (those murderous mirrors), the phrase refers to Laura's two eyes rather than a literal mirror imagined again as a rival suitor (46.7). Her eyes function as mirrors for the speaker's own lethal entrapment. Insofar as he is trapped by her eyes, the obsession of the Petrarchan speaker is not simply a desire for Laura but also a narcissistic fixation on his own status—which is defined by her attitude toward him.

In *Amoretti* 45, Spenser echoes Petrarch's forty-fifth poem by inviting the lady to replace her "glasse of christall clene" with the poet's "inward selfe" (1–3). Unlike a mere mirror, the poet can reflect the "fayre Idea" of her person rather than the mere outward appearance (7). The rest of the poem reveals this Neoplatonic rhetoric to be wryly coercive: if the addressee continues to be cruel, then the poet will make public a deformed version of her image—or, at least, of her reputation. Yet Spenser comes closer than Petrarch in admitting that the male sonneteer, and not the aloof woman, may be the true narcissist.[14] In *Amoretti* 35 and 83, which are close to identical, the speaker is explicitly described as a Narcissus-like gazer. Yet at the end of these sonnets, gender difference emerges as the decisive distinction between vain self-love and love for another person. "This rather enigmatic sonnet," Calvin Edwards remarks, "leaves us wondering why the speaker thinks his situation is like that of Narcissus . . . and why he cannot be satisfied with his view of the lady."[15] The task of the poem is to correct the opening impression that the speaker's dissatisfaction marks his desire as narcissistic. The speaker begins with a complaint, but after the emphatic volta, he declares that he is satisfied by the sight of his beloved to the disparagement of all else. Only the repetition of this sonnet later in the sequence, after the speaker has ostensibly won her over, suggests his lasting dissatisfaction. Yet in neither iteration of the sonnet does the source of his dissatisfaction lie specifically in her person. Her overwhelming appeal is the initial cause of the speaker's narcissistic predicament, but it is eventually called upon to be the solution as well.

To the question of why this person should be overwhelmingly attractive to the point that "this worlds glory seemeth vayne" by comparison, Spenser's Narcissus sonnets offer a tautological answer: she is a "she" (35, 83.13–14). By recasting the female object of desire into a grammatical subject, the poem's last word affirms that insofar as the poem's speaker is male, his desire cannot strictly be like Narcissus's. As Michael Warner has shown, the conflation of gender difference with the self/other distinction amounts to a "staggeringly primitive confusion."[16] The confusion of gender for identity in toto—and the conclusion that desiring someone of the same gender as oneself is tantamount to desiring oneself pathologically—underwrites the alignment in psychoanalysis of homosexuality with narcissism as well as with autoeroticism. Centuries before Freud, Spenser strategically develops a version of this confusion.[17] In sonnets 35 and 82, what fulfills the speaker's narcissistic tendencies while also precluding narcissism is the emergence of a *she*, an emergence that is entirely predictable but still meant to register as a minor epiphany.

Appealing to the fact of gender difference cannot, however, resolve why the speaker should seek to marry this particular woman. Between the two nearly identical Narcissus sonnets, *Amoretti* 67 works to confer more substance on this "she"—not, however, by providing concrete details about her but instead by describing the speaker's surprisingly successful pursuit of her. Despite operating through the conventional motif of the male pursuer-as-hunter, this sonnet works to establish the space of some personally meaningful reciprocation. An asymmetrical form of mutual desire provides a different impression of the desired woman's singularity. The poem achieves this impression through a half-spoken allusion to Actaeon. The opening of *Amoretti* 67 signals the possible relevance of the Actaeon myth through a deviation from its two closest precedents, Petrarch's *Canzoniere* 190 and Thomas Wyatt's adaptation, "Whoso list to hount." Following Wyatt, Spenser describes erotic frustration as a metaphorical hunt that has failed. Yet Spenser adds the detail of "panting hounds beguiléd of their pray" (67.4). In *Canzoniere* 190, the Petrarchan speaker is not hunting at all when he is dazzled by the sight of a white doe; in Wyatt's sonnet, no hounds are present and the speaker hunts only with a net. By introducing an Ovidian element missing in Petrarch's and Wyatt's precedents, Spenser balances his celebration of mutual love with his affirmation of male agency. In Ovid's narration, hounds are central to the subject/object reversal that Actaeon suffers. Just before Actaeon is killed by his own hounds, Ovid provides a mock epic catalog of the dogs' names. This suggests a grim joke in which the hounds emerge as something like the true heroes of this episode. In and of itself, Spenser's mention of hounds would not amount to a clear allusion to the Ovidian myth. After line 4 of *Amoretti* 67, the hounds seem to disappear from the poem entirely. Yet the word "beguyld" recurs emphatically as the poem's last word, this time describing the pursued woman rather than the hounds:

> Strange thing me seemd to see a beast so wyld,
> So goodly wonne with her owne will beguyld. (67.13–14)

This conclusion reveals that Spenser has added the detail of the hounds to enact a twist on the Actaeon myth. In Spenser's poem, the metaphorical hunt is initially unsuccessful but then gives way to the real triumph that the poet enjoys regarding his future wife. Because of this unexpected success, the subject/object reversal does not transform the male hunter into a victim. Instead, the beloved woman herself is half-transformed when she is caught by her pursuer. She continues to occupy a status that blurs the line between human and beast. Even by the end of the poem, the beloved woman does not emerge out of the metaphorical hunt with her human agency completely intact.

Spenser locates this precarious balance of reciprocal desire and gender asymmetry in the different meanings of "beguyld." Whereas the early phrase "beguiling hounds" had been straightforward in its meaning, the later use of the word is meant to convey a dynamic form of desire. "Beguiled" can describe either the agent or the victim of guile, and beguiled victims can be deluded either by another or by themselves. The hounds in line 4 have obviously been the victim of the "deare's" elusiveness, but it remains unclear in what sense the deare herself has been beguiled. It is possible that she has been "goodly wonne" because she has been deceived by her own will when she chose to approach her pursuer. Yet perhaps she has been won over "with" her own will in the sense that she has concealed her own erotic desire in a coy game. (This reading is possible in part because "will" can denote not just agency in general but carnal and sinful desire.[18]) If this is the case, then she has beguiled the speaker into thinking he has accomplished some sort of coup. By locating the oscillations between subject/object and human/beast within the desired woman, Spenser alters the patterns of the Actaeon myth. He does so to amplify the affective reversals involved in the erotic hunt and to channel these energies toward a supposedly happy ending.

This roundabout allusion to the Actaeon story helps to explain a more basic deviation from Wyatt's and Petrarch's precedents. The first word of *Amoretti* 67 explicitly points out that the hunt is a simile: "Lyke as a huntsman after weary chase" (1). By contrast, neither Petrarch nor Wyatt signals explicitly that he is speaking metaphorically. In Spenser's sonnet, the second quatrain explicitly brackets off what should be the end of the simile:

> So after long pursuit and vaine assay,
> When I all weary had the chace forsooke. (5–6)

This should mean that we have left the vehicle for the tenor, moving from the metaphorical hunt to the speaker's real concerns. Within this transition, the *I* that emerges in the sonnet contains some degree of uniqueness if only through negation: this *I* should stand apart from the mere trope of the hunter. As a result, this *I* functions as an analog to the *she* that concludes *Amoretti* 35 and 83—the Narcissus sonnets. In those poems, Spenser avoids the use of the first-person *I* even at the expense of logical coherence. The speaker only likens his eyes (rather than his *I*) to Narcissus. This comparison threatens to become dizzyingly illogical because Narcissus is then described as having eyes himself. In the Narcissus sonnets, *she* must emerge as the real subject/object of desire. As the subject/object, *she* defines the male speaker's identity, at least insofar as his whole being, his *I*, is not like Narcissus after all.

In *Amoretti* 67, the poetic speaker's *I* develops more fully at the expense of the woman's subjectivity. The actual content of both *I* and *she* remain open-ended, yet they are brought into relief against the backdrop of what or who they are not.[19] Spenser works to provide the open-ended *she* and *I* with some diacritical fixity: *she* is not a *he*, and *I* is not a generic Petrarchan huntsman. What distinguishes the "deare love" from a deer is dear love— an affective exchange that promises to stabilize the beloved's identity as Elizabeth Boyle even within a series of poetic tropes. Ironically, however, the establishment of this love turns the desired and desiring woman back into a "beast so wyld." Only in this way can Spenser describe how the canine instruments of his pursuit have been replaced by his future wife: she remains a "beast" insofar as she serves as the object of his desire. From this subordinated position, however, she must maintain a "wyld" form of agency. She may be goodly won, but a pun underscores that she is goodly one, a unified self—if only so that her independent will can fulfill the speaker's desire for reciprocation.[20] "Goodly wonne" forms an ironic echo with the description of her "owne goodwill," with which she is "fyrmely tyde" (12). The dear assents to her binding, but she is also bound up as if her own goodwill has been deployed against her, as if it were a rope or a net.

Love Is the Lesson

The goal is not just to celebrate the speaker's satisfaction but also to celebrate mutual beguiling under the auspices of Christian love. When Spenser appeals directly to Narcissus or indirectly to Actaeon, he takes part in a long tradition of interpreting Ovid morally and theologically, often through the resources of Neoplatonism. When it comes to the myth of Actaeon, these varied interpretations produce revealing inconsistencies. As Leonard Barkan reminds us, the fourteenth-century *Ovide moralisé* holds up Actaeon as a cautionary tale against bad habits by likening him to a "riche hom[m]e" who suffers an unhappy fate because he keeps idle dogs around him.[21] In sixteenth-century England, Abraham Fraunce includes this interpretation in his list of moral lessons to be drawn from Actaeon's story. Fraunce explains that the myth can also teach us not to be "*ouer curious and inquistiue in spying and prying into those matters, which be aboue our reach.*"[22] Yet Christian interpretations could view Actaeon not just as a cautionary figure but also as a Christlike one. *Ovide moralisé* also offers a Christian allegory whereby

> *Dyane, c'est la Deité*
> *Qui regnoit en la Trinité,*
> (Diana, she is the deity who reigned in the Trinity)

and Actaeon is identified as "*li filz Dieu*" (the son of God) who sees the Trinity in its uncovered state.[23] Barkan observes that "Actaeon/Christ becomes the hero of a Platonic initiation story in which the highest masquerades as the lowest. That individual is vouchsafed a vision of the Trinity and as a result must die to the world."[24] This interpretive tradition suggests that the Actaeon myth can be rendered compatible with Christian belief, but not necessarily in a way that firmly links divine truth to human love. Equating the punitive Diana with the Trinity does turn Christ-as-Actaeon into a sacrificial victim, but there is nothing necessarily loving about this lethal encounter with the bare truth.

In *Amoretti* 67, Spenser devises an alternative way to align the Actaeon-like hunt with Christian love. He does so by echoing William Langland's late fourteenth-century vocabulary of beguiling and beguilement in the eighteenth passus of *Piers Plowman*—a passage that had already served as a precedent for multiple episodes in *The Faerie Queene*. This passus explores how Christ's triumph might be rendered compatible with reason, legality, and property rights—modes that seem more compatible with law than with grace. At the gates of hell, Truth and Mercy debate the possibility of salvation. Truth asserts that nobody can exit hell, citing Job's declaration,

"Quia in inferno nulla *est* redemp*cio*."²⁵ Mercy, however, points out that because humanity was "bigyled" through the devil's trickery, grace can legitimately operate through a seemingly paradoxical mode of "gode sley3te" (18.164–65). Soon afterward, Satan expresses his fear that Lucifer's legal claim on humanity is tenuous because it is the result of trickery. A goblin confirms Satan's fears by observing that "god wil nou3t be bigiled" (18.294).

When Christ arrives to assert his right to harrow hell, he confirms that Lucifer's wicked guile makes the gracious repossession of humanity possible:

Theueliche þow me robbedest : þe olde lawe graunteth.
Þat gilours be bigiled : and þat is gode resou*n*. (18.340–41)

Christ then explains the mechanism through which he will beguile the guiler. Perfecting the eye-for-an-eye accounting of justice ("Dente*m* p*ro* dente *et* oculu*m* p*ro* oculo"), Christ will pay member for member, and life for life (18.342). Only a logical slippage, however, allows Christ to assume this sacrificial role. As the rhetoric of the beguiler being beguiled gives way to eye-for-an-eye logic, it becomes evident that vengeance should be exacted from Lucifer the felonious thief, and not from Christ. Christ sanctions a paradoxical form of counterguile with the claim that "grace gile destruyeth" (18.350). Once grace destroys guile, Christ can assert that he will "bi ri3t and resou*n* : raunsou*n* here [his] leges" (18.352). Yet the questions of why and to whom Christ must pay a ransom remain mysterious even as he repeats that he can recover Adam's issue "thoru3 raunsou*n*" (18.356). If Christ were to pay a ransom to Lucifer, then he would be honoring a fraudulent claim to humanity; if God demands ransom, then the legal and moral objections to Lucifer's illegitimate use of guile have been rendered moot, as his possession of humanity has proven to be binding in God's eyes. The only way to claim that law, reason, and grace can coexist is to propose sacrifice as God's way of stymying legalistic reasoning with a mysterious action.

In Spenser's view, the ransom theory of atonement, attributed to the second-century Church Father Irenaeus, should have been long obsolete. Even in the fourth century, Gregory of Naziansus had already articulated the problem with this theory: "since a ransom belongs only to him who holds in bondage, I ask to whom was this offered, and for what cause? If to the Evil One, fie upon the outrage!"[26] Protestant theology had largely (but not exclusively) adopted some version of the later penal theory of atonement. The concept of indebtedness, intrinsic to the very notion of redemption, does remain operative within this line of thinking. As the metaphor of indebtedness coexists with an emphasis on Christ's having suffered corporal and capital punishment in the place of sinful humanity, the appeal to economic payment tends to become more incongruous.[27] Yet *Amoretti* 68 may appeal to the outdated ransom theory as a provisional way to balance Christ's heroic harrowing of hell with a Protestant view of justification. This negotiation allows Spenser to imagine salvation as a form of wholesale purchasing power that, in turn, helps him downplay his class anxieties with regard to his future wife.

Around the question of mutual but asymmetrical love, Spenser can subordinate directly economic concerns to religious understandings of freedom as they bear on erotic desire. The questions of the deare's goodwill in *Amoretti* 67—to what extent she invites the speaker's love and to what extent she is trapped—implicitly bear upon theological questions concerning free will and irresistible grace.[28] At the same time, the classical question of displaced wrath that looms over book 3 of the *Metamorphoses* also informs Spenser's reworking of motifs from the Actaeon and Narcissus myths. In his handling, the potentially tragic problems of fate, chance, and constraints on freedom become the positive condition for love based on an individual preference that still remains governed by providence. The narcissistic aspects of Spenserian love suggest a fixity of affect that would be pathological were it not ordained by a higher power. In the place of fatal fixity, *Amoretti* 67 emphasizes chance and the freedom of the deare, who approaches the speaker only because she thinks she might quench her thirst "at the next brooke" (8). This choice or chance encounter deflects the sense that God has paired Elizabeth Boyle with an undeserving suitor in a way that is unfair to her.

In this sonnet, the partial abstraction of divine intervention, which accommodates meaningful choice in love, gives rise to a political message about the limits of sovereignty over intimate affairs. Missing from Spenser's poem is the interdiction of Caesar—or, as Wyatt's sonnet of the failed hunt suggests, of the joint interdiction of Christ and Caesar. Wyatt's speaker finds that he must not approach the object of his pursuit, which bears the message, "*Noli me tangere* for Caesar's I am."[29] This line has long tantalized readers. The prohibition against the speaker's erotic desire echoes Christ's command to Mary Magdalene not to touch him. Wyatt may also be hinting dangerously at Henry VIII as the English Caesar who forbids contact with Anne Boleyn—his mistress but not yet his queen.[30] These injunctions might work in concert, as both Christ and Caesar forbid transgressive contact in the name of sanctity. Yet Wyatt's tone of weary frustration invites a different interpretation, at least at the level of feeling: the English Caesar may have gone beyond the limits of propriety, failing to render unto God what belongs to God, and, in the process, spoiling the hunt for the speaker and for many others.

In the absence of any prohibition, Spenser's speaker is surprisingly free to touch the deare. His twist on his English precedent implies that the prerogative of an earthly Caesar would have hindered love, which takes hold within a delicate balance of fate, free choice, and will. Any possible clash between the wills of God and of Caesar in matters of love disappears when the English monarch ceases to meddle. In *Amoretti* 33, Spenser admits that his love may exist in a state of conflict with his service to the queen. He writes to his friend Lodowick Bryskett that he has done a "[g]reat wrong" to his "sacred Empresse" by taking time away from *The Faerie Queene* to celebrate his own love (33.1–2). Given the importance of his personal experiences, writing of the queen properly would require "another wit" or "another living brest" (33.9, 14). The *Amoretti* not only demands all of Spenser but also celebrates a love that promises to confer on him a new identity. This is the experience of individuating Christian love that *The Faerie Queene* cannot confer on the queen, whose poetic images multiply in the absence of the fixity that marriage supposedly provides.[31] In the following sections, I look back to the 1590 *Faerie Queene*, which offers an allegorical mirror for the unmarried Elizabeth I and defers the happily ever after that Spenser claims for himself in his sonnet sequence. Reading across the *Amoretti* and *The Faerie Queene* in this way, we can discern the development of Spenser's poetic vocabulary defining conjugal love around an affirmation of personal singularity and against replaceability.

Love Interrupted

The first book of *The Faerie Queene* leads the reader to expect a conjugal conclusion only to postpone that celebration. This book teaches allegorical lessons about the challenge of holiness by narrating Redcrosse's struggle to live up to his calling as Una's future husband.[32] In telling this allegorical story, Spenser develops the language of beguiling and goodwill that he would subsequently deploy in *Amoretti* 67. In the early cantos, the wicked Archimago tricks Redcrosse into abandoning Una as unfaithful to him. Archimago then disguises himself as Redcrosse. Archimago orchestrates this confusion in identity to underscore the question of why Redcrosse—so susceptible to falsehoods—should be the object of Una's loyal love in the first place. Disguised as Redcrosse, Archimago approaches Una with words of reconciliation:

> My dearest Dame,
> Far be it from your thought, and fro my wil,
> To thinke that knighthood I so much should shame,
> As you to leaue, that haue me loued stil,
> And chose in Faery court of meere goodwil,
> Where noblest knights were to be found on earth. (1.3.28.1–6)

Archimago suggests that Redcrosse's destiny and actions have been shaped entirely by Una's choice to love him—by her "meere goodwil." This may be a piece of deceptive flattery on Archimago's part. His claim tends to conflict with Spenser's own description of the initial pairing of Una and Redcrosse in his letter to Walter Raleigh. In the letter, Spenser describes how Gloriana and Una work in tandem to transform "*a tall clownishe younge man*" initially "*vnfitte through his rusticity*" into Redcrosse.[33] Una brings the Christian armor that can transform an unfit man into a proper hero, and the queen (albeit somewhat begrudgingly) designates him as the man that Una should select as her champion. Redcrosse's identities as hero and future husband are conferred upon him by the queen, whose sovereign choice works in cooperation with the will of Christian truth personified.

The opening canto of book 1 seems to confirm Spenser's gloss in his letter to Raleigh. We learn that Redcrosse is

> [u]pon a great adventure . . . bond,
> That greatest *Gloriana* to him gaue. (1.1.3.1–2)

Yet Una does not correct Archimago's description of her relationship with Redcrosse as having been premised on her own mere goodwill. Instead, she takes pleasure in his "louely words," which seem to her

> due recompence
> Of all her passed paines. (1.3.30.1–2)

If Archimago partially occludes the full truth, he nonetheless offers Una a satisfying fantasy of her free choice in love. When Una accepts that fantasy without mentioning Gloriana's role, she sidesteps a more resounding affirmation of sovereignty's compatibility with Christian truth. Una seems to prefer a narrative based on her goodwill. In the context of *The Faerie Queene*, however, the longing for this kind of autonomy in love might be a problem for a celebration of Gloriana's sovereignty.

There is no simple solution to this problem, only the one offered by the unfolding allegory. Redcrosse must emerge as the suitable object of Una's faithful affections by undergoing the travails of holiness. Here, Spenser transforms the problem of husbandly merit into the basis of a national allegory. Redcrosse is not just any future husband seeking to be holy but, it turns out, the patron saint of England. The question of husbandly merit—made familiar to all Christian husbands by Pauline teaching—opens onto an investigation of how and why Protestant England should have emerged as the champion of Christian truth. The opening canto of *The Faerie Queene* immediately signals a slippage between Redcrosse's own merit and the symbol of Christ's atonement that shields him. The blood on Redcrosse's breast, Darryl Gless observes, "represents either Christ's merits applied to the faithful (imputed righteousness) or His virtues enacted in and by them (actual holiness of life)."[34] Later in book 1, Duessa and Sansjoy openly mock imputed righteousness as inimical to knightly valor and to love. Sansjoy accuses Redcrosse of winning Duessa (disguised as Fidessa) to "augment the glorie of his guile" and of defeating his brother Sansfoy "with guilefull snare" (1.4.42.1, 47.5). Guile is, at this stage in the narrative, a trait associated with figures like Archimago and Duessa; the logic of beguiling the beguiler as a redemptive act has yet to be established. As a result, Redcrosse's enemies are able to claim that being imputed with Christ's righteousness is a fraudulent form of heroism.

This accusation is a travesty of a Protestant understanding of justification, but it stings enough to form the basis of Redcrosse's despair. The question of Redcrosse's personal fitness and real merit comes to a head when Arthur has to liberate him from bondage to Orgoglio.[35] As A. C. Hamilton notes, when Arthur embarks on "a deepe descent, as darke as hell" to rescue Redcrosse, he is being likened to Langland's victorious

Christ (1.8.39.7–9n). After redeeming Redcrosse in a manner reminiscent of Christ's harrowing hell, Arthur transmits to the lesser knight a version of the challenge that Christian husbands confront as they are called to be Christlike when, in fact, they are sinners in need of salvation. Redcrosse's apparent lack of personal merit renders him vulnerable to Despair. Despair teaches Redcrosse that his knightly heroism has been characterized by bloodshed that will require punishment, "For life must life, and blood must blood repay" (1.9.43.6). A few stanzas later, Despair asks,

> Is not he iust, that all this doth behold
> From highest heuen, and beares an equall eie?
> Shall he thy sins vp in his knowledge fold,
> And guilty be of thine impietie? (1.10.47.1–4)

Despair is certainly right that Redcrosse is a sinner but lures him into forgetting that he has been justified and that he is in the process of being sanctified. After having been redeemed, Redcrosse cannot see how he can live up to the calling of being a deserving husband. Una herself has to intervene to snap Redcrosse out of his state. Before she teaches Redcrosse the lesson, "Where iustice growes, there grows eke greter grace," she reminds him of his knightly duty to perform his quest as her champion (1.9.53.6). Prompted by Una, Redcrosse will eventually conjoin his heroic quest with the rhythms of Christian typology. He will emerge both as a proper champion and as a kind of second Adam through marriage to Adam's daughter.

Yet even as Spenser gives us intimations of an eschatological conclusion, he cannot celebrate the end of redemptive history in his opening book. Redcrosse's allegiance to Gloriana, which prompts his abrupt departure from his bride, serves as shorthand for the forces preventing the allegory and the narrative of marriage from coming together. Deferral is required so that the perfection of England's religious identity is not fully achieved in this narrative; the late sixteenth-century present would then be a gratuitous postscript rather than a time of necessary Christian reform.[36] This fact concerns Elizabeth directly: through the poem's dynastic chronicles, history reaches out beyond the poem to confer on Elizabeth the role of perfecting the union between nation and church. Gloriana must defer the consummation that underwrites the holiness of dynastic marriage so that Elizabeth I can eventually emerge as Protestant England's heir apparent.

By forming but also undermining the link between Queen Elizabeth and the poem that celebrates her, marriage functions as a key site of politico-theological thinking within the allegorical poem.[37] In the proem to book 1, Spenser hails the queen as a mirror of divine grace and majesty and locates in Gloriana her "true glorious type" (4.7). Yet the proem to book 2 describes the poem itself as a mirror in which Elizabeth is invited to behold herself. This poetic mirror, however, refracts as much as it reflects. Elizabeth's iconography as the Virgin Queen makes it a strenuous exercise to bring chastity and love together in Spenser's allegory. Eventually, the splitting of the queen's image into the figures of Gloriana and Belphoebe opens onto a complex interplay of virginity, chastity, and marriage. As John King observes, this interplay serves as a basis of the poem's meditation about the monarch's two bodies.[38] King's observation offers a useful corrective. In an important earlier study, Marie Axton elaborates on Kantorowicz's theory by detailing how a theory of Queen Elizabeth's two bodies was developed not just in legal discourses but also in the drama of the period. Axton examines how appeals to the queen's two bodies were useful in negotiating the drawn-out crisis of succession. Yet Axton shows that this quasi-mystical notion remained controversial as it competed with other, less mystifying notions. (If, for example, Elizabeth "justified her single life by claiming the kingdom as her spouse" in the 1560s, both the House of Commons and dramatists at Gray's Inn tended to reject that metaphorical claim because they remained "impatient for a real child born of their Queen."[39]) If a theory of the queen's two bodies did become ascendant, it tended to do so late in Elizabeth's reign or even posthumously.

In *The Faerie Queene*, the disconnect between the drive toward a conjugal conclusion and the celebration of the unmarried Elizabeth reminds us of the poem's inability to unite the female monarch's two bodies in a stable fashion. Axton's study is primarily concerned with drama, and Spenser only makes a few appearances in it. When Axton does devote attention to *The Faerie Queene*, she treats it as an Arthuriad—one that affirms the legendary line of succession from Arthur to Elizabeth. Affirming Arthur's historical reality, Axton observes, furnishes legal theorists in the sixteenth and seventeenth centuries a way to teach "that a king had always had two bodies and that ever since the time of Arthur allegiance had been sworn to the king's body natural."[40] Yet Axton does not mention how, in *The Faerie Queene*, the line of descent from Arthur to Elizabeth is not direct but rather takes a detour through Artegall, whose union with Britomart is perpetually deferred in the extant narrative. John King subsequently reminds us that by fostering an identification between Elizabeth and Gloriana, Spenser disrupts a linear story of descent. Spenser divides the image of the queen into a personal self destined for chastity (but with a twin destined for marriage) and a sovereign self destined for a marriage to the deserving hero Arthur.

In book 1, the question of why Una should be attached to Redcrosse already begins to suggest how an allegory of Christian marriage cannot serve to unify the queen's two bodies. Even before the introduction of the virgin Belphoebe in the poem, the queen's reflection is already split when Una—rather than Gloriana—models the proper bearing of a chaste queen:

Who in her self-resemblance well beseene,
Did seem such, as she was, a goodly maiden Queene. (1.12.8.8–9)

As an allegorical bride, Una seems destined for a nonliteral and mystical form of marriage; this form would be compatible with Elizabeth's self-presentation as a wife and mother to her nation. Yet the identification of Una and Elizabeth as nonliteral brides is unsettled by Una's willingness to love an initially undeserving bridegroom. It is important for the narrative that Una is not merely an allegorical bride but also a character who grapples with a version of the practical problem that all Christian wives confront within Pauline marriage. The interruption of Una's betrothal is necessary both for Redcrosse's service to Gloriana and for Spenser's poetic service to Queen Elizabeth. This interruption allows the subsequent books to look for (but never perfect) alternative ways for sovereignty and love to function together across the queen's divided personae and reflections.

In book 2, Guyon embodies a provisional solution, but only by suspending the question of love. We know Guyon to be the only protagonist of *The Faerie Queene* without a conjugal destiny; his mission calls him to avoid love as "a monster fell," as the Palmer calls it (2.4.35.3).[41] Guyon's heroism is so practically effective because it is limited. His mission is to conjoin temperance with retributive justice rather than to render that form of justice compatible with conjugal love through a logic of Christian redemption. Guyon's heroism makes it easier to harmonize epic patterns with soteriological questions, all under the aegis of service to the queen. As I go on to argue, this becomes especially apparent at the center of book 2, when Guyon descends into Mammon's Cave. Within this *descensus* episode, Guyon establishes the logic of beguiling the beguiler, which Spenser deploys again to celebrate his personal love in the *Amoretti*. By echoing Langland's account of Christ's victory over the devil, Spenser opens the question of how Guyon's limited version of Christlike heroism might render atonement compatible with reason. Yet even if Guyon succeeds in doing so, he has no interest in securing a link between redemption and love. Guyon's success results from self-preservation and political service in the name of just anger. For the sake of expediency, Guyon temporarily suspends the dangers of the subject/object reversal that function within Spenser's promotion of conjugal love.

To put this in the Ovidian terms discussed earlier, Guyon avoids the trappings of Narcissus and serves only as a faithful hound-like instrument of his queen. In the proem to book 2, Spenser addresses not only the queen but also his general readership. Whereas Elizabeth should continue to use the poem as a mirror, other readers might be motivated by inclinations toward objective knowledge as well as self-knowledge. Spenser specifically addresses the reader who may be skeptical of Faery Lond's existence:

> ne let him then admyre
> But yield his sence to bee too blunt and bace
> That no'te without an hound fine footing trace. (2, proem, 4.3–5)

Spenser declares that an acute reader might not need a hound to find Faery Lond while, at the same time, describing the poem as a hound-like instrument for a reader with cruder sensibilities. In the first canto of book 2, this question of the necessity of a hound-like instrument is applied to Guyon himself. Archimago lures Guyon into believing that a knight has defiled a lady. Guyon asks,

> Where may that treachour then . . . be found,
> Or by what meanes may I his footing tract?
> That shall I shew (sayd he [Archimago]) as sure, as hound
> The stricken Deare doth chaleng by the bleeding wound. (2.1.12.6–9)

Temporarily duped by Archimago, Guyon proves himself "bace" enough to require the fine footing of a hound—a role that Archimago is eager to fill. In the final canto of book 2, Guyon finds himself momentarily in danger of an Actaeon-like predicament. As he approaches the Bower of Bliss,

> *Guyon* hapned by the same to wend,
> Two naked Damzelles he therein espyde. (2.12.63.5–6)

One damsel hides while the other tempts Guyon with a partial display of her body. Yet the Palmer intervenes to snap Guyon out of this transgressive gaze. Just as Guyon's speech to Archimago in the first canto suggests, the proper object of his hunt is not an object of erotic desire but a target of just retribution. His destiny is not to be an Actaeon-like hunter who stumbles onto erotic experience but rather to maintain his mission as an instrument of justice.

Guyon's mission does not call him to rewrite the fates of Actaeon and Narcissus but rather to steer clear of both. Guyon, in other words, stops short where the Spenserian speaker of the *Amoretti* will resume in order to arrive at a satisfying sense of Christian love. Guyon's avoidance of love defines his position with respect both to his queen and to Christian belief. When Archimago craftily positions himself as a kind of hound, he leads Guyon first to Duessa, and then to Redcrosse. Guyon comes perilously close to jousting with the knight of holiness. Guyon repents that he has almost leveled his "cursed steele" against the "sacred badge of [his] Redeemers death" while Redcrosse describes how his hand almost

> did haynouse violence
> On that fayre ymage of that heauenly Mayd. (2.1.27.5–6, 28.6–7)

Queen Elizabeth should function as a mirror of the divine, but here, Gloriana's image comes close to clashing with the symbol of Christ's sacrifice. After this fight is averted, Redcrosse describes Gloriana's image providing Guyon with "faire defence" and then concludes, "Your court'sie takes on you anothers dew offence" (2.1.28.8–9). The respective meanings of Redcrosse's and Guyon's shields disclose the differences between their missions. Redcrosse's task has been to align himself with the righteousness that has been imputed to him; only then will he be a Christlike future husband. As Redcrosse comments, Guyon does take upon him another's due offence, but this does not make him Christlike in self-sacrificing love. Guyon does not suffer the punishment due properly to others but instead carries out just vengeance on behalf of others' wrongs—with an affective intensity that he feels vicariously. By curbing the dangers of that intensity, he renders himself fit to express justice, but not grace that exhibits the meaning of love.

Questions concerning Guyon's freedom versus obedience do arise, in ways that parallel the earlier question of whether Una freely chose to love Redcrosse out of her mere goodwill or whether she was directed to do so by Gloriana. Guyon volunteers to punish Acrasia on behalf of Amavia and Ruddymane, but Spenser's letter to Raleigh describes Gloriana's appointing Guyon to carry out the task of vengeance. This discrepancy seems to echo the question concerning who or what, exactly, paired Una with Redcrosse. In this latter case, however, less friction arises because anger proves more readily transferable than love; anger can be felt genuinely even if it is commanded by another. Guyon discovers, in fact, that just wrath is dangerously transferable—its objects too slippery. This is in contrast to the affective fixity that love demands as it aims toward marriage. The language of goodwill recurs as Redcrosse and Guyon reconcile and describe their respective motivations for service. As Redcrosse tells Guyon,

> More then goodwill to me attribute nought:
> For all I did, I did but as I ought. (2.1.33.4–5)

For Una, as we have seen, goodwill serves as a partially fantastical basis for her free choice in love. For Redcrosse, by contrast, an appeal to goodwill helps him negotiate his religious calling with his political service; even if he deploys the rhetoric of modesty, he is claiming a balance of religious and political duty as emanating from his will.

Guyon's mission is clarifying insofar as it remains unburdened by the demands of free choice and reciprocity within love. In the second canto, Guyon and Medina seem well suited for each other: he is the knight of temperance, and she embodies the virtuous mean. When Medina asks Guyon to tell his story, he responds,

> This thy demaund, O Lady, doth reuiue
> Fresh memory in me of that great Queene. (2.2.40.1–2)[42]

Guyon echoes famous words uttered by Aeneas to Dido, but in a way that underscores that Guyon will not become entangled in an erotic relationship.

When Aeneas complains, "Infandum, regina, iubes renovare dolorem," the *regina* that Aeneas addresses is Dido herself.[43] Guyon's queen, by contrast, is the absent Gloriana, whom he hails as "th'Idole of her makers great magnificence" (2.2.41.9). In the ensuing story told to Medina, Guyon revises the previous canto by revealing that Gloriana originally did send him, at the Palmer's request, to punish Acrasia. In this instance, the confirmation of Spenser's explanation in his letter to Raleigh subordinates Guyon's vow to Amavia to his service to his sovereign. The conclusion of canto 2 confirms that Guyon's allegiance to Gloriana is a defense against love. In contrast to the way Aeneas inflames Dido's desire with his speech, Guyon speaks strategically so that the night

> [t]hose guests beguyled, did beguyle their eyes
> Of kindly sleep, that did them ouertake. (2.2.46.6–7)

Through the allure of speech devoted to his queen, Guyon starts to recuperate beguiling—the act that had, in the previous book, been aligned with un-Christian treachery. Guyon's allegiance to Gloriana functions as a form of beguilement that allows him to escape erotic entanglement of the sort that had delayed Aeneas.

For Guyon, justice sundered from love is more expedient than the attempt to harmonize the two through Christlike self-sacrifice. The theological and literary logics of his mission become more apparent in Mammon's Cave. In this epic descent, beguiling the beguiler borrows the structure or logic of Christ's redemptive heroism but does not secure any form of love. Within the cave, Guyon must resist wealth as the offered means to achieve narcissistic self-satisfaction. In book 1, Avarice personified had been likened to Narcissus, "whose plenty made him pore" (1.4.29.4). It is no surprise that Mammon is similarly aligned with Narcissus. Mammon is shaped

> to feede his eye
> And couetous desire with his huge threasury. (2.7.4.8–9)

Mammon declares that narcissistic appreciation of hoarded wealth can satisfy the longings of those who "hauing not complaine, and hauing it vpbrayd" (2.7.14.9). Spenser goes on to echo this exact line in *Amoretti* 35 and 83 to describe the predicament of Narcissus-like unhappiness in love. As a sonneteer, Spenser does admit the possibility of his own economic ambitions through the language of greed and "covetize." Yet the speaker disavows such motivations by declaring that "all this worlds glory" proves an empty show next to the only true object of his desire—not a reflection of himself but rather an external "she." In *The Faerie Queene*, Mammon presents Guyon with a more candid conflation of desire and greed in his presentation of Philotime. She not only is fair in and of herself but also represents a path to "all this worldes blis" (2.7.48.8). Initially, Guyon relies on an association between wealth and guile to reject Mammon's offers. Guyon deems all riches the

> roote of all disquietness;
> First got with guile. (2.7.12.2–3)

His rhetoric softens just a bit when he rejects Mammon's wealth out of the mere possibility that it has been obtained from

> rightfull owner by vnrighteous lott,
> Or that bloodguiltness or guile them blott. (2.7.19.4–5)

The vocabulary of beguiling reveals the basis of Guyon's rhetorical maneuvers. Regarding this exchange, Paul Alpers remarks that if it stages "a debate between contending moralities, Guyon seems rather stupid to respond solely to Mammon's offer of money and not to his broader claims."[44] Yet Guyon is preparing himself not just to reject the fruits of alleged guile but also to deploy a just form of guile himself.[45] At the conclusion of the canto, the poet remarks that Guyon did not suffer

> lust his safety to betray;
> So goodly did beguile the Guyler of his pray. (2.7.64.8–9)

The immediate occasion for this comment is Guyon's refusal of Proserpina's silver seat, but the word "lust" echoes Mammon's offer of his daughter:

> Thy spouse I will her make, if that thou lust,
> That she may thee aduance for works and merit iust. (2.7.49.8–9)

Guyon's refusal of Philotime begins with an appeal to decorum:

> But I, that am fraile flesh and earthly wight,
> Vnworthy match for such immortall mate
> My selfe well wote, and mine vnequall fate. (2.7.50.2–4)

In the *Amoretti*, Spenser finds in Christian grace a way to overcome his lower economic station and his spiritual unworthiness. Guyon recognizes, by contrast, that Mammon's "offerd grace" (2.8.33.1) is spurious and rejects it with a guileful claim of his own:

> yet is my trouth yplight,
> And loue auowd to other Lady late. (2.7.50.6–7)

Guyon implies that his vassalage to Gloriana is plighted love. This is a half-truth, and it allows Guyon to shield himself from love (the combination of narcissistic self-regard, economic gain, and heterosexual union that Mammon offers) with the absent person of Gloriana.

The limitations of Guyon's achievement, however, are brought into relief by comparison with two precedents, Aeneas and Christ. When Guyon sees Tantalus on the banks of the Garden of Proserpina, the hero is explicitly likened to Aeneas at the river Phlegethon.[46] Spenser's hero goes further than Aeneas had by interacting with Tantalus directly, but the encounter is hardly redemptive. In this grimly comic moment, the only consolation that Guyon offers the damned spirit is the advice to endure his punishment and to serve as an "[e]nsample" of "mind more temperate"—the same virtue that Guyon himself must learn to embody in the world above (2.7.60.4). Tantalus responds by railing against divine injustice. The subsequent pairing of Tantalus with Pilate underscores the shortcomings of Guyon's temperance in an epic underworld that is classical and also demands a Christian understanding. Pilate's inability to wash his "filthy feculent" hands links him to Ruddymane, whose bloody hands serve as an image of hereditary sin (2.7.61.4). Pilate's presence reminds us that Christ alone removes the imprint of sin, and that he did so by becoming the victim of displaced punishment. Pilate recalls how he

> [d]eliuered vp the Lord of life to dye,
> And did acquite a murder felonous. (2.7.62.6–7)

In authorizing the punishment of the innocent instead of the guilty, Pilate unwittingly advances redemptive history but stains himself as culpable in the process.

Both Pilate's condition and the solution offered by Christ's atonement raise questions about the transferability of guilt. If this episode were tasked with harmonizing redemption with love, then these questions about transferability would complicate the Pauline teaching that the meaning of marriage is perfected by Christ's sacrifice. In contrast with the affirmation of a uniquely personal love, Christ's sacrifice might imply a kind of fungibility when it comes to personhood and agency. Guilt is mysteriously transferable to all of us, as Ruddymane's condition exemplifies. Atonement can operate through just wrath being taken out on the innocent.[47] Guyon's quest demonstrates that displaced vengeance can establish a tenable mode of personal feeling and political service. Yet Guyon sidesteps the challenge of showing how this kind of displaced affect can be compatible with love, especially in a form that longs for personal fixity. Like Langland's Christ, Guyon effectively beguiles the guiler in the underworld. Yet Guyon's descent does not redeem anyone or anything in particular. His calling is only to avoid contact with defilement. He deploys guile and counterguile to avoid the dangerous reversals of agency involved in an attempt at free and mutual love.

Love Beguiled

Both the efficacy and the limitations of Guyon's heroism become apparent at the end of book 2, when he destroys Acrasia's bower. Guyon does prove himself more resistant to sexual temptation than one of his predecessors in Christian epic. In Torquato Tasso's *Gersualemme liberata*, the Christian knight Rinaldo succumbs to the temptress Armida and needs to be rescued.[48] As his rescuers Carlo and Ubaldo learn, Rinaldo's transgressive desire expresses itself as a narcissistic form of Petrarchan frustration. Armida's desire for Rinaldo is sparked as she looks at him "sí che par Narciso al fonte" (as Narcissus [gazed at his own reflection] at the fount).[49] Rinaldo, in turn, comes to wear a crystal mirror for Armida to behold herself while he implores her to see a truer reflection in his own person. He insists that the mirror on his breast will reflect her *forma* (form) and *meraviglia* (wonder) better than her own crystal can.[50] Later, a superior form of narcissistic self-regard offers a remedy for Rinaldo's condition. Upon seeing his reflection in the diamond shield Ubaldo presents before him, Rinaldo finally recognizes his error and begins the process of renewing his heroism. When, in *Amoretti* 45, Spenser implores his beloved to put away her "glasse of christall clene," he casts himself not just as a generic Petrarchan lover but also as one specifically resembling Tasso's Rinaldo. Yet Spenser claims to have found a solution to the peril of narcissism within a Protestant form of marriage that corrects Petrarchan desire. In *Amoretti* 35 and 83, he does not need external intervention to rescue him from narcissistic fixation because he appeals to gender difference itself to disclaim his Narcissus-like tendencies.[51] By contrast, by the time Guyon approaches the Bower of Bliss, he has already learned to avoid narcissistic self-regard and the dangers associated with redounding desire. The speaker of the *Amoretti* and Guyon advance two different resolutions to the dilemma posed by Tasso's Rinaldo—the one seeks Christian marriage, and the other destroys the site of erotic desire.

In *The Faerie Queene*, the partial resemblance between Rinaldo and Guyon opens onto broader questions about how a Christian romance epic should conclude—and how decisive a conjugal celebration should be. This chapter opened by mentioning the importance of Ariosto's precedent in achieving poetic closure through a marriage of conversion. As Ariosto's translator, Harington praises this conclusion as it brings to an end the allegorical, moral, and narrative trajectories of the *Orlando* poems, all while fulfilling an ambition of Virgilian epic. Like Ariosto before him, Tasso writes in praise of the House of Este. In contrast to *Orlando furioso*, however, the ending of *Gerusalemme liberata* leaves tantalizingly unclear what role a triumphant marriage plays in harmonizing the narrative with the allegorical designs of a poem that also looks ahead to the House of Este. We do not learn whether Rinaldo's relationship with Armida is redeemed through marriage. The poet leaves unspoken whether Armida accepts Rinaldo's marriage proposal and whether she converts to Christianity.[52]

My aim has been to detail what it means for Spenser to claim for himself the triumph of marriage in a form that never materializes in *The Faerie Queene*. As book 3 of *The Faerie Queene* moves beyond Guyon's avoidance of love to redirect us toward allegorical heroism with a conjugal destiny, Britomart comes to face a potentially insurmountable task. It falls on this female Narcissus to establish mirroring as the grounds for Christian love while, at the same stroke, securing a dynastic marriage that secures Elizabeth's legendary ancestry. Britomart's introduction to erotic desire challenges her to become the master rather than the dupe of guile. In canto 1, Britomart fails to understand the "guilfull message" embedded in Malecasta's glances, and Britomart's innocence renders her susceptible to her hostess's more overt advances (3.1.51.9). "Who meanes no guile," the poet comments,

> be-guiled soonest shall
> And to faire semblaunce doth light faith annexe. (3.1.54.6–7)

Only by handling guile more strategically can Britomart perfect narcissistic desire for and an Actaeon-like pursuit of her future husband. Only then can she attempt the calibration of love that Spenser subsequently claims to have achieved in the *Amoretti*.

Britomart's heroism does promise to allow Spenser's religious and literary treatment of marriage to surpass Tasso's and to rival Ariosto's. Whereas Guyon has avoided the temptations that ensnare Tasso's Rinaldo, Britomart goes on to perfect a version of the role that Clorinda plays with respect to marriage in *Gerusalemme liberata*. In the second canto of Tasso's epic, the lovers Sofronia and Olindo act out in Jerusalem a version of the Pauline link between Christ's sacrifice and conjugal love. Sofronia offers herself up as a sacrificial victim on behalf of her people, and Olindo in turn desires to take upon himself the punishment leveled at his beloved (or to join her in death). Clorinda arrives to redeem this couple and to allow them to live rather than die as husband and wife. Yet her pagan identity threatens to turn this episode into a parody of the true meaning of marriage being exhibited through Christ's redeeming love. Much later, in the twelfth canto, the reader learns that Clorinda had been conceived by a Christian mother under the iconography of Saint George. It turns out that Clorinda's destiny has always been a Christian one. Yet Clorinda converts only as she dies from the wounds that she has suffered from her would-be Christian husband, Tancredi. The redemptive meaning of marriage and the earthly experience of love must remain sundered until—as the spirit of Clorinda explains to Tancredi in a dream—the afterlife.

If Britomart can redeem others to chaste love and also secure her own union with Artegall—and a dynastic line that points to Queen Elizabeth—then she might harmonize Tasso's transcendent impulses (particularly when it comes to the perfection of love's meaning) with Ariosto's celebration of marriage on earth. The implications of Britomart's mission as a redeemer-wife are clarified in the 1596 installment of *The Faerie Queene*. The argument of book 5, canto 5 tells us that Artegall is "*subdewd by guile*" when he succumbs to the Amazon Radigund (line 2). Radigund works to corrupt Artegall's capacity to love Britomart freely and by choice. Clarin serves as a go-between in Radigund's attempts at seduction. Clarin explains to her mistress that she seeks "by his freedome to get his goodwill" (5.5.32.7–8). Radigund then orders Clarin to deliver a token through Eumenias, whose name means "goodwill". Clarin, however, beguiles the guileful Radigund as she attempts to win Artegall's goodwill for herself. This is the context in which Britomart, at the opening of the very next canto, labors to beguile herself—and ends up resembling Christ in the process. In Artegall's absence,

> her grief with errour to beguyle,
> She fayn'd to count the time againe anew. (5.6.5.3–4)

This seems like a minor affective negotiation, a mere attempt to distract herself. Yet Britomart's self-beguiling assumes a greater significance when it mediates between biblical meaning and a poetic myth of love:

> Ye guilty eyes (sayd she) the which with guile
> My heart at first betrayd, will ye betray
> My life now to, for which a little whyle
> Ye will not watch? false watches, wellaway. (5.6.25.1–4)

These lines suggest how Britomart can be simultaneously like Christ and like his imperfect followers. On the night before his crucifixion, he asks his disciplines to pray, but they succumb to the weakness of the flesh by falling asleep. The allusion is confirmed when the poet describes the hour when the

> bird, that warned *Peter* of his fall,
> First rings his siluer Bell t'each sleepy wight. (5.6.27.2–3)

When Britomart attempts to be a kind of Christlike master over her wayward eyes, she shuttles direct echoes of the gospels into Spenser's allegory of chastity accommodating Christian love. As we have seen, in *Amoretti* 35 and 83, the Spenserian speaker likens his eyes rather than his whole self to Narcissus. The speaker is estranged from his eyes as part of the sonnet's attempt to overcome the impression that the speaker is truly like Narcissus. This estrangement is even more pronounced in Britomart's case as she works to make her status as a kind of female Narcissus more recognizably Christian. As a result, an interplay of righteous beguiling and narcissism operates within Britomart's person as a kind of affective circuit. Even in isolation, Britomart's love for Artegall allows her to progress from the role of fleshly and erring disciple to that of a Christlike teacher.

The configuration of Christlike heroism and vulnerable love embodied by Britomart promises to resolve some of the problems concerning marriage established in book 1. If Britomart and Una share the question of why they should love fallible husbands, Britomart provides a new answer: she loves her future husband not only as the masculine image she has seen in her mirror but also in the way that Christ loves his bride. This is a gender-bending solution to the problems posed by Pauline marriage. Yet for that reason, the solution ends up handing a challenge back to Britomart's future husband, Artegall. After Britomart defeats the Amazon Radigund, Artegall must depart from his redeemer-wife not only to fulfill his service to Gloriana but also to clarify his heroic status. The basic problem of a husband's personal merit with respect to his wife ends up resurfacing in the poem. In the 1590 *Faerie Queene*, Britomart achieves a provisional triumph by redeeming another future wife, Amoret. Yet Spenser goes on to rewrite the book's happy conclusion by undoing Amoret's reunion with Scudamour. Even the original version reminds us that this allegorical narrative of marriage remains imperfect when it describes Britomart's sense of half envy at the happy conjugal conclusion that she has brought about. When Amoret and Scudamour embrace, their hermaphroditic union tends to recall the definition of marriage as "one flesh" in Genesis rather than the redefinition in the New Testament (Gen. 2:24). The marriage of Amoret and Scudamour should not succumb to a typological regression: their union has been made possible by a Christian or even Christlike heroine. What remains unclear, however, is how Britomart should secure a Christian form of heterosexual union for herself.

When Britomart liberates Amoret at the end of book 3, she prepares herself to become a Christlike wife. In Busirane's antechamber, however,

Britomart begins to define her station not through a direct appeal to Christian belief but again with respect to Ovidian myths. Among the stories that she sees in the tapestry demonstrating Cupid's might is the story "Thebane Semelee" (3.11.33.1). In book 3 of the *Metamorphoses*, the story of Semele mediates between the stories of Actaeon and of Narcissus. I have been arguing for the importance of the interplay between these two myths in Spenser's imagination. Up to this point in *The Faerie Queene*, Spenser has offered no explicit comparisons between the story of Britomart and her nurse, Glauce, with that of Semele and her nurse, Beroë. The book's penultimate canto suggests the reason for such avoidance. Semele's story reveals the danger of mistakenly seeking and then experiencing direct erotic contact with the divine: "she with death bought her desire" (3.11.33.5). Semele's story reveals to Britomart how her own form of mediated desire, Narcissus-like in origin but also capable of real fulfillment, will be more safely chaste. Conjugal love should participate in divine love and be an index of it, but the erotic contact between a husband and wife should be a safe-sex reflection of the love between Christ and his Church.

Yet even if Britomart's conjugal destiny exists at a safe remove from the fate of Semele, she is unable to model a suitable synthesis of Narcissus and Actaeon under the aegis of chaste Christian love. When Britomart goes on to confront Cupid as an idol of love, she "euermore and more vpon it gazed" (3.11.49.8). This idolatrous fixation then gives way to the riddle of how a knight of chastity should comport herself—a visual riddle that teaches her to be bold, but not too bold. As she begins to consider this puzzle, Britomart cannot

>   satisfy
> Her greedy eyes with gazing a long space. (3.11.53.3–4)

Because erotic love still functions as an idolatrous trap, she begins to regress into a futile rather than productive form of narcissism. Spenser immediately associates Britomart's Narcissus-like predicament with the breakdown of an Actaeon-like pursuit that should, ideally, redefine subject and object within love:

> But more she meruaild that no footings trace,
> Nor wight appear'd, but wastefull emptinesse. (3.11.53.5–6)

In *Amoretti* 67, Spenser's speaker is surprised that his pursuit results in his "deare" love turning back to meet him: "Strange thing me seemd," he remarks,

> to see a beast so wyld,
> so goodly wonne with her owne will beguyld.

For Britomart, by contrast, the "[s]traunge thing" is not reciprocation but instead the conspicuous absence of an other who might pursue her or be pursued by her (3.11.53.8).

The pattern of similarities with and divergences from Spenser's triumph in the *Amoretti* continues in book 3's final canto. The turning point in Spenser's sonnet sequence makes erotic love sufficiently compatible with Christ's work of salvation, while affirming the free choice and contingency that make reciprocal desire possible despite gender asymmetry. Such dynamics work differently for Britomart as she suffers in Amoret's place in order to save her. Busirane may embody loose, unchaste desire, but his vengefulness seeks a fixed object. Yet the force of his violence alights on Britomart inadvertently, as "Vnwares" his weapon

> stroke into her snowie chest,
> That litle drops empurpled her faire breast. (3.12.33.3–4)

Owing to this stroke of mischance, an eroticized form of vengeful violence becomes transferable, from Amoret to Britomart. Britomart, in turn, experiences a desire for retribution when "life she him enuyde, and long'd reuenge to see" (3.12.34.12). Within Britomart's experience as a heroic victim, a feeling of vengeance becomes compatible with a desire to liberate love.

Within this configuration of desire, revenge, and sacrificial bloodletting, Britomart does allow love to prevail in the 1590 ending of book 3. A satisfying subject/object reversal occurs when Scudamour meets Amoret,

> Like as a Deare, that greedily embayes
> In the coole soile, after long thirstinesse. (3.12.44.7–8)

Yet even this conclusion leaves Britomart's quest unfulfilled. Britomart may have freed others so that they might love, but she will have to work in the later books to clarify what it means to be both a redeemer and a chaste wife. It is fitting that before developing Britomart's Christlike heroism further in the 1596 *Faerie Queene*, Spenser needs to undo the union of Scudamour and Amoret. The revised 1596 ending of book 3 uses a familiar word to describe the frustration of Amoret's love: Scudamour's sudden absence leaves her "beguyld" and "fild with new affright" (3.12.44.9). In contrast to the *Amoretti*, the 1596 *Faerie Queene* picks up where Spenser left off by regressing to a beguilement that speaks to disappointment in love rather than to its surprising fulfillment.

* * *

In book 6, canto 4, Spenser underscores what is missing from so many of the provisionally satisfying unions that his poem offers: a way to harmonize the dynastic functions of marriage with the longing for personal love. Sir Bruin's lordship is imperiled by his loving but childless marriage to Matilde. Calepine's delivery of a surrogate son—who will "[b]e *gotten, not begotten,*" as the prophecy foretells—will restore the couple's personal and political happiness (6.4.32.7). The surrogate child does not only embody a practical solution. His origins also suggest that he serves as a redemptive substitute for Ruddymane, the orphaned infant marked by the hereditary stain of original sin. At the same time, the terms of the prophecy make a clear distinction between this baby and God's only begotten Son. Perhaps, as Pauline teaching suggests, only an appeal to mystery can resolve the affective contradictions involved in the story of a Son who gives himself up as a sacrifice to paternal wrath to redeem his metaphorical wife. If redemptive sacrifice perfects conjugal love, the possibly redefined meaning of regulated reproduction remains uncertain. Even in the *Amoretti*, Spenser's celebration of Christian marriage's capacity to elevate a highly personal love is limited. Spenser had once been married to a woman named Maccabaeus Childe, and the couple had had two children together, but such facts are pushed to the side as he declares his love for his one true Elizabth.

2

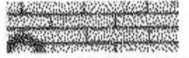

Jealousy against Substitution in *Othello* and *The Winter's Tale*

Elizabeth I's refusal to name a successor generated fears of instability for many years. Yet upon her death in 1603, the accession of James VI of Scotland to the English throne proved to be a relatively smooth affair. Religious strife and economic uncertainties persisted, and the Gunpowder Plot would reveal the extent of the threats to James. Yet his reign still promised to resolve the turmoil over succession unleashed by Henry VIII. James took the English throne married and the father of sons who could continue the Stuart dynasty. He did not only occupy the literal status of husband and father but also attempted to make marriage part of his mythology of kingship. Shortly after his coronation, he declared before the English Parliament that the entire island was his lawful wife. Yet at the more literal register of royal marriage, it would prove difficult to uphold James and his wife, Anna of Denmark, as exemplars of love. Their marriage had proven notoriously tempestuous. As Alan Stewart recounts, James had, as the Scottish king, written in "shockingly unguarded" terms of his decision to marry in 1589 as a practical and political matter.[1] Reports of "'an open diffidence'" between the royal couple as well as their "'very evil menage'" came to circulate.[2] As the Scottish queen consort, Anna had even been suspected of playing a role in the Gowrie conspiracy, the mysterious plot in 1600 to kidnap or to assassinate James. Once James and Anna became English monarchs, rumors intensified about Anna's harboring of Roman Catholics (and of her own conversion), her political machinations, and her sexual infidelities. James worked to attenuate her influence; his own sexual dalliances have famously been the basis of rumor and speculation.

This chapter turns to Shakespeare's two great Jacobean plays of jealousy, *Othello* and *The Winter's Tale*. According to extant records, *Othello* was first performed at court in November 1604; *The Winter's Tale* was composed some six or seven years later. Yet this chapter does not examine the treatment of jealousy in these plays alongside the details of James's rule and his married life. I consider how these two plays advance religious and political thinking about Christian marriage by dramatizing jealousy as the exaggerated form of a love that insists on fixity and recoils at the idea of replacement. At the outset of *Othello*, loving marriage promises to perfect the hero's conversion to Christianity and his assimilation in Venetian society. Tragedy arises when Othello's need for personal affirmation cannot be fully accommodated by Christian marriage. Pauline teaching locates within all marriages an oscillation between personal love and a higher, corporate truth. Othello and Desdemona's particular marriage arises out of office-based forms of vocational identity; Othello discovers that his longing for permanent and absolute singularity in love cannot be fulfilled. Yet the tragedy that ensues has little effect on the prevailing order because Venice's republican polity, as the play imagines it, has no essential stake in marriage as the vehicle of continuity. In the aftermath of Othello's tragedy, Venetian authorities have no trouble replacing him in his stations. In *The Winter's Tale*, by contrast, jealousy is the by-product of a hereditary monarchy in which the legitimacy of the royal heir is a vital concern. Leontes's lapse into an obsession with his wife's fidelity is famously sudden and irrational. Yet the obsession results from a pervasive anxiety about his singular status as king. The presence of another king may be the effective catalyst for jealousy, but that affective state registers Leontes's awareness that his marriage has already produced his own replacement. The only solution to the destructiveness unleashed by Leontes's jealousy lies in a Christian form of grace that promises to redeem royal marriage, even within the play's overtly pagan setting.

In both plays, jealousy reveals how the longing to be permanently affirmed as a singular individual is not fully compatible with Christian marriage. In a study of monotheism and violence, Regina Schwartz describes how, in the Hebrew Bible, Yahweh's jealousy maintains an exclusive national identity. Schwartz turns to the story of King David, Bathsheba, and

Uriah to illustrate the link between the jealousy attributed to God and the politics of human jealousy. "Monotheistic theology is obsessed with the possibility and actuality of betrayal," Schwartz observes, "and it is in that context that the king of Israel goes astray." Schwartz concludes that in Uriah's fidelity, "desire for God and human desire are made analogues of one another."[3] Within a Christian outlook, however, it remains unclear what role jealousy should play after the typological redefinition of marriage. In my introductory chapter, I observed that John Donne's *Holy Sonnet* 18 concludes with a memorable formulation of the disjunction between Christ's love for his church and the earthly experience of conjugal love. Jealousy lies at the heart of this disjunction, as Donne unsettles the norm of monogamous fidelity by proposing that Christ should properly be a witting and eager cuckold.

Othello and *The Winter's Tale* dramatize the political consequences of the unresolved question of jealousy. In these plays, jealousy produces a double bind for republican and monarchical polities: personal intimacy is rendered untenable both by a state that is relatively indifferent to conjugal love and by a form of sovereignty excessively invested in marriage for its own perpetuation. This is a bind that may still remain familiar to us in some form. Although we may deem state power an unwelcome encroachment on personal intimacy, we may still call on the state to provide love with legal, practical, and even affective forms of public legitimacy. *Othello* and *The Winter's Tale* remain two of the most influential treatments of jealousy in the history of drama in the English language. It is beyond the scope of this chapter to detail how these plays would—through print, performance, adaptation, and more diffuse patterns of influence—shape understandings of marriage in subsequent centuries. Yet this chapter does propose that by attending to the vocabulary of love against substitution, we can reconsider how our reading practices link the religious past to a less overtly religious modernity. This chapter advances a particular corrective by describing how the demand for personal love in these plays resists Carl Schmitt's efforts to subordinate art and aesthetic experience to so-called objective historical reality. In the 1956 *Hamlet or Hecuba*, Schmitt conscripts Shakespearean tragedy for his view of political history. He claims that we can account for *Hamlet*'s lasting aesthetic force through a political understanding of taboo (the verboten content of the play amounting to James I's fraught relationship to his mother, Mary, Queen of Scots) rather than a psychoanalytic one. He sees history functioning as the "objective reality of the tragic action."[4] By reading *Hamlet* in this way, he works to subordinate *Hamlet*'s tragic power to his historical narrative—one that looks ahead to the inadequacies of Stuart kingship and, beyond, to the necessity of a modern form of state power.

Othello helps us to discern the distortions in Schmitt's claims about Shakespearean tragedy. More specifically, *Othello* helps us pinpoint in his thinking the racist and sexually anxious fascination that he would attempt to occlude with his call for an objective understanding of tragedy.[5] Even as *Othello* has long functioned as a template for racial anxieties at the limits of civic incorporation, the play reveals a disjunction between the hero's need to privilege the personal experience of love, on the one hand, and the shared realities of the state, on the other. Even as the play limits the tragic effects of jealousy to Othello and Desdemona's marriage—with no real effects on the political stability of Venice—that conclusion offers no affirmation of the supervenience of state power. *The Winter's Tale* subsequently dramatizes jealousy as a problem for hereditary monarchy. Yet this play resists Schmitt's claim that Shakespearean tragedy registers the problems of the Stuart dynasty in ways that look ahead to the advent of modern state power. Read together, Shakespeare's plays of jealousy reveal marriage to be a site "where religion is no longer working—but neither are the secular solutions designed to replace it," to quote Julia Reinhard Lupton and Graham Hammill's working definition of political theology.[6] Yet *Othello* and *The Winter's Tale* undermine any attempt to turn the tragic or tragicomic consequences of the demand for personal love into a mythology of state power. Instead, both plays reveal how narratives of state power generate their affective appeal by masquerading in the name of objective reality.

A State of Substitution

At the end of *Othello*, the tragic hero recounts the error that led him to murder his wife. Othello likens himself to "the base Indian" (according to the 1622 First Quarto) or to "the base Iudean" (according to the First Folio) who

> threw a pearl away
> Richer than all his tribe. (5.2.347–48)[7]

This crux has presented two modes—religious, on the one hand, and ethnic or racial, on the other—through which Othello understands his descent into murderous jealousy.[8] If he likens himself to the "base Indian," he appeals to a form of ignorance affiliated with racial difference; the effects of that difference have persisted in spite of his conversion and admission into Venetian society. The First Folio's "Iudean" locates Othello's downfall within a scriptural framework, likening him either to Herod the Judaean or to Judas Iscariot. An allusion to the story of Herod would offer a direct link to a previous conjugal tragedy. Herod is lured by Salome into suspecting his wife Mariamne and eventually ordering her execution. Early editors such as Alexander Pope and Lewis Theobald prefer this interpretation as they rely on the Fourth Folio text and the "Iudean" variant.[9] The other readings, which have since gained prominence, do not allude to stories concerning marriage. Instead, they describe wrongheaded judgment concerning worth and value: the Indian cannot fathom the worth of the pearl, while Judas Iscariot betrays Christ for thirty pieces of silver.

All these interpretive possibilities can speak to Othello's condition because his marriage exhibits a specific version of a general problem concerning personal value—not the value of a Christian wife but rather that of a Christian husband in his wife's esteem. Pauline teaching instructs wives to view their husbands as Christlike while reminding husbands that they, too, are in need of redemption. Othello, however, desires to manifest real rather than mysteriously imputed merit. From beginning to end, he wishes to be revealed as he truly is. After Iago's machinations render him an undeserving husband, Othello struggles to reconcile his lack of merit with his heroic sense of self-worth. Insofar as he likens himself to an ignorant Indian, he deflects the question of his own worth by emphasizing Desdemona's inestimable value. If Othello likens himself to Judas Iscariot, he expresses just how un-Christlike he has been with respect to Desdemona. In either case, Desdemona's worth has ended up stymying Othello's quest to be honestly good, and his final recourse is an act of self-sacrifice. Although Othello narrates his suicide as an act of service to Christian Venice, he reaffirms his inability to make himself worthy of Desdemona's love by redeeming her.

Even if the Pauline definition of marriage contains a core of mystery or untruth, it is still called on to be tenable. Ideally, the irresolvable problem of personal merit should energize a dynamism between individual love and collective belonging as members of Christ's redeemed body and wife. Jealousy, however, functions as the vehicle that drives Othello and Desdemona's Christian marriage to catastrophe. Marriage should have been the culmination of Othello's acceptance into Venetian society. Recent scholarship has attended to the way that Othello and Desdemona's marriage mirrors Ruggiero and Bradamante's in *Orlando furioso*. In the Italian romance epic, marriage had crowned the conversion of a Muslim hero to Western Christendom. "Beginning with the marriage that should end a romance," Benedict Robinson observes, *Othello* "dramatizes the disintegration of that marriage" and "marks the failure of romance."[10] Dennis Britton details how, under Iago's sway, Othello "ceases to participate in transformative romance" as a vehicle of conversion.[11] This attention to the literary, religious, and racial logics at play in the unraveling of Othello's romance adds historical substance to Stanley Cavell's influential claim that *Othello* anticipates the tragic possibilities of Cartesian skepticism. For Cavell, Othello spuriously tries to overcome all doubt by placing "a finite woman," Desdemona, "in the place of God"—or, as it turns out, in the place of Christ.[12] Cavell does cite A. C. Bradley to refer to Othello as "the most romantic of Shakespeare's heroes" and Norman Rabkin to call Othello "the most Christian of the tragic heroes."[13] Yet Cavell only glances at the cultural histories that enable Shakespeare to channel theological and philosophical meaning into the drama of a husband's overreliance on his wife.

Othello turns the triumph of romance into the grounds of an epistemological tragedy by exacerbating the tensions within Pauline marriage. The slippage between Othello's claim to merit and his awareness of insufficiency registers early in the play, when Othello appears before the Senate to account for his secret wedding. Othello testifies how, upon hearing his stories of heroism, Desdemona

> wish'd
> That heaven had made her such a man. (1.3.162–63)

If Desdemona had desired to be a man like Othello, she indirectly fulfills such desires by becoming his sweet warrior, the general's general. Yet Desdemona may have articulated a desire not to be a man but rather to be wooed by a man like Othello—a hypothetical friend of Othello's who would, presumably, be a more appropriate object of her affections because he is a countryman rather than a foreigner. Othello explains that he interpreted Desdemona's remark as a coy hint and then wooed her. Even by his own account, however, love contains the possibility of self-estrangement. The role of beloved husband may be an open-ended office that Othello has merely come to occupy. This fleeting admission eventually gives way to Othello's fuller realization that he is not Christlike even as a Christian husband. Othello's dependence on his wife's love reveals not merely the universal defect of sin but also the pressures that beleaguer him as a Moorish convert. We eventually learn alongside Iago that Cassio had played a key role in the formation of Othello and Desdemona's love. Cassio may have functioned in the gap that Othello's testimony had only suggested as a grammatical placeholder—between Othello and "such a man" as him. Iago overhears Desdemona describing how Cassio "came a-wooing" with Othello and took his part when she had spoken "dispraisingly" of him (3.3.71–72). Othello may have needed an active intercessor to win Desdemona's love all along; the occlusion of this fact in Othello's earlier testimony reveals the anxieties that Iago is able to exploit. By the time Iago learns of Cassio's earlier role, he has already initiated a plot to turn him into a target of Othello's jealousy.

Jealousy operates in the slippage between Othello's sense of meriting Desdemona's love, on the one hand, and his public claim to worth as a military leader and a Venetian citizen, on the other. The Venetian Senate does confer legal sanction on Othello and Desdemona's union. The duke is even sympathetic enough to remark that his own daughter would have been won over by Othello's tales. Yet *Othello* depicts the republic of Venice as lacking an essential stake in marriage and thus lacking the affective force to provide closure to the union it legitimizes. We can discern how the play portrays the Venetian government as relatively indifferent to marriage by turning to one of Shakespeare's source texts, Lewes Lewkenor's 1599 English translation of Gasparo Contarini's *Commonwealth and Government of Venice*. Contarini describes ducal marriages being deemed so important that a 1327 law prevents the doge from marrying the daughter of a "straunger" even if that foreigner has "obtained the right and tytle of a Venetian gentleman."[14] A 1383 law prevents the doge from marrying "the daughter, sister, or kinsewoman of any forraine prince" without special permission (197). Although a republic does not, at least in theory, rely on dynastic marriage for its continuity, the exclusivity of ducal marriage is nonetheless a crucial matter. *Othello* presents a form of marriage to an assimilated foreigner that does not concern the duke directly. Brabantio objects to Desdemona's choice of a stranger, but this is a personal concern that is deemed an unseemly interruption of the Senate's public business. In Contarini's account, the Venetian nobility consider marriage to be a practical affair, arranged "for the most part alwaies . . . by a third person, the bride being neuer suffered so much as to behold her future husband" until contractual matters are settled (194). Othello and Desdemona's marriage does not conform to the practices of the Venetian nobility. Or, more accurately, Othello wishes to narrate his marriage as having arisen purely from Desdemona's personal choice. Only later do we become aware that Cassio might have brokered their union as a kind of "third person." In this light, Othello's initial desire to suppress Cassio's role and his lapse into jealousy both manifest an impulse to privilege individual love over public concerns.

The framing of act 1, scene 3, which takes place at the Senate, underscores the disparity between personal and state affairs. In the scene's opening, the duke and the senators are able to see through a Turkish naval ruse. Venetian power expresses itself as an ability—expressed through dialogue and skepticism—to discern rational motives lurking behind pretenses. Perhaps for this very reason, this kind of state is poorly equipped to prop up conjugal love as an enabling fiction mediating between Christ's love and its imperfect manifestations. The aftermath of this scene highlights the Venetian state's lack of affective sway when it comes to intimate matters. When the duke offers the begrudging father-in-law Brabantio rhyming commonplaces of comfort, the latter mocks the Senate's ineffectiveness when it comes to intimate rather than tactical affairs. Brabantio offers ineffective couplets of his own:

> So let the Turk of Cyprus us beguile,
> We lose it not, so long as we can smile. (1.3.210–11)

Even though Brabantio officially accepts his daughter's marriage, he still bequeaths unhappy jealousy to his new son-in-law. In this case, however, his rhyming couplet proves more effective:

> Look to her, Moor, if thou hast eyes to see;
> She has deceiv'd her father, and may thee. (1.3.292–93)

Brabantio exhorts Othello to apply the Venetian mode of rational skepticism within his own married life. Brabantio, in Lupton's reading, proves himself to be "a type of the Jewish Christian, uneasy with the universal fellowship promised by his faith" and desiring to uphold a narrower "national brotherhood."[15] Brabantio's desire for exclusivity is not rendered obsolete by the triumph of a Christian marriage but is rather communicated to his foreign son-in-law. The advice to intermingle love and the tactics of statecraft turns out to be a form of sabotage.

When this seed of suspicion develops into full-blown jealousy under Iago's manipulation, the reemergence of a sensibility that could have been rendered obsolete (at both the civic and the religious registers) exposes the limits of Shakespeare's imagined republican polity. Venetian authority unwittingly allows the residue of paternal jealousy to stain Christian marriage. According to Andrew Hadfield, *Othello* follows republican theory by dramatizing how "individual virtue . . . can only flourish if nurtured and protected by powerful state institutions."[16] Jealousy is the vehicle through which Iago manifests himself as an "antirepublican villain."[17] Yet Othello's tragedy does not reaffirm that individuals should be nurtured by state institutions but instead reveals the contradictions within the Venetian polity. In response to scholarship linking *Othello* to early modern republicanism, Andrew Sisson has called for more attention to the "specifically republican problematic of the citizen's other as the *functionally specialized professional*"—that is, the professional soldier or mercenary.[18] Sisson traces a dichotomy between the ancient Roman citizen-soldiery (as championed by Niccolò Machiavelli) and the Venetian separation of citizenship from a military establishment (advocated by Contarini). In Sisson's account, Othello suffers from a distinctively Venetian inability to perfect the transition from being a professional soldier to being a citizen. In the terms of my argument, jealousy reveals the religious patterns behind Venice's inability to assist Othello after his marriage should have elevated his merit as a soldier-turned-citizen. Othello finds that he cannot translate his military valor—the basis of his civic identity—into a conviction of Christlikeness in his wife's eyes. Defined primarily by skeptical reason, Venetian authority is ill-equipped to provide the affective assistance that Othello would need in order to balance awareness of imputed Christian merit with his heroic sense of genuine personal worth.

If Iago's assault on Othello's marriage makes Iago a recognizably antirepublican villain, he succeeds by turning Othello's insecurities as an assimilated Black Venetian into an acute case of the discrepancy between any husband and Christ. Nobody in the play is more aware of the problem of personal merit than Iago. The play opens with his complaint that Cassio has been unjustly promoted ahead of him. As Bradley has reminded us, however, we have no real way to test Iago's initial claim to have been more deserving than Cassio.[19] Rather than making his own merit conspicuous, Iago finds ways to translate his possibly baseless vocational envy into Othello's sexual jealousy. Othello's sense of merit has already linked military standing and a claim to love; by stoking Othello's jealous demand for singularity in Desdemona's affections, Iago produces a discord between these private and public registers. This discord manifests itself when Othello decries the breakdown of his vocation even before receiving so-called proof of Desdemona's infidelity. He feels that he can no longer occupy the role of general when he can merely imagine "the general camp" having sex with his wife (3.3.345).

Iago trains Othello's jealousy on Cassio, his lieutenant and erstwhile intercessor in love. In act 2, scene 3, Cassio unwittingly articulates the religious logic that allows Iago to turn otherwise petty vocational envy into the grounds of a profound travesty. Cassio confuses his military standing for the condition of his soul. When Iago expresses his desire to be eternally saved, Cassio gratingly insists that "the lieutenant is to be sav'd before the ancient." (2.2.109–10) This is a drunken quip on Cassio's part, but it reveals how Iago has reshaped his own envy into a shared confusion between one's military office and one's spiritual condition. This travesty becomes tragic rather than farcical when Iago brings it to bear on Othello and Desdemona's marriage. Pauline teaching confers on marriage a soteriological dimension by defining it around Christ's sacrificial love. Christ atones for the members of his corporate body by exposing his literal body to divine punishment. Iago gives the audience special access to the way he perverts this link between atoning sacrifice and love. In his second soliloquy, he reveals a plan to exact revenge either by cuckolding Othello or by implanting jealousy in him. Willing himself to heed the baseless suspicion that Othello has slept with his own wife, Emilia, Iago declares that

> nothing can or shall content my soul
> Till I am even'd with him, wife for wife;
> Or failing so, yet that I put the Moor
> At least into a jealousy so strong
> That judgment cannot cure. (2.1.298–302)

The "wife for wife" retribution that Iago imagines is never attempted, but its logic haunts the play nonetheless. He wants to think of wives as interchangeable in an economy of sex as displaced vengeance: he declares his need to have sex with Desdemona not because he desires her, per se, but because he might be able to get back at Othello this way. This misogynistic logic is initially localized in Iago but proves powerful insofar as it can pervert the meaning of redemptive Christian love. Ultimately, killing replaces sexual vengeance as the more direct way to distort the soteriological meaning of Christian marriage. Under Iago's influence, Othello tries to think of the killing of Desdemona not only as erotically charged violence but also as a righteous sacrifice. He realizes too late that his actions expose him as an unworthy husband while elevating the innocent Desdemona to a Christlike station.

In a final irony, Othello's excessive desire for merit and fixed love costs him not only his marriage but also his official standing. At the end of the play, Cassio "rules in Cyprus" (5.2.332). The promotion may be just recompense for what Cassio has suffered, but it is also of a piece with the way state power remains estranged from love. Nothing in the play (including Iago's unexplained description of Cassio as "almost damn'd in a fair wife") suggests Cassio's commitment to love outside of his professional bonds (1.1.21). Cassio's dealings with Bianca—and his willingness to mock her affections—suggest that he views women as instruments for satisfying his desires. Even Cassio's interactions with Desdemona confirm this instrumental view of women. His final promotion reveals that Venetian power (as the play imagines it) exists at a remove from Christian love. Venice is not attached to individuals through durable bonds of love but can replace them with facility. The Senate, as we learn in act 4, had already decided to put Cassio in Othello's seat as governor of Cyprus. From the Senate's viewpoint, Othello's tragedy is a curiously unpleasant twist in a preordained replacement.

Othello against the Sea

Othello translates biblical jealousy into a plot that retains a sense of profundity even as it repeatedly upends any supernatural claims of causation. By doing so, the play shuttles between theological and more modern-facing forms of the incompatibility between individual experience and corporate realities. Othello's religious and racial difference operates between these registers. Julia Reinhard Lupton elaborates on the importance of a detail suggested only in Othello's final speech—the suggestion that he is a circumcised convert to Christianity. Othello's body bears the marks of an older register of meaning; his flesh is supposed to serve as the medium of a new, spiritual truth and yet still resists full conversion. Lupton relates Othello's circumcision and his suicide to the textual transmission of Christian truth. His circumcision serves as a "reinscriptive cut" that "does not disappear into its typological sublations, instead reinstating the Hebraic function of a signature."[20] His final act of bloodshed-as-narration does complete his incorporation into Christian Venice, but at the expense of his life. Building on Lupton's discussion, Urvashi Chakravarty discusses Othello's circumcision within an examination of the role of natality in Shakespearean drama.[21] Natality is a divided concept. It can promote the sense that we are all born into a shared humanity, but it also governs the sense that we are born into particular tribes, nations, and races. Circumcision places on the male reproductive organ a permanent reminder of particularity. Othello tragically discovers that rebirth into a Christian community has not perfected the link between spiritual and physical liberation. In Chakravarty's reading, Othello's final speech and act attempt a death that might (the unacceptability of suicide notwithstanding) achieve a fuller rebirth into a spiritual life.

Whereas Lupton and Chakravarty both describe Othello as embodying the problems of particularity and racial difference for the supposedly universal claims of Christian truth, Christopher Pye describes Othello's predicament as looking ahead to a modern form of aesthetic subjectivity.[22] Pye's reading relies on a strategic anachronism to describe how Othello privileges his subjective impressions—the only real basis of his mounting certainty of Desdemona's unfaithfulness—over juridical fact. This makes Othello resemble modern subjects who seek to privilege the supposed autonomy of their aesthetic experiences, apart from legal and political realities. Othello's proto-modern anagnorisis includes the realization that his experiences have, in fact, always remain enmeshed within political power. According to Pye, we can find *Othello*'s clearest expression of a modern aesthetic sensibility in Montano's description of waiting for the general's arrival in Cyprus:

> As to throw out our eyes for brave Othello,
> Even till we make the main and th'aerial blue
> An indistinct regard. (2.1.38–40)

Montano's words reveal how reality (in this case, Othello himself as an object of perception) can vanish or dissolve into a subjective experience—not through inattention but rather through an intensity of focus.

Before the late disclosure of Othello's circumcised status, a recognizably religious notion of jealousy shapes the play's consideration of the limits of inclusivity. At the same time, the drama of jealousy shapes the play's capacity to anticipate a proto-modern form of subjectivity. I argue that the intensification of a love that insists on fixity turns Christian marriage into a dramatic form capable of generating the proto-aesthetic experience that Pye discerns. When Othello finally arrives on the shores of Cyprus, he speaks about his own recent experience:

> And let the laboring bark climb hills of seas
> Olympus-high, and duck again as low
> As hell's from heaven! (2.1.187–89)

Othello translates the horizontal crossing of the seas into a vertical axis of absolutes. In doing so, he translates his sea voyage into a hypothetical scenario, described in the subjunctive. He does this to underscore the reality of his present satisfaction upon being reunited with Desdemona. He desires to arrest time in the name of a consummated love:

> If it were now to die,
> 'Twere now to be most happy. (2.1.189–90)

This intensity of feeling generates within a new Christian marriage an imbalance between personal experience and corporate reality. Othello's celebration of loving permanence contains the kernel of a disruptive, antisocial effect. Othello ignores the political and military realities of the sea voyage—and everyone else involved other than Desdemona—in order to fantasize about fixity. This is not a minor oversight, as the sea has not only imperiled the lives of Othello's followers but also handed Venice a decisive victory by wiping out the Turkish fleet. Othello's solipsism contrasts with Cassio's behavior, which manages to express joy over Turkish defeat, deep concern for Othello, and admiration for Desdemona all at once. Othello comes to admit that he "prattle[s] out of fashion" (2.1.206). Even before jealousy effectively takes hold, Othello's demand for a singular experience of love generates feelings that are estranged from shared Christian belief and from political realities.

We can look beyond *Othello* for confirmation that Shakespearean drama generates appeals to an intensely subjective experience out of the distortions produced by frustrated conjugal love. In *Cymbeline* (first performed in 1611), Imogen is divided from her new husband Posthumus, and she describes how she would have seen him off as he involuntarily set sail:

> I would have broke mine eye-strings, crack'd them, but
> To look upon him, till the diminution
> Of space had pointed him sharp as my needle;
> Nay, followed him till he had melted from
> The smallness of a gnat to air, and then
> Have turned mine eye and wept. (1.3.17–22)

This description serves as the counterpart to both Montano's and Othello's accounts of the sea voyage. Within the form of perception that Imogen imagines, Montano's aesthetic sensibility and Othello's desire for permanent love converge. Imogen longs to have fixed Posthumus in her loving gaze as long as possible until his complete disappearance. In Imogen's speech, this imagined perception of disappearance merges seamlessly with an affective state: his melting away gives way to weeping in her eyes. At the end of the play, Imogen will finally reunite with Posthumus after a long series of romance digressions.[23] In this conclusion, wife and husband are finally able to embrace and to freeze themselves into a visual emblem of fidelity.

In *Cymbeline*, Imogen's intensely subjective demand for love can be accommodated once her marriage is no longer necessary for dynastic succession. Because the same romance narrative that restores Posthumus to Imogen also restores her missing brothers, Imogen is no longer Cymbeline's sole surviving heir. She is destined to be, instead, a "piece of tender air," or *mulier*—a woman whose destiny is to be a "most constant wife" (5.5.446–49). In the handling of the Soothsayer, the imagery of fixed love giving way to a vanishing but then being restored as a new fidelity is reshaped into a specifically political metaphor. Just as

> the Roman eagle
> From south to west on wing soaring aloft,

>   Lessen'd herself, and in the beams o' th' sun
>   So vanish'd,
>
> so should
>
>   our princely eagle
>   Th'imperial Caesar

reunite "[h]is favor with the radiant Cymbeline" (5.5.470–75). The play concludes with this image of an eagle vanishing in the beams of the sun, reemerging, and then reuniting with the sun once again. This imagery celebrates a renewed Roman-British alliance, but in a way that signals the future ascendancy of Britain. Imogen can remain fixed in love with Posthumus, and at a remove from the Soothsayer's political iconography, only after a romance plot magically liberates her personal love from its dynastic function.

Whereas Imogen's marriage is finally freed from the pressures of hereditary succession, Othello's story begins as he seeks full integration into a republican polity in which merit, not legitimate birthright, should be the basis of civic belonging.[24] If Imogen's romance and Othello's tragic undoing form a chiastic pattern around the intimate experience and public utility of marriage, one specific site of that crisscrossing is on the seashore. Imogen and Othello are linked by having their respective marriages temporarily sundered by the sea, in a way that leads them to privilege their own impassioned perceptions over shared realities. I propose that this particular configuration of love, subjective experience, and the reality (or dramatic fiction) of the sea offers us an occasion to revisit an old question regarding *Othello*: the relevance or irrelevance of the Venetian ritual known as the Sposalizio del Mare. This is a question that editors debated in previous centuries. In the first act, Othello tells Iago that were it not for his love for Desdemona, he would not have married her "[f]or the sea's worth" (1.2.28). Samuel Johnson refers to the Sposalizio del Mare when he glosses this line as, "I would not marry her, though she were as rich as the Adriatic, which the Doge annually marries."[25] Yet Henry James Pye subsequently dismisses the Sposalizio del Mare as irrelevant, and Horace Howard Furness's own remarks in the variorum edition indicate that he sides with Pye and the case for irrelevance.

By considering the clash between a highly personal love and shared, corporate realities, we can clarify the relationships among history, political mythmaking, and dramatic feeling as they relate to this question of relevance. The Sposalizio del Mare, the celebration of Venice's marriage to (and dominion over) the sea, seems to have originated around the year 1000 as a blessing of the Adriatic Sea on Ascension Day (the Sensa). By the 1260s, this blessing had evolved into a ceremony celebrating the marriage of the Venetian doge and the sea. By the sixteenth century, as Edward Muir explains, "the marriage of the sea was the carefully orchestrated apogee of the state liturgy."[26] This ceremony transforms the tenuous balance between love and subservience within Christian marriage into a celebration of the doge's beneficent dominion. Ducal power remains expansive but also carefully bounded: "In espousing the sea," Muir observes, "the doge was marrying the subjects of the Venetian maritime colonies and establishing that he was the *padrone* of the sea lanes, but he was most certainly not espousing the people of Venice."[27] Overseas power is celebrated in a way that allows Venetians to imagine that dominion back at home remains within the proper limits of republicanism. The "notion of matrimonial consent" underlies this metaphorical marriage of the doge and the sea and helps to affirm this balance of power and restraint.[28] The Marriage of the Sea is mentioned in Contarini's *Commonwealth*. In the ceremony, the "prince," as Lewkenor's translation refers to the doge, "throwing a ring of golde into the sea . . . doeth betroth him|selfe to the sea."[29]

Regardless of whether Shakespeare had the Marriage of the Sea specifically in mind, we know that the perilous sea crossing is an original addition to the existing stories behind *Othello*'s plot. This addition does not affirm a Venetian myth of marriage but reveals how decisive military victory can give rise to a personal tragedy. As we have seen, the same sea that destroys the Turkish fleet also sunders Othello from Desdemona. State triumph will never fully coincide with a feeling of conjugal love in this play. Instead, the kind of turmoil that the sea represents continues to function in Othello's personal experiences in Cyprus. In a study of the meanings attached to the sea in Shakespearean drama, Steve Mentz labels Iago "the anti-God of the sea" because he deliberately activates the chaotic, destabilizing force that the sea represents early in the play.[30] In my reading, Iago nurtures a form of jealousy that heightens Othello's solipsistic reaction against what the sea has meant for him—for him as a husband rather than as a Venetian general and governor.

The prefatory materials in Lewkenor's translation of Contarini show us what might have been more interesting to an English readership than the specific details of the Sposalizio del Mare: Venice's own relationship to the sea reimagined as a way to describe the transmission of knowledge to England. In the process of crossing the seas and a linguistic divide, this transmission becomes a matter of politically charged artistry. One prefatory sonnet imagines Venice not as the husband of the sea but rather as a sea nymph whose "virgin state ambition nere could blot"—at least in the past. "Now," the poet continues,

> I prognosticate thy ruinous case, When thou shalt from thy Adriatique seas,
> View in this Ocean Isle thy painted face. (Contarini, Commonwealth, 4v)

Because of Lewkenor's work of English translation, Venice will be able to behold a reflection of its or her own face across the sea. This would seem to flatter Venice by making English translation nothing but a form of mirroring and cosmetic enhancement. Yet the sonnet's final couplet ominously declares to Venice, "Enamour'd like *Narcisssus* thou shalt dye" (Contarini, *Commonwealth*, 4ᵛ). The conclusion implies that Lewkenor will benefit England not only by translating information about Venice but also by helping Venice succumb to excessive self-admiration through a foreign reflection.[31]

In *Othello*, the presentation of the sea reminds us of how the play actively mediates between knowledge about Venice and the gendered tropes involved in political mythmaking. For this reason, *Othello*'s dramatic presentation of the sea can help pinpoint some of the key deficiencies of Carl Schmitt's reading of *Hamlet*—and of the calibration of art, affective impressions, and political history that Schmitt attempts. At the outset of this chapter, I mentioned that Schmitt makes the case for an understanding of Shakespearean tragedy that locates the aesthetic power of drama within a supposedly objective historical narrative. Schmitt argues that *Hamlet*'s tragedy can remain durably powerful long after its time because of the "structurally determining, genuine *intrusions* [*Einbrüche*]" of history in the play.³² These intrusions refer to incendiary topics concerning James's legitimacy as the future English monarch; the scandalous past of his mother, Mary, Queen of Scots; and her eventual execution as authorized by Queen Elizabeth I. These incendiary matters could not be handled directly, but their presence is nonetheless felt as political taboos that energize the play. The aesthetic force of this kind of taboo does not become inert over time as explicit topical allusions might. By advancing this historical rather than psychoanalytic interpretation of taboo, Schmitt situates *Hamlet* within a political trajectory that looks beyond the Stuart monarchy, and the crises it would confront, and toward the advent of modern state power.

In attempting this reading, Schmitt must present a highly selective account of *Hamlet*'s tragic power. As Victoria Kahn observes, some of Schmitt's claims about history and aesthetics—and his attempt to position *Hamlet*'s tragedy between medieval theology and the rise of the nation-state—might seem sensible to us until "we remember that all of Schmitt's 'historical reality' comes at the price of any serious attention to the language or form of the play."³³ Schmitt's responses to his interlocutor Walter Benjamin make clear some of the deliberate distortions at play. Benjamin had argued in his study of allegory and *trauerspiel* (bourgeois tragedy) that "Hamlet alone is a spectator by the grace of God," and that "Shakespeare was capable of striking Christian sparks from the baroque rigidity of the melancholic."³⁴ Reading *Hamlet* as Benjamin does would locate the source of its tragic force in the tension between transcendence and the immanence of human power. Schmitt subsequently works to strip Hamlet of the partially transcendent outlook that Benjamin attributes to him via Christian grace.³⁵ To reaffirm a historical narrative aiming toward modern, increasingly secularized sovereignty, Schmitt insists that neither *Hamlet* nor Hamlet is Christian in any meaningful sense. Evidence to the contrary within the play must be denied or ignored.

It is particularly meaningful that Schmitt entirely overlooks Hamlet's sea voyage—the interrupted voyage toward England that allows him to return to Denmark with a renewed belief in providence. This oversight facilitates the conscription of *Hamlet* for Schmitt's claims about history, in which the ocean serves as an explanatory device for historical events. As an island backwater, England lagged behind the Continent in the transition from a so-called barbarism to genuine politics. Only in this context, Schmitt argues, could *Hamlet* have arisen as a tragedy of the monarch's legitimacy. Yet England's belatedness ultimately affirms the forward thrust of history; England would cast off its belated status by emerging as a global engine of modernity as an overseas empire.[36] This treatment of the sea offers one example of the way Schmitt's historical narrative of the modern state is grounded on mythic and affective appeals—while also denying that this is the case. Before turning to *Hamlet*, Schmitt had initiated his expansive study of the origins of modern European sovereignty, the 1950 *Nomos of the Earth*, with the distinction between the land and the anarchic sea. He bases his political history on the way "the solid ground of the earth is delineated by fences, enclosures, boundaries" whereas the "*sea* knows no such apparent unity of space and law."[37] In this opening gambit, the sea operates as a mythopoetic source of causation on which Schmitt can base his historical claims—including his later claims about English sovereignty as shaped by England's maritime existence. The sea functions not only as a geographic reality but also as a primordial form of chaos against which sovereignty defines and legitimizes its operations. When, in *Hamlet or Hecuba*, Schmitt subsequently turns to Shakespearean tragedy and its relationship to history, he insists on the objectivity of his interpretation by ignoring one of the most famous sea voyages in literary history—an imagined crisscrossing not just between Denmark and England but also between a providential worldview and a proto-modern subjectivity.

Schmitt chose to elaborate his claims about tragedy through a reading of *Hamlet*, but we now know the extent to which, earlier in his life, he had grappled with *Othello*. This earlier engagement sheds light on his motivations for rejecting a psychoanalytic understanding of taboo in favor of a supposedly objective explanation. After studying Schmitt's personal diaries, Andreas Höfele observes, "From 1921 to 1924 his diaries contain just two references to Hamlet but over sixty to the Moor of Venice."[38] Höfele traces Schmitt's fascination with Othello during a period of intense, sometimes suicidal self-berating and of numerous sexual trysts. Schmitt's first marriage, to a Serbian woman who falsely claimed aristocratic pedigree, ended in personal embarrassment in 1916. Schmitt's eventual attempts to remarry resulted in his excommunication from the Roman Catholic Church in 1926.[39] I have no interest in Schmitt's personal life, but I mention these forays into his diaries because they provide us with clear evidence that a configuration of marriage, jealousy, and racial difference furnished the grounds of his intense interest in *Othello*. "A déraciné cannot marry," reads an entry on Othello, referred to here as a stranger without stable civic identity, from February 1923. "[I]f he does, he kills the woman. Jealousy becomes the form of her execution."[40] Schmitt finds Othello's alienation personally fascinating, and his diary entries labor against positive identifications with him. Schmitt's entries develop what Höfele calls a "case for Othello as stranger-and-therefore-enemy."[41] The indictment of Othello as inassimilable to Christian Venice links Schmitt's views about the Moorish hero to his antisemitism, and to his theoretical elaboration of the friend/enemy distinction. An April 1924 diary entry twists Othello's self-understanding (whereby chaos threatens to return if he should not love Desdemona) to give the tragedy of interracial marriage a mythic cast in Schmitt's own thinking: "Chaos and monster are the terms of Othello."[42] This same entry identifies excessive sensuality as a trait that Othello shares with the proletariat and with Jews.

One diary entry from October 1923 reveals clearly how Schmitt negotiates his lurid fascination with Othello. Schmitt remarks that Othello "has had an Emilia already, although she also lived in loneliness."[43] In the play, the relationship between Othello and Emilia is the basis of a rumor that Iago reports in an early soliloquy. Yet far from corroborating this rumor (whose validity even Iago acknowledges to be uncertain), the play leads us to suspect it or reject it outright. Schmitt, however, gives credence to Iago's jealous anxiety. Schmitt then remarks, "One must view this in institutional terms, not psychologically."[44] "This" refers here not only to the adulterous union of a lonely woman with the Black foreigner but also to Othello's need for additional validation through a loving interracial marriage. The appeal to an "institutional" understanding—whereby Othello's inability to be incorporated into Venice is a structural inevitability—deflects a fuller recognition that Schmitt has turned Iago-like in his anxiously racist view of Othello. When viewed in this light, Schmitt's turn to *Hamlet* in the 1950s rejects a psychosexual understanding of taboo not only to advance his account of political history but also to culminate his earlier process of dis-identifying himself with Othello through a sexually anxious form of racism that insists that it is attempting a properly institutional understanding.[45]

If we return to *Othello*'s presentation of jealousy, we can discern how the play actively resists the subordination of Shakespearean tragedy to an interpretation like Schmitt's—one that rejects psychoanalytic understandings in favor of a teleological narrative of state power. By translating the problems internal to Christian marriage into a tragic plot, *Othello* drives a wedge between the perpetuation of the state (along with its overseas extensions of power) and deeply felt personal experience. In the tragedy that arises out of this bifurcation, the most pertinent question is not, as Schmitt's reading of *Hamlet* might have it, whether Shakespeare invites Jacobean kingship to perfect the synthesis of marriage's political and personal meanings or whether Shakespeare exposes the gap between these registers. Schmitt's own political narrative insists on James's divine view of kingship as doomed to fail; this is how both Jacobean kingship and the political taboos energizing *Hamlet* are said to look forward to modernity. What is more important is how, in the typological meanings of marriage, Shakespeare finds a dramatic structure in which the supervenience of state power—in this case, in an imagined republican form—is something that cannot be celebrated. *Othello* has long been and continues to operate as a template for the confluence of xenophobic, racist, and sexual anxieties. Yet the play can still teach us to reject a mode of interpretation that props up its claims to historical objectivity by occluding its own investments in mythologies—religious, secular, or somewhere in between.[46] These political mythologies attempt to subordinate intimate feeling to structures of belonging that demand exclusion in the name of restricted incorporation.

Camillo's If

The Winter's Tale locates the problem of jealousy squarely within hereditary monarchy. At the outset of the play, the obsession with fidelity coincides with paranoia about legitimate reproduction. The first words that Polixenes utters inform us that he has been in Sicily for "[n]ine changes of the wat'ry star" (1.2.1). This makes it possible for Leontes to suspect that the baby that his wife, Hermione, is carrying is Polixenes's. Yet the need for legitimate offspring becomes indistinguishable from the demand for a love that might permanently affirm personal singularity. Leontes's fit of jealousy is preceded by banter in which Polixenes offers a myth of male friendship. The two kings are described as having been entirely interchangeable, "twinn'd lambs" who exchanged "innocence for innocence" (1.2.67–69). In this account of a prelapsarian absence of individuation, the fact of mortality is denied in a way that allows women to be identified as the sources of the fall. Hermione understands this and silences Polixenes before he can propose that she and his own wife are "devils" (1.2.82). Yet Polixenes has already given voice to a fantasy in which marriage is not a remedy for but instead the original cause of mortality as well as the need for individuation.

When Leontes subsequently confronts his son, Mamillius, the political and personal solutions that marriage has presumably offered in the past now conflict with one another. The visual evidence of Mamillius's legitimacy—his likeness to his father—is now proof that Leontes will need to be replaced after his death. Understanding Leontes's jealousy through his thwarted desire for permanent uniqueness clarifies the play's politico-theological significance. Christopher Pye, as we have seen, locates the political meanings of *Othello* in the way that the play anticipates aesthetic subjectivity in its mystified relationship to the law and the state. What this means for an early modern drama of hereditary monarchy becomes clearer when Pye turns to *The Winter's Tale*.[47] Whereas Schmitt's political theology centers on the sovereign decision, Leontes's jealousy, Pye argues, amounts to an aesthetic experience akin to Othello's. In Leontes's case, proto-aesthetic experience operates in a register of knowledge that undermines his sovereign decision. In this reading, Mamillius functions as a mimetic object for Leontes. By privileging subjective impressions over reality, Leontes can twist evidence of his son's legitimacy into the grounds for suspecting his wife further. The king must subsequently learn that the coincidence of aesthetic subjectivity and sovereignty is tragically imperfect. Leontes must be subjected to a higher law that does not bend to his corruptible, subjective decision-making.

When Leontes speaks to his son, his words reveal not only the misogyny that Polixenes has activated but also the way that his view of kingship shapes the affective crisis surrounding replaceability. Looking at Mamillius, Leontes declares,

> yet they say we are
> Almost as like as eggs; women say so—
> That will say any thing. But were they false
> As o'er-dy'd blacks, as wind, as waters, false
> As dice are to be be wish'd by one that fixes
> No bourn 'twixt his and mine, yet were it true
> To say this boy were like me. (1.2.129–135)

In Leontes's jealous mind, women are not identified directly with the imagined male swindler but rather with his instruments of deception, the loaded dice. Sexual fidelity and legitimacy are, ultimately, proxies for different forms of paranoia about male competition. The false dicer is not just a hypothetical figure but a placeholder for Polixenes, who is under suspicion of having cheated his friend. Yet the feared violation of the "bourn" between them reveals other underpinnings of sexual jealousy; this boundary is suggestive of the limits of the two sovereign's proper kingdoms. Polixenes's presence imperils the link between Leontes's supposedly unique personhood and the bounded limits of his kingship. Polixenes's myth of prelapsarian friendship has suggested that their two distinct sovereignties amount to a political reality based on no essential truths about their persons. Even the trickery of the

> one that fixes
> No bourn

cannot dislodge the conspicuous truth of Mamillius's legitimacy. Yet his legitimacy affirms a different kind of threat to Leontes—the unavoidable facts of mortality and replacement.

Out of this breach between a longing for uniqueness and awareness of replaceability, *The Winter's Tale* draws forth not only a mad form of jealousy but also alternative forms of agency that elude sovereign authority. This agency is predicated on an "if," and Camillo is the character who exercises it most meaningfully. The entire play begins with an open-ended question concerning the distinction between Sicilia and Bohemia. "If you shall chance, Camillo, to visit Bohemia," Archidamus offers, "you shall see (as I have said) great difference betwixt our Bohemia and your Sicilia" (1.1.1–4).[48] Camillo's response anticipates Polixenes's myth of male friendship: the two kings "were train'd together in their childhoods; and there rooted betwixt them then such an affection, which cannot choose but branch now" (1.1.22–24). This response is ambiguous. Perhaps the single affection that roots them together shows that Sicilia and Bohemia are, contrary to Archidamus's claim, identical. Or, perhaps, their branching off has subsequently established their distinctiveness. We will never be able to adjudicate with certainty whether the claim of difference or of identity would have been more accurate. By the time Camillo does travel to Bohemia, its relationship to Sicilia has altered drastically. Leontes's jealousy has effectively driven a wedge between him and Polixenes, generating the distinctiveness that was in question when the play begins.

The opening exchange already begins to confer on Camillo a certain power as a subject—a power that will emerge fully when Leontes turns tyrannical. After the play begins with a conditional and an appeal to contingency ("If you [Camillo] shall chance"), the second scene opens with Polixenes's deploying the language of chance to explain why he seeks to return home:

> I am question'd by my fears of what may chance
> Or breed upon our absence. (1.2.11–12)

Polixenes's appeal to chance is straightforward, as he fears unanticipated events in his kingdom. His use of the word "breed," by contrast, is metaphorical. This rhetorical flourish signals a conceptual pairing between randomness and birth or origins. This pairing proves crucial for the affective logic of the ensuing action. For Leontes, Hermione's pregnant body becomes a maddening sign of the forms of contingency—chance and breeding—beyond his control. Perversely, insisting that Hermione is carrying Polixenes's baby is the way for Leontes to insist on his mastery, jurisdictional and epistemological, over reproduction. Leontes tries to overcome the awareness that what distinguishes his own sovereignty from Polixenes's is the mere chance of his breeding.

In an attempt to shore up his embattled sense of sovereign selfhood, Leontes conscripts Camillo to affirm his jealousy. He tries to turn Camillo into an instrument for his wishes by offering him something that sounds like a choice but is not a choice at all:

>   If thou wilt confess,
> Or else be impudently negative,
> To have nor eyes nor ears nor thought, then say
> My wife's a hobby-horse. (1.2.273–76)

By making Hermione's unfaithfulness a binding fact, Leontes tries to nullify Camillo's agency within the form of a seeming if/or choice. What

Camillo thinks or chooses should not matter; he has to say what Leontes wants him to say. When left to himself, however, Camillo reasserts the power of his choice. Confronted with the dilemma of having been ordered to poison Polixenes, Camillo reasons,

> If I could find example
> Of thousands that had struck anointed kings
> And flourish'd after, I'ld not do't. (1.2.357–59)

Camillo seems to rely on an if/then logic but then affirms his absolute decision: *even* if he could find an example of a successful regicide, he would not follow Leontes's orders. This is not a choice based on examples or reason. It is an expression of his conviction. Camillo subsequently detaches the external considerations that might legitimize a decision to disobey ("but since / Nor brass nor stone nor parchment bears not one") from his predetermined imperative ("I must / Forsake the court") (2.2.359–62).[49] When Polixenes returns to the stage, Camillo's rhetoric underscores how the foreign king is now entirely dependent on him:

> If therefore you dare trust my honesty,
> That lies enclosed in this trunk which you
> Shall bear along impawn'd, away to-night! (1.2.434–36)

Camillo positions himself as the guarantor of a trust that must lead to a decision:

> Be not uncertain
> For by the honor of my parents, I
> Have utter'd truth. (1.2.441–43)

Neither Polixenes nor Leontes can directly confront the simple truth that his personal and political destiny is conferred on him by his birth, over which he could have had no control. Camillo, by contrast, articulates a way to suture familial honor and personal choice together—by defying rather than obeying his sovereign's command.

When Camillo invokes his familial honor as a power that Polixenes must rely on absolutely, he points to a broader dynamic in the Shakespearean drama of political power: honor as a competitor to kingly prerogative. I would like to revisit in particular the opening act of *Richard II*, in which Mowbray and Bolingbroke resist the king's wishes in order to persist in their claims of treason against each other. This scene captures how honor mediates between the individual and the family in a way that defies the wishes of the king. As Richard II tries to quell the feud between Bolingbroke and Mowbray, he instructs the latter,

> Rage must be withstood,
> Give me [Bolingbroke's] gage. Lions make leopards tame. (1.1.173–74)

Mowbray responds:

> Yea, but not change his spots. Take but my shame,
> And I resign my gage. My dear dear lord,
> The purest treasure mortal times afford
> Is spotless reputation; that away,
> Men are but gilded loam or painted clay.
> A jewel in a ten-times-barr'd-up chest
> Is a bold spirit in a loyal breast.
> Mine honor is my life, both grow in one,
> Take honor from me, and my life is done. (1.1.175–83)

Mowbray appeals to reputation and honor in ways that make them analogous to the status of a king. Although their effects are powerful, their essence is elusive, making it necessary to blur the lines between flesh and spirit. Reputation and honor are said to exist deep within one's body, but this entire exchange tends to make bodies themselves metaphorical. If reputation is a metaphorical jewel, it is difficult to locate not only because it is elaborately hidden but also because it is, in fact, a spirit. In my introduction, I argued that Kantorowicz's reading of *Richard II* overlooks the roles of wives and mothers within the so-called tragedy of the king's two bodies. He also overlooks the possibility that Mowbray and Bolingbroke confer on themselves a nonmonarchical analogue to the king's two bodies. The union of body with honor is not necessarily mystical, nor does it derive its power from a Christological basis. Far from asserting the indissoluble link between honor and life leading to immortality, Mowbray appeals to its fragility. Yet the imperative to maintain this fragile bond gives Mowbray a reason to defy his king.

When Bolingbroke speaks in turn, he emphasizes the familial basis of his honor:

> Shall I seem crestfallen in my father's sight?
> Or with pale beggar-fear impeach my height
> Before this outdar'd dastard? (1.1.188–90)

He declares that preserving his dignity in his father's eyes is more important than obeying his king. This conviction provides Bolingbroke with an occasion for a rhetorical maneuver that he deploys often: appealing to violence in a way that fosters the impression that his metaphors are, in fact, binding on the body. Bolingbroke declares that before he would allow his tongue to utter dishonorable words, his

> teeth shall tear
> The slavish motive of recanting fear,
> And spit it bleeding

in Mowbray's face (1.1.92–94). Mowbray's appeal had acknowledged honor to be a kind of metaphor that needed to be sustained within his body. Bolingbroke, by reducing words to the tongue and then uttering his willingness to bite it off, conveys the sense that he is more extreme in his commitment to the reality of honor—which is not his alone but also his father's.

When Bolingbroke later usurps the throne, he must paper over the very problem that he has helped to expose: a noble prerogative to uphold familial honor can compete with the king's two bodies. This competition has been possible because honor is, like Christlike kingship, a metaphor that seeks purchase on bodies. I suggest that this appeal to honor in *Richard II* anticipates—in a narrowly aristocratic rather than a democratic form—what Eric Santner describes as arising after monarchy and out of "the shift from royal to popular sovereignty": a belief in the people's two bodies necessarily includes a slippage between the political representation of all citizens and the actual physical lives of the people.[50] This splitting becomes evident in the absence of a royal Christology that binds the king's flesh to his mystical body. When this mythic union is no longer viable, postmonarchical subjects are left grasping for representational modes that might relate the fullness of their actual, bodily lives to their subjecthood within political representation.

If we return now to *The Winter's Tale*, we can observe how Camillo's appeal to familial honor is potentially more radical than the appeals of Mowbray or of Bolingbroke in *Richard II*. When Camillo unfolds the story of Leontes's jealousy to Polixenes (but before Camillo presents him with the choice to believe), the Bohemian king responds,

> Camillo,
> As you are certainly a gentleman, thereto
> Clerk-like experience'd, which no less adorns
> Our gentry than our parents' noble names,
> In whose success we are gentle, I beseech you. (1.2.390–94)

The certain fact is that Camillo is a gentleman rather than a nobleman; even from within the gentry, he can leverage familial honor against the demands of his king. As a result, Camillo's prestige lowers the foreign king's self-regard. Polixenes equates the way knowledge enriches the gentry to the way hereditary birthright confers legitimacy on the nobility. He applies the word "gentle" to his own noble and royal derivation, affirming some equality between him and the gentleman Camillo. All of this may function in the key of nervous wordplay, with Polixenes flattering Camillo because he possesses crucial knowledge. By the end of this scene, however, Polixenes declares more emphatically that he

> will respect thee [Camillo] as a father, if
> Thou bear'st my life off. (1.2.461–62)

Camillo has leveraged his personal and familial honor to gain a sort of patriarchal prestige with respect to a king.

Long before the restoration at the end of the play, Hermione tries, but fails, to reestablish honor as a distinctive characteristic of the royal family—and in a way that reasserts the role of women in particular. Summoned to testify, she declares that she would have remained silent even at the threat to her own life, except

> for honor,
> 'Tis a derivative from me to mine,
> And only that I stand for. (3.2.43–45)

She attempts to regain control over a situation in which Leontes has obsessively located dishonor in her womb. She describes both her honor and her offspring as her own ("from me to mine"), rather than shared with her husband. Only in this trial scene does the audience learn that she has, in fact, always been of royal descent. When she describes herself as "a great king's daughter" and then wishes that her father, the "Emperor of Russia," were alive, she signals how Leontes's jealousy has achieved a retrograde function (3.2.39, 119). The effects of jealousy make her want to retreat from the bond of marriage back to her father's auspices.

Yet Hermione can find no effective way to avoid the dishonor that her husband has brought on her family. To overcome the tragic effects of jealousy, *The Winter's Tale* shuttles the play toward a Christian redemption of marriage—or, at least, a simulacrum of it. What the play attempts, as Sarah Beckwith details, is "a new theatrico-religious paradigm of resurrection" that draws on the gospels as well as a tradition of Christian drama to communicate the possibilities of human forgiveness.[51] Beckwith argues that Shakespeare's drama of resurrection is "not doctrinal" and "does not articulate a set of beliefs about the Resurrection."[52] Instead of becoming mired again in questions about Shakespeare's Protestant or Roman Catholic inclinations, she describes how *The Winter's Tale* reshapes religious belief into a grammar of forgiveness. My own focus is on the ability (or inability) of marriage to mediate among a recognizably Christian form of grace, personal love, and intergenerational replacement. In this light, it is revealing that Paulina's role is limited to restoring the possibility of Leontes's and Hermione's love by orchestrating a resurrection. Paulina lives up to her biblical namesake by making possible the overlay of Christian forgiveness onto the play's pagan settings. Yet the redemption that she oversees cannot restore the intergenerational relationships that have been sundered by jealousy. This tragicomedy needs to end not only with a restored marriage but also with the rediscovery of a missing child.

Camillo is the one who orchestrates Perdita's return, and his achievement is more difficult to locate within the alignment of Christian grace and conjugal love. His achievement is to make personal desire compatible with political stability after all. His own motivations are not necessarily erotic or familial. Yet as he deals in an underhanded way with Florizel and Perdita, he explains to the audience that "a woman's longing" to see Sicily again is compelling him to be dishonest (4.4.667). He scapegoats an idea of female weakness to explain his dubious actions; what he has gestated in Bohemia is a seeming violation of his honor. This violation may be surprising given his early actions in the play, but it is useful or even necessary for the restoration of Sicilian monarchy. For Camillo's plan to work, he must violate Florizel's trust; the ending of the play is magical in part because Camillo does (regardless of his intentions) lead Florizel to the site of a happy conjugal conclusion. Before all of this unfolds, however, Camillo reasons that he is staking his happiness, his honor, and his political loyalty on an uncertain wager:

> Now were I happy if
> His [Florizel's] going I could frame to serve my turn,
> Save him from danger, do him love and honor,
> Purchase the sight again of dear Sicilia
> And that unhappy king, my master, whom
> I so much thirst to see. (4.4.508–13)

In the opening act, Camillo had evaded Leontes's demand for obedience. He had done so by posing to himself an if-statement that actually revealed his preordained decision on the basis of his sense of honor. Here, however, Camillo is willing to make a wager on a genuinely uncertain "if."

His exposure to real chance is expedient for the play not only because it has unintended consequences but also because it confers on Leontes a renewed authority—even above those who have restored his wife and his daughter to him. At the end of the play, Leontes attempts to surmount the challenge to sovereign authority that Camillo has embodied throughout the play. Leontes does so by unexpectedly inviting (or ordering) Paulina to marry Camillo. In Camillo, Leontes claims to have found an "honorable husband" for Paulina (5.3.143); the king tells Camillo, in turn, that Paulina's

> worth and honesty
> Is richly noted. (5.3.144–45)

Neither Camillo nor Paulina has a chance to respond. Yet by stymying Camillo's and Paulina's capacities either to assent dutifully or to disagree, Leontes works to shore up his prerogative even as a penitent, chastened king. He attempts to harmonize the recognizably Christian grace that Paulina has brought into the play with the political utility that Camillo represents. Marriage is the most obvious form in which to attempt this kind of integration. By pairing Camillo with Paulina, Leontes also works to differentiate his tragicomedy from that of his classical predecessor Admetus. The story of Admetus and Alcestis ends in a state of unresolved awkwardness: we do not know how Alcestis responds to a husband who has violated his oath not to accept another woman into his household after his wife's death. Admetus is innocent of this violation only by virtue of ignorance. Herakles has not told him that the veiled woman to be admitted into his household is, in fact, Alcestis brought back from the dead. In *The Winter's Tale*, Leontes has clearly been guilty, but he has dutifully refused remarriage in the aftermath of his wife's death. At the very end of the play, he makes his difference from Admetus more conspicuous by foisting an awkward question of remarriage onto Paulina. If the classical precedent of the Alcestis myth speaks to an unresolved predicament between reconciliation and remarriage, Leontes's final gesture seeks to assert his control over such affective complications. By arranging a remarriage, Leontes attempts to control the very dynamics that motivated his own descent into jealousy: the clash between the absolute fixity he had sought in love and the practical reality of replacement.

Yet his final gesture amounts to an unsatisfying display of restored authority. Paulina has never exhibited an impulse to remarry; Camillo, in turn, has never suggested his desire to marry anyone, let alone Paulina in particular.[53] The final twist of *The Winter's Tale* reminds us that the work of harmonizing love and substitution under the aegis of monarchy may still be performed at the expense of real personal love—at least among subjects. At the same time, Leontes's jarring proposal of a remarriage may function to distract the audience from the fact that he can do far less about the other haunting loss that qualifies the play's tragicomic conclusion—the death of Mamillius. This irretrievable loss threatens to open onto an entire series of questions that have no answers. It remains unclear in what sense Leontes has truly gained an heir, as the oracle has promised. He may have gained a son-in-law, but Florizel has been restored to the status of being Polixenes's heir as well. The future of Sicilian sovereignty remains uncertain. In Shakespeare's Bohemia and Sicilia, the only precedent offered for a marriage between a prince and a foreign princess (that of Leontes and Hermione of Russia) does not clarify the possibilities of the latter maintaining the boundaries of her father's kingdom. If such concerns do not register emphatically by the end of the play, that is largely because our attention remains fixed on the narrative of a restored marriage, followed abruptly by the possibility of remarriage after the death of a spouse.

Florizel and Perdita at Sea

Up to this point, I have not discussed the most famous crux in *The Winter's Tale*, found in the speech in which Leontes announces to Mamillius the onset of jealousy:

> Can thy dam?—may't be?—
> Affection! thy intention stabs the centre.
> Thou dost make possible things not so held,
> Communicat'st with dreams (how can this be?),
> With what's real thou co-active art,
> And fellow'st nothing. (1.2.137–42)

As Stephen Orgel argues, the editorial history around this speech manifests the "will, or even willfulness, involved in selecting from among the ambiguities of an open and fluid text a single, paraphrasable sense."[54] Around this speech, any desire to impose a stable meaning on the text coincides with Leontes's jealousy. As Leontes obsesses about the threat to his singularity, anxious readers might want to stabilize the meaning of his words even if he is voicing the onset of confusion. One basic ambiguity in these lines concerns whether "[a]ffection" is a predicate nominative (with Leontes apostrophizing an abstract concept, as he does in the text quoted above from the *Riverside* edition) or whether it refers to Hermione's own affection, now suspected of being wayward. These two possibilities do not have to be discrete. Even if "affection" is an abstract concept, it remains linked with Hermione in such a way that "thy intention" seems to refer simultaneously to affection personified and to Hermione. Leontes's grammatical slipperiness conveys his fear that affection is not a fixed power but rather a fluid, interpersonal reality. The opening of the play locates affection within the challenges to his uniqueness as embodied by Polixenes. Camillo declares that between the two kings, who were initially brought up together, "there rooted . . . such an affection which cannot choose but branch now." Affection has the force of destiny between the two kings, but the word "branch," as Camillo uses it, makes it ambiguous whether their destiny is to be divided (branching out from one another) or unified in organic growth. Leontes comes to fear that through Hermione's erotic choice, affection has collapsed this dynamism of sameness and singularity.

If affection is to mediate successfully between an insistence on personal uniqueness and recognitions of sameness and replaceability, it requires the passage of time to do so. The necessity of time passing is already suggested by Camillo's description of the gradual "branching" of the two kings out into their respective kingdoms; it is confirmed by the play's famous break with temporal verisimilitude. In Sicilia, the imagined passage of sixteen years allows Leontes to affirm the fixity of his penitent love. In Bohemia, this same passage of time allows Florizel to mature as the inheritor of the questions surrounding the identities of princes and husbands. Yet because Leontes's actions have led to the loss of his son, Florizel does not compete with a prince whose existence will qualify any claim of personal or political singularity. Instead, Florizel's insistence on marrying the object of his love defines him against intergenerational substitution within his own family:

> From my succession wipe me, father, I
> Am heir to my affection. (4.4.480–81)

Leontes's jealousy had led him to fear the transferability of affection, with Polixenes present as the alternate object. Florizel expresses a longing to exit the cycle of replaceability even though he is an heir. He wishes to be born from affection itself—reborn as a husband rather than as a prince, out of the love between him and Perdita.

By insisting on his choice in love, Florizel claims for himself a permanence that he can try to will into existence. When his plan to marry Perdita has been discovered by Polixenes, he insists, "What I was, I am" (4.4.464). Yet even before being thwarted, Florizel understands the need to conjoin this feeling of permanence with the passage of time, and the contingencies that it brings. He uses the vocabulary of the sea to imagine how this fusion could take place within Perdita as he perceives her:

> When you do dance, I wish you
> A wave o' th' sea, that you might ever do
> Nothing but that; move still, still so,
> And own no other function. (4.4.140–43)

In *Othello*, the sea is the chaotic force that serves Venice while imperiling Othello and Desdemona's marriage. After arriving safely on the Cypriot shore, Othello wishes to arrest time completely to enjoy permanent love. Florizel, by contrast, imagines Perdita as conjoining flux and stasis artfully within her person. Yet he can only articulate this as a fanciful wish, and soon, the couple will find themselves crossing the sea toward a destiny that remains uncertain. When they arrive in Sicilia, conjugal love will, contrary to Florizel's fantasies, be returned to its place under patriarchal auspices. Even before the revelation of Perdita's identity, Leontes affirms Florizel as his "father's image" and his "very air" (5.1.127–28). An obvious pun undercuts Florizel's previous claim to be the heir to his own affection. Because Polixenes's fatherhood needs to be reaffirmed, Leontes's penitence has not exorcised from the play the obsession with female fidelity. In the final act, Leontes feels that he can celebrate Florizel as Polixenes's image and heir because his "mother was most true to wedlock" (5.1.124).

In retrospect, the perilous crossing of the sea seems to have served the aims both of personal love and of political continuity. Yet this is not a straightforward resolution. I have argued that, early in the play, Camillo deploys the language of "if" in a way that thwarts Leontes's claim to absolute power over his subjects. Even as the end of the play restores kingship, it reaffirms a transcendent authority beyond the reaches of any human authority. Leontes can do nothing to thwart or to bring about the oracular "if": "'and the King shall live without an heir, if that which is lost be not found'" (3.2.134–36). The dramatic sea in *The Winter's Tale* helps to explain why even the affirmation of a chastened monarchy must remain a half-satisfying conclusion. Florizel has desired to cast himself as resolutely singular, above and beyond the demands of succession. The unique object of his love, imagined as a tide in the sea, would make stasis possible within a world of flux; Florizel wishes that Perdita would "own no other function" than this. In *Cymbeline*, Imogen can finally fulfill her longing for fixed love because she has been freed from the necessity of being an heir; Florizel is not afforded a similar luxury. It is unclear whether being restored to the status of a princely heir fulfills, modifies, or violates the terms of Florizel's desire. This question is not so much addressed as it is diverted toward the restoration of Leontes and Hermione's marriage. Perdita participates in this deflection. Instead of affirming her future husband's desire for fixity in an explicit way, she does not address Florizel at all in the final scene. She focuses her attention instead on her restored mother.

In Hermione's return, irreplaceable personhood and the passage of time are conjoined in a different way than Florizel had been able to imagine. They are conjoined in the wrinkles that mark her appearance. Leontes marvels that "Hermione was not so much wrinkled" when she ostensibly died sixteen years earlier (5.3.28). Paulina explains that the addition of wrinkles is merely a sign of the "carver's excellence" which could anticipate the passage of time to perfect verisimilitude (5.3.30). This extraneous moment seems to offer clumsy exposition that explains away an inconvenient reality. Yet the reality of Hermione having aged sixteen years is, of course, not a reality at all but part of the dramatic fiction and of the play's flagrant violation of verisimilitude. Hermione both has and has not aged sixteen years. If wrinkles are visible to us, they are the product neither of Giulio Romano's painting nor of the passage of time but rather of stage cosmetics. The poignancy of this moment derives not from Leontes's guilt giving way to wonder in the reality of his wife's continued existence (we might merely register that as maudlin) but instead in the way that his affective transformation underwrites within our viewing experience a rapid oscillation between what we know to be real and what we know to be false. In other words, Leontes's stubborn rejection of substitution has been redeemed from the status of mad jealousy if his penitence over the imagined years can effect within the audience a momentary inability to distinguish between real duration and the fictive passage of time. This seemingly gratuitous detail is important because it prepares Hermione's durable existence across time to become the object of faith—not just for Leontes but also for us—around which this play attempts a tragicomic restoration. It is possible to relate this particular dynamism of the perceived, the real, and the fictive to the Pauline definition of marriage. The Epistle to the Ephesians teaches that Christ transformed his bride into "a glorious church, not having spot, or wrinkle, or any such thing" so that she could be worthy of union with him (Eph. 5:27). (The same language of spot and wrinkle appears in both the 1568 Bishops' Bible and in the 1599 Geneva Bible.)

Hermione's wrinkles are not direct evidence of Leontes's deficiencies as a husband, but they do manifest the long period of estrangement that he has caused. Even on the cusp of faith, Leontes's remark about his wife's wrinkles may signal to us that he continues to fall short of Christlikeness, and that he has done nothing to redeem her or the losses she has incurred.

The Winter's Tale openly signals its awareness that its dramatic experiments with time might strike audiences as utterly incongruous. Yet insofar as the presentation of Hermione as a resurrected queen, wife, and mother manages to strike us as poignant, then that affective claim on us leads us to realize the difference between what we see before us and what we might want to see. When brought back to life, Hermione will embrace Leontes. Yet what remains for the restoration of their marriage or for the nature of his kingship in the future is entirely unclear, regardless of what Leontes wants to believe. Hermione simply has no words for him; in this sense, she will be like Euripides's Alcestis. Yet Hermione does have words, directed to Perdita alone. If we have suspended our disbelief about the passage of time to feel that Hermione has aged, the play channels the complex feelings arising out of that half belief in a fictive duration toward an affirmation of a bond between mother and daughter, queen and princess, with any questions about political succession remaining open-ended and uncertain.

3

Gondibert and the Biopolitics of Marriage

We may still remember William Davenant for his claim to being Shakespeare's illegitimate son. John Aubrey records Davenant's habit of declaring over wine that he seemed to write "with the very spirit [of] Shakespeare" because Shakespeare was his father.[1] This was hypothetically possible because Davenant's mother, Jane, was the hostess of an Oxford tavern that Shakespeare visited. As Aubrey remarks, Davenant's self-aggrandizing gossip conferred on his mother "a very light report."[2] In the preface to *Gondibert* (published separately in 1650, a year before the poem), Davenant certainly does not announce his claim about Shakespeare but places himself instead in an artistic lineage of epic poets from Homer to Spenser. The influence of Shakespeare does register indirectly when Davenant signals his intention to produce a "Heroick Poem" that is structured like a play, "proportioning five bookes to five *Acts*."[3] Whereas Davenant's gossip about Shakespeare persists as a source of curiosity, his bid to succeed Spenser in the history of epic seems simply to have been doomed. *Gondibert* was a target of ridicule from its inception, and Davenant never completed it.

This chapter does not dwell on Davenant's varied attempts to affiliate himself with the previous two authors studied in this book. It attends to the way that Davenant takes up and adapts the existing vocabulary of conjugal love as a rejection of substitution. He does so to comment on the altered realities of England after the civil wars. *Gondibert* initiates an elaborate critique of Christian marriage as an instrument of political cohesion. Davenant celebrates eros as the vehicle of reproduction and reproduction as the vehicle of succession. Yet in his view, marriage has clearly failed to promote stability. Like Spenser before him, he initiates a long heroic poem that never arrives at the promised conjugal conclusion. In *Gondibert*, a change of heart is the central plot device that thwarts the possibility of closure. The titular hero seems destined to win the hand of the princess Rhodalind, the only child of King Aribert. By bringing valor, love, and dynastic stability under the aegis of marriage, Gondibert should allow Davenant to unite Mars and Venus in a heroic poem that also follows the rhythms of comedy. Instead, Gondibert falls in love with Birtha, who nurses him back to health after he has combatted his rival in the quest to marry Rhodalind.

Around this plot twist of affective replacement, *Gondibert* explores the fictive dimensions of Christian marriage. The poem describes how awareness of that fictive nature can disrupt political authority. In the preface, Davenant asserts his plan to reject the supernatural in favor of the practical. Within the narrative, resurrection proves to be a Christian belief that has little purchase on worldly reality; the closest approximation of resurrection lies in knowledge that can save lives on earth. This bears directly on the question of marriage as Gondibert falls in love with Birtha after she has helped to save his physical life. Birtha knows how to do this because her father's house is an archive of scientific knowledge. Even as religious belief is being subordinated to practical knowledge, Davenant cynically teaches that poetry still has a role to play. Poetry is needed to persuade women like Birtha to revere their husbands more than they deserve. Yet the resulting myth of husbandly superiority does not serve the interests of the monarch. The extant narrative of Davenant's poem ends with Gondibert working with Birtha's father to flatter and deceive King Aribert. After redirecting conjugal love away from a belief in Christ's salvation and toward literal lifesaving, Davenant reaffirms a basic truth: the human sovereign might be able to cut natural life short but cannot give or extend it. When it comes to feelings such as gratitude over the preservation of life, the king has less of a claim than those who possess practical knowledge.

Davenant could not have truly foreseen the extent to which modern state power would seek to manage life itself. Yet in the latter half of this chapter, I argue that *Gondibert*'s commentary on mid-seventeenth-century religion, science, and politics presents us with an occasion to revisit our genealogies of modern biopolitics. I refer specifically to Giorgio Agamben's well-known elaboration of the theory of biopower that Foucault left unfinished. Neither marriage nor reproduction plays a significant role in Agamben's account. Yet marriage has long served not only to regulate the generation of human lives but also to shape collective attitudes about the appropriate (or ardently desired) configuration of biological and civic life. Writing in the aftermath of the civil wars, Davenant describes the conditions in which royalist ideology can no longer command affective sway over the realities of sex and reproduction within Christian marriage. The incomplete narrative of *Gondibert* serves as a reminder that scientific knowledge can coexist with religious myths and art in a way that thwarts the will of the sovereign.

I do not mean to propose an unduly optimistic lesson about the possible autonomy of scientific learning allied with intimate feeling. As *Gondibert* drives practical knowledge as a wedge between feeling and authority, it also registers the persistence of Christian typology within a view of marriage that is becoming less overtly theological. As Gondibert works to deceive King Aribert, he imagines his choice to pursue personal love as being of a piece with his father's failure to achieve his highest military ambition: to secure a universal empire. Because worldwide unity through conquest has proven impossible, Gondibert will forsake political life and choose loving marriage instead. His thinking seems muddled, but Davenant's preface offers some clarification. Davenant praises expansionism as an outlet for the kind of energy that might lead to strife at home. More pointedly, he criticizes Jews as exemplifying a nation-specific form of dominion without universalizing ambitions. There are no Jews in *Gondibert*, yet Davenant's remarks in the preface signal the relevance of the universalizing claims of typology as it structures a Christian understanding of marriage. By registering the broadly political implications of Pauline marriage, *Gondibert* shows us how conjugal narratives serve a divided role in the early glimpses of a modern biopolitics. If natural life and practical learning come to elude the will of the sovereign in the name of love, the form of love that persists still contains within it a kernel of ambition that is expansionist in nature and exclusionary in its frustration.

Gondibert alerts us to the work that conjugal narratives perform in shaping a sense of which lives should enjoy the benefits of singularity and belonging at once, and which lives can be deemed expendable for the sake of love. This chapter concludes by turning to the alternative myth of singularity, replaceability, and stability that Davenant promotes after the Restoration. He participates in the celebration of economic expansion as the grounds of a new myth of monarchical prestige and makes especially clear that commerce promises to replace a political myth of marriage. Charles II might be able to occupy a unique station by presiding over a world otherwise defined by fungible goods. Affirming the king's status in this way offers an alternative to the failed project of upholding royal uniqueness within loving marriage.

The Disappointment of Marriage

Charles I and Henrietta Maria were married by proxy in May 1625, but their marriage eventually promised to turn a brokered union into a site of real personal affection. Yet this affection ended up being a key source of contention owing to Henrietta Maria's Catholicism and political activity. During the First English Civil War, the parliamentary forces under General Thomas Fairfax sought to weaponize Charles's love for his queen by publishing, in 1645, *The King's Cabinet Opened, or Certain Packets of Secret Letters and Papers Written with the King's Own Hand*. In these letters, the king addresses his wife as "Dear Heart" and mingles military and strategic matters with personal ones. In a letter dated April 9, 1645, for example, Charles writes, "I pray thee consider, since I love thee above all earthly things, & that my contentment is unseperably conjoyned with thine, must not all my Actions tend to serve and please thee?"[4] Royalists decried the publication of *The King's Cabinet Opened* as an outrageous breach of decorum.[5]

For Cavalier poets, the civil wars did not just fray and then sunder the union of Charles and Henrietta Maria. These poets describe cultural upheaval as shattering the harmony between private love and public honor throughout the realm. Even among royalist poets, Davenant had especially good reason to become disillusioned with marriage as an instrument of cohesion. He had been more properly of the queen's party than of the king's. The title page of the masque *The Temple to Love* (published in London in 1634–35) publicly identifies Inigo Jones as the "Surveyor of his Majesties Workes" and William Davenant as "her Majesties Servant." Before and during the civil wars, Davenant's hope in Henrietta Maria shaped his literary endeavors in promoting marriage as a vehicle of ideological coherence. As Kevin Sharpe notes, Davenant was anomalous insofar as he personally claimed not to understand Platonic love and celebrated sexual desire as a wholesome natural phenomenon. Yet Davenant was willing to subordinate his own sensibilities to accommodate Henrietta Maria's investments in Neoplatonic love.[6] Davenant's earlier dramatic works appeal to marriage as "the metaphor employed for the ordering of the private virtue and the commonweal," as Sharpe puts it, and also as the practice that can "cement alliances, mend friendships and unite contending families or rivals."[7]

Davenant's service to the queen could be directly political as well as literary. In 1641 he was arrested for having taken part in a plot to free the Earl of Strafford from imprisonment. In the ensuing *Humble Remonstrance*, Davenant seeks clemency from Parliament by pointing to his published work appealing to Charles I to abandon his Personal Rule. Davenant reminds us that "it is not long since [that he] wrote to the Queenes Majesty in praise of her inclination to become this way the Peoples advocate."[8] Davenant refers to his recent (1640 or 1641) poem "To the Queen," one of the many he addressed to her. This poem elevates the queen to the position of the "Judges Judge, and Peoples Advocate."[9] The queen is sociable, in a manner that contrasts with the tendencies of kings who are often "peculiar and alone" (1) and prone to "extreame obdurateness" (19). Marriage exists to "cure this high obnoxious singleness" (11). Because queens live

> in Monarchs breasts
> Tenants for life, not accidental Guests,

royal marriage is a key first step toward an inclusive and corporate form of kingship (13–14).

Davenant's hopes would, however, prove misplaced. Henrietta Maria's views would increasingly coincide with Charles's unwillingness to make concessions to Parliament. Yet Davenant persisted as long as he could in his promotion of royal marriage and of the person of the queen. In the 1639–40 *Salmacida Spolia* (the last masque of the Caroline court before the civil wars), the arrival of Charles as Philogenes, the lover of the people, is preceded by celebration of the Queen Mother, Marie de Médicis. The chorus sings that even though the blessings emanating from the queen's own person are *"too great to last"* in their sight, it can rejoice in the Queen Mother, *"from whom they are deriv'd."*[10] The masque does conclude with Henrietta Maria, "representing the chiefe Heroin," descending and joining Philogenes in dance (D2ʳ). This expression of conjugal harmony brings the remote *"musick of the Spheres"* down to the human plane: the chorus celebrates how "[a]*ll that are harsh, all that are rude*" have finally been "*subdu'd*" in this effective display (D4ᵛ). Royal union does not only mediate between the king and the people. It also mediates between continuity and rupture in a time of mounting civil strife. When the queen descends, the chorus remarks that her beauty has frozen everyone around her. Only her dance with Philogenes allows time to resume decorously, in a way that attracts public adoration:

> *Move then like Time, for Love (as well as he)*
> *Hath got a Kalender.* (D3ʳ)

The chorus concludes with a lesson not only about the royal couple's graceful movement in time and space but also about intergenerational continuity in the service of national cohesion. The people will learn from the royal couple's example,

> *Till we so kinde, so wise, and carefull be,*
> *In the behalf of our Posteritie*
> *That we may wish your Scepters ruling heere.* (D4ᵛ–D4ʳ)

Yet even in poems written long before the civil war, strains become visible when Davenant relates Charles I to a celebration of his queen and her maternal status. Davenant seems to have written only one poem addressed to Charles, titled "To the King on New-Yeares Day 1630." This poem encourages the king to rule in Parliament, although he had initiated his Personal Rule in 1629. The ode begins,

> The joyes of eager Youth, of Wine, and Wealth,
> Of Faith untroubled, and unphysick'd Health;
> Of Lovers, when their Nuptials nie,
> Of Saints forgiven when they die;
> Let this yeare bring
> To *Charles* our King:
> To *Charles*; who is th'example and the Law,
> By whom the good are taught, not kept in awe. (lines 1–8)

The first couplet seems entirely conventional in a poem of flattery, introducing glimmers of trouble and illness only to banish them. Yet the next couplet proves a bit more puzzling. Even in wishing Charles well, Davenant seems to summon problems that should be irrelevant. Charles had married Henrietta Maria in 1625; he was only twenty-nine years old at the beginning of 1630. If the wish for extended youthfulness explains the oddity of wishing this king the erotic anticipation of a marriage, the following image of deathbed absolution clashes with that impulse.

This pairing of an anticipated wedding with death expresses in fragmentary form some of the problems with marriage that would become much more evident in *Gondibert*. Royal marriage registers the fact of the king's mortality. In early 1630, Henrietta Maria was pregnant with the son who would eventually go on to succeed Charles, if only after a remarkable interruption. As we have seen, Davenant would go on in the 1640 or 1641 poem "To the Queen" to describe Henrietta Maria as a tenant of the king's breast. This occupancy is called on to be a basis of the king's communal or corporate reign. Yet Davenant could also reverse the roles of container and contained to suggest the king's mortal limitations. In a mid-1630s poem titled "To the Queen, Presented with a Suit," Davenant hails Henrietta Maria as a benevolent patroness. He imagines the queen's being attended by historical and mythical women: Tomiris, the sixth-century Scythian queen who defeated Cyrus the Great; Penelope, identified as "Queene of Ithaca" (line 45); and Artemisia II of Caria. Penelope is said to embody "chaste desires," but she is flanked by powerful women who are threatening or morally dubious (46). Artemisia II married her own brother, Mausoleus, the Persian satrap, but Davenant mentions neither the incestuous nature of Artemisia's marriage nor her reign after Mausoleus's death.

He focuses instead on the legend of Artemisia's consuming Mausoleus's ashes after his cremation. After referring to Artemisia as "a living Tomb unto her Lord" (48), he looks ahead to the time

> when
> The Destinies are so much vex'd with Men
> That the just God-like Monarch of [Henrietta Maria's] breast
> Is ripe, and fit to take eternall rest. (49–52)

Artemisia's precedent allows Davenant to imagine a time when the queen will serve as Charles's living mausoleum. Davenant celebrates this as a particular form of immortality: the poet will "court [Charles's] spirit" as if he were the "mighty *Julius*" (53–57). The comparison to Julius Caesar ominously suggests what Davenant could not have genuinely foreseen in the 1630s—the political killing of King Charles. By imagining a Caesarian form of premature death leading to apotheosis, Davenant insists on the king's mortality while praising the queen's capacity to survive, if only to serve as his vessel.

The portrayal of the king as incapable of resurrecting himself except through his wife anticipates the problems of marriage in *Gondibert*. If queens and mothers are the guarantors of succession imagined as a form of immortality, then even kingly husbands cannot truly maintain a Christlike position over them. This simple point about reliance on the female reproductive body furnishes the grounds of a complex meditation. If royalist ideology seeks to align the awe owed to a king with the reverence owed to a husband, then that claim is based on a fictive likeness between a husband and Christ. Awareness of this fictive dimension undercuts sovereign awe. We can discern the faint outline of these notions in the opening stanza of Davenant's 1630 poem "To the King." After invoking the pairing of marriage and mortality through the rhyming pair of "Lovers, when their Nuptials nie," and "Saints forgiven when they die," Davenant establishes the refrain for the entire poem. The refrain ends by celebrating Charles as "th'example and the Law" but also by stripping him of the power to rule by awe—or, more specifically, to rule the good by awe. Over the already good, Charles may have no legitimate grounds to strike awe.

Revenge against Love

Davenant's *Gondibert* is the story of the fictiveness of husbandly merit and its implications for kingly awe. The poem opens by presenting marriage as the solution to King Aribert's dynastic impasse in eighth-century Lombardy.[11] Because Aribert has no son, the man who marries his daughter, Rhodalind, must succeed him. This premise establishes the basis both of a familiar romance plot and of an equally familiar comic pattern. Rhodalind has two male suitors, Gondibert and Oswald. "*Oswald* as reward of merit sought" the hand of Rhodalind, the poet tells us, "[w]ith Hope, Ambition's common Baite, beguild" (1.1.40.3–4). Gondibert, by contrast, feels "Love's fire" in his breast (1.1.46.1). Davenant repeatedly describes Oswald and his soldiers as old, Gondibert and his followers as young. The formulas of comedy dictate that the young suitor should prevail, and this generic impulse leads the reader to accept a breach of class hierarchy. Duke Gondibert should prevail over Prince Oswald by winning the hand of the princess.

Gondibert does defeat Oswald in battle, but this amounts to a pyrrhic victory for the cause of aligning personal love with succession. Before Gondibert realizes in the next book that he loves Birtha and seeks to marry her instead of Rhodalind, the first canto establishes internal problems that thwart a conjugal conclusion. The initial problem seems to lie in a split between hidden, private feeling and public awareness:

> Love's fire [Gondibert] carry'd, but no more in view
> Then vital heat which kept his heart still warm. (1.1.46.1–2)

Yet it turns out that the real problem is that Gondibert's love might never have been attached to Rhodalind to begin with:

> As yet to none could he peculiar prove,
> But like an universal Influence
> (For such and so sufficient was his love)
> To all the Sex he did his heart dispense. (1.1.48)

The reader is suddenly asked to root for a suitor who seeks the hand of a princess he may not love in any "peculiar" way. This seems like a puzzling disclosure, but Davenant's preface offers some clarification: "Love in the Interpretation of the Envious, is softnesse; in the Wicked, good men suspect it for Lust; and in the good, some spirituall men have given it the name of Charity: And these are but termes to this which seemes a more consider'd Definition; that indefinite Love is Lust; and Lust when it is determin'd to one, is Love."[12] The good suspiciously think of eros as sinful desire, and they valorize instead the more spiritual *agape*. Yet Davenant believes that lust is substantively the same as love. Love is lust that happens to be fixed on a singular object. When Gondibert's desire has yet to be fixed on Rhodalind, the fire that he feels may amount to lust in the popular understanding of the term. My reading of *Gondibert* details how Davenant applies his cynical understanding of marriage to realign goodness with a naïve faith in love, but in a way that undercuts kingly authority.

The fixity of love and heroic marriage will never converge in *Gondibert* to stabilize the future of the monarchy. By entering into a contest against the ambitious Oswald, Gondibert participates in a form that makes Rhodalind a negotiable object of political desires. This is true not only for the two antagonists but also for their followers, who understand marriage as a shared form of competition:

> The royal *Rhodalind* is now the Prize
> By which these Camps would make their merit known;
> And think their Gen'ral's but their Deputies
> Who must for them by Proxy wed the Crown. (1.1.77)

Marriage by proxy is possible on the battlefield. The ensuing contest between Gondibert and Oswald drives a wedge between the heroic merit that men seek in conflict and the highest form of merit that defines Christian marriage. The grounds for discerning this difference are initially established not in a scriptural echo but rather in a set piece, in the second canto, that affiliates *Gondibert* with Virgilian epic. In book 7 of the *Aeneid*, Ascanius's killing of the stag of Silvia provokes a war between Aeneas's men and the residents of Latium. Aeneas and his son, Ascanius, achieve victory in the battle that they have sparked through an indecorous act of hunting. Davenant reshapes the ambivalence of this Virgilian precedent to speak to the consequences of the recent civil wars. In contrast to the episode in the *Aeneid*, the local residents at the site of Gondibert and Oswald's confrontation are the ones hunting a "Stagg made long since Royall in the Chace" (1.2.32.3). A political allegory links pity for the executed Charles I to pity for this hunted stag. Davenant announces this identification emphatically but temporarily in this episode. The reader is made aware that *Gondibert* does grapple with urgent concerns, but the poem's questions regarding ambition, violence, and love will not be pursued in a consistently topical manner. Davenant decries violence against the stag as the act of "Murdrous Man" and of "Tirranique Man" (1.2.37.4, 1.2.38.1). The hunt results in the stag's being killed by "the Monarch Murderer" (1.2.52.1). Gondibert certainly does not participate, but he recognizes the local hunters as his father's old rangers and embraces them. The rangers then warn Gondibert—albeit too late—that Oswald and his men are waiting in ambush for him. Gondibert must now navigate a situation in which an act likened to regicide has already occurred, with a new form of violence being targeted against him. He should rise above the threats against him, but he is assisted by those who have already committed a form of violence denounced by the poet as a travesty.

In the ensuing parley with Oswald, Gondibert tries to promote love and sacrifice over more bloodshed. Gondibert invites Oswald to satisfy his "love, or lust of Empire" by taking "[t]he Crown, which is the worst of *Rhodalind*" (1.3.26.1–4). Gondibert seems to indicate that he is happy to marry Rhodalind for her person alone and will relinquish a claim to the crown. This offer fails to secure a resolution. When Oswald scoffs at Gondibert, the hero tries to avert general bloodshed through an offer of single combat:

Let your revenge onely on me be spent,
And hazard not my Party, nor your own. (1.3.31.3–4)

It is important that Gondibert describes single combat as a ritual of sacrifice:

Ambition else would up to Godhead grow,
When so profanely we our anger prise,
That to appease it we the blood allow
Of whole offenceless Herds for sacrifice. (1.3.32)

This attempt to reshape single combat into a religious rite is far from coherent. If Gondibert presents himself as a sacrifice to appease Oswald's vengeance, then he assumes a self-defeating posture that undermines his heroic merit. Perhaps the rhetorical shift from appeasing Oswald's personal revenge to appeasing ambition personified suggests that either Gondibert's or Oswald's blood might indifferently be shed as sacrifice. Yet if Gondibert dies, then he would be incapable of actualizing his love for Rhodalind, making it "peculiar" through marriage. If Gondibert kills Oswald, he would have earned marriage to Rhodalind through an act of killing that has only been relabeled as expiation.

For the time being, Davenant leaves implicit the contrast between Gondibert as a would-be husband and the way that Christ, according to Pauline teaching, perfects conjugal love through self-sacrifice. In book 3, as

I go on to discuss, the seeming irrelevance of the resurrection reveals the extent to which Pauline teaching is unhelpful for Gondibert's quest for marriage. In book 1, Gondibert fails in his bid to conjoin love and self-sacrifice simply because neither Oswald's nor Gondibert's followers will allow their leader to engage in personal combat. Oswald's men clamor to display their valor. Gondibert's men, by contrast, are motivated by love in various configurations. Count Hurgonil loves Gondibert's sister, Orna; Gondibert's niece inspires reciprocated love from Arnold as well as unreciprocated love from Hugo. (The name of Gondibert's niece, Laura, identifies Hugo's futile desire as Petrarchan.) Young Goltho has yet to feel love, but Tybalt keeps the object of his love a secret. The fact that some of Gondibert's followers seek to marry his sister and his niece reveals how the form of love he champions is still enmeshed in the politics of kinship that the ambitious Oswald pursues. Gondibert should model for his followers a superior form of heroism that leads to both loving marriage and political stability.

When Gondibert kills Oswald, this seeming victory gives rise to another order of challenge to the logic of Christian marriage. This challenge emanates from the person of Oswald's sister, Gartha, who arrives in book 2 demanding revenge. She finds a way to embed vengeance within the economy of marriage when the aged hero Hermegild arrives to offer her a marriage pact. Earlier in book 2, King Aribert laments the violence between Gondibert and Oswald; he decrees that Hermegild should be the heir to his throne. Davenant disorients the reader by withholding any information about Hermegild's identity. Only later does the reader learn that Hermegild has long loved Gartha without the hope of reciprocation. Hermegild appears offering the crown to Gartha's surviving brother, Hubert, but only if Gartha will agree to marry him:

> The Crowne on thee, adorn'd with *Rhodalind*;
> Which yet for *Gartha* is a price too low. (2.4.24.3–4)

When Gartha accepts, the problem is not simply that her marriage pact is ersatz because it is not based on fully mutual love. The union of Hermegild's love and Gartha's vengefulness can take hold so effectively because it exposes the unresolved questions of merit within Christian marriage. Gondibert's bid to turn himself into a worthy husband has given rise not only to Gartha's longing for vengeance but also to her ability to negotiate with her own person in a contractual form of marriage. Hermegild, in turn, understands the utility of the political marriage that he is brokering. He discerns that Hubert's "merits are too light" to lay claim to King Aribert's throne, yet he may still "get in *Rhodalind* the Peoples part" (2.4.42.1–4). Davenant's earlier poetry, as we have seen, celebrates Queen Henrietta Maria's capacity to serve as "the Peoples advocate." In *Gondibert*, Hermegild articulates the openly cynical belief that if Rhodalind marries Hubert, she can sway public opinion regarding her undeserving husband. For the time being, Hermegild directs Gartha to display herself before the people first, in anticipation of the role that Rhodalind might fulfill later, to "prepare their pity" for Hubert (2.4.46.1). Relying on the yearning for vengeance, Hermegild brokers a union whose function is to prop up a false sense of merit—both personal and political. This configuration proves tenable because a morally superior alignment of merit and love within marriage does not materialize in the poem.

In the seventh canto to book 3—composed after Davenant's 1652 release from imprisonment, and not published until 1685—jealousy functions as the instrument for Hermegild's and Gartha's attack on marriage. Gartha seeks to sabotage the union of Gondibert's sister, Orna, with his loyal follower Hurgonil. This pairing has, in fact, been the most promising synthesis of personal love and political expediency in the poem. In the previous chapter, I argued that Shakespeare's treatments of jealousy expose the rift between communal realities and individual experience, between the supposed inclusivity of Christian truth and the realities of exclusion. In Davenant's addition to *Gondibert*, Gartha manufactures jealousy through a plot reminiscent of two Shakespearean plays. She dresses up as a young man and appears in the window of Orna's bedchamber while Hurgonil looks on. This is a variation of the trick that fools Claudio into doubting his betrothed Hero's faithfulness in *Much Ado about Nothing*.[13] After being smuggled into Orna's bedchamber by an unscrupulous servant—one who sells "[t]he Jewel Honour at a common price"—Gartha appears once Orna is asleep (3.7.45.3). Here, Gartha poises herself to be like Iachimo breaking into Imogen's bedchamber in *Cymbeline*. Yet unlike Claudio in *Much Ado* and unlike Imogen's husband, Posthumus, Hurgonil cannot be duped into jealousy. Gartha's ruse fails, much to the frustration of the men around her. They had called for direct, violent action against the king. Davenant's extra canto does not narrate the tragic triumph of jealousy over love. Neither does it show that love can fully triumph over jealousy. Hurgonil and Orna's union is neither sabotaged nor perfected in marriage. Gartha, after her failure, negotiates with the aggrieved men in her party so that they will not pursue a campaign against Aribert. Davenant's added canto ends with a stalemate between love and vengeance.

Making Birtha Jealous

Ironically, Hermegild, Gartha, and Hubert have no need to sabotage the titular hero directly. After defeating Oswald, Gondibert ends up falling in love with Birtha, who nurses him to health. Romance epic plots are full of wayward lapses in desire. Gondibert's love for Birtha recalls book 2 of *The Faerie Queene*, in which Timias is nursed to health by the virgin Belphoebe and then foolishly expresses his desire for her. Yet in Davenant's poem, Gondibert's love is reciprocated and threatens to arrest the central plot. This threat is all the more serious because the poem has admitted that Rhodalind had never been the "peculiar" object of Gondibert's love. The poem stops without explaining whether the hero ends up marrying Rhodalind after all, or whether Gondibert's true destiny is to marry Birtha. In the latter case, the refusal of an expedient marriage would secure a comic ending at the expense of epic ambitions. In book 2, once love between Gondibert and Birtha takes root, Gondibert's new mission is to find a suitable way to trick King Aribert, who wants him to be his son-in-law. The comic impulses informing the reader's expectations have altered: the obstacle to Gondibert's desire is no longer the rival Oswald but instead the king as an unwitting *senex*.

Before attending to Gondibert's love for Birtha, it will be useful to turn to Thomas Hobbes's remarks about the poem, which Davenant published with his preface. Hobbes declares that he wants to avoid detailing "every excellent picture of virtue" *Gondibert* offers, but that he "cannot forbeare" to mention "the Description of Love in the person of *Birtha*, in the seventh *Canto* of the second Booke."[14] Hobbes adds that there "has nothing bene sayd of that subject neither by the Ancient nor modern Poets comparable to it."[15] Hyperbole may undercut the sincerity of his praise, but the fact that Hobbes singles out this story of love—whether for praise or for sly ridicule—seems remarkable. As Victoria Kahn has shown, Hobbes's *Leviathan* is structured around a rejection of romance and of love as binding political instruments. For Hobbes, the romance genre shows love to be one of the "self-aggrandizing passions" that lead to the "dilemma of mimetic desire."[16] Love is an emulous form of desire and identification. Fostering a subject's love for the ruler can end up motivating ambition—the desire to become the ruler. Kahn details how, in response to this perceived threat, *Leviathan* promotes a social contract that severely limits the forms of identification between subject and sovereign and is defined instead by fear.

Within this illuminating reading of *Leviathan*, Kahn mentions the exchange between Hobbes and Davenant. She argues that "Davenant must have thought of *Gondibert* as a Hobbesian poem"—one that reveals an incompatibility between the emulous love of romance and political stability.[17] It is true, she acknowledges, that the "prefatory letter to Hobbes told a different story" by affirming poetry's role in the promotion of love.[18] Yet she concludes that Hobbes praises *Gondibert* for being a "properly chastened" romance, one that "adheres to the truths of history and philosophy and excludes all supernatural machinery."[19] In my reading of *Gondibert*, marriage complicates the subordination of religious myth to practical knowledge. I will go on to discuss how Davenant exposes Christian marriage as a myth that relies on deception; at the same time, he still shows that poetry is valuable because it advances the fictions that prop up an unstable sense of male superiority. He teaches this divided lesson through an appeal to jealousy, which is not just a problem for marriage but also an inducement for it. Jealousy functions, more specifically, as a useful device for making Gondibert seem worthier than he truly is in Birtha's eyes.

What Hobbes singles out in *Gondibert* may prove more revealing than what Kahn's brief remarks about Davenant suggest. In the thirtieth chapter of part 2 of *Leviathan*, Hobbes makes a concession to the desirability of having the people feel that their sovereign loves them. Initially, Hobbes seems to proscribe mimetic desire in just the way that Kahn describes: subjects "are to be taught that they ought not to be led with admiration of the virtue of any of their fellow subjects . . . so as to defer to them any obedience or honour appropriate to the sovereign only."[20] Yet he adds a rationale for curbing emulation and envy among subjects: "For that sovereign cannot be imagined to love his people as he ought that is not jealous of them, but suffers them by the flattery of popular men to be seduced from their loyalty."[21] Even if love is not a defining characteristic of sovereignty, it is still important that the sovereign can be imagined as loving his subjects jealously. In describing this useful projection of affect, Hobbes appeals to a specifically religious understanding of conjugal jealousy. He adds that popular flatterers have often proclaimed "marriage with [the people] *in facie Ecclesia* . . . by preachers" even though this amounts to a form of political adultery.[22] The people should be made to feel that they are exclusively bound to a jealous sovereign. This moment in *Leviathan* suggests the possibility that Hobbes and Davenant share an interest in a vocabulary that pits substitution against a politically useful form of love. Both writers understand that love has proven deficient as an instrument of cohesion. Yet both exhibit—albeit to very different degrees and ends—a willingness to promote a fictive sense of love. For Hobbes, a perception of jealous love is a useful accessory to sovereignty. For Davenant, promoting religious myths of love confers value on poetry, even poetry that has largely discredited the relevance of the supernatural.

In book 2 of *Gondibert*, Davenant explores how the merely metaphorical aspects of Christian marriage undermine its political utility. After Gondibert is seriously wounded in his fight with Oswald, he learns that resurrection is, at best, a remote reality that exists as an object of religious belief and artistic representation. The practical alternative lies in scientific knowledge that can provide bodily healing in this world. Gondibert's life is literally saved at the House of Astragon—"an obviously Baconian establishment," as Lois Potter describes it—and falls in love with Astragon's daughter.[23] For the sake of Gondibert's heroism, however, Davenant goes on to manufacture an affective reversal whereby Birtha not only loves Gondibert but also falls into jealousy, in a way that leads her to regard him as superior. Davenant touts poetry as the vehicle for upholding such convenient nontruths as the superiority of a would-be husband over the woman who has saved his life. Yet at the same time, Davenant's frankness concerning the need to deceive Birtha (and wives in general) undercuts any sincere belief in the form of conjugal love that poetry promotes.

Davenant begins this line of thinking by describing the House of Astragon as a site devoted primarily to natural learning:

> Here Art by such a diligence is serv'd,
> As does th'unwearied Planets imitate;
> Whose motion (life of Nature) has preserv'd
> The world, which God vouchsaf'd but to create. (2.5.7)

In this expression of an early deist sensibility, the art of natural learning promises to reveal the principles of nature because the divine creator stands at a remove from the workings of creation. At the outset of his preface, Davenant criticizes poetry that deals with the supernatural—beginning with Homer, who talks so much of "Heaven, and Hell" and of "Gods and Ghosts" that "he sometimes deprives us of those natural probabilities in Story, which are instructive to humane life."[24] Davenant, by contrast, seeks to impart worldly lessons. In book 2, the description of the House of Astragon surveys the different branches of natural learning. Most relevant to Gondibert's condition is medical knowledge. In Astragon's library,

> [books written by] *Physicians* stood; who but repreive
> Life like a Judge, whom greater pow'r does awe;
> And cannot an Almighty pardon give
> So much yeilds Subject Art to Nature's Law. (2.5.63.1–4)

This seems like a sobering lesson about human knowledge, which can merely extend mortal life temporarily. Yet Davenant's simile is already beginning to reshape this lesson into a political meditation concerning the limitations of sovereignty. He invokes the limitations of scientific knowledge to draw a parallel: in extending lives, physicians exhibit the kind of power of reprieve that belongs to judges. Yet physicians do not have any absolute power to decree life rather than death. It is unclear whether Davenant is truly attributing the almighty power of pardon to the sovereign (as the analogy likening physicians to judges would suggest). It is possible that, despite Davenant's deist outlook, these lines are meant to remind us that only the Almighty has power over natural life—natural life being the tenor of the simile in which juridical life is only the vehicle. The last line replaces divine prerogative over life with "Nature's Law," to which the art of the physician is always subject. Even if the possible relevance of divine agency retreats from the stanza, the reader can still observe that the human sovereign (and the supposedly almighty power of pardon) is not able to sway the natural laws of life and death.

Davenant does not clarify this point in detail, but instead moves ahead to show that religion does have a place in the House of Astragon. It occupies the status of poetry, which is repeatedly deemed inferior to scientific knowledge. After the "long survay" of natural learning in Astragon's library, Davenant describes the refreshment offered by a turn to "pleasant *Poets*" (2.5.65.1–2). The first poet mentioned is the psalmist David, identified as "Heav'n's lov'd *Laureat*, that in *Jewry* writ" (2.5.66.2). The promotion of poetry through an appeal to the psalmist David is conventional. Yet Davenant may have previously half alluded to David in announcing that Astragon's knowledge of the natural world is actually superior to the knowledge contained in scriptures. Astragon's nursery

> seems to grow all that in *Eden* grew; And more . . .
> Then th'Hebrew King, Nature's Historian knew. (2.5.28.3–4)

David Gladish suggests that Davenant is referring to Solomon's wisdom, but the invocation of a Hebrew king might also anticipate the later mention of David's poetic authorship.[25] Davenant is establishing a hierarchy in which practical learning (like horticulture) is superior to both religious teaching and poetry, even though all three discourses coexist in Astragon's archives. Davenant declares that scientific knowledge chastens "Man's pride (grown to Religion)"; he praises the Copernican revolution for resituating "our lov'd Earth, which we think fix'd" (2.5.19.1–2).

The most humbling lesson that science offers to a religious mindset concerns the inevitability of death. Astragon's collection of "*Skelitons* of ev'ry kinde" offers a visual lesson undercutting the prideful belief in human superiority over other species (2.5.32.2). Davenant follows this lesson with a surprising illustration:

> Yet on that Wall hangs he too, who so thought;
> And she dry'd by him, whom that He obay'd. (2.5.33.1–2)

As Gladish notes, "The implication would seem to be that these are the skeletons of Adam and Eve."[26] The hesitant nature of this gloss is warranted. Davenant suggests that Adam was prideful in believing himself to be superior to other animals. Davenant does not clarify whether he deems Genesis misguided in teaching that God originally gave humans dominion over animals, or whether he believes that even before the Fall, Adam misunderstood the extent of the dominion conferred on him. Instead, Davenant quickly turns our attention to the more familiar lesson of Adam having obeyed Eve in eating the forbidden fruit. The significance of this brief mention of the Eden story becomes clearer in the next canto, when Davenant surveys the three religious temples in Astragon's house. Here, the Christian narrative of salvation might promise to undo the results of the Fall—but not in a way that affirms religious teaching to have a greater purchase on the world than natural learning. Instead, Davenant reminds us that religion is aligned with artistic representation rather than with scientific knowledge. Astragon's Temple of Praise contains artistic renderings of creation and of redemption. In one of these paintings, Christ is

> in ascension shown;
> When Hell he conquer'd. (2.6.72.2–3)

After describing Christ in triumph, Davenant reminds us that what we are dealing with is artistic representation rather than truth: "By Pencills this was exquisitely wrought; *Rounded* in all the Curious would behold" (2.6.73.1–2) Christ's ability to redeem life from hell is subordinated to the ability of the artist to simulate reality convincingly:

> Where life *Came out*, and *Met* the Painters thought;
> The *Force* was *tender*, though the strokes were *bold*. (2.6.73.3–4)

Gondibert directs all these strands of thought concerning knowledge, mythic belief, and art toward the topic of marriage. In the depiction of the Genesis story found in Astragon's temple, divine creation and human *poiesis* converge on Eve's origins. Davenant signals the operations of art even in the institution of Adamic marriage. Whereas the first chapter of Genesis describes God conferring benevolent dominion over creation on Adam and Eve, Davenant describes Adam's pride as triggering fear from the animals. Davenant is repeating his claim that the superiority of humans over animals amounts to a proud delusion. Eve is then described as having been designed to curb Adam's tendencies toward pride even before the Fall:

> But here (to cure this Tyrant's sullennesse)
> The Painter has a new false Curtain drawn,
> Where, Beauty's hid Creation to expresse;
> From thence, harmlesse as light, he makes it dawn.
> From thence breaks lov'ly forth, the World's first Maid. (2.6.62–63.1)

These lines leave it unclear whether the painter accurately captures God's intentions in presenting Eve to Adam, or whether the painter is taking interpretive liberties. This ambiguity may be the point: divine creation and human art may work together in a joint attempt to curb the original impulse toward tyrannous pride—in this case, over the animals of Eden. This claim reminds us of Davenant's earlier political poetry, which elevates royal marriage as a vehicle for curbing the characteristically antisocial tendencies of kings like Charles I. When, here in book 2 of *Gondibert*, Davenant describes the original institution of marriage, the same notion recurs but with far less grounds for optimism. By this point, Davenant has repeatedly described Adamic pride (the root of "this Tyrant's sullennesse") as existing before the Fall, and Eve is being tasked with an impossible role in which she will be blamed further, for helping to cause the Fall.

When the narrative returns to the possibility of Birtha and Gondibert marrying, the focus shifts from Edenic marriage to the question of why any wife should love an imperfect would-be husband as if he were Christlike. Birtha confronts in a literal form the burden of untruth that the Pauline redefinition of marriage places on all wives: she has redeemed Gondibert, and not the other way around. What motivates her to revere him nonetheless is a form of superstition:

> She fashions him she lov'd of Angels kinde;
> Such as in holy Story were imploy'd
> To the first Fathers. (2.7.33.1–3)

She thinks of "how her imagin'd Spouse and she" will enjoy immortality, "[t]hat they by Time shall ne'r o'retaken be" (2.7.41.1–3). She indulges such fantasies despite having been trained in scientific learning at her father's house. Even from the standpoint of Christian belief, these fantasies amount to a typological regression: Birtha bypasses the kernel of untruth in Pauline marriage by hoping that marriage might simply undo the Fall. When she considers the prospect of marriage, "[s]he thinks of *Eden*-life" (2.7.43.1). To the extent that marriage still requires faith in myths, Davenant promotes poetry as the way to generate that faith. In practice, this means that the third book of *Gondibert* must make Birtha succumb to jealousy. Jealousy is not merely an instrument for Gartha to deploy in her later attempt to sabotage marriage. It is first a vehicle for Davenant to reinforce the fragile claim of husbandly superiority. When Birtha comes to fear that Gondibert will forsake her to marry Rhodalind, her jealousy may be justifiable. When Gondibert swears to Birtha in book 3 that "*Rhodalind* [he] never sought," the reader has to recall in what sense this might possibly be true (3.2.74.3). Even though Gondibert fought against Oswald for Rhodalind's hand, Gondibert's personal love (or lust) had not been fixed on her. From Birtha's perspective, this could just mean that Gondibert is fully capable of switching his aims in marriage yet again.

Birtha's jealousy is useful, however, because it leads her to downplay her merit as the savior of her husband's life. Gondibert may find a way to gain the upper hand despite having no real claim to superiority. At first, Gondibert tries to effect this gendered reversal through the gift of a magical emerald passed down from generation to generation in his family. When worn by "the neglected wife," this "Bridal Stone" visibly manifests any infidelity on her husband's part through "faintness, and a pale decay of life" (3.4.49.4, 3.4.50.2–4).[27] This explanation confirms that Gondibert is the one who needs to prove himself faithful. At the same time, he puts Birtha in a perpetual state of doubt concerning her status in his affections. Yet she is not entirely naïve, and her claim on Gondibert's grateful love widens the disparity between personal affection and the public utility of marriage. She declares that the simplest way for Gondibert to prove himself worthy is by not marrying Rhodalind. Even as Birtha hopes that this will be the case, she laments what this would entail:

> Why stoop you down,
> My plighted Lord, to lowly *Birtha's* reach,
> Since *Rhodalind* would lift you to a Crown? (3.4.55.2–4)

Gondibert enjoys a newfound opportunity to earn Birtha's reverence. Birtha declares that if Gondibert forsakes Rhodalind and the crown, then he will live up to her earlier fantasies about him:

> your vertue has with Angels place,
> And 'tis a virtue to aspire at Heav'n. (3.4.56.3–4)

Birtha's jealousy has reshaped into a religious myth her awareness of the sacrifices that Gondibert might need to make in order to marry her. He has been effectively promoted from the status of a mortal man whose life Birtha has saved.

It is possible that the emerald and the crown—the two instruments whereby Gondibert can prove himself worthy—form the basis of a biblical allusion that confirms his mythic elevation in his wife's eyes. In the fourth chapter of Revelation, John sees Christ on his throne; Christ looks "like a jasper and a sardine stone: and there was a rainbow round about the throne, in sight like unto an emerald" (Rev. 4:3). The enthroned Christ is surrounded by twenty-four elders who initially wear golden crowns, yet they soon "cast their crowns before the throne" and then praise him as worthy (Rev. 4:10). If this allusion is operative in Davenant's poem, then it suggests that by forsaking any literal crown, Gondibert will prove to be closer to Christ in Birtha's esteem. She declares that she is the one who will owe Gondibert "a debt that shall be hourly paid"—and not the other way around (3.4.59.3). Because Gondibert can earn such esteem only by forsaking a literal crown, however, the alignment of loving marriage and political continuity eludes the poem.

The ensuing conversation between Birtha and Gondibert confirms that the political usefulness of marriage is being undercut even as husbandly superiority is reaffirmed as a poetic myth. Birtha explains that the reverence she would pay to Gondibert would offer him an alternative to the experience of being a sovereign:

> And as tow'rds Heav'n all travail on their Knees;
> So I tow'rds you, though Love aspire, will move:
> And were you crown'd, what could you better please
> Then aw'd obedience led by bolder Love? (3.4.57)

When the alignment of husband and Christ becomes somewhat closer to real, love is joined by "aw'd obedience." Yet if wifely obedience is analogous to the awe inspired by a sovereign, Birtha's rhetorical question makes clear that her awe can only exist as an alternative to political power. Gondibert is asked to remain satisfied with a domestic form of awe even if he has forsaken the crown to merit it. By this point in the narrative, the alignment of sovereignty with husbandly prerogative has already been undermined at the rhetorical level. In the previous canto, the king tries to assert his prerogative over marriage. He greets Gondibert, his would-be son-in-law, in such a way as

> to have it understood
> That Kings, like God, may chuse whom they wil chuse;
> And what they make, judg with their own Eies good. (3.3.51.2–4)

Aribert is the victim of irony because he is unaware of Gondibert's new love for Birtha. He deems kings godlike both in their ability to choose—suggesting a parallel between sovereign decision-making with predestination—and in their capacity to judge "what they make." When he describes kings as judging what they make "with their own Eies good," he suggests an echo of Genesis, in which God deems every aspect of his creation to be good. Yet Aribert unwittingly exposes a fundamental distinction between divine and human forms of sovereignty: if kings are capable of judging "what they make," their power may be limited to human constructions. Unlike God, human rulers may be unfit and unable to exert control over forms of life that they had no hand in making. Gondibert's speech goes on to alter the terms of kingly prerogative. He declares to Aribert,

> A King you are o're Subjects, so as wise
> And noble Husbands seem o're Loyal Wives. (3.4.22.1–2)

The king has declared himself to be godlike, but Gondibert casts him in the position of a husband who only seems like a lord from his wife's perspective—and only as long she remains loyal. This subversive flattery initiates Gondibert's attempt to persuade the king, without asking him overtly, to marry his daughter Rhodalind off to some other suitor.

Gondibert has been learning to renegotiate the alignment of God and sovereign under the tutelage of the "kinde and prudent *Astragon*" (3.2.65.1). Astragon knows how to defy the king as an archivist of scientific knowledge, of religious myth, and of poetry. These forms of knowledge converge in a way that allows Astragon, too, to flatter the king deceptively. In one encounter, Astragon declares to the king that

> when thus his Beams he does dispence
> In lowly visits, like the Sun he shows
> Kings made for universal influence. (3.3.47.2–4)

In book 2, as we have seen, Davenant promotes heliocentrism as one example of an error-prone religious outlook being humbled by scientific knowledge. Here, Astragon seems willing to turn his knowledge into the basis of a trite simile of flattery. Aribert's response reveals that he is unaware of the nature of the threat that Astragon poses to his authority. Davenant describes how

> [Astragon] with renown the King for Science pays,
> And Vertue; which Gods likest Pictures bee;
> Drawn by the Soul, whose onely hire is praise;
> And from such Salary not Heav'n is free. (3.3.48)

Aribert is again the victim of irony, as he is grateful to a subject who is in the process of flattering and deceiving him. Davenant also presents a more nuanced point about the limitations of sovereignty in relation to science. Those who pursue knowledge may not seek worldly forms of gain, but they do seek praise. When it comes to the economy of praise, however, heaven itself may be obligated to reward those who seek knowledge of the natural world. Such knowledge is, in Davenant's deist outlook, the most accurate understanding of the creator ("Gods likest Pictures"). As a result, this stanza suggests not only that the king feels indebted to Astragon, but also that the king might be somewhat irrelevant to the economy of praise in which a somewhat aloof creator nonetheless rewards those who seek to learn about creation. This helps to explain the case of an archivist of knowledge who seeks no reward from the monarch but instead a degree of autonomy that would allow his daughter to fulfill her love.

 Davenant develops this understanding of praise in book 2 by describing how the Temple of Praise at Astragon's house allows science and religion to coexist. Davenant defines praise as the artful mediation between accurate knowledge of nature and mythic belief in the creator. Praise prevents worldly knowledge from lapsing into outright cynicism and disbelief. In the preface to *Gondibert*, Davenant quotes his own description of the Temple of Praise to declare that poetry "is so much the uttermost and whole of Religious worship" because it is "usefull . . . to Men."[28] By "usefull," he refers to the capacity to connect knowledge and belief in a way that stabilizes authority. Poetry needs to assume this function because the clergy have "fail'd in governing Princes" and also "in ruling the People; by whom of late, Princes have been govern'd."[29] His idea of praise confirms that King Aribert is unwittingly exposing his weakened position when he affirms the value of Astragon's learning. Heaven itself may owe Astragon a "[s]alary" of praise for his efforts, but this economy threatens to operate not just at a remove from the king but in covert defiance of his wishes.

The Biopolitics of Conjugal Love

The split between science and mythopoetic belief working together, on the one hand, and the myths that sustain sovereign awe, on the other, anticipates some of the impulses behind the formation of the Royal Society soon after the Restoration of the Stuart monarchy. The society's First Charter of 1662 expresses Charles II's hope that "the whole world of letters may always recognize us not only as the Defender of the Faith, but also as the universal lover and patron of every kind of truth."[30] Thomas Sprat opens his 1667 *History of the Royal Society* with a dedication to Charles II, praising him for being the first of "*all the Kings of* Europe" to establish such a society.[31] Sprat (who would go on to be appointed bishop of Rochester) observes that "the True God *himself*" reveals "*his value of* Vulgar Arts" through numerous biblical stories concerning "Natural *or* Mechanical Invention."[32] The dedicatory epistle concludes that Charles II "*will certainly obtain* Immortal Fame, *for having establish'd a perpetual Succession of* Inventors."[33] To use the terms that Davenant prefers, the establishment of the Royal Society should ensure that the king will play a key role in the economy of praise, which promotes the useful belief that scientific knowledge is a form of reverence for the creator. Sprat's sincerity in praising the king and the degree to which his *History* is constrained by political pressure have been matters of long-standing debate.[34] Yet the *History* does confirm what *Gondibert* anticipates: the perceived need to reclaim for the monarchy the positive affects— including gratitude and love—surrounding the practical benefits of science.

I propose that the narrative of science, political authority, and personal feeling in *Gondibert* can offer lessons that look far beyond the seventeenth century. Even as the purchase of Christian belief on marriage erodes, marriage still shapes collective feelings about sacrifice, the acceptability of certain forms of nonsacrificial killing, and desirable configurations of personal love and social cohesion. Questions about these matters surface between the first two books of *Gondibert*. As we have seen, Oswald is killed after Gondibert's attempt to unite heroic love and peace through a heroic form of religious sacrifice fails. In the aftermath of the violence, the status of the dead remains uncertain. Back within the walls of Verona, where King Aribert holds court, priests refuse to give Gondibert's fallen soldiers a proper burial:

> These by their bloody marks in Combat di'de;
> Through anger, the disease of Beasts untam'd,

the priests reason (2.1.44.1–2). The refusal to bury those who have died in unsanctioned violence has classical precedents, but the priests in Verona articulate what sounds more like a Christian rationale. They go on to explain:

> Here the neglected Lord of peace does live;
> Who taught the wrangling world the rules of love. (1.2.45.1–2)

For King Aribert to be aligned with Christ under the title of "Lord of peace," Gondibert's men must be dishonored and dehumanized in death. This decree, however, proves unpopular with the people of Lombardy and with Gondibert's surviving followers. Davenant leaves unclear whether Gondibert's fallen soldiers are buried. The first canto of the second book ends with an unresolved problem whereby the failure to contain violence through sacrifice has led to an impasse between the people's sense of what is proper and the joint decision of religious and political authorities.

We come to learn, however, that Oswald does receive a burial. He is guiltier of sparking unsanctioned violence, yet his funeral is designed to reintegrate him into the polis. Hubert, Oswald's brother,

>   does declare
> How oft and well, he for the *Lombards fought*. (2.4.60.3–4)

This form of civic reincorporation after death cannot take place in a Christian form. Davenant tells us that

> *Oswald* (whose illustrious *Roman minde*
> Shin'd out in life, though now in dying hid) (2.4.55.1–2)

received

> *Roman* fun'ral rites . . .
> Which yet the World's last law had not forbid. (2.4.55.3–4)

Oswald is burned on a pyre and receives rites befitting a classical hero rather than a Christian one. When Davenant refers to the "World's last law," he is likely referring to a decree of Charlemagne that made cremation punishable by death in the year 789; this would be a few decades after the action of *Gondibert* ostensibly takes place. Oswald can be reintegrated after death as a hero rather than as a pariah, but only in a conspicuously pagan form that a Christian ruler would soon outlaw.

In contrast to the suspended fate of Gondibert's slain followers, Oswald's funeral makes narrative sense for two reasons. The first is that Gartha has arrived as a spokesperson for her brother, demanding both a proper burial and retribution. She insists that her brother is not someone who should have been killed with impunity. The second reason lies in Gondibert's subsequent change of heart. When Aribert deems Oswald's killer, Gondibert, worthy of marrying his daughter, he tacitly acknowledges that Oswald's death is acceptable for the sake of securing a heroic marriage. If *Gondibert* were to celebrate the union of the titular hero and Rhodalind, it would have to deem not only Oswald's death but also the death of Gondibert's followers acceptable for the union of personal love and dynastic continuity. In the absence of narrative closure, however, these problems have no available solution except through a nostalgic recourse to a classical, Roman past that is now deemed unacceptable. As Aribert's own priests teach, the king should seek to be a Lord of peace who teaches the world the rules of love.

These concerns about the acceptability of violence in the pursuit of love are not addressed in a straightforwardly political meditation but instead through a literary vocabulary of marriage, one that crisscrosses between classical and Christian registers. Gartha's role in demanding burial for her slain brother makes her partially resemble Antigone. Yet in contrast to Antigone, who sacrifices not only her life but also her conjugal destiny to her dedication to her brothers, Gartha has a desire for vengeance that forms the basis of her entry into marriage. Her presence in this poem unsettles any sense of whose deaths should be felt as acceptable sacrifices in the name of achieving a desired conjugal union—the union between the two subjects we as readers are initially trained to affirm. A straightforward affirmation of Pauline marriage might have confirmed that the highest form of sacrifice has already established the mysterious dynamism between personal love and corporate truth; no additional bloodshed should be required. Yet in *Gondibert*, this question of acceptable or unacceptable death comes to be located within the form of a conjugal narrative because Pauline marriage has proven untenable—first because the hero could not negotiate a viable form of sacrifice and peace in the name of love, and then because he learns that Christian belief may have less of a claim on his personal love than the practical forms of knowledge that preserve his natural life.

Especially around Gartha, questions about sacrifice and unsanctioned (or even seemingly pointless) violence suggest that conjugal narratives become a site of biopolitical negotiations within the transition from a Christian to a less straightforwardly religious outlook. If we treat *Gondibert* as something more than a curiosity or an artistic failure, it can serve to remind us that we should consider marriage more methodically within our genealogical accounts of biopower and biopolitics. I have in mind Agamben's influential discussion of the *homo sacer*, a figure in ancient Roman law who *"may be killed"* with impunity *"and yet not sacrificed."*[35] This figure plays a central role in Agamben's attempt to revise Foucault's unfinished account of biopower. As an alternative to Foucault's bifurcation between premodern and modern forms of sovereignty, Agamben suggests that the convergence between techniques of power and technologies of the self has always been an aim of sovereignty. He hypothesizes *"that the production of a biopolitical body is the original activity of sovereign power."*[36] The *homo sacer* might be dimly recognizable even in modernity insofar as he or it "preserves the memory of the originary exclusion through which the political dimension was first constituted. The political sphere of sovereignty was thus constituted through a double exclusion, as an excrescence of the profane in the religious and of the religious in the profane, which takes the form of a zone of indistinction between sacrifice and homicide."[37] For Agamben, the modern manifestation of this zone of indistinction is the concentration camp. The camp is not an aberration but rather a necessary exception to modern sovereignty as it continues the work of producing a biopolitical body.

I do not claim that *Gondibert* alludes in any way to the Roman concept of the *homo sacer*. Instead, I argue that Davenant's poem can lead us to consider early modern marriage as a site where questions of sacrifice, personal feeling, and civic belonging are turning biopolitical—as the normative force of Pauline marriage is being questioned. By attending to marriage as a form in which a theological structure gives rise to various biopolitical negotiations, we can address one basic matter that Agamben's turn to the *homo sacer* leaves unresolved: the question of relevance. Agamben admits that the *homo sacer* is an "obscure figure of archaic Roman law," and it remains unclear how this ancient concept should have remained relevant for a modern expression of power that is exemplified in the concentration camp.[38] Attention to marriage can also refine our understanding of how personal feelings operate in tandem with techniques of state power. As Agamben observes, Foucault's unfinished theory does not fully address how state power works in concert with "*technologies of the self* by which processes of subjectivization bring the individual to bind himself to his own identity and consciousness and, at the same time, to an external power."[39] Norms concerning marriage have long been sites in which certain configurations of the personal and the corporate are sanctioned, under the force not only of external discipline but also of intimate feelings that promise to define and redefine subjects.

Attention to marriage can help to account for another deficiency in Agamben's elaboration of biopolitics. As Heather Latimer argues, "the reproductive body is a blank spot in Agamben's definition of bare life."[40] Karen Weingarten elaborates on this claim in a study of abortion in the United States. Focusing on the mandate to maintain a majority White nation, she describes how American women were viewed as "national vessels of reproduction"—with the result that women who threatened the future of White fetuses were deemed guilty of a "crime against their own bodies" and "risked being designated bare life."[41] Agamben's attenuated attention to reproduction is a structural feature of the way he theorizes the relationship between sovereignty and life. His twinned focus on the ancient figure of the *homo sacer* and on the modern concentration camp often allows him to treat human lives as if they arrive ready-made, available for the work of biopolitics.[42] When, for example, Agamben revisits Foucault's description of premodern sovereignty being defined by the right to decide life and death, he reminds us that the Roman *vitae necisque potestas* described the unconditional authority of the father over his son. Agamben is not invested in describing how paternity exists in a state of asymmetrical competition with maternity; this is the case even though the Roman concept of *vita*, in contrast with an Athenian understanding, "brings together the meaning of both *zoë* and *bios*."[43] Instead, he describes how the Roman precedent of patriarchal prerogative reveals something crucially important about the nature of sovereignty.

When he turns to the theory of the king's two bodies, he argues that Kantorowicz deliberately ignores the Roman precedent of imperial consecration and apotheosis. In my introductory chapter, I described to what end Kantorowicz neglects the role of women, marriage, and motherhood in *Richard II* as he reads the play as the tragedy of the king's two bodies. I argued that he avoids recognizing how, around the question of marriage and reproduction, the tragedy of the king's two bodies coexists with a tragicomedy that reveals how notions of godlike kingship can persist even within comical or even farcical forms of veneration. For Agamben, by contrast, what Kantorowicz deliberately avoids is an understanding of "the political body . . . as the cipher of the absolute and inhuman character of sovereignty."[44] In Agamben's theory, sovereignty tends to be a paradoxical formation with a hidden force of nearly transhistorical causation, with the result that even a genealogy of biopolitics can remain largely abstracted from questions about reproduction and gender.[45]

It is true that Agamben discusses Nazi eugenics, remarking that the project to control heredity in the name of national health reveals how biopolitics operate not just in the concentration camp but also within the citizenry. He quotes a portion of the October 1933 legislation (which was passed as an extension of the earlier July 1933 Gesetz zur Verhütung erbkranken Nachwuchses, or Sterilization Law) that bans marriage to anyone identified as contagious and unsound. He remarks on the "immediately political character" of such legislation and proposes that the seeming enigma of Nazism can be explained only if we understand the full scope of its "biopolitical praxis."[46] Yet in this brief account, he overlooks how the impulse to control reproduction needs to speak (in this case, to clarify and speak again) in the name of marriage. As a result, his emphasis on the politicization of life neglects another, related enigma: how a cultural form like marriage can link intimate affects including familial love or even a sense of a desired comic conclusion to thanatopolitics at the national level. Marriage is not only a readily available vehicle for regulating reproduction but also a form that directs personal feelings of love and belonging toward upholding the distinction between legitimate and illegitimate lives.

The extant narrative of *Gondibert* does not explore in great detail the link between marriage and scientific understandings of reproduction. Yet marriage is the form that is supposed to mediate between personal feeling and political stability through legitimized reproduction. For Gondibert, however, marriage becomes the node around which scientific knowledge is overshadowing a theological worldview while, at the same time, aligning with intimate affect in a way that thwarts the will of the king. The king's inability to control marriage signals the limitations of his power as it concerns the ability to make or even to regulate natural life. I have argued that *Gondibert* promotes knowledge of the natural world not simply to undercut the sway of Christian belief but to expose the fictive claims of sovereignty. Even if poetic mythmaking can shore up Gondibert's fictive superiority, that same combination of affect and mythmaking provides him with a rhetorical mode that ironizes the prerogative of his king. Within a broader genealogy of biopolitics, the fictive dimensions of sovereignty's claim over natural lives and over affect help to remind us why the project to regulate life can become so tenaciously obsessive. The core of untruth regarding control over life itself keeps the goal of biopolitics ever elusive. At the same time, the reminder that scientific knowledge can coexist (however uncomfortably) with religious myths in a way that resists the sovereign will shows how, under particular circumstances, biopower itself can become partially unmoored from state power. This reminder is useful insofar as it complicates any fatalism about how modern power entails inevitable encroachments on life—as if the form of power represented by the concentration camp is necessarily or equally ever present in all modern states. Yet the lessons that I draw from *Gondibert* are not straightforwardly optimistic ones—that science and personal mythmaking might lead to liberating impulses. Instead, Davenant's poem suggests that as Christian marriage gives way to a less overtly theological configuration of personal experience and corporate realities, that configuration can foster a connection between personal feeling and what has been labeled necropolitics. As Achille Mbembé has argued, biopower is insufficient to account for the project of modern sovereignty. Whereas Agamben identifies concentration camps as exemplifying the internal state of exception, Mbembe points to the constitutive exercises of power outside the boundaries of the state, in colonies and other contested zones. Outside its proper borders, sovereignty defines itself through necropower, the manifestation of the power over death, which was never truly left behind in the transition from premodern sovereignty to modern biopolitics.[47]

Davenant describes how marriage—and in particular, a largely disenchanted view of Christian marriage—can channel contradictory inclinations toward inclusion and exclusion into a personal register of love. When Gondibert defies the wishes of his king to pursue the new object of his desire, he does not establish a clear bifurcation between the personal and the political. Gondibert's insistence on love is energized paradoxically by a frustrated desire for global empire. When Astragon asks Gondibert why he would forsake Rhodalind to pursue marriage with Birtha, Gondibert explains the source of his disillusionment with the crown. His own father "ment to chastise Kings, and States" and

> [t]o overcome the world, till but one Crown
> And universal Neighbourhood he saw;
> Till all were rich by that alliance grown;
> And want no more should be the cause of Law. (2.8.35.4–36)

His father apparently longed to conquer the entire world with the aim of rendering not just all law but also all human difference obsolete. A truly universal empire would have eliminated any divisions among natural reproduction, family, and sovereignty by restoring humanity to an Edenic state: "One Family the world was first design'd" (2.8.37.1). The shattered fantasy of universal unity through dominion has led Gondibert to prefer a personal expression of conjugal love—one that defies the wishes of the king. When Gondibert insists on pursuing love, he is not simply forsaking a communal sphere of political obligations. He is pursuing in an alternative form a frustrated desire for imperial mastery.

In the preface, Davenant expands on this aspect of Gondibert's story to announce aspects of his own moral and political theory. He hails "that Element of greatness and honor, *Empire*" as the proper outlet for the ambitious "Mindes of Men," which "are more monstrous, and require more space for agitation and the hunting of others, then the Bodies of Whales."[48] When he points to America as an outlet for these energies that can lead to turmoil at home, he is not at all making a theoretical point. In early 1650, he prepared to set forth on a journey to serve as colonial governor of Maryland. He had received a commission, signed by the exiled Charles on February 16, to replace the insufficiently loyal Lord Baltimore. Several months earlier, Davenant had been appointed to serve as the treasurer of Virginia. He would be apprehended by English parliamentary forces in his subsequent attempt to sail to America; he continued to work on the third book of *Gondibert* while imprisoned.[49] When he was composing his preface before all these events unfolded, the New World remained a viable outlet for imperial ambitions. Yet his preface does not elaborate on the point about ambition by discussing the New World at length.

He reverts instead to a typological structure, in which the Christian affirmation of the universal prevails over a supposedly outdated Hebraic past. Even though imperial ambition can motivate a beastly, monstrous form of destructiveness, he declares that "narrow Dominion breeds evil, peevish, and vexatious minds, and a nationall self-opinion, like simple Jewish arrogance; and the *Jewes* were extraordinary proud in a very little Countrey."[50] There are no Jews in *Gondibert*. This commentary makes sense only insofar as it refers to the typological structure that still matters for Davenant's conjugal narrative. If Gondibert's love for Birtha expresses a viable form of heroism, then that love should contain within it a noble desire for conquest—one that distinguishes his heroism from the narrowness of Jews, who are relegated to obsolescence. If marriage offers a way for individual spouses to affirm each other as unique even within a corporate form of belonging, the exclusive nature of that corporate identity still functions to demarcate outsiders. Within this context, Davenant's remark about "the narrow Dominion" of the Jews is not a non sequitur. Even as a by-product of Christian typology, his remarks reveals how an idea of Jewish difference can be embedded in the relationship between personal love and political ambitions. His poetic treatment of heroic love links the patterns of Christian typology with a longing for conquest in the name of overcoming all law.

Davenant certainly had little stake in offering a critique of how, within the structure of Christian typology, positive affects such as love and peace can continue to harbor an impulse toward expansionist aggression. Yet his cynicism motivates him to be candid about how poetry is required to attempt these affective mediations. In his later writings, he would find other, more concrete occasions to celebrate expansionism abroad as the vehicle for English growth and stability. He was aware that expansionism involved destructive forms of brutality and enslavement. Yet in dramatic entertainments such as *The Cruelty of the Spaniards in Peru* (1658) and *The History of Sir Francis Drake* (1659), he took part in the familiar strategy to celebrate English expansionism (including Oliver Cromwell's Western Design), as a more benevolent alternative to Spanish conquest.[51] By writing such plays, the royalist Davenant managed to find a degree of approval from the Interregnum government.

Love or Trade

In closing this chapter, I do not turn to Davenant's dramas of anti-Spanish and pro-English feeling but instead to his poetry after the Restoration. Davenant takes part in the Restoration project of making overseas trade the basis of a renewed myth of royal splendor. In *Astraea Redux* (1660), John Dryden couples a celebration of the monarchy with the promotion of energized maritime expansionism. Davenant's own contributions to this political mythology reveal the extent to which the affective claims previously associated with Christian marriage can (and cannot) be shuttled into an economic register.[52] Davenant renegotiates questions about personal uniqueness and replaceability by promoting Charles II's singular capacity as king to regulate the trade of fungible goods. Davenant managed to get his own "Poem upon His Sacred Majestie's Most Happy Return to His Dominions" into print only days after *Astraea Redux* in June 1660. His poem, like Dryden's, turns to myth and history to affirm Charles II's return to the throne. Charles I had been a "*perfect Father*" and exhibited "God-like pitty, near his *Martyrdom*," and now Charles II has emerged as a kind of resurrected heir (lines 11–12). Insofar as Charles II has "out-done" the art of "Great *Julius* in disguise," he has proven himself not just a truer version of Julius Caesar but rather a new Augustus (9–10). Davenant goes on to enumerate the many benefits promised by Charles II's official program of reconciliation.

Only after this calibration of the mythic and the practical does the poem belatedly acknowledge the presence of Henrietta Maria, both as the mother of the new king and as a living repository of Charles I's memory. When Davenant describes the queen in "*Mourning Widowhood*" as exhibiting "[h]er care o're all the *Pledges* of *their* love," he seems to return to some of the central concerns—the utility of royal marriage, and the person of the queen—of his writings from the 1630s (254–56). Yet Davenant immediately aligns Charles II more narrowly with his father once again:

You, in your Manhoods bloom, exprest an aw,
Not of his *Regal* but of *Natures* Law (257–58)

The appeal to the natural bond of patriarchal descent is meant to attenuate the maternal presence of Henrietta Maria and the memory of her controversial marriage with Charles I. In the remainder of this poem, the appeal to patriarchal piety as a natural phenomenon underwrites a new configuration of love, family, and kingly authority—one that does not rely on Christian marriage. This avoidance becomes conspicuous when Davenant relegates the women of the royal family to a gender-specific form of praise that puts them at a remove from hereditary succession. He invokes "[t]wo, of the gentler *Sex*," who

> remain to grace
> The matchless number of his *Royal Race*. (285–86)

The first, unnamed woman is identified as Henrietta Maria only when Davenant describes her as having exemplified "*prudent* Widow-hood" (290). The second woman

> has fit vertue to dispence,
> Even to a Cloyster'd Virgin, *innocence*;

this refers to Charles II's sister Henrietta Anne, not yet married to Philippe, Duke of Orleans (291–92). Davenant, who had previously been known as her majesty's servant, now affirms Charles II as a successor to his martyred father while casting the women of the royal family primarily as widows and virgins rather than as wives and mothers.

In "Poem to the Kings Most Sacred Majesty" (1663), Davenant elaborates on how the affective work that Christian marriage had failed to perform for the sake of political stability might be achieved by a myth of benevolent commerce. This poem does dutifully rehearse the motif of Charles II as the resurrected son:

> The truth of Resurrection is by *You*
> Confirm'd to all, and made apparent too. (lines 171–72)

Whereas *Gondibert* had subordinated belief in the resurrection to the life-saving work of medicine, Davenant is willing to reengage with a political mythology of the resurrected king. This makes Charles II the Christlike head of a corporate body:

> The Church *You* have reviv'd: for well we may
> Confess it more than rescu'd from decay,
> Since having lost, by Martyrdom, the *Head*,
> The *Limbs* had all the signs of being dead. (174–77)

Yet Davenant does not make any connections between the Christlike status as the head of an ecclesiastical body and the Christlike status of a loving husband. This avoidance is conspicuous insofar as this poem was published in the year following Charles II's marriage to Catherine of Braganza. Charles had followed his father in marrying a foreign, Roman Catholic princess, but it was still too early to know that this royal marriage would produce no heirs. It was certainly known, however, that Charles entered into this marriage as the father of numerous illegitimate children. Elevating the king as a Christlike husband is not viable, and Davenant pursues other, practical ways to harmonize individual experience and collective belonging under the restored monarchy. He describes the king as instilling a sense of individual importance even among lowly subjects. Charles is described as listening to subjects who come to him pleading with "a tedious narrative" (241); the king leads this kind of suitor

>   to believe
> His Case is not as others cases are,
> But intricate, and very singular. (242–44)

Even if these lines sound cynical, they express the need for an enabling fiction of singularity among all subjects. The locus of this enabling fiction has shifted from conjugal love to displays of political favor.

"Poem to the Kings Most Sacred Majesty" goes on to describe naval power and maritime commerce as more compelling ways not only to expand Charles II's power but also to strengthen the affective claims of the monarchy.

> All that by Naval Art men strive to learn,
> *You* with peculiar Glory, will obtain,

Davenant advises (274–75). His 1640–41 poem "To the Queen" had described Charles I as "peculiar and alone" and thus prone to obdurateness;

this is a condition that Davenant had hoped marriage could moderate. In the opening book of *Gondibert*, the reader had learned that the titular hero's love is not "peculiar." Peculiarity, in other words, serves to indicate both the problems of kingly authority and the appeal of singularity in love. In 1663 Davenant seeks to advise the king about a practical way to secure his royal singularity against the practical realities of substitution and fungibility. Trade is promoted as an alternative to the economy of eros and regulated reproduction. Under Charles's control, ships build networks of trade "[m]ore fruitfully than Sexes do by love" (302). The king remains uniquely fixed in his seat of naval power, which he exercises to impose order on the trade of fungible goods. Davenant is eager to take on a kind of advisory role. He seeks to clarify the political and affective gains achieved by a supposedly harmonious form of trade. After announcing trade as more beneficial than natural reproduction, he offers the prospect of a worldwide network of mercantile productivity:

> Ships, which to farthest distances are sent,
> Are so concern'd with their number to augment,
> That they by nought but Number can dispence
> The vital heat of Trade, Intelligence.
> By pow'r of Number they themselves disperse
> For a Collection, through the Universe,
> Of all the *Freights* which ev'ry Country yeilds. (303–9)

The phrase "vital heat" had, early in *Gondibert*, described the protagonist's desire—which was not merely hidden or private but never "peculiar" to Rhodalind. After the Restoration, Davenant shifts the locus of questions concerning uniqueness or replaceability to a commercial register so that the king's affective sway over his subjects might be newly enhanced. By presiding over a commercial network, Charles II might maintain his singular glory over the "pow'r of Number."

Imposing control over the seas requires not just benevolence inspiring love but also sovereign awe. Within the English navy, Davenant explains that

> *Sea-men*, in loudest Storms, are not dismay'd
> When they are even *oblig'd* to be *afraid*. (317–18)

Dutiful allegiance overpowers even the natural instinct of self-preservation. As a result, these English seamen can confront pirates who,

> with a Frantick courage, dare
> Maintain against the World continual War. (323–24)

A naval force that subordinates natural self-concern to political reverence strikes fear among these pirates, who are otherwise lawless:

> But though they dare all other Tempests meet,
> Yet still they fear the Thunder of your Fleet. (327–28)[53]

Davenant, who had downplayed England's participation in colonial violence while celebrating the heroic energy of expansionism, now praises a benevolent form of trade that reserves the resources of fear, awe, and force, to be deployed against the unruly agents of chaos.

Yet the final rhetorical act of "Poem to the Kings Most Sacred Majesty" is to undercut itself—not by admitting the messy violence involved in expansionism and mercantilism, but by describing how poetic praise of Charles II might prove inferior in quality when it focuses on trade. Davenant initially makes this suggestion by reverting to language proper to love: he declares that because many poets strive to immortalize Charles II, they will invariably be jealous of each other. Davenant then satirizes what it would be like if an assembly of poets had to elect a single ambassador of fame for the king:

> Th'Election likely is to end in vain;
> All loosing that which each presum'd to gain. (451–52)

Davenant reshapes jealousy into financial greed to describe why he produces inferior poetry within this Restoration context. He likens himself to a generic man who,

> o're-joy'd at sodain sight
> Of Treasure found, grows jealous, and through care
> Lest others in his Prize should claim a share,
> Bears hastily from that which he did find
> Much less away than what he leaves behind. (464–68)

Davenant may be echoing the Parable of the Hidden Treasure. Yet in the parable, the man who rejoices in discovering the treasure of the kingdom of heaven can sell all that he has to purchase the field in which it lies. The prize of Restoration poetry, by contrast, is something that Davenant cannot purchase for himself. Out of his jealous suspicion of other poets, Davenant publicly proclaims only a few of Charles II's virtues, while "many more are left behind unprais'd" (471). Davenant is, of course, being coy about poetry written to the tune of commerce. He is suggesting that if he were to be celebrated as a singularly favored (and well-paid) poet, he would reveal the full extent of his praise. Yet the self-effacing gestures go beyond modesty and come close to self-sabotage. Rather than serving as an effective solicitation to an exclusive poetic relationship with Charles II, the turn to a desire for self-aggrandizement suggests that poetry mythologizing the king's singularity might never achieve the same appeal as a poetry that affirms love. An alignment of a king's prestige with Christlike love is a fiction susceptible to debunking, yet Davenant hints that a royal myth based on commerce will lack even more affective intensity. Davenant, previously the faithful servant of the queen, might now be sanctioned to think of himself openly as a self-serving agent and his poetry as an instrument for his own ends.

4

Love against Succession in *Paradise Lost*

John Milton almost never writes of Christ as the exemplary husband.¹ His 1645 divorce tract *Colasterion* contains an exception that proves the general rule. He does cite the Pauline definition of marriage, but only in the course of summarizing a counterargument to his own case for divorce: "*If the husband ought to love his Wife, as Christ his Church, then ought shee not to bee put away for contrariety of minde.*"² In response, Milton declares that the Pauline "similitude" undercuts the argument because "if the husband bee as Christ to the Wife, then must the wife bee as the Church to her husband." When the wife does not live up to this calling, "Christ himself threat'ns to divorce such a Spouse, and hath often done it" (*CPW* 2:732). By implying that Christ divorced the Roman Catholic Church, Milton tries to strengthen his Protestant argument for divorce and remarriage in cases of spiritually incompatibility. In his own life, he would eventually remarry twice—not after divorce, which remained inaccessible, but after the deaths of his first two wives.³ Whereas Milton's earlier tracts argue for the benefits of divorce and remarriage, his later poetry communicates more ambivalence about replacing a spouse. As I go on to discuss in his chapter, Milton's sonnet "Methought I saw my late espoused saint" expresses a diffuse sense of guilt that is associated with remarrying after the death of a wife. This guilt persists even though both Christian teaching and English norms sanction this form of remarriage.

This chapter focuses primarily on *Paradise Lost*, which places an impassioned rejection of replacement at the center of Edenic marriage. This feeling of love helps Milton to explain the Fall. After eating the forbidden fruit, Eve decides to share it with Adam out of her jealous fear that she might die alone and be replaced by a new wife. Adam, in turn, declares that he cannot tolerate losing Eve even though he expects that God would create a second wife for him. Adam's decision is condemned, but *Paradise Lost* finds ways to elevate his sinful choice as heroic. In the final books, an explicit appeal to the *felix culpa* serves to affirm God's goodness, but it also fosters the impression that Adam's loyalty to his first wife may have led to a happier outcome. The poem achieves closure by elevating reconciliation within the original marriage as a key feature of God's redemptive plan. This presentation of conjugal love bears on matters of salvation, despite the fact that Milton continues to avoid aligning Christ and husband. The prophecy of a Son who must be born underwrites the reconciliation of Adam and Eve's marriage.

When Pauline teaching announces the higher truth of Christ's love, conjugal love is tied to questions about the nature of redemptive sacrifice—in what way Christ gave himself to purify his metaphorical wife. Milton had long grappled with the irrational account of an innocent victim taking on punishment owed to the guilty, and divine justice being satisfied with that displacement. He had shared his ambivalences by publishing his early poem *The Passion* in unfinished form. In *Paradise Lost*, however, Milton has God articulate a demand for "rigid satisfaction, death for death" in the name of justice.[4] Here, Milton seems to affirm the doctrine of substitutionary atonement, whereby Christ suffers capital punishment on behalf of guilty humanity. When Milton elevates conjugal love as a rejection of substitution, however, he drives a wedge between the satisfaction of divine justice—which can fully admit of replacements—and a human love defined by affective fixity. He works around but also puts pressure on the Pauline definition of marriage by questioning how compatible Christ's sacrifice can be with the original form of human love.

This affective problem energizes Milton's critique of hereditary succession. "Out of a great early modern period of confessional and political strife," Sharon Achinstein observes, "the couple in marriage becomes for Milton a site of wholly human concern."[5] This chapter considers how and to what end Milton's poem alienates human love from a divine outlook. Milton's God is overwhelmingly concerned with the promotion of his Son as his rightful heir. God's mysterious insistence on succession becomes enmeshed with other forms of substitution and affective displacement, all of which conflict with what Adam and Eve feel to be most urgent in their experience. My reading touches on familiar interpretive questions surrounding *Paradise Lost*—the problem of Milton's aloof God as well as the question of how we are to understand Milton's presentation of divine monarchy. When it comes to the political meanings of *Paradise Lost*, it has been possible to discern Milton's disillusionment with radical politics and a turn toward proto-bourgeois individualism or even quietism after the Restoration.[6] Yet readers have also felt that Milton's republican values remain intact, with divine kingship being a singular case that disproves the legitimacy of human monarchy, and with Satan expressing a fraudulent commitment to republican values.[7]

By focusing on the antagonism between conjugal love and the logics of substitution in *Paradise Lost*, I seek to weave among these interpretive possibilities in a specific way. My reading discerns a coherent antimonarchical critique within the affective challenge that Milton presents to the reader. Yet it also locates an incoherence in Milton's presentation of Christian marriage. Whereas Pauline teaching explicitly makes soteriology the basis of Christian marriage, Milton seeks an alternative way to link the salvation achieved by the Son to a tenable form of human love. Toward the end of this chapter, I argue that Milton finally relies on a temporal inversion—or even an affective sleight of hand—to achieve this. Adam and Eve reconcile so that the Son can be born in the future, but Milton also aims to disentangle conjugal love from the utility of regulating reproduction. The ending of *Paradise Lost* tries to overshadow the fact that Adam and Eve eventually reproduced by generating a vivid impression that their marriage was a site of personal love outside Eden. Even as Milton conveys this feeling, he cannot offer any proof of their mutual love in a fallen world. The poem's ending invites the belief or fantasy that all our existences ultimately derive from redemptive love rather than from physical reproduction alone. After describing this crossover, I turn briefly to *Paradise Regained*, in which the Son of God seeks to reveal himself as the true heir to God's throne. In his attempt to prove that merit and birthright are entirely compatible, love hardly registers as a motivation. Instead of perfecting the meaning of marriage, Milton's second epic confirms the pattern established by his first: human love flourishes at a remove from hereditary succession.

I close this chapter with a suggestion that the relationship between Milton's two epics can speak to our present-day concerns about love and the politics of reproduction. More specifically, I pair *Paradise Regained* with Lee Edelman's reading of *Hamlet*, which describes the protagonist as the tragic child of reproductive futurity. I propose that Milton's Son occupies this status even more paradigmatically than does Hamlet. In Milton's outlook, the impulse of reproductive futurity could have been rendered obsolete after the birth, death, and resurrection of the promised Son. Yet Milton does not fully sunder conjugal love from the forward-looking demands of reproduction. Instead, he inverts the chronology of Christian typology to embed the demands of a future-oriented reproduction within his elevation of married love. He stops short of appealing to the fait accompli of the Son's mission by leading the Christian reader to feel (if not strictly to believe) that marriage and reproduction are necessary for the future. Calling attention to this slippage in Milton's promotion of heterosexual union should play a part in historicizing how the logic (or illogic) of reproductive futurity has been communicated to us.

Reconsidering Remarriage

After Charles I was executed in January 1649, basic questions became newly urgent: How should rulers be replaced? Can sovereignty remain continuous without relying on heirs? The Interregnum government ultimately proved unable to secure a viable alternative to hereditary succession. Nearing death, Oliver Cromwell seems to have named his son Richard to succeed him as Lord Protector.[8] Although Cromwell had previously refused the crown, his Protectorship became a hereditary title nonetheless. Long before these developments played out, Charles I's fate immediately unleashed a reconsideration of the nature and utility of Christian marriage. Abiezer Coppe, for example, began prophesying in London in 1649 not just against disparities in wealth and power but also against monogamy. In *Some Sweet Sips, of Spirituall Wine* (1649), Coppe prays to God to "give a bill of divorce to all carnall, fleshly fellowships. . . . Divorce them from Type, marry them to *Truth* [O the truth, as it is in *Jesus!*]."[9] Coppe relies on typological thinking to argue that the truth of Christ as a corporate bridegroom should nullify any earthly marriages. In *A Fiery Flying Roll* (also 1649), Coppe teaches that partaking in extramarital affairs is a sign of Christian freedom. "But thou Precisian . . . do but blow a kisse to thy neighbours wife . . . if thou dar'st," Coppe taunts.[10] Such attacks on monogamy led to the so-called Ranters being condemned and reviled.

By contrast, by the time the Diggers William Everard and Gerrard Winstanley led the communal occupation and cultivation of St. George's Hill in Surrey in April 1649, their published writings had already explained why monogamous marriage is an exception to their rejection of all things proprietary. In *The New Law of Righteousness* (published in January of that year), Winstanley anticipates the fear that abolishing property would lead to the erosion of monogamy: "If it be thus, then saith the scoffer, mens wives shall be common too? or a man may have as many wives as he please?"[11] The notion expressed by this hypothetical scoffer is widespread; earlier in the century, Shakespeare's *The Tempest* has the scoffers Sebastian and Antonio draw the same conclusion when presented with an utopian fantasy of a realm without laws or property.[12] To argue that monogamy is divinely ordained and also reasonable, Winstanley cites the definition of marriage found in Genesis. (From Coppe's point of view, this would amount to a regression from Christian liberty to the Old Testament.) In February 1649, Winstanley would publish a separate short treatise devoted exclusively to differentiating the Diggers from the Ranters. *A Vindication* appeals to religious ideologies of what counts as natural behavior but also to very practical concerns. After decrying sexual license as hindering "the pure and naturall Generation of man," Winstanley argues that "the mother and child begotten in this manner, is like to have the worst of it, for the man will be gone and leave them."[13] Coppe, by contrast, is largely indifferent to the burdens of reproduction and child-rearing. In a letter to his disciple Mrs. T. P., published in *Some Sweet Sips*, he celebrates a spiritual form of conception that both men and women can experience: "When the *Man-Child Jesus* is brought forth *In Us*."[14] Although he preaches egalitarianism when it comes to wealth and power, his appeal to spiritual truth overshadowing physical reality allows him to ignore the asymmetries of reproduction.

Milton's earlier divorce tracts had gained him a reputation for immorality, but he had certainly never advanced the kind of attack on monogamy that Coppe preaches. In 1649 Milton was not at work clarifying his positions regarding the purpose and practice of Christian marriage. He was busy justifying the execution of Charles I. Milton's polemics do attack Charles's marriage, criticizing the king as having been swayed by his

French, Roman Catholic wife. In *Eikonoklastes*, Milton recalls the publication of Charles's seized correspondence in the 1645 publication *The King's Cabinet Opened*. Charles's letters reveal how "*constancy to his Wife is set in place before Laws and Religion*" (*CPW* 3:541). In *The Doctrine and Discipline of Divorce*, Milton deems the suggestion that divorce in the Mosaic law was granted only for the sake of relieving wives "[p]alpably uxorious"—because, he argues, God designs marriage to meet the spiritual needs of men, starting with Adam, rather than of women (*CPW* 2:324). In 1649 uxoriousness proves to be a political failing and not just a basis of misunderstanding marriage as God instituted it. By the time Milton was composing *Paradise Lost* in the late 1650s and 1660s, however, it would have been entirely clear that attacks on Charles I as an uxorious king had not swayed the English people. Milton's epic needs to go further by undercutting the mythic appeal of kingship. *Paradise Lost* attempts this by exerting affective pressure on the notion of substitution; substitution is a logic that, in varied forms, underlies both sacrificial atonement and hereditary succession. If the Pauline definition of marriage does not explain fully how the truth of Christ's self-sacrificing love should coexist with the call for intergenerational replacement found in Genesis, marriage is still called upon to make this coexistence tenable. Milton's narrative, by contrast, shows how personal love must exist at a remove from a concern for succession—even in the highest case of divine kingship.

In book 4 of *Paradise Lost*, Milton does celebrate "wedded love" as the

> mysterious law, true source
> Of human offspring, sole propriety,
> In Paradise of all things common else. (4.750–52)

This particular definition of marriage conforms to the one that Winstanley had promoted. Marriage is, for the sake of regulating reproduction, a unique exception to the goodness of prelapsarian communalism.[15] Yet Milton's appeal to marriage as the true source of offspring is slightly incongruous in the context of describing Adam and Eve's marriage; no possibility of illegitimate offspring exists in Eden. More to the point, these lines tend to clash with Milton's broader tendency to subordinate reproduction as a rationale for marriage.[16] In *The Doctrine and Discipline of Divorce*, Milton scoffs at the notion that God provided Adam with a wife in order "to joyn him with an accidentall companion of propagation, which his sudden word had already made for every beast" (*CPW* 2:309). In sharp contrast to the view Winstanley expresses, Milton ridicules the notion that a key distinction between humans and animals lies in the regulation of reproduction; spiritual and intellectual companionship should be the definitively human trait. In *Paradise Lost*, these earlier ideas are put to the test. In book 8, Adam recalls how, when he asked for a companion, God tested him by inviting him to enjoy companionship with the animals that "reason not contemptibly" (8.374). In response, Adam observes that some animals are paired off ("lion with lioness") in a way that might be replicated by humans. Although *Paradise Lost* does celebrate marriage as a source of true offspring, Adam passes God's test by sidestepping the conclusion that he needs a human reproductive partner. God praises as uniquely human Adam's recognition that what he needs is a form of intellectual "fellowship" (8.442).

In *Paradise Lost*, the claim that Edenic marriage is anomalously proprietary does not open on to an extended case for marriage's necessity in legitimizing reproduction. Instead, that anomalous propriety is shuttled into the affective register of love fixed between husband and wife. Milton heightens the possessiveness of conjugal love at the climactic moment of the Fall. After Eve eats from the tree of knowledge, she speculates about the consequences of her transgressive act. The threatened punishment of death remains mysterious to her. By contrast, the possibility of being replaced by "another Eve" registers sharply; it is for Eve a "death to think" (9.828–30). Eve's newly sinful nature manifests itself as jealousy, and her fear of being replaced eclipses a fear of dying. When Eve approaches Adam, she fails to deceive him with her claims about the fruit. Milton adapts the biblical lesson, "And Adam was not deceived, but the woman being deceived was in the transgression" (1 Tim. 2:14). Milton's Adam fully recognizes that eating the forbidden fruit will result in death. Yet he still chooses to fall because he cannot tolerate the prospect of replacing Eve:

> Should God create another Eve, and I
> Another rib afford, yet loss of thee
> Would never from my heart. (9.911–13)

Adam concludes that it is better (or more necessary) to disobey God than to lose his first wife. Milton presents the reader with a case in which proper reasoning conflicts with impassioned feeling. Part of Adam's reasoning must be correct: he should separate himself from his fallen wife and trust in God to provide him with another. Yet Milton makes the correct option unappealing, and he does so in such a way that blurs the crucial distinction between remarriage after divorce and remarriage after death. In Adam's singular case, remarriage after separation and remarriage after the death of a spouse are all but identical. No wider incompatibility could exist than the one between unfallen, immortal Adam and fallen, newly mortal Eve. Yet Adam ponders remarriage as the right option only to decry it as intolerable. Around the feeling that love rejects substitution, Eve's jealousy finds common ground with Adam's undeluded reasoning.

When the Son of God descends to issue judgment after the Fall, he condemns Adam for his choice. "Was she thy God, that her thou didst obey," the Son asks rhetorically (10.145), adding,

> that to her
> Thou didst resign they manhood? (10.147–48)

If Milton's imagination remains consistent from 1649 to the 1660s, there may be a connection (however indirect) between Adam's uxoriousness and Charles I's. The mythic Fall should serve as an explanation for the later failing. When Adam insists that nature prevents him from separating from his wife, he may be appealing to necessity in a way that the poem explicitly associates with the lies that tyrants tell. In book 4, Satan asserts that he must, for the public good of all the fallen angels, pervert Adam and Eve even though he personally sympathizes with them. Milton clarifies that this a spurious appeal to

> necessity,
> The tyrant's plea. (4.393–94)

Yet Adam's claim that nature compels him to join his wife does not serve as the grounds of a straightforward critique of his uxoriousness. When Adam chooses Eve over God, he is presented as sympathetic, even heroic. David Quint stakes an intricately detailed reading of *Paradise Lost* on the opening premise that Adam's transgressive choice is the "central human heroic act" of the poem—one that allows Milton to redefine epic around love.[17]

Although Adam is criticized for being unduly swayed by his wife in book 10 of *Paradise Lost*, the same book goes on to present his misogyny—not his excessive love—as the problem that needs to be corrected.

The conclusion of *Paradise Lost* does not reinforce the lesson that Adam needs to love Eve less intensely. Instead, it elevates reconciliation within marriage as a vehicle of grace. The final books remind us repeatedly that the Son of God will be born specifically as the "woman's seed."[18] Eve must assume her place as the mother of humanity so that the second Eve, Mary, can give birth to the Son. Yet a forward-looking faith in God's plan should encourage Adam and Eve not merely to reproduce but also to love each other genuinely. In the final book, Adam responds to the lesson about the redemptive future with his version of the *felix culpa* paradox:

> Full of doubt I stand,
> Whether I should repent me now of sin
> By me done and occasioned, or rejoice. (12.473–75)

Adam may not explicitly connect the logic of the fortunate fall to his choice to stay with Eve. Yet the poem as a whole invites the sense that Adam's sinful choice has led to a superior outcome than the alternate reality of remaining immortal in Eden with a second wife.

If *Paradise Lost* exhibits a shift in Milton's attitudes toward remarriage, that shift may be informed by his personal experiences as well as his political convictions. I do not mean to advance a sentimental or moralizing claim that reconciling with Mary Powell taught Milton that it is better to stick with a difficult marriage than to pursue divorce. I turn instead to the ambivalence that Milton's writings express regarding remarriage after the death of a spouse. Milton's sonnet "Methought I saw my late espoused saint" reports a dream that the poet has had of his recently deceased wife.[19] The poem suggests the surviving husband's sense of guilt through an early allusion likening Milton's late wife to

> Alcestis from the grave,
> Whom Jove's great son to her glad husband gave. (lines 2–3)

Alcestis volunteers to die on her husband Admetus's behalf. Before dying, she makes Admetus promise never to remarry. When "Jove's great son" Herakles rescues Alcestis from the underworld, he brings her back to Admetus veiled and unidentified. Admetus, under the weight of his promise, is reluctant to let a woman into his household, but Herakles prevails. Euripides's *Alcestis* ends abruptly after Admetus recognizes the veiled woman as his own wife. We do not learn the extent to which Alcestis disapproves of Admetus for having accepted her in the guise of another woman; this tragicomic conclusion remains a tense, awkward one. The allusion to this myth at the opening of Milton's sonnet is startling. Milton's wife had certainly not volunteered to die on his behalf. If the comparison between Milton's wife and Alcestis is to make emotional sense rather than proving simply incongruous, it does so by communicating the poet's diffuse sense of guilt—in having played a role in his wife's death by impregnating her, and, perhaps, also in considering remarriage after her death.

We do not know for certain whether Milton's sonnet concerns his first wife Mary Powell or his second wife Katherine Woodcock.[20] Both died soon after giving birth. We do not know whether the sonnet conveys some sense of guilt over the mere potential of remarriage or over the prior reality of remarriage and the prospect of remarrying yet once more. In either case, this sonnet suggests that Christian belief does not resolve the affective problems surrounding remarriage. Milton's sonnet moves on from the allusion to Alcestis to biblical forms of redemption—from Jove's son to Yahweh's. Yet the poem renders unsatisfying one answer concerning remarriage found in the gospels. The Pharisees seek to stymy Jesus by asking what would happen to a man who married multiple women after their successive deaths but were all resurrected together. Jesus answers that "in the resurrection they neither marry, nor are given in marriage, but as are angels" (Matt. 22:30). Milton, however, imagines in his sonnet that he might enjoy the sight of his resurrected wife in heaven "without restraint" (line 8). The poem does not offer a meditation on how this wish (which blurs the line between a longing to see and a desire for erotic contact) conflicts with Christ's teaching.[21] Instead, the poem ends with a deflating return to earthly existence. The vision of the late wife has only been a dream: "I waked, she fled, and day brought back my night" (14). If this poem is in any way a candid disclosure of some of the poet's feelings, then it gives voice to Milton's guilt about remarriage in a form that Christian teaching cannot alleviate.

As the abrupt ending of the sonnet brings us from the promise of resurrection back down to earthly disappointment, it does so in a way that suggests a number of classical precedents. One is found in the dream that Aeneas has of his wife Creusa in the *Aeneid*.²² "[S]he left me weeping and eager to tell her much," Aeneas recalls at the end of book 2, "and drew back into thin air."²³ Creusa had been killed in the destruction of Troy when Aeneas had let her trail behind. By contrast, Aeneas had hoisted their son Ascanius on his shoulders while leading his father Anchises by the hand. This scene offers a tableau of Aeneas's priorities: patriarchal descent over his wife. By calling this precedent to mind, the unsatisfying ending of Milton's sonnet looks forward to the expansive reconsideration of marriage in relation to epic heroism presented in *Paradise Lost*. The story of Adam and Eve rejecting remarriage advances Milton's redefinition of Virgilian epic.²⁴ In the *Aeneid*, Aeneas's destiny as a widower is to remarry for the sake of political expediency rather than for love. Some of the most memorable episodes in Virgilian epic involve Aeneas's struggle to leave Dido behind, her suicidal despair upon being abandoned, and her subsequent refusal to interact with Aeneas in the underworld. The shade of Dido turns away from Aeneas and towards her first husband, Sychaeus. Whereas Virgilian epic accepts the possibility of a bad conscience when it comes to the hero's treatment of women, Milton elevates conjugal love as a key epic virtue— even after that love has motivated disobedience against God. At the end of Milton's epic, Eve emerges as a conduit of divine grace; she is the one who helps to spur Adam out of his descent into misogyny and despair. In her final speech, Eve echoes Aeneas's father Anchises in book 2 of the *Aeneid*. "[B]ut now lead on; / In me is no delay," Eve tells Adam (12.614–15).²⁵ Milton has Eve echo the words of Anchises as he promises to follow his son out of burning Troy: "Now, now there is no delay; I follow, and where you lead, there I am."²⁶ Even as Eve's speech declares her willingness to follow, this echo still suggests that she has assumed a privileged role once occupied by the arch-patriarch. Milton's Eve, as Quint puts it, is "no Creusa to be left behind."²⁷ The ending of *Paradise Lost* confirms that Milton has prioritized the fixity of love over the utility of remarriage and over a concern for patriarchal descent.

Substitution against Love

In *Tetrachordon*, Milton describes Edenic marriage as having synthesized fleshly and divine understandings of love—without the delay, necessary in a fallen world, of a typological unfolding of truth. "*Adam* spake like *Adam* the words of flesh and bones, the shell and rinde of matrimony," Milton writes, "but God spake like God, of love and solace and meet help, the soul both of *Adams* words and of matrimony" (*CPW* 2:603). In *Paradise Lost*, however, conjugal love ends up exposing a rift between Adam and his creator. This may be true not only within Adam's own experiences leading to the Fall but also in the reader's sympathies. Whereas Adam's transgressive choice in the name of love may register as tragically heroic, Milton's God is notoriously aloof or callous. My reading proposes that Milton's God is alienating not only because he has a defensive tone but also because he insists on various iterations of the principle of substitution. The pressure that Milton places on substitution through his presentation of conjugal love leads, in turn, to a multilayered investigation into the nature of Christ's atonement and into the mythic basis of hereditary succession.

In book 3, God foresees the Fall and articulates his plan for redeeming humanity. Divine mercy cannot merely dispense with justice, but justice can accept forms of displacement:

> [Man] with his whole posterity must die,
> Die he or justice must; unless for him
> Some other able, and as willing, pay
> The rigid satisfaction, death for death. (3.209–12)

In an earlier essay on the atonement, C. A. Patrides quotes these lines as exemplifying the legalistic voice of Milton's God. Patrides argues that Milton's description of the "rigid satisfaction" that divine justice requires is consistent with the "penal-substitutionary theory of the Atonement."[28] This theory had its origins in Anselm's medieval theology and was subsequently developed both by Luther and Calvin. Anselm had theorized atonement as a debt of honor that sinful humanity could not render to God, and that Christ paid instead. The later adaptations of this doctrine emphasize the way Christ suffers a corporal and capital punishment in the place of sinners. The notion of a debt having been paid remains an active simile in the very notion of redemption; the simile is useful insofar as it mitigates the sense that there is something incongruous and unjust about an innocent victim suffering death in the name of satisfying divine justice. Although Patrides denies that he seeks to recuperate Milton's depiction of God, his reading nonetheless suggests that if we find something distasteful about Milton's God, that might be because the penal theory of atonement has become less familiar—or less palatable—to us.

Recent scholarship tends to focus more on Milton's engagement with the heterodox theologies that flourished in the seventeenth century. We have some evidence that Milton played a role in licensing the *Racovian Catechism* for publication in 1650.[29] This catechism advances Socinian teachings, including the teaching that Christ's death does not appease divine justice but rather serves as an example of perfect obedience. In a reconsideration of Milton's views on the atonement, Gregory Chaplin concludes that *Paradise Lost* does not fully yield to the Socinian critique but rather seeks a middle ground between an acceptance and a rejection of substitutionary atonement. "Milton rejects the traditional Anselmian understanding of atonement as a debt . . . that Christ must pay," Chaplin argues, "and adopts a position similar to the one Hugo Grotius presents in *De satisfactioni Christi* (1617): God rules creation as a political state and has an obligation to punish crimes against that state."[30] For Chaplin, Grotius's precedent shows that a demand for atonement can be understood as a rational expression of justice rather than an irrational satisfaction in bloodshed.

In my reading, the affective challenges emanating from Milton's depiction of God cannot be contextualized away—by situating God's demand for "rigid satisfaction" within a shared belief in penal atonement, or alongside Grotius's modifications of that doctrine to render it more compatible with reason. I believe that we should understand the poem as strategically estranging our understanding of God from a comprehensible form of love. Milton works toward these ends by pitting God's satisfaction in substitution against a human form of love that recoils at the very principle. The formula "death for death" speaks a language of equivalence, but it also describes a willingness to accept difference—differences as significant as innocence standing in for guilt. Divine justice accepts a form of displacement that we might colloquially refer to as taking it out on someone else; taking it out on someone else is especially egregious if the target of displaced retribution is blameless. In book 4 of *Paradise Lost*, Milton goes on to suggest that displacing wrath on innocent parties is a tendency that God and Satan share. When Satan first encounters Adam and Eve, he imagines Hell receiving the human pair and their future progeny. Satan then declares,

> Thank him who puts me loth to this revenge
> On you who wrong me not for him who wronged. (4.386–87)

Satan's sarcasm suggests that he is parodying divine goodness even as he blames God as the true source of this chain of displaced vengeance. Satan's wrath needs to be deemed wicked whereas divine justice should be righteous. One key distinction, which I go on to discuss, lies in the fact that Adam and Eve are naïve victims whereas the Son volunteers to take punishment upon himself. Yet despite this key difference, God and Satan are presented as being locked in a contest, affective and political, that makes humanity a kind of bargaining chip.

The contest between God and Satan opens onto a rationale for the very existence of humanity. The poem reveals in stages that the imperative to replace may have motivated God to create us in the first place. In book 4, Satan expresses his aggravation that God has replaced the fallen angels:

> behold instead
> Of us outcast, exiled, his new delight,
> Mankind created. (4.105–7)

In book 1, however, Satan had mentioned

> a fame in Heaven that [God] ere long
> Intended to create, and therein plant
> A generation. (1.651–53)

It is unclear if Satan is suggesting that God originally intended humanity to replace the fallen angels or if this replacement was something of a convenient coincidence. Later, however, the angel Raphael specifies that God created humanity to demonstrate his ability to

> repair
> That detriment

caused by the expulsion of the rebel angels (7.152–53). This is the first clear answer that Adam and Eve (the primary recipients of Raphael's lesson) receive as to why God has created them. Milton had, in a very early poem, expressed the sense that offspring can be replaced in the affections of their parents. "On the Death of a Fair Infant" closes by advising a bereaved mother (likely Milton's sister) that if she patiently renders back to God the baby whom he only lent temporarily, then God

> will an offspring give
> That till the world's last end shall make thy name to live. (lines 76–77)

Replacing a dead infant with a superior child is the final solace that the poem offers. I have discussed how Milton gives us hints in his poetry that his feelings (if not his avowed beliefs) about remarriage changed as a result of his experiences. It is less clear if losing his only son, John, altered the kind of view he had expressed in his very early poem.[31] In *Paradise Lost*, Adam and Eve are taught to accept the suggestion that God has created them as replacements; this suggestion should not contradict the sense that God loves his latest offspring. Yet for fallen readers if not for Adam and Eve, it may be a challenge to accept that we were created only because a depopulated heavenly kingdom might have diminished God's prestige.

If we are to be faithful readers, then we must accept that we can genuinely be loved by God even while we serve as bargaining instruments in his contest with Satan. This is Milton's poetic iteration of what it means for all creation to exist for God's glory. When, in book 3, the Son volunteers to die on behalf of humanity, his willingness promises to make divine justice compatible with love—and in a way that might harmonize the affective and intergenerational logics of replacement. Pleased with the Son's choice, God declares that he

> hast been found
> By merit more than birthright Son of God,
> Found worthiest to be so by being good. (3.308–10)

Two seeming paradoxes emerge in this singular case of divine succession. First, there should never have been any cleavage between birthright and merit. The legitimacy of God's only begotten Son should never have been in doubt, as true merit should be the only possible outgrowth of his identity. If this is the case, when God explicitly prioritizes merit over birthright, he may be serving as a kind of mouthpiece for Milton's own republican values. Second, it remains mysterious why an immortal God would have an heir at all. This mystery is amplified when God foretells how the Son will, after the final judgment, assume the reign he has merited only to give it up:

> Then thou thy regal sceptre shalt lay by,
> For regal sceptre then no more shall need,
> God shall be all in all. (3.339–41)

If these paradoxes puzzle us, we are invited to be content with the fact that humanity will participate in the Son's triumph; he will

>   reign
> Both God and man, Son both of God and man. (3.315–16)

Only in book 5 does Raphael go on to reveal that a challenge to God's promotion of his Son as heir had initiated cosmic prehistory. Raphael remembers that God declared,

> This day I have begot whom I declare
> My only Son,

and that dissatisfaction with this public elevation eventually resulted in the war in heaven (5.603–4).[32] Insofar as Adam and Eve are happy to exist, they might (upon receiving this new information from Raphael) feel grateful or pleased that Satan once challenged the promotion of God's Son and ended up depopulating heaven. Such a feeling would tacitly function as a prototype of the *felix culpa* while, at the same time, registering a highly subversive form of a republican sentiment that questions birthright and insists on proof of merit. Raphael makes it possible for Adam and Eve to conclude that they owe their existence to Satan having insisted on the proof of the Son's merit—even if Satan only did so for entirely corrupt reasons.[33] When we as readers encounter Raphael's lesson, we recognize that the promotion of merit over birthright in book 3 had not been a gratuitous distinction after all but one made necessary by a heavenly civil war.

In light of Raphael's story, the voluntary nature of the Son's choice to die proves all the more essential to Milton's theodicy. His choice should display his merit and confirm that divine kingship accommodates a republican esteem for merit-based office holding—in a more genuine way than satanic despotism offers in its sham of consensus building. In book 2, Milton presents a debased version of the heroic choice that the Son will subsequently make. Down in Hell, Satan rules "[h]igh on a throne of royal state," yet he nonetheless calls for a parliamentary debate regarding the course of action the devils should pursue (2.1). This debate turns out to be a ruse. Together with his companion Beelzebub, Satan dissuades the devils from the decision they collectively reach under the advice of Belial and Mammon—to remain in Hell and to hope for the best. When Beelzebub sways the devils to attack God indirectly through his newest creation, the poet reminds us that this idea had been

> first devised
> By Satan, and in part proposed: for whence
> But from the author of all ill could spring
> So deep a malice? (2.379–82)

Satan is not merely a tyrant who manufactures false consensus. He galvanizes support by volunteering for the genuinely dangerous mission to the new world. This act of volunteering may be ersatz only to the extent that Satan has responded to his own call, which no other fallen angel has dared to answer. Yet even if Satan displays real courage, that display serves to reinforce his "monarchal pride" and his blasphemous sense "of highest worth" (2.428–29).[34] False consensus building and displays of genuine bravery can operate together as the ruses of a manipulative despot.

The Son's choice needs to rise above the satanic pattern. It does so, in part, because the Son is not answering his own call but rather that of his Father. Yet the relationship between the Father and the Son still raises questions about how free, exactly, the Son's response can be. Milton prefaces the heavenly colloquy by reminding us that the Son is "the radiant image" of God's glory, just as the Epistle to the Hebrews teaches (3.63; cf. Heb. 1:3). In the appearance of the Son,

> all his Father shone
> Substantially expressed. (3.139–140)

The Son reflects the Father not just in visible appearance but also in the acoustic register of language. The Son's first speech in the poem is a kind of echo:

> O Father, gracious was that word which closed
> Thy sovereign sentence, that man should find grace. (3.144–45)

His ensuing words make this echo effect more pronounced. After raising the possibility of destroying humanity after its satanic perversion, the Son urges,

> That be from thee far,
> That far be from thee, Father. (3.153–54)

Because the Son manifests what is already in the Father, the nature of his choice needs to be defined more carefully. My discussion of free choice will deviate further from the topic of marriage, and I want to signal in advance how I plan to return to Milton's definition of love against substitution. I ask what it means for the Son to volunteer to die alongside Aristotelian notions of free choice—notions that are related to Milton's own republican ideals. Milton does not apply these existing understandings straightforwardly but rather challenges the reader to consider how, exactly, the Son's choice to die on behalf of humanity differs from Satan's corrupt version. This distinction is not only framed as a rational matter; it also involves irrational forms of personal identification and desire. Regarding the irrational passions underlying free and unfree choices, Milton resorts to mythopoetic fabrications as much as he offers systematic explanations. All of this establishes the grounds for understanding the human test case of real versus corrupt freedom. For Adam and Eve, an intense feeling that love must reject substitutes blurs the lines between free choice and compulsive necessity. Insofar as this love motivates disobedience against God, it is contaminated by a satanic form of irrational passion. Yet at the same time, Milton affiliates this transgressive love with the possibility of redemption. This is not a straightforward recuperation of irrational love as the grounds for a renewed freedom. Long before Adam can exhibit the undeluded but wrongful choice to join his wife in sin, Eve has been rendered unfree from the start. In their original union, Adam's sense that Eve is irreplaceable leads to the violation of her choice—her decision not to unite with him. By the end of the poem, Eve's violated freedom is compensated through her elevation as a privileged vehicle of divine grace. Yet here as elsewhere, the nonlogic of the *felix culpa* asks us to be content with a happily ever after when questions of fairness cannot be fully resolved.

I begin this line of thinking by noting that the Son's free choice does not conform neatly to Aristotle's working definition of *eleutheria* ("liberty" or "freedom"). In the *Politics*, Aristotle contrasts *eleutheria* both with the condition of household slaves and with so-called natural slavery, an innate deficiency in intellect and character.[35] *Eleutheria* requires the ability to deploy reason (something the natural slave is said to lack) and to apply rational choices toward one's own self-directed aims. Even if the Son reflects and echoes his Father's wishes, Milton must not present him as a servile yes-man. The Son echoes the Father's words, but in a manner designed to promote grace. The chiastic pattern in the Son's speech ("That be from thee far, / That far be from thee Father") suggests that he deploys rhetorical skill to advance his ends. In his earlier political writings, Milton had elevated the Aristotelian concept of *eleutheria* even while adapting it to suit his Protestant values. The frontispiece to *Areopagitica* contains an epigraph from Euripides's *Suppliants*. "This is true Liberty," Milton's English translation begins,

> when free born men
> Having to advise the public may speak free. (*CPW* 2:485)

Milton translates *touletheron* (which attaches the definite article to *eleutheria*, with "the free thing" referring to the condition of freedom) as "true Liberty."[36] In appealing to an Athenian model, Milton may be tacitly endorsing the idea of limitations placed on democratic participation. Aristotle's definition of *eleutheria* promotes a form of democracy in which only male heads of households—who preside over women, children, and slaves—enjoy the linked privileges of self-direction and of civic participation. *Areopagitica* does appeal to the liberties and dignities of a male citizen (one who is indignant about the possibility of being treated like a schoolboy). Yet Milton's desire to limit freedom is not strictly based on gender and class but rather on sectarian affiliation. The writings that Milton seeks to exclude from the freedom from prepublication censorship are not those by women (or by those of a certain class) but, instead, writings by anyone seeking to promote Roman Catholicism. This is deemed an affront to real freedom from the outset.

Milton's political writings go on to manifest a tension between a call for freedom and a desire to restrict decision-making even further—not just to Protestants but more narrowly to the righteous few who are said to be pursuing freedom. In the opening of *The Tenure of Kings and Magistrates*, Milton declares that slavery consists of a lack of reason and deference of human customs; if this is a natural or domestic form of slavery ("within doors"), it also fosters blind acceptance of political tyranny (*CPW* 3:190).[37] As the republican experiment would eventually veer toward collapse, Milton's arguments for restricted decision-making would intensify—most notably in *The Ready and Easy Way* (1660). When the majority of citizens desire a return to kingship (a longing that Milton can only deem a form of madness) then their choice should be overruled by that of a more virtuous minority, in the very name of freedom. If this kind of belief has any chance of being valid (rather than lapsing entirely into self-righteous partisanship), then it needs to appeal to a truth or judgment existing above human disagreement. Only this higher judgment could confirm as binding the conviction that Roman Catholicism is incompatible with a free exchange of ideas, or the political conviction that a return to Caroline monarchy would be a return to bondage.

In *Paradise Lost*, Milton attempts to show how freedom can be of a piece with obedience to God's verdicts. Applying reason to consider how best to please God should be the most appropriate form of pursuing one's own aims. This is true even when pleasing God seems to conflict with self-interest—as in the case of the Son's volunteering to die—because God elevates those who abase themselves to please him. In Aristotelian terms, this might mean that when the Son chooses to die on behalf of humanity, he exhibits a freedom that does not conform neatly to the political notion of *eleutheria* but still does express *hekousios* ("voluntary choice"). In Adriel Trott's summation, "Freedom [*eleutheria*] as Aristotle takes it up in a political context is the capacity to do what we want to do." On the other hand, "[c]hoice [*hekousios*], as defined in *Nicomachean Ethics* III.3, concerns that which depends on our efforts and follows as a result of deliberation."[38] Yet within the interplay between Milton's theological and political concerns, a balancing act between *eleutheria* and *hekousious* might not produce a fully satisfying answer as to how, exactly, the Son's choice to die models a republican form of liberty as well as heroic merit within a divine monarchy that insists on obedience.

To this point, I have focused on the contrast between the corrupt forms of consensus building and volunteering that Satan models in book 2 and the Son's superior choice in book 3. This pattern of distinctions relates philosophical and theological questions about reason to the political tension between individual merit and the hereditary claims of kingship. Yet when it comes to Satan's original decision to rebel against God, Milton presents us first with a poetic myth—and not a rational explanation—of the original transgressive choice as having been rooted in libidinal identification and desire.[39] In book 2, Satan reunites with the other members of the evil Trinity that he has spawned. When his daughter, Sin, narrates her origins, we recognize that Milton is rewriting the myth of Minerva being born from the head of Jove. At the same time, the story of Satan and Sin is an early twist on the Narcissus motif, which will become so prominent later in the poem. Sin describes to Satan how, after giving birth to her, he used her as a narcissistic mirror:

> full oft
> Thy self in me thy perfect imagine viewing
> Becam'st enamored. (2.763–65)

Because this episode parodies the Trinity, the description of satanic narcissism threatens to cast a shadow over God's relationship to his Son as described in the following book. That relationship, too, is defined by the Father's pleasure in interacting with his own image. Yet Sin is neither a reflective surface nor a radiant son but, instead, a female body capable of allegorical reproduction. The "joy" that Satan takes in Sin ends up filling her womb with a "growing burden" (2.765–67). Milton is allegorizing in a literal, even incongruous fashion the teaching found in the Epistle to James that "when lust hath conceived, it bringeth forth sin: and sin, when it is finished, bringeth forth death" (James 1:15).

More rational questions of angelic freedom do persist as an important part of Milton's theodicy. God deems the freedom to make bad choices necessary:

> Freely they stood who stood, and fell who fell.
> Not free, what proof could they have given sincere
> Of true allegiance. (3.102–4)

Even as the Son's choice is primarily contrasted to Satan's debased leadership, the freedom of the faithful angels who did not rebel also matters. None of the good angels dare to volunteer to die on behalf of humanity. When God asks for a willing sacrificial victim, "all the heavenly choir stood mute" (3.217). This exact moment is anticipated by book 2, when none of the fallen angels dare to volunteer to journey to the new world. Only Satan proves courageous enough to do so. In the divine version, the Son shows himself to be distinctively meritorious. After volunteering, the Son reveals the knowledge or faith underlying his choice:

> Though now to Death I yield, and am his due
> All that of me can die, yet that debt paid,
> Thou wilt not leave me in the loathsome grave. (3.245–47)

Milton relies on a Christian reading of Psalm 16 to suggest that if the psalmist David could express a proto-Christian faith that God "wilt not leave [his] soul in hell," then the Son of God surely could have known or believed this (Ps. 16:10). The Son's awareness of his future resurrection manifests his unique status regarding the Father. At the same time, this awareness raises a question about the manner in which he alone has volunteered heroically—in contrast to all the good angels. If the angels in heaven were less dutiful, they might wonder if they, too, could have volunteered to die if they had been aware that the death in question would only be temporary. Milton emphasizes how Satan faces genuine risk and uncertainty in the mission for which he volunteers—in contrast to the conviction that the Son has regarding the merely temporary death for which he is volunteering.

This might seem like a projection of excessively cynical attitudes onto the faithful angels. Yet in book 5, when we learn that the merit of the Son had been the original matter of heavenly contest, Raphael's narration makes it explicit that that the civil war had been rigged by God for the benefit of his Son. God had allowed the fighting to take place—going as far as weakening the innate strength of the good angels—so that the

Son could arrive on the third day in victory. That interval signals how, in Milton's imagination, the war in Heaven is linked to the three-day experience of death that the Son will undergo. Whereas the Son is praised for choosing what will turn out to be three days of death, the good angels had unwittingly fought in a three-day war that they could not win, through no fault of their own. By the time the colloquy in heaven takes place, the good angels may have fully accepted (as a condition of their loyalty, and upon pain of punishment) their role as innocent foils to the Son. Yet for the reader, the later lesson provided by Raphael might reactivate the question of how, exactly, the Son's heroic choice perfects not only freedom in the abstract but also a politically meaningful sense of choice in particular.

For the purposes of my argument, it is important to note how the Son articulates a very specific configuration of soteriological, economic, and contractual terms—not to resolve all of the questions regarding choice and merit in relation to the divine hereditary monarchy, but instead to offer a provisional rhetorical workaround. When the Son declares,

> Though now to Death I yield, and am his due
> All that of me can die, yet that debt paid,
> Thou wilt not leave me in the loathsome grave,

he seems to imply some version of the ransom theory of atonement. The Argument to book 3—added by Milton to the poem in 1668—confirms this: "The Son of God freely offers himself a ransom for man."[40] The ransom theory of atonement should register as long obsolete in Milton's imagination. Yet in a poem that personifies Death at length, the Son's appeal to the ransom theory cannot simply be dismissed as a loose manner of speaking. The issue is not that the Son has made his choice based on a mistaken understanding of salvation. Instead, I argue, Milton's Son briefly appeals to an outdated soteriology to reframe his voluntary mission within a contractual mode. I will go on to discuss how this mode subsequently links the question of the Son's freedom with the questions surrounding Adam and Eve's conjugal union. Here, I want to suggest that the Son is making a kind of performative speech act that generates a binding contractual debt relationship with Death. This would explain the force of the "now" in the Son's statement, "now to Death I yield, and am his due." Although the incarnation of the Son lies far ahead, the Son's words have made his obligation to Death binding at the present moment of utterance.

The Son provisionally casts his death as a ransom owed to Death personified to define what part of him is negotiable and what part is not. The Son's choice involves a distinction between "all that of [him] that can die"—and will thus be rendered as payment—versus the aspects of self that will persist after corporeal death. This distinction may be tenuous given Milton's inclinations toward Mortalism. Milton does not tell us if the Son is speaking coyly when he refers to that undefined part of himself that cannot die, or whether the Son has yet to determine whether or not the soul is capable of undergoing suspension.[41] What we do know is that the Son relies on the Father to preserve the continuity of his identity. God will guarantee that some part of the Son's being is nonnegotiable in its permanent singularity and cannot be rendered as payment to Death. When book 4 of *Paradise Lost* shifts its attention to Eden, all of these matters surrounding the essential or intrinsic self and contractual obligations converge on marriage. A love that rejects replaceability establishes the new, human context of the difficult lessons concerning free choice and obedience or disobedience to God.

On Me, Me Only

In *Paradise Lost*, the intensity of human love blurs the lines between choice and compulsion. This is true when Eve conflates jealousy with love in her choice to tempt Adam with the forbidden fruit. Unfallen Adam, in turn, feels that his love for an irreplaceable wife compels him to sin even when he is aware of the consequences. These decisions, which bridge the gap between freedom and unfreedom, culminate a longer narrative in which the problems of gender hierarchy help to explain how the Fall could have taken place—supposedly at a safe remove from divine culpability. Much of this narrative involves Adam's struggle to maintain his supposed superiority as a husband. The challenge to Adam's self-esteem (to use the phrase that Milton may have introduced into English parlance) begins in earnest when Eve narrates how reluctant she had been to unite with him at first. Eve's initial speech has proven so memorable because she describes herself as the original, sinless Narcissus—one who actively preferred her reflection to Adam.[42] This speech suggests how Eve's beleaguered freedom occupies a very particular place in Milton's poem. Because Eve is innocent, her narcissism should not align her with Satan. We can easily differentiate their two forms of narcissism by focusing on the different erotic and reproductive logics involved. In the allegorical myth of Satan giving birth to Sin and then consummating their relationship, Milton had aligned Satan with lust itself. ("Then when lust has conceived, it bringeth forth sin," the Epistle to James teaches.) Eve's narcissism, by contrast, is so chaste—or, at least, so sterile—that it is a hindrance to sex and reproduction. Eve's narcissism is deemed a threat even as it promises to unleash nothing in particular on God's creation.

Yet Eve's narcissistic satisfaction needs to be deemed inferior to the satisfaction that the Father takes in his own radiant image as expressed in his Son. As we have seen, the exchange between Father and Son needs to feature enough grounds for agency to accommodate a true conversation as well as a voluntary decision. Eve recalls her interaction with her reflection as a kind of conversation:

> pleased I soon returned,
> Pleased it returned as soon with answering looks
> Of sympathy and love. (4.463–65)

Yet this seems to be a naïve understanding of what constitutes a productive conversation. Eve's narcissism may not only be intrinsically inferior to the divine version but also kept that way in a deliberate fashion. It is remarkable that the disembodied voice never mentions knowledge of God as the ultimate reason that Eve should leave her reflection behind.[43] The disembodied voice only instructs Eve to assume her role as Adam's image and as a future mother. In this sense, the voice plays a part not just in confirming Satan's conclusion about gender hierarchy but also in working to keep it true: "He for God only, she for God in him" (4.299).

Whereas the voice limits the scope of Eve's knowledge and choice merely by omitting any mention of God, Adam is actively coercive in violating Eve's agency. Eve recalls that she had initially sought to reject Adam's advances, and to return to her pleasing reflection, but that Adam had seized her hand and claimed her as his own. In a poem that relies on free choice to exculpate God, this violation of Eve's sinless choice registers as ominous. This is true despite Eve's qualifications that Adam had seized her with a "gentle hand" and that she has since accepted the lesson that "manly grace" excels beauty (4.488–90). I have argued that, in the divine colloquy in book 3, the Son explains or rationalizes the grounds for his heroic choice to volunteer to die by appealing to a language of debt, ransom, and contract. The Son reshapes questions about his voluntary choice into questions about what aspect of his being (bodily or spiritual) is negotiable and can be rendered as payment to death. In book 4, Milton brings this conceptual apparatus to bear on Adam's and Eve's asymmetrical forms of freedom. If Adam's seizure of Eve can be justified at all (at least in his own mind), it is by imagining it as a seizure of assets that belong to him. We recall that later in book 4, Milton goes on to celebrate marriage as an anomalous form of "propriety" in an otherwise communitarian paradise. As Alison Chapman notes, the verb "to seize" was "primarily a legal term meaning to come into ownership of, as evident in the tenure of seisin."[44] Chapman argues that in "the sole propriety model of Eden, for Adam to 'seize' Eve's hand does not mean that Eve is being reduced to a thing he owns. Rather, she becomes one of the attributes or characteristics of him, and he also becomes one of the attributes or characteristics of her."[45]

My reading is less sanguine about the possibility of an asymmetrical but mutual possession when it comes to Eve's first encounter with Adam. As Eve recalls, Adam had pursued her while crying out,

> Whom fly'st thou? Whom thou fly'st, of him thou art,
> His flesh, his bone; to give thee being I lent
> Out of my side to thee. (4.482–84)

Eve had been unaware of her bodily origins, but Adam appeals to the notion of contractual lending to stake a claim upon her:

> Part of my soul I seek thee, and thee claim
> My other half. (4.487–88)

The questions about negotiability, the body, and the soul that were previously raised by the Son (in relation to death) are now amplified as they play out across two separate people and across a hierarchical understanding of gender. Eve obviously could not have been a willing party to the contractual form of lending to which Adam appeals. Later, fallen Adam will register some version of the complaint that Eve might have issued regarding her congenital indebtedness:

> Did I request thee, maker, from my clay
> To mould me? (10.742–3)

More to the point, Eve feels nothing approximating a reciprocal feeling about Adam: she flees from his claims on her.

When Paul, in the Epistle to the Ephesians, cites Edenic marriage to impose a Christian meaning on it, he leaves it especially unclear why any Christian wife would honor any particular husband as if he were like Christ. In Milton's handling, the Genesis narrative already furnishes the basis of that asymmetry. Adam feels that he has a right to seize Eve as an irreplaceable object; this feeling is indistinguishable from his love for her. Yet even though Adam is the source of Eve's physical being (in a way that no other husband can claim of his wife), she does not deem him desirable. In the absence of mutual desire, the language of debt and repayment functions as a rhetorical device to allow Adam, like the Son before him, to uphold some distinction between what about his person is negotiable and what is essential to his being. For Adam, however, the relationship between the negotiable and the nonnegotiable concerns his own body and another person all at once. This does not make Eve his property in a simple (or material) way. Adam declares that he must reclaim his flesh as it exists in Eve's person—but as part of his soul. Eve remains absolutely nonnegotiable in Adam's eyes to the extent that she is inseparable from the wholeness that he seeks. In articulating this claim, Adam renders himself fragmented in his self-understanding. What does prove negotiable, however, is Eve's volition over her own body. The disembodied voice has already taught Eve that she has been born into a state of partial objecthood, designed to be another's image. Adam's economic and legal appeal subsequently recasts her unfreedom as both just and necessary to him in his quest to achieve his sense of wholeness, body and soul.

All of the problems besetting Adam and Eve's initial union will require correction far beyond Adam's selective and self-serving retelling of the same story in book 8. The genuine correction must happen in stages, with Adam and Eve separately reaffirming their capacity for free choice around their love for each other as irreplaceable objects. When Adam decides to disobey God in favor of remaining married to Eve, he exhibits a freedom that is neither satanic nor like the Son of God's. Adam's choice is distinctively human. His wrongful but free choice is not based on faulty reasoning; Adam knows that the Fall has already made Eve mortal and will lead to his own death. He simply prefers to live and die with Eve rather than enjoying immortality with a second wife. Adam's deliberation reveals that he displays not just *hekousios* but also *eleutheria*—except in a manner that defies God. Adam proves himself to be distinctively unlike the Son. Adam has decided that he knows what is best for himself, and he will pursue his self-directed aims despite God's warnings.

We can now revisit the way that Adam's appeal to a feeling of necessity ("So forcible within my heart I feel / The bond of nature") threatens to align his decision-making with the rhetoric of tyrants. Milton offers us two ways to distinguish Adam's deliberations from Satan's disingenuous rhetoric. The first way concerns the contrast between displaced and fixed affect. Milton deems "necessity" as the "tyrant's plea" immediately after Satan declares it regrettable but necessary to pursue revenge on Adam and Eve (who have not wronged him) as a roundabout means of attacking God. Milton does not condemn this displaced violence against innocent victims so much as he condemns the dishonesty involved in Satan's claim that he must carry out this distasteful act. When Adam feels that he is compelled to join Eve, he insists on the fixity of his affect. Affective fixity is, in turn, aligned with sincerity, as Adam seems to be uttering his impassioned feelings rather than dishonest rationalizations. The second distinction between Satan and Adam involves the split between the public and the private. Satan's dishonest appeal to necessity is based on his rhetoric of advancing the public good of the fallen angels, through "[h]onor and empire with revenge enlarged" (4.390). Adam, by contrast, feels bound to intimate attachments. This sense of obligation not only overrides his sense of duty to God but also undercuts his future status as the patriarch of a human empire. In the final books of *Paradise Lost*, the angel Michael teaches Adam,

> this had been
> Perhaps thy capital seat,

but "this preeminence thou hast lost" (11.342–43). In contrast to Satan's proto-tyrannical rhetoric, Adam does not justify his wickedness with an appeal to public reason, but rather sacrifices his public-facing prestige to remain with his wife.

As I have noted, the concluding books of *Paradise Lost* spend less time rebuking Adam's decision than affirming it after all. After hearing of the salvation to come from the angel Michael, Adam declares that he has learned his lesson:

> that to obey is best,
> And love with fear the only God. (12.561–62)

Adam tacitly expresses penitence for his earlier choice of Eve over God. Yet when the angel Michael subsequently teaches that Adam

> shalt possess
> A paradise within [him], happier far,

he reopens the rhetoric of the *felix culpa* (12.587–88). It is once again unclear whether Adam should repent or rejoice in his transgression. Subsequently, when Adam rejoins Eve, she affirms that the happier condition that God has graciously produced is not merely an inward contentment but instead an interpersonal love. Eve insists to Adam that

> with thee to go,
> Is to stay here; without thee here to stay,
> Is to go hence unwilling; thou to me
> Art all things under heaven, all places thou. (12.615–18)

If Adam's insistence on remaining with Eve resulted in the loss of Eden, Eve now declares that conjugal love can transform any place into paradise.

Eve's eagerness at the end of the poem to be led by Adam is meant to overcome (or, at least, to render more palatable) the earlier violations of her choice. Eve's desire to exercise some form of *eleutheria* has always been constrained by her role as the object of desire that makes Adam's willful but free choice possible. This is patently unfair to Eve. Adam is eventually able to exercise free choice even if it means disobeying God. Eve is unable to decide what is best for herself even in a case in which her decision cannot be labeled as sinful. This unfairness arises out of a pattern of thinking that Milton had established in his earlier writings about marriage. In the preface to the revised 1645 publication of *The Doctrine and Discipline of Divorce*, for example, Milton appeals to Parliament with an analogy: "as a whole people is in proportion to an ill Government, so is one man to an ill marriage" (*CPW* 2:229). Given the realities of male-dominated marriage, it would have made far more sense to liken the unhappily governed people to suffering wives.[46] Yet Milton constructs an appeal specifically to male agency—both when it comes to the private matter of initiating divorce proceedings and the public matter of refusing an oppressive form of government—by disavowing and also arrogating for his own purposes a normatively female form of unfreedom. Milton was certainly aware that unhappy wives are victims of unfreedom. In the later divorce tracts *Judgment of Martin Bucer* and *Tetrachordon*, Milton makes explicit concessions to cases in which wives are more prudent than their husbands and should have the power to initiate divorce.[47] Yet these concessions are exceptions to Milton's focus on male unhappiness, private and political. At the end of the seventeenth century, Mary Astell remarks critically on the disingenuous twist within Milton's deployment of marriage and divorce as political metaphors. In *Some Reflections upon Marriage* (1700), Astell observes that even if men often decry living under arbitrary power, "not *Milton* himself wou'd cry up Liberty to poor *Female Slaves*, or pleased for the Lawfulness of Resisting a Private Tyranny."[48]

Even as *Paradise Lost* narrates the mythic basis of Milton's male-centered view of marriage, it keeps us aware that the violation of Eve's agency functions as a rationale for divine grace. In book 3, God announces his intention to offer mercy to humanity while offering the fallen angels no hope of salvation:

> man falls deceived
> By the other first. (3.130–31)

If God's use of "man" does not contradict the biblical teaching that Adam fell without being deceived, then God must be implying that Eve—and not Adam—is the representative of humanity. If the violation of Eve's agency is a problem for Milton's rational theodicy, God is already turning her victimization into the grounds of a happier conclusion for humanity. Like the *felix culpa* itself, however, this is not a logical explanation; it does not explain why Eve should have been born unfree with respect to Adam. The conclusion of *Paradise Lost* can only invite the reader to feel that the problems surrounding Eve's choice have been surmounted by an expression of conjugal love renewed by divine grace. As noted earlier, Milton emphasizes this point by conferring on Eve a kind of patriarchal prestige: in expressing her willingness to follow Adam's lead, she does not echo Aeneas's lost wife, Creusa, but rather his father, Anchises.

The allusion to the *Aeneid* near the very end of *Paradise Lost* culminates a sequence of Virgilian allusions, at the end of which Eve belatedly emerges as free (or, at least, freer) under the auspices of the Son's redemptive mission. In book 3, as the Son volunteers to die on behalf of humanity, he implores the Father,

> Behold me then, me for him, life for life
> I offer, on me let thine anger fall. (3.236–37)

The Son's tendency toward repetition has led him to echo not only the words of the Father but also, in this instance, the words of the faithful friend Nisus. In book 9 of Virgil's epic, Nisus and the younger Euryalus take part in a nighttime raid. They succeed, but Euryalus is distracted by the spoils of victory and ends up being captured. Nisus refuses to flee to safety but rather approaches Volcens, king of the Rutulians, and pleads for Euryalus's life:

> *me, me, adsum qui feci, in me conuertite ferrum*
> *o Rutuli!*
> me, me, here I am, the one who has done the killing.
> Turn your sword on me, Rutulians![49]

Noting this parallel between Virgil's Nisus and Milton's Son, Chaplin argues that Milton mitigates the harsh illogic of sacrificial atonement by appealing to the Son's friendship with humanity. Christ's teaching, "Greater love hath no man than this, that a man lay down his life for his friend" (John 15:13) informs Milton's attempt to show how, in the Christian redemption narrative, "*caritas* subsumes *amicitia*."[50] Chaplin also cites the story of Damon and Pythias, whose loyal friendship inspires the tyrant Dionysus of Syracuse to free them. Yet the problem with Milton's promotion of the Son's friendly disposition is that it threatens to align God with Volcens. Nisus is unsuccessful in attempting to save his friend by taking the punishment upon himself; Volcens kills both of his prisoners in an act of vengeful punishment. Milton is, of course, suggesting that the Son's self-sacrificial act is superior to classical analogues. Yet we can note why it would not make sense for Milton to allude explicitly to the happier example of Damon and Pythias to announce the Son as a superior friend. Unlike Dionysus, who makes an uncharacteristic act of clemency, Milton's God has insisted that someone must die, or else "justice must." If the Damon and Pythias story registers as an indirect precedent, it may only underscore the similarity between God and the cruel Volcens.

Later in *Paradise Lost*, Milton provides us with the grounds for reorienting our understanding of the Nisus and Euryalus episode—in a way that disassociates God from Volcens. This reorientation does not involve a divine act of clemency that rises above the need for sacrificial death, but instead a shift in emphasis from *amicitia* to conjugal love. In book 10, Eve expresses her penitence as well as her concern for Adam by volunteering to take the punishment of sin on herself:

> on me exercise not
> Thy hatred for this misery befallen,
> On me already lost, me than myself
> More miserable; both have sinned, but thou
> Against God only, I against God and thee,
> And to the place of judgment will return,
> There with my cries importune heaven, that all
> The sentence from thy head removed may light
> On me, sole cause of thee of all this woe,
> Me me only just object of his ire. (10.927–36)

Of all the echoes of Nisus found in *Paradise Lost*, Eve's, as Leah Whittington observes, "is the closest to Vergil in both syntax and situation."[51] Eve's speech is the pivot around which Milton recalibrates *amicitia*. At first, Eve is not exactly aligned with Nisus insofar as she is not seeking to rescue her friend from wrath. She is, instead, asking Adam to stop putting so much blame on her. As a result, this echo of Virgil initially suggests that Adam is the one being unduly tyrannical toward his wife. Only at the end of the speech does Eve declare that she will ask God to put all the punishment for sin on her shoulders. She insists that she will be a self-sacrificing friend even if Adam has failed to exhibit grace. When we recall that Nisus is Euryalus's older friend, we understand that Eve is attempting a rhetorical reversal in primacy over her husband.

As *Paradise Lost* redeems a transgressive human love that insists on affective fixity, Eve's echo of Nisus momentarily shifts the site of fixity from marriage to a sacrificial economy. Yet Eve's singular status ("Me me only") will not be affirmed through self-sacrifice; that mission belongs to the Son alone. Eve's uniqueness will instead be reaffirmed in reconciled marriage. Only after the Fall—and after having attempted a form of self-affirmation through self-abasement—is Eve afforded this opportunity to display a form of freedom even roughly analogous to the form Adam has always enjoyed. It is important for Milton's poem that Eve's belated attempt at heroic choice is neither transgressive (like Adam's) nor fully heroic (like the Son's). She volunteers for a form of self-sacrifice that God has already rendered unnecessary. Eve's declaration is useful precisely because it is gratuitous; in this case, God will bear absolutely no resemblance to Volcens. The triumph of Eve's attitude is confirmed when Adam scrambles to reestablish his superiority over his wife. Adam declares that

> [i]f prayers
> Could alter high decrees (10.952–53)

then he would already have implored God,

> That on my head all might be visited,
> Thy frailty and infirmer sex forgiven,
> To me committed and by me exposed. (10.955–57)

Adam provides the poem's final echo of Nisus, but he is only parroting Eve defensively. Eve's posture of self-sacrifice has, however, already started to snap Adam out of his despair. Adam remembers the clue about the redemptive future offered in the *protoevangelium* and makes it a basis for reconciliation with his wife. As Whittington puts it, "By the end of Adam's response, the first couple have moved into new emotional and rhetorical terrain in which the language of heroic self-suffering has been replaced with the language of charity and unity in suffering."[52]

This promotion of love is possible because Milton has gone to such lengths to circumvent the Pauline teaching that Christ's self-sacrificial love perfects the meaning of marriage. In Milton's handling, the Son's sacrifice is the distant object of faith that allows Adam and Eve to redefine their marriage after the Fall. In this light, the altered Virgilian language of "on me" (and me alone) takes an even sharper resonance. When Eve has called for punishment to fall on herself exclusively, she has attempted a form of singularity through self-negating penitence. Milton's God might continue to operate on the principle of displaced affect when it comes to punishing his Son. At this divine register, a sacrificial logic of substitution and a mysterious logic of hereditary succession work together: by offering to die on behalf of humanity, the Son has ostensibly proven himself to be the unique and rightful heir of an undying God. On the human plane, however, personal singularity must be affirmed through love. When Eve brings closure to *Paradise Lost* by declaring her willingness to follow Adam—in such a way that the two are united as one—she affirms that God has generated a happier conclusion out of the transgressive fixity of human love.

This promotion of a love that rejects substitution advances a political critique that goes further than any attack on a single monarch—against the uxoriousness of Charles I or the debauchery of Charles II. Instead, Milton describes human love as flourishing only when it develops at a remove from the effort to make birthright compatible with merit. Yet this celebration of love still relies on a final affective twist. Despite Eve's final eagerness to follow Adam, the reader can only expect (and hope) that she will disagree with him at times. The poem says little about the content of this marriage even as it entices us into feeling that gender hierarchy has somehow been stabilized in a new, rarefied way. If this bid for closure succeeds, it does so by tacitly making the reality of reproduction stand in for evidence of love. As readers, we only know that Adam and Eve's postlapsarian marriage must have succeeded, in some sense, because they eventually reproduced. The conclusive proof lies not only in the birth of the incarnate Son, but also in our own existence. Milton's poem ends by leading readers to fantasize that our existence ultimately originates out of love—fallen but somehow perfected—rather than the mere fact of reproduction. When Eve echoes Anchises, she confirms that Milton's celebration of marriage still retains a reproductive and dynastic core even if that impulse is not straightforwardly patriarchal or imperial. Adam has been invited to subordinate his hopes of being the father of a global empire to inward and conjugal forms of happiness. Yet Milton secures a satisfying conclusion for his poem not necessarily by abandoning imperial teleology completely, but rather by refocusing it on two human subjects who affirm each other's singularity.

The Dilemma of the Son

Whereas the silent conflation of a reproductive future with genuine love is designed to shuttle *Paradise Lost* toward a happy ending, that conflation also explains the problems that the hero of *Paradise Regained* inherits. Milton's Jesus struggles to understand how he should define and display his unique status as God's Son. Yet most of the brief epic takes place in the wilderness in which Satan tempts the Son with practical means to reveal his station publicly. A basic disagreement between Satan and Jesus concerns the nature of the throne that the Son of God should seek to occupy. Satan urges,

> thy kingdom though foretold
> By prophet or by angel, unless thou
> Endeavor, as thy father David did,
> Thou never shalt obtain. (3.351–54)

Yet Jesus insists that he does not seek David's literal throne. As the heir to a divine father, the Son seeks a throne whose spiritual (or allegorical) nature baffles Satan. When it comes the Son's fulfillment of his status as heir, *Paradise Regained* offers us a highly restrictive, even ambivalent form of triumph. The poem's final lines are famously anticlimactic:

> he unobserved
> Home to his mother's house private returned. (4.638–39)[53]

The conclusion of *Paradise Lost* should inform our understanding of the limited scope of the Son's triumph in *Paradise Regained*. Richard Strier articulates a crucial point when he observes, "Perhaps what is most striking in Milton's presentation of Jesus is what is missing from it. Totally absent is love as a topic or motive."⁵⁴ For Strier, Jesus's indifference to saving sinners out of love suggests Milton's valuation of classical magnanimity over Christian humility. My reading emphasizes how Jesus's indifference to love extends the political critique of hereditary succession initiated in *Paradise Lost*. Jesus's mission is to reveal himself as God's unique Son. When the balance of birthright and merit continues to be the primary source of contestation, love for humanity is subordinated to the point of irrelevance. The affective separation between the divine concern over succession and the human experience of love widens in *Paradise Regained*, even though the divine Son has been born as a man.

The Son does not display the kind of self-sacrificing friendship that exemplifies love. Nor does Jesus offer a tenable way to redefine marriage by transforming self-sacrificing friendship into the exemplary form of husbandly care. The Son of God triumphs over Satan on top of his "Father's house" (as Satan refers to the Temple) only to return home to his mother's (4.552). This anticlimactic conclusion emphasizes a curious feature of Christian typology: Jesus, identified as the second Adam, is not the husband but rather the son of the second Eve. The final book of *Paradise Regained* does teach us that Jesus has redefined what it means to be a man. Milton implicitly likens Jesus to Oedipus when he likens Satan to

> that Theban monster that proposed
> Her riddle. (4.572–73)

Whereas Oedipus solves the Sphinx's riddle with the answer, "man," Jesus stands to display himself as Son of both God and man. Yet the gendered twist involved in identifying Satan with the female Sphinx looks ahead to the true riddle of Jesus's identity: what it means for him to be the son of the second Eve. Insofar as we reject any resemblance between Jesus's and Oedipus's fates out of hand, we tacitly reaffirm a basic fact: Jesus has no conjugal or reproductive destiny of his own. The end of *Paradise Regained* confirms what Milton means when he initially promises a story of Jesus successfully raising "Eden . . . in the waste wilderness" (1.7). The paradise that Jesus restores is not the paradise of Adam and Eve's prelapsarian union. Instead, the metaphorical Eden that Jesus makes possible is the capacity to be a human Son of God, by the side of but also at a partial remove from a human mother. As the maternal care of the second Eve typologically supersedes the role of the first Eve, however, the meaning of marriage remains imperfect in Milton's second epic.

I conclude this chapter with a forward-looking suggestion about how we might consider Milton's presentation of marriage, reproduction, and typology alongside our present-day negotiations of political, familial, and sexual lives. The conclusion of *Paradise Lost*, I have argued, operates through a silent reversal. Adam and Eve's forward-looking mandate to reproduce stands in for a coherent rationale for Christian marriage and reproduction. If Milton's happy ending requires this typological inversion, the Son in *Paradise Lost* subsequently finds himself unable to resolve, for the future of Christianity, the mystery surrounding love and reproduction. I want to pair this unresolved problem in Milton's poetry with our present-day political imagination by way of Lee Edelman's critique of reproductive futurity. Edelman describes how so much of our discourses appeals to "the survival of the social in the Imaginary form of the Child."[55] Yet this rhetoric defers the collective good that is promised rather than ever securing it. Reproductive futurity functions as a screen for the destructive streak within our modes of life—partly through a homophobic scapegoating of queerness as inimical to the Child. Edelman's critique pinpoints how a key aspect of our discourse not only fails to secure positive change but seems designed to fail. Yet his polemic has also been criticized for insisting that queerness can only have a negative and antisocial status.[56]

I want to focus specifically on the way Edelman deploys reproductive futurity as an instrument for an antigenealogical mode of literary analysis. He does so in a reading of Shakespeare in which Hamlet tragically discovers that he must occupy the role of the child anticipated by reproductive futurity.[57] Edelman rejects a cultural genealogy that would be receptive to historical particularity as it structures the relationship between past and present. A critical view of reproductive futurity underwrites a certain mode of antihistoricism. Edelman's turn to *Hamlet* is informed not only by psychoanalysis but also, more specifically, by the theory of the archive that Jacques Derrida develops alongside both *Hamlet* and Freud. In *Archive Fever*, Derrida reminds us that the power of archival consignation—the power to determine what does and does not belong together—involves a form of violence. Even as the archive preserves a supposedly unified body of memory for the sake of an open-ended future, it "must also import there, *in the same stroke*, the death drive, the violence of forgetting, *superrepression* (suppression and repression) . . . in short, the possibility of putting to death the very thing . . . which *carries the law in its tradition.*"[58] The archive necessarily takes from what is supposedly excluded and then represses the memory of that violence. Locating the "*superrepression*" of the death drive within the demand to preserve a patriarchal legacy, Edelman reads *Hamlet* as illustrating how textual transmission is bound up with the tragic burdens of genealogy. Hamlet shoulders the burden of remembering his father, but (as both Freud and Derrida remind us) when he seeks to wipe his mind of anything but his father's memory, he still relies on a writing tablet as a prosthetic device of familial memory.[59] For present-day readers of *Hamlet*, a patriarchal demand may continue to operate within the imperatives of a historicism that insists that we inherit the burdens of the past when we read.

Milton's Jesus has obviously proven to be less influential than Hamlet as an early modern Oedipus figure. Yet I argue that the suspended fate of the Son in *Paradise Regained* can help us account for the illogic embedded in the narrative of reproductive futurity. In my previous work, I have detailed the usefulness of *Archive Fever* in considering Milton's 1671 publication, *Paradise Regained, to Which is Added Samson Agonistes*, as a kind of miniature archive—one that challenges us to reconsider how the Christian archive claims Hebraic scriptures as its own.[60] Milton's Jesus registers the Hebraic past not only textually but also on his body. He is a circumcised Jewish man who conforms to all laws of purity even as he seeks to secure spiritual liberation from those laws. The joint publication of *Paradise Regained* and *Samson Agonistes* underscores the question of how Jesus should perfect the heroism that Samson had previously embodied—a form of heroism that mysteriously displays sanctioned forms of lawlessness, lust, and violence in the name of a holy nation. My previous reading was concerned with the typological problem of universal truth claiming to subsume an archive of ethnic particularity and conflict—of Christianity reclaiming a Hebraic legacy within an archive it relabels as its own and also claims to be open to all nations.

The matter of marriage troubles Jesus's capacity to redefine the Jewish archive. In the biblical narrative, Samson's first marriage to a Philistine woman is a form of impurity that is mysteriously motivated by God's Spirit—ostensibly to foster occasions for violence against the Philistines. In *Samson Agonistes*, Milton not only amplifies the questions surrounding

Samson's first marriage but also deviates from scriptures to describe the Philistine Dalila as Samson's second wife. *Samson Agonistes* is a tragedy of interethnic remarriage. Milton's Jesus, by contrast, avoids all impurity and erotic entanglements. When we consider the partly occluded role of reproductive futurity in Milton's religious imagination, we can discern a way that Jesus might have assumed and perfected elements of Samson's story. Both Samson and Jesus suspend a linear narrative of reproductive futurity. After Samson's violent death, Manoa declares his intent to bring Samson's corpse "[h]ome to his father's house" and to transform this house into a perpetual monument for his son (line 1733). In death, Samson will assume control of the father's house without having become a patriarch in his own right. Manoa concludes his vision of his son's future archive by describing virgins who will

> [v]isit his tomb with flowers, only bewailing
> His lot unfortunate in nuptial choice. (1741–42)

Manoa imagines his son's legacy as inspiring not just militant heroism but also a suspension or even rejection of marriage.

This suspension of patriarchal descent is meaningful because Samson's Israel is not ruled by a hereditary line of kings. As the refrain of the Book of Judges tells us, "In those days there was no king in Israel, but every man did that which was right in his own eyes" (Judges 17:6; cf. 18:1, 19:1, 21:25). In *Paradise Regained*, Milton could have described the Son as perfecting the suspension of reproductive futurity not through self-annihilating violence but rather by a life of perfect obedience. This suspension would facilitate Milton's critique of political succession. Milton's Son is, bafflingly, the heir to a throne that needs no heirs at all; he is never meant to rise to the status of patriarch. Yet at the same time, the Son has proven his merit and legitimacy by volunteering for a self-sacrificing death. He could prove to be the sole and final tragicomic child of reproductive futurity—in a more decisive and paradigmatic fashion than Hamlet. For Milton, the possibility of Jesus's having suspended the mandate to reproduce among Christians was not just hypothetical. A younger Milton had taken the possibility of lifelong virginity seriously.[61] Even after Milton abandoned celibacy for marriage and fatherhood, his writings display a desire to subordinate reproduction to spiritual companionship. Yet this subordination would never be complete. *Paradise Lost* reveals the unstable compromise between love and reproduction that Milton ends up attempting. Milton does not grapple openly with the rationale for reproduction—for Christians in general, or for godly republicans who reject hereditary succession in particular. In this regard, Milton is less honest than Gerrard Winstanley, who had attempted to produce an explicit rationale for making marriage an exception to Christian communalism on the basis of regulating reproduction, with an awareness of gender asymmetries.

As Milton's Jesus is unable to perfect the meaning of Christian marriage, his story offers glimpses of configurations of sexuality that are unmoored from a reproductive imperative. For the project of historicizing queerness, *Paradise Regained* presents an especially revealing moment in which the classical prestige of homoeroticism persists—if only to be dismissed as irrelevant along with heterosexual desire. In book 2, Satan presents Jesus with the temptation of a banquet that features

> stripling youths rich-clad, of fairer hew
> Than Ganymede or Hylas. (2.352–53)[62]

Yet the point is not merely that classical homoeroticism is a satanic temptation; the same banquet features "[n]ymphs of Diana's train" as well as versions of the women pursued by the knights of Arthurian romance (2.355). Jesus is impervious to any configuration of the heroic and the erotic. This categorical indifference, in turn, emphasizes the possibility that heternormativity is somewhat of a demonic trait. Belial,

> the dissolutest spirit that fell,
> The sensualest,

had initially proposed tempting Jesus with beautiful women (2.150–51). Satan dismisses the suggestion, proclaiming,

> Belial, in much uneven scale thou weigh'st
> All others by thyself; because of old
> Thou thy self dot'st on womankind. (2.173–75)

The subsequent banquet scene and its erotic traps make it clear that Satan is taking exception only to Belial's gender-specific logics of identification and desire. The possibility of Jesus's indifference to sex and reproduction suspending the distinction between classical homoeroticism and modern heternormativity might seem to be a lesson with a limited purchase for us now—limited, perhaps, to a subset of Christians who are willing to heed literary-historical lessons about shifting religious attitudes toward sexuality. Yet this kind of scholarly inquiry might prove newly helpful as asexuality, apart from religious celibacy, is being legitimized as a form of personal and political identification. Asexuality has become a topic of discussion among literary scholars, but it remains to be seen how and how far asexuality will prevail as a socially viable, visible form of identification—and the extent to which historically minded scholarship will help to theorize that viability.[63]

The less speculative lesson that Milton's presentation of the Son offers us concerns the contingent configurations of reproductive futurity across different political and religious modes. Edelman's reading of *Hamlet* is largely unconcerned with the status of Hamlet as a prince whose access to his father's throne has been delayed. This antihistorical reading is underwritten by Freud's promotion of Hamlet as a proto-modern Oedipus figure, with Hamlet's specifically political concerns being subsumed within psychosexual dynamics. In well-known versions of literary history, Milton has been identified as a transitional figure between aristocratic and bourgeois worldviews, with the conclusion of *Paradise Lost* shuttling us out of the world of epic and toward the world of the bourgeois domestic novel.[64] In *Paradise Regained*, however, Milton reminds us that, in his view, the transition from a world defined by hereditary birthright and a world defined by love is anchored by a forward-looking expectation of the Son of God. This Son confronts the tragic possibilities not merely of being an anticipated child but rather of being an heir to a throne. In Milton's outlook, the Son should have decisively proven himself to be the one and only heir capable of conjoining merit and birthright. The contest over his ability to do so functions as a myth of the primordial origins of history as such; his return to earth to fully claim his throne should mark the end of history. From this vantage point, the bourgeois modernity that *Paradise Lost* supposedly anticipates should be nothing more than a temporary holdover. Reproductive futurity should not be the normative way to anticipate the future but rather an anachronism—one that is binding only if we fantasize that the Son's birth is a future event.

Yet in Milton's poetry, reproductive futurity still remains embedded within the promotion of love supposedly at a remove from the demands of succession. Related forms of confusion may persist even within our secular (or quasi-secular) imaginations concerning the foreseeable ends of history. We might refer to our twenty-first-century discourses about climate change, in which the pervasive rhetoric of reproductive futurity coexists with outright apocalypticism. As the future scale of human habitation on earth seems uncertain, reproductive futurism itself is undergoing epochal changes. Transhistorical explanations underwritten by psychoanalytic modes of reading should not prevent us from discerning how relations among queerness, heteronormativity, reproduction, and personal freedom are being reshaped within particular political, economic, and affective structures. It also remains to be seen if contingent alliances will counteract the atavistic impulses toward patriarchal kinship—equally alive in much of our reactionary politics, public discourses, and popular entertainment. Milton's poetry should remind us of how such cultural struggles have been prefigured by a literary vocabulary that elevates individual love without fully severing it from the imperative to reproduce in the name of a mythic form of succession.

5

Lucy Hutchinson and the Imperfection of Christian Marriage

In *The Memoirs of the Life of Colonel Hutchinson* (completed ca. 1671), Lucy Hutchinson writes of her late husband not just as a devoted husband but also as a heroic leader in the republican cause. At the same time, Hutchinson insists that she writes of her late husband accurately and honestly. This may help to explain why she needs to sidestep the Pauline teaching that wives should regard their husbands as Christlike. This is true even when John Hutchinson is described as a political martyr after the Restoration. A more emphatic alignment of husband and Christ in the eyes of a loving wife would undercut claims about truthful reporting. An excessive promotion of John Hutchinson's status as a Christlike martyr would align the *Memoirs* with an idolatrous tendency that, in Lucy Hutchinson's view, should only characterize royalist representation. This chapter begins by detailing the vocabulary that Hutchinson develops as an alternative to the Pauline definition of marriage. When claims about John Hutchinson's virtues become strained by recognition of his shortcomings, the *Memoirs* resorts to a number of maneuvers, including the presentation of corrupt and venal foils who should make Hutchinson's singular merit conspicuous if only by negative contrast. Lucy Hutchinson constructs a complex apparatus that involves self-reflexivity about the distortions involved in promoting her husband's supposedly singular public and private virtues.

In Hutchinson's republican outlook, the promotion of genuine personal merit should facilitate a critique of hereditary monarchy, in which heirs are born into positions of power that they might not deserve. Yet in the *Memoirs*, she qualifies her critique of succession. She does so, I argue, because the *Memoirs* is thoroughly invested in affirming John Hutchinson's claims on his familial property as the oldest surviving son of his late father. Lucy Hutchinson affirms primogeniture when it comes to property while rejecting it as the basis of leadership. There is no absolute contradiction between republican politics and a belief in inherited property. Yet in the *Memoirs*, an insistence on the rights of the firstborn generates tensions with the commitments both to merit and to freedom of conscience for all. These tensions emerge in episodes concerning John Hutchinson's relationship to his younger brother George, and also in the disagreements between the Hutchinsons and more radical Protestants who call for class leveling. Hutchinson offers no systematic explanation of why her economic principles better suit the ideals of godly republicanism. She relies instead on the sense that calls for radical egalitarianism are expressions of class envy, of which her husband had been an undeserving target. Some of Hutchinson's rhetorical gestures may remain familiar to us insofar as strong affirmations of individual merit within a republican polity continue to coexist uneasily with the realities of intrafamilial wealth.

The second half of this chapter turns to Lucy Hutchinson's biblical epic *Order and Disorder* (published in unfinished form in 1679). In this work, she explores how Christian theology might accommodate a highly personal love within the spiritual truth of marriage. In contrast to the *Memoirs*, this epic appeals repeatedly to the Pauline teaching that Christ's love perfects the meaning of marriage. Yet typological interpretation ultimately fails to accommodate the kind of loving, republican marriage that she upholds in the *Memoirs*.[1] Early in *Order and Disorder*, she works to reaffirm the desirability of marriage and reproduction for Christian women while, at the same time, advancing a critique of hereditary succession. This critique becomes less coherent when she narrates the dynastic concerns narrated in Genesis. Love is certainly a feature of the marriages of Abraham and Sarah, of Isaac and Rebecca, and of Jacob, Leah, and Rachel. Yet these unions are also vehicles of patriarchal filiation. Hutchinson should render these stories of marriage compatible with a spiritual reinterpretation anchored by Christ's love. *Order and Disorder* stops short, however, just as Jacob prevails in usurping the blessings of his older brother, Esau. Pauline teaching reinterprets the blessing of the younger Jacob as a precursor of God's election of the Gentiles as members of the new, spiritual Israel (see

Rom. 9:1–16). The triumph of a younger son might have linked Pauline typology to Hutchinson's critique of hereditary kingship. Yet the abrupt ending of *Order and Disorder* suggests that Hutchinson's commitment to the property rights of the oldest son continues to pose an impasse within her religious and political imagination.

In the previous chapter, I described how Milton defines love against substitution in ways that put affective pressure on the form of succession that God practices in elevating his Son. Hutchinson is, in key ways, more candid than Milton in dealing with the asymmetries of Christian marriage. This is true when it comes to the burdens of reproduction and to the demand that wives regard their imperfect husbands like Christ. Hutchinson can be quite open about the way her affirmation of Christian marriage relies on half-truths or fabrications while still insisting that it is based on truth. This chapter shows how Hutchinson deploys these combinations of the true and the untrue to advance her ideals while negotiating them with her economic interests. When the fictive core of her understanding of marriage threatens to become too evident, however, Hutchinson relies on one of the basic resources offered by typological interpretation. She insists, despite clear evidence to the contrary, that the unresolved contradictions between love and substitution belong to a Jewish understanding that must be deemed outmoded and superstitious, in contrast to the truth of Christian interpretation.

All These Things Being Notoriously True

Lucy Hutchinson's avoidance of remembering her husband as Christlike becomes conspicuous toward the end of the *Memoirs*, which relates the protracted end of John Hutchinson's life. He had been a signatory to Charles I's death warrant, and his life hung in the balance in 1660 as the Convention Parliament debated whether he should be one of the exceptions to the general pardon offered by the Act of Oblivion. Lucy Hutchinson records how her husband was "ambitious of being a publick sacrifice," one whose death might appease the royalists and foster national peace.[2] Yet she reports that she, "herein only in her whole life, resolv'd to disobey him, and to emproove all the affection he had to her for his safety, and prevail'd with him to retire" (229). The hyperbolic claim that she had never before disobeyed her husband draws attention to Lucy Hutchinson's effort to undermine her husband's wish in this one instance. John Hutchinson would, in fact, go on to die as a prisoner in 1664, after being detained under suspicion of joining a rebellion. In 1664 Lucy Hutchinson is the one convinced that her husband is near death. He, by contrast, believes that God will preserve his life. Yet he resolves, "'[B]ut if I doe [die], my blood will be so innocent, I shall advance the cause more by my death, hasting the vengeance of God upon my unjust enemies, than I could doe by all the actions of my life" (264). He can still think of himself as an innocent victim—but in a different manner than he had wished to think of himself in 1660. In 1664 he does not think of himself as a sacrifice who is willing to die to bring about peace, but rather as an unwilling victim whose innocent blood will cry out for just retribution. Lucy Hutchinson's stubborn love for her husband postpones his death, and her intervention renders him less overtly or effectively Christlike in his later political martyrdom.

In materials added to the *Memoirs*, Lucy Hutchinson reveals how a Christian view of conjugal love could have tied her theology to her political critique more firmly. In an autobiographical sketch, Hutchinson begins with the lesson that what the foolish deem to be common events are in truth the workings of providence. The union of her own parents had been the result of providence working through seeming accidents. Her mother, Lucy St. John, was the third wife of Sir Allen Apsley. After Apsley's second wife died, his friends planned for him "a match of a very rich widdow" until "something in her person and behaviour" led him to demur (284). Lucy St. John, in turn, could have ended up marrying one unnamed suitor "of greater name, estate, and reputation than the rest" (284). Yet this suitor had a sudden change of heart and married another woman—"whom, when he recover'd his reason, he hated" (285). Sir Allen Apsley met Lucy St. John "accidentally" while she was staying with some relatives at the Isle of Jersey; in this household, she became a Calvinist (285). Lucy Hutchinson turns the story of her own origins into a Calvinist fairy tale, whereby inexplicable changes in heart are expressions of God's will. In this same sketch, Hutchinson suggests that marriage can secure national myths of providential origins as well as personal ones. Her father, she tells us, traced his ancestry back to "those Saxons that remain'd subjects to the Norman conqueror" whereas her mother's family descended from the conquering Normans (280). She celebrates the intermarriage of Normans and Saxons and praises the form of government that arose in the British Isles: "a mixture of monarchy, aristocratie, and democracy, with sufficient fences against the pest of every one of those formes, tiranny, faction, and confusion" (280). Hutchinson does not elaborate on the suggestion that intermarriage between the Saxons and Normans actively contributed to a mixed form of government. She does, however, contrast the situation in England with those of neighboring kingdoms, in which princes rule over their brethren "rather as slaves than subjects, and are only serv'd for feare, but not for love" (280).

The materials added to the *Memoirs* also speak to why she must sidestep the Pauline alignment of husbands with Christ. Hutchinson's prefatory note to her children warns of an excessive love that could turn the memory of their late father into an idol. To avoid this pitfall, Hutchinson presents a "naked undrest narrative, speaking the simple truth of him" (1). John Hutchinson was a singularly loving husband, and yet not excessive in his affections: "Never man had a greater passion for a woman, nor a more honourable esteeme of a wife; yet he was not uxorious" (10). The perception of uxoriousness was hardly a theoretical danger. The *Memoirs* echoes the kind of sentiment that Milton had expressed earlier in the century in writings such as *Eikonoklastes*. Hutchinson describes Charles I as having been "a most uxorious husband"; she also describes the menace that Queen Henrietta Maria had posed to the republican cause (46). When Lucy Hutchinson writes of her late husband, she must balance claims about his uniquely loving nature with a counterbalancing note of moderation.

Hutchinson's note to her children contains an artful negotiation of these divided impulses. Writing of herself in the third person, she proposes, "If he esteem'd her att a higher rate than she in her selfe could have deserv'd, he was the author of that vertue he doted on, while she only reflected his owne glories upon him; all that she was, was him, while he was here, and all that she is now at best is but his pale shade" (10). This is a reworking of a description found in the main text of the *Memoirs*. There, Hutchinson describes herself as "a very faithfull mirror, reflecting truly, though but dimmely, his owne glories upon him, so long as he was present" (32). She elaborates, "The greatest excellencee she had was the power of apprehending and the vertue of loving his. Soe, as his shaddow, she waited on him every where, till he was taken into that region of light which admitts of none, and then she vanisht into nothing. 'Twas not her face he lov'd, her honour and her vertue were his mistresses; and these (like Pigmalion's) images of his owne making" (33). These descriptions of the wife serving as a mirror or shadow of the husband have played a prominent role in scholarly discussions. N. H. Keeble, for example, offers an influential account of the distinction between the wife described as a mere shadow and "the creatively independent, defiant and opinionated narrator" whose writings preserve her husband's memories.³ For my own argument, Hutchinson's formulas of conjugal love are revealing in the way that they circumvent Pauline teaching. She is more inclined to liken her husband implicitly to a kind of Narcissus figure or explicitly to Pygmalion rather than to Christ. By appealing to various metaphors and myths to describe a loving but male-centered form of marriage, Hutchinson redirects a question that Paul leaves unanswered for Christian wives: why they should love any particular and imperfect husband as if he were like Christ. (She only presents the other half of the gendered equation—how her husband imputed or magnified virtues that might have been deficient in her own person.) Her model of conjugal love promotes a belief in her husband's unique merits while also conferring on herself some capacity to disobey when she deems it necessary—and in accordance with God's higher will.

If, however, we pursue the question of a husband's merit in his wife's eyes, we have the grounds to revisit the two particularly memorable episodes in the *Memoirs*. In both, literal acts of replacement put John Hutchinson's supposedly singular merit to the test. The first episode takes place in 1642, after Hutchinson has helped prevent Viscount Newark from seizing the stock of gunpowder at Nottingham. Upon learning of a warrant for his arrest, Hutchinson flees from Leicestershire, leaving behind his pregnant wife. Lucy Hutchinson admits having felt "something aflicted to be left alone in a strange place" (64). She finds relief when it turns out that her royalist brother is leading the nearby Cavalier forces. Yet when the royalist Captain Welch visits Lucy Hutchinson, he denounces her husband as being "so unworthy of her as to enter into any faction which should make him not dare to be seene with her" (65). In an attempt to mend her husband's reputation, she arranges for her husband's younger brother, George, to impersonate him. In response, Welch "seiz'd Mr. George by the name of Mr. John Hutchinson" (66). Even when George and Lucy Hutchinson confess the truth, Captain Welch persists in the arrest because he desired "to revenge himselfe of Mrs. Hutchinson"—even if it means punishing "an innocent gentleman" (66). This episode begins with John Hutchinson's cowardice and devolves into a farce of substitution energized by a misdirection of punishment that he is said to deserve as an unworthy husband.

The much later episode of substitution, by contrast, concerns the exact way in which Lucy Hutchinson thwarts her husband's desire to die as a martyr in 1660. She not only "prevail'd with him to retire" but went so far as to forge a letter in her husband's name and addressed it to the Speaker of the House of Commons. She describes this forged letter as helping to save her husband's life, at least for the time being. This episode has become a focus of renewed scholarly interest. Reviving earlier doubts about the truthfulness of this particular story, Derek Hirst concludes that it is more plausible that John Hutchinson had himself submitted a letter of recantation to the Convention Parliament.[4] According to this skeptical account, Lucy Hutchinson is lying to preserve her late husband's reputation as an unflinching republican hero. In response to Hirst, David Norbrook offers a meticulous reconsideration of the available evidence.[5] Norbrook concludes that it is plausible that Lucy Hutchinson did forge the letter. Yet all assessments of plausibility must rely on circumstantial evidence, as the letter in question was destroyed in a fire in 1834. The terms that both Hirst and Norbrook deploy make it very clear that our factual assessments of plausibility continue to be tangled up with value judgments about religious, gendered, and literary matters. Hirst charges that editors and scholars who accept Hutchinson's story as valid "must add arrant hypocrisy, as well as forgery, to Mrs. Hutchinson's sins."[6] Norbrook concedes that Lucy Hutchinson downplays the extent to which John Hutchinson was criticized by other republicans of betraying the cause. Yet Norbrook asks rhetorically, "Writing to inspire her children with their father's example, Lucy Hutchinson was guilty of major sins of omission. But how far did she go toward overt fabrication?"[7] Norbrook dissuades us from thinking that the devout wife, mother, and writer would have committed a more egregious sin.

Instead of adding my sense of what is and is not plausible, I want to disentangle the religious and literary logics through which Lucy Hutchinson negotiates her claimed merits and failings—as related to but also distinct from her husband's. When Hirst and Norbrook both deploy the language of sin, they appeal to Hutchinson's religious sensibilities as we imagine them. In her own self-presentation, however, she never describes her forgery as sinful. Instead, she describes it as a unique act of disobedience that displeased her husband. The distinction between a sin against God and disobedience to a husband is, I argue, an outgrowth of the vocabulary of conjugal love that she develops in the *Memoirs*. Around the issue of the forged letter, the difference between God and husband is amplified. Lucy Hutchinson attributes the clemency that her husband received in 1660 to divine will: "Yet though he very well deserv'd it, I cannot so much attribute that universall concurrence that was in the whole House to expresse esteeme of him . . . as to an over-ruling power of him that orders all men's hearts" (231). Hutchinson argues that her husband did, in truth, deserve Parliament's clemency, yet the expression of this claim as a caveat suggests a cleavage between his personal merit and divine grace. Hutchinson then breaks from her tendency of talking about herself in the third person to express her opinions in the first. She subordinates the claim that she had forged the letter to her conviction that Providence spared her husband's life. As she teaches at the outset of her autobiographical sketch, only fools attribute to accidents what are truly the expressions of God's will. All of this might merely speak to an antinomian streak in Lucy Hutchinson—at least when it comes to saving her husband's life. Yet the willingness to suspend moral rules by appealing to Providence results in a story of a wife who saves her husband, and this singular instance of wifely disobedience undermines the alignment of husband and Christ.

At the same time, this episode of righteous fraudulence confirms the relevance of romance for the mode of writing that Lucy Hutchinson develops to remember her husband as a republican hero. Hirst asserts that "Mrs. Hutchinson constructed a romance out of her husband's life," and it is clear that this assessment is a critical one.[8] Erin Murphy subsequently reminds us that the *Memoirs* does openly register the relevance of romance in propping up John Hutchinson's worth—but only to disavow it quickly as a royalist mode of writing. Lucy Hutchinson recounts how, in January 1645, her husband, faced with royalist plots and cowardice in his own ranks, still routed the forces led by the Sir Charles Lucas. She then observes, "If it were a Romance, wee should say after the successe that the Heroes did it out of excesse of gallantry, that they might better signalize their vallour upon a foe who was not vanquisht to their hands by the inclemency of the season; but while wee are relating wonders of Providence wee must record this as such a one as is not to be conceived from a relation, in the admirable mercy that it brought forth" (114). As Murphy remarks, this comment reveals how Hutchinson "does not merely reject romance as a royalist mode of telling history, she reclaims it by recasting it in another genre."⁹ The way Hutchinson appropriates the resources of romance in the *Memoirs* establishes the terms in which she would, in *Order and Disorder*, celebrate the pious fraud of Jacob in deceiving his father, Isaac. Following Murphy's insightful reading, I want to pay closer attention to the exact mechanism of disavowal that Hutchinson deploys. By disassociating her own writing from the corrupt, royalist genre of romance and by appealing to the true workings of Providence instead, Hutchinson enhances the impression that she is telling the truth of her husband's comportment—not by offering any additional evidence but rather through a knowing reference to a genre that she dismisses as politically suspect.

The strategy of borrowing from romance while disavowing it intensifies toward the very end of the *Memoirs*, as John Hutchinson's life hangs in the balance. At one point, Lucy Hutchinson intrudes on her own narrative, remarking, "I cannot here omitt one story, though not altogether so much of the Collonell's concerne" (242). This tangent concerns a noncomformist preacher named Palmer being imprisoned under the order of John Toplady, mayor of Nottingham, who "had formerly bene a Parliament Officer but was now a Renegado" (242). The preacher gathers increasing attention when he refuses to be silent in prison. Hutchinson attests, "I heard [on] oath, to the Councell, that a thousand of the country came in armed to the Towne, and marcht to the prison window to heare the prisoner preach" (243). In response to such reports, troops are prepared to be sent into Nottingham. Confusingly, however, Hutchinson adds that "one who had a relation to the Towne being then at Court, and knowing this to be false, certified to the contrary and prevented the Troope" (243). It becomes unclear what the truth concerning the noncomformist minister is, and which source of information is reliable. Instead of adjudicating these matters, however, Hutchinson wraps up this episode with a wild story of her own: Mayor Toplady began vomiting blood until he "languisht for a few months and died" (243). Hutchinson illustrates the violent retribution that renegades against the cause of religious freedom will experience. Simply by inviting the discerning reader to consider the slippage between truth and falsehood, she tries to foster the impression that her story of divine justice is true even if it sounds fabulous.

When the narrative returns to the central matter of John Hutchinson's fate, the strategy of disavowing romance gives way to a practical justification of subterfuge. Lucy Hutchinson describes how both she and her husband deploy a number of underhanded tactics as they deal with the royalists who persecute them. During John Hutchinson's final imprisonment, Lieutenant Robinson demands monetary payment for Hutchinson's family to visit him. Negotiations ensue, but before a deal is reached, the eldest son sneaks in to tell his father that Robinson has been spreading malicious lies about him. The implication is that royalist malice justifies the Hutchinsons' own dubious actions. John Hutchinson blackmails Robinson by threatening to expose his embezzlement of money from those under his charge. Lucy Hutchinson observes, "All these things being notoriously true, this letter put [Robinson] into a greate rage" (259). John Hutchinson's blackmail does not work exactly as intended. Instead of waiving the demand for a bribe to let the Hutchinsons visit the Colonel, Robinson begrudgingly gives back some of his embezzled funds. Yet this leads to an unexpected form of esteem for John Hutchinson: "the soldiers, understanding that Collonell Hutchinson's observations of his frawd had procur'd them this satisfaction, us'd to give him thankes" (259).

The Hutchinsons have jointly brought their understandings of truth and justifiable fraud full circle. Previously, Lucy Hutchinson enhanced her claims about the accuracy of her husband's reported merit by contrasting her narration to the distortions of romance. Now, however, she celebrates her husband's ability to turn the "notorious truth" of royalist wickedness into the grounds of his own commendable act of blackmail. Casting her own morally questionable work as an expression of divine will, she is able to engage in various forms of dishonesty while still insisting that the royalist forms of distortion are the truly unacceptable ones. Her multiple roles—allegedly forging a letter to save her husband's life and writing to defend his posthumous reputation—belie her claim to having served as a passive mirror for John Hutchinson's virtues. Instead, she actively deflates her husband's normatively Christlike status in the process of affirming the republican virtues that he supposedly possessed.

The Work of a Lifesaving Wife

In the *Memoirs*, the two memorable episodes of substitution—the first involving George Hutchinson's arrest, the second involving Lucy Hutchinson's forged letter—raise questions about John Hutchinson's merit both as an older brother and as a husband. In between these episodes, contestations over John Hutchinson's public merits take up the bulk of the text. At stake are Hutchinson's claim to being the governor of Nottingham, his status as a military leader in the face of insubordination within his ranks, and his commitment to republicanism and religious freedom as a Member of Parliament. These challenges require John Hutchinson to exhibit various combinations of personal virtue and external, official sanction. They also provide opportunities to show that he deserves the higher position that he enjoys regarding his younger brother. At one point in the narrative, John Hutchinson travels from Nottingham to seek clarification from the Committee of Safety. George Hutchinson is asked to take his brother's place, but he ends up proving far less effective as a leader. John Hutchinson, according to his wife, had "a certeine spiritt of Government, in an exterordinary manner which was not given to others," so that "the Garrison was much disorder'd by his absence" (155–56). Lucy Hutchinson appeals to her husband's je ne sais quoi to distinguish him from George, who tried his best to lead, "but in a different way from his brother" (156). This episode presents the reader with one long overdue corrective to the earlier story of John Hutchinson's cowardice and desertion.

Later in this chapter, I will detail how the question of the younger and older brothers' respective merits is not just a practical matter for Lucy Hutchison but also a theological one. Here, it is sufficient to note that the question of John Hutchinson as a worthy older brother coexists with questions about his worth as a husband—and in a way that shuttles us from domestic concerns to public affairs. The connection between familial and political matters becomes especially evident when Lucy Hutchinson presents a series of corrupt men within the army ranks who should, as foils, reveal her husband to be virtuous by way of contrast. Much later, these same men emerge as full-blown conspirators against John Hutchinson. Within the early preview, the first two villains mentioned—Sir John Gell and Charles White—exemplify how husbandly failings go hand in hand with political corruption. Hutchinson accuses Gell of "being a fowle adulterer" who only switched to the parliamentary side out of self-interest (67). White, in turn, was "a man who was of meane birth and low fortunes" who grew up to be "addicted to many lusts, especially to that of woemen." Hutchinson adds that "God, to shame him, gave him up to marrie a wench out of one of the Ale-houses he frequented" (69).[10]

The latter two conspirators in this list—Huntingdon Plumtre and James Chadwick—exemplify more complicated configurations of private and public corruption. When Lucy Hutchinson denounces Chadwick as the final villain in the sequence, she takes the condemnation of his class climbing to rhetorical extremes: "Never was a truer Judas since Iscariott's time than he, for he would kisse the man he had in his heart to kill" (72). The remark seems to set up a comparison of John Hutchinson and Jesus at their respective moments of betrayal. Yet Lucy Hutchinson eventually puts a twist on the comparison that she leads the reader to expect. Later, she describes how General Fairfax commissions her husband to raise a regiment of twelve hundred men. Chadwick is supposed to carry messages between Fairfax and Nottingham, but he takes this opportunity quietly to procure for "himselfe a Commission for a Regiment, and a joynt commission for himselfe and Collonell Pierrepont to be Governors of the Towne and Castle" (105). Chadwick, in his attempt to muster troops for himself, "cheated the country of pay for I know not how many hundred men: for which, if he had not stollen away in the night, he had bene ston'd, and as his wife passed through the townes, she was in danger of her life" (105). The sudden mention of Chadwick's wife leads us to realize that he does not function in Hutchinson's narrative simply as a Judas-like betrayer. He is instead a useful contrast to John Hutchinson insofar as he proves to be a bad husband, one whose corrupt dealings have ended up jeopardizing the safety of his wife. Even if we remember that John Hutchinson had also acted in a cowardly fashion by deserting his wife, we are led to feel that Chadwick is publicly and privately corrupt in a way that Hutchinson had never been.

We finally learn in what sense Chadwick does prove to be Judas-like when Lucy Hutchinson relates how, in September 1644, he was motivated by his own conscience to hand over to George Hutchinson documents revealing the conspiracy to discredit his brother's authority (see 141–42). Yet Chadwick ends up resembling Judas less emphatically than the reader was originally led to expect. Chadwick has come to repent before rather than after his betrayal has fatal consequences. The conclusion to Chadwick's treacherous plot allows Lucy Hutchinson to negotiate once again the virtues of the older and younger Hutchinson brothers. George Hutchinson again proves himself to be capable and reliable. At the same time, by helping to expose Chadwick's Judas-like betrayal before it can take effect, George Hutchinson short-circuits a more straightforward alignment of his older brother with Christ in unjust victimhood.

The third future conspirator in Lucy Hutchinson's early list is the most revealingly ambivalent figure. Hutchinson labels Huntingdon Plumtre a "horrible Atheist," yet she qualifies this condemnation with praise of his skill as a physician (70–71). Plumtre had, it turns out, made an unnamed appearance in the account of John Hutchinson's earlier years. He had cured the younger brother George Hutchinson of "an Epileptick disease" that had frustrated "the skill of the best Doctors in England" (71). Even though Plumtre's moral failings cast a pall over his talents, "Mr. Hutchinson and his brother, in pitty to him, and remembrance of what God had done by him, still own'd him, and protected him . . . though it was impossible for his darkness and their light long to continue mix'd" (71). John Hutchinson's indebtedness to an atheist amplifies the question of his merit regarding his brother: his inability to save his younger brother's life in any direct way contrasts with the ways in which George Hutchinson would go on to defend him. Yet the challenge that Plumtre embodies does not only concern the greater worth of the older brother. I argue that Plumtre's moral threat also concerns John Hutchinson's relationship to his wife, even though Plumtre is the only one of the four conspirators who is not accused of any sexual impropriety. In chapter 3, I argued that William Davenant exposes the fictional kernel of Pauline marriage by contrasting the practical skill of medicine with a religious belief in the resurrection. Lucy Hutchinson intuits similar possibilities of a worldview in which literal lifesaving has more of an affective purchase than the promise of salvation. For Lucy Hutchinson, physical lifesaving must not pose a viable challenge to Christian salvation, and the temporary relationship between the Hutchinsons and Plumtre (between light and dark) must be sundered.[11]

For this very reason, however, Plumtree serves as a wicked contrast or moral foil for Lucy Hutchinson herself. As we have seen, Hutchinson goes on to describe how she preserved her husband's life at the expense of his desire to die as a public sacrifice. She achieves this preservation of life through forgery rather than through medicine. Yet earlier, she recounts how, in September 1643, she (in her capacity as the governor's wife in Nottingham) had stepped in to practice medicine "for want of another Surgeon" (99). She reports having applied "some excellent balsoms and plaisters in her closett, with the assistance of a gentleman that had some skill." She implies that she was, provisionally, a surgeon in her own right, whereas the skillful gentleman serves as her assistant. Having had "such good successe," she managed to save all five in her charge (99).

Plumtre is not just a morally corrupt but capable physician. He is dangerous because he leverages both practical learning and literary artistry against a belief in God. In the earlier section of the *Memoirs*, Lucy Hutchinson describes him as "a young phisitian, who was a good schollar and had a great deale of witt, but withall a profest atheist" (26). Plumtre is one of the charming men in John Hutchinson's social circle during his time in London, yet "through the grace of God," they "had not power to infect him, who, like a bee, suckt a great deal of honie from these bitter flowers" (26). Lucy Hutchinson does not mention that Plumtre was a poet who had published a volume of Latin epigrams in 1629. It was through the discourse of poetry that Hutchinson herself had grappled with a materialist worldview and its atheistical inclinations. She had produced what was likely the first English translation of Lucretius's *De rerum natura*, undertaken at some point between the mid-1640s and the late 1650s.[12] When she describes her husband as having been like a bee sucking honey from a bitter flower, she may be revisiting a simile that Lucretius deploys twice. In the opening book and again in book 4, Lucretius compares his work of communicating Epicurean philosophy in verse to that of a physician putting honey around a cup of wormwood to entice a patient into taking bitter medicine.[13] Hutchinson would eventually conclude that the wormwood of Lucretian atheism was harmful rather than medicinal. In the preface to her biblical epic *Order and Disorder*, she criticizes her earlier labor, deeming "it to be a very unsafe and unprofitable thing for those that are young . . . to exercise themselves in the study of vain, foolish, atheistical poesy."[14] According to the *Memoirs*, the younger John Hutchinson had been immune—naturally, by way of the grace of God—to the dangers posed by Plumtre. By contrast, Lucy Hutchinson had worked through the intertwined threats of poetry, science, and atheism much more consciously—and, by her own account, with greater risk to her Christian beliefs and morals.

By the time Lucy Hutchinson was composing the *Memoirs*, atheism does not seem to have posed a serious threat to her worldview. Yet the portrayal of Plumtre emphasizes how the appeal of literal lifesaving still challenges the calibration of individual merit and Christian love that Lucy Hutchinson attempts as she remembers her husband—without reference to the Pauline alignment of husbands with Christ. All of this comes to a head when she goes on to thwart her husband's wishes to die as a Christlike martyr because she values his mortal existence. She insists on her fixed love for her husband by keeping him alive. She is a lifesaving (or, at least, life-preserving) wife, but what this means for John Hutchinson's supposed merits as a Christian husband and as a republican leader needs to be negotiated. The ambivalent presentation of Plumtre earlier in the *Memoirs* suggests the extent to which Lucy Hutchinson takes on the threat of morally transgressive behavior while shaping her husband's legacy, both during his life and after his death.

Love and Property

There are moments in the *Memoirs* in which Lucy Hutchinson's views about marriage coincide squarely with her critique of the Stuart monarchy.[15] Yet criticism of Charles is not a sustained topic in this text. By the time Lucy Hutchinson was composing the *Memoirs*, she (like Milton) would have realized that mocking Charles I as an uxorious husband had not been effective in dislodging the public sentiment that he had died as a Christlike martyr. Hutchinson's primary targets are, instead, those within Parliament and the army who betrayed the cause. The narration of events following the Battle of Naseby in June 1645 reveal clearly how the danger of uxoriousness is not just a royalist problem but also a republican one. Hutchinson relates that General Fairfax and his wife visited Nottingham. Within the span of a single sentence, Hutchinson turns Anne Fairfax from a potential ally into an enemy of religious liberty.[16] Lady Fairfax "was exceeding kind to her husband's Chaplaines, Independent Ministers, till the Armie return'd to lie neerer London; and then the Presbiterian Ministers quite chang'd the lady into such a bitter aversion against them that they could not endure to come into the Generall's presence while she was there, and the Generall had an unquietst, unpleasant life with her" (168). These estranged independent chaplains receive support from John Hutchinson. Yet "Lady Fairfax caress'd with so much kindnesse" one "bitter Presbiterian" minister and his brethren that they felt emboldened to complain to Hutchinson directly about the toleration of nonconformism in Nottingham (168).

In this instance, the Hutchinsons can present themselves as a godly counterexample to Anne Fairfax's undue influence over her husband.

When "some notes ... concerning Pedobaptisme" are discovered in Nottingham, they become a matter of heated contention for the Presbyterians (169). In a response befitting a Protestant leader, John Hutchinson "searcht the Scriptures alone" to reconsider the question of child baptism (169). The word "alone" redirects an appeal to *sola scriptura* toward a contrast between reading in isolation versus reading within godly marriage: when Lucy Hutchinson joins her husband, she turns the reading of scriptures alone into a shared enterprise. After careful study, the Hutchinsons jointly declare "themselves unsatisfied in the practise" of infant baptism (169). Because, however, they do not go further in denouncing child baptism, they are branded as anabaptists and zealots by the angered Presbyterians. Lucy Hutchinson implies that she and her husband were willing to wear these inaccurate labels as badges of their commitment to freedom of conscience.

Yet Fairfax's concessions to his wife eventually have consequences that are harder to correct with supposedly godlier behavior. For much of the *Memoirs*, Fairfax is a sympathetic figure who supports John Hutchinson. Yet as Lucy Hutchinson narrates the rise of Oliver Cromwell, she again blames Anne Fairfax's undue influence over her husband. Initially, the issue seems to be the contested matter of John Hutchinson's becoming the governor of the Isle of Jersey. Rather than affirming Hutchinson's new position, Fairfax, "perswaded by his wife and her Presbyterian Chaplains, threw up his Commission at such a time when it could not have been bene more spitefully and ruinously to the whole Parliament interest" (195). It turns out that the ambiguous phrase "his Commission" is shuttling us quickly from the question of Hutchinson's governorship to that of Fairfax's own commission as general. Lucy Hutchinson blends the contestation over her husband's governorship with the more momentous matter of Fairfax's resignation in 1650. She clarifies that "this greate man" Fairfax "was then as unmooveable by his friends as pertinacious in obeying his wife; whereby he then died to all his former glory" (195).

In this decisive instance of a wife's excessive influence, the Hutchinsons cannot provide a clearly superior counterexample. Much of John Hutchinson's story during the Protectorate and after the Restoration consists of swings between active public service and domestic retirement. When, in April 1653, Cromwell disbands the Rump Parliament, John Hutchinson retreats to his familial estate, Owthorpe, and enjoys the "innocent recreations" of domesticity "during Oliver's mutable reigne" (207). Lucy

Hutchinson's qualification that his household, in return, loved him "with such a feare and reverence as restrein'd all rude familiarity" strikes a defensive note against her husband's diminished status in domestic retreat (208). Later, in October 1659, when Colonel Lambert disbands the Rump Parliament, John Hutchinson severs himself from all but the most basic political obligations and "stay'd att home, and busied himself in his own domestick employments" (216).[17] Hutchinson's final retreat into domesticity in 1660 proves entirely involuntary—brought about not just by exigencies but also by the machinations of his wife and her forged letter. By the end of the *Memoirs*, it remains unclear how fully Lucy Hutchinson can disassociate her husband from uxoriousness and its public consequences.

The greatest contrast to John Hutchinson's virtue as a republican hero does not, however, lie in Thomas Fairfax but in Oliver Cromwell. In Lucy Hutchinson's presentation, Cromwell embodies a different imbalance between domestic concerns and public ones than Thomas Fairfax or even Charles I does. Whereas those men are excessively swayed by their wives, Cromwell seems to treat marriage as an instrument of power. One exception to Cromwell's indifference to love ends up affirming the rule. After describing Cromwell as having gotten rid of his "triumvirs" (Major General Harrison and Lambert), Lucy Hutchinson blames his family for unworthily inflaming his political ambitions: "His wife and children were setting up for principallity, which suited no better with any of them than scarlett on the Ape; only, to speak the truth of himselfe, he had much naturall greatnesse in him, and well became the place he had usurp'd" (208–9). At this particular moment, Cromwell's excessive ambition is of a piece with his susceptibility to his wife's influence. Yet Hutchinson goes on reinforce how Cromwell is generally indifferent to personal love and views marriage as a vehicle of his ambition. She describes him as having exercised "arbitrary power" not only by sending out his major-generals across England, but also by matching his daughters to various lords in an effort to render them "pittifull slaves" (209). At the same time, Cromwell continued to delude followers like Lambert "with hopes and promises of succession" (209).

Within this configuration of family, marriage, and excessive ambition, Hutchinson's ambivalence intensifies around the matter of Richard Cromwell's succeeding his father to become Lord Protector. Hutchinson tends to downplay one of Oliver Cromwell's potentially gravest violations of republican values—his apparent choice of a hereditary successor to the title of Lord Protector. She memorably describes Richard Cromwell as "a peasant in his nature, yet gentle and virtuous," a son who "became not greatnesse" (209). She presents Oliver Cromwell's ambition as inimical to republicanism and to love while, at the same time, qualifying Richard Cromwell's failings by referring to him as virtuous but incapable and lowly in nature. The qualified critique of Richard Cromwell is partly the result of personal loyalty. The *Memoirs* describes the younger Cromwell encouraging John Hutchinson to reemerge into public life as sheriff of Nottinghamshire. Yet Lucy Hutchinson's qualifications about Richard Cromwell are not only a matter of gratitude. The note of ambivalence results, I argue, from Hutchinson's attempt to balance her commitments to republican merit and to individual conscience with her economic interests—which include a defense of primogeniture and of class hierarchy. She turns Richard Cromwell's inability to live up to the role of Lord Protector into an occasion for her to express a particular version of class prejudice. Even if he was "gentle and virtuous," Richard Cromwell was "a peasant in his nature" rather than an innate leader. She may have in mind Richard's lack of military experience, which distinguishes him both from his father (whose great successes led to excessive ambition) and from John Hutchinson, who supposedly remained principled as a leader.[18] The divided judgment of Richard Cromwell's character speaks to the ambivalent role that he occupies in Hutchinson's imagination. She needs to find a way to blame Oliver Cromwell for turning a position of leadership—rather than familial property—into an inheritance. Richard Cromwell is a victim of his father's failure to uphold this distinction; Richard may have proven gentle and virtuous enough rather than manifesting his peasant nature had he inherited his father's property and not his high political office.

Lucy Hutchinson's critique of succession needs to be roundabout in a text that affirms the property rights of John Hutchinson as the eldest surviving son of Thomas Hutchinson and his first wife. John Hutchinson did succeed his father as MP for Nottinghamshire, but Lucy Hutchinson promotes this as a desirable alignment of birthright and publicly acknowledged merit. John Hutchinson's ardent republicanism differentiates him from his father. Political character is not necessarily passed on from a father to the eldest son, but property, in Lucy Hutchinson's view, should be. Questions of remarriage and inheritance dominate the early account of John Hutchinson's upbringing. Thomas Hutchinson remarries after his wife's death, and this second marriage generates practical problems. John Hutchinson eventually realizes "that his father's second love and marriage to a person of such quality, as requir'd settlement for her sonne, must needes to be a lessening to his expectation" (24). Later, we learn that Thomas Hutchinson, upon his death in 1643, bequeathed "all his personall estate and all that was unsettled at Mr. Hutchinson's marriage to his second wife and her children; at which his two sons [John and George] had not the least repining thought, but out of tender love, were very much afflicted for his loss" (90). Lucy Hutchinson insists that her husband did not receive his full due, but that he still loved his father nonetheless. This claim about filial piety (which John shares with the younger George) is of a piece with her repeated insistence that her husband had never sought personal gain during his loyal service as a colonel, governor, and MP.

None of this prevents the Hutchinsons from being acutely concerned with financial matters. By the end of the *Memoirs*, economic accounting intensifies as Lucy Hutchinson details the losses that the family incurred and the charges that the royalists exacted as they imprisoned her husband. She can be so open about her calculations because she has described how far she has gone to uphold the singular identity of her husband. The stubbornness of her love makes it acceptable for her to worry openly about how the life of her husband becomes a financial burden. As Hutchinson describes how she helped to prolong her husband's life in 1660, she recalls that friends had urged him to surrender himself so that his estates might not be jeopardized. She, however, "would not yet consent the Collonell should give himself into custody, and she had wrought him to a strong engagement that he would not dispose of himselfe without her" (229). This refusal to trade her husband's well-being for the sake of property immediately precedes her decision to forge the letter in her husband's name.[19]

Despite her commitment to conscience and freedom of belief, Hutchinson repeatedly affirms intergenerational transfers of wealth. There is no absolute contradiction between a republican commitment to individual merit and a belief in primogeniture. Yet tensions between these commitments surface in the *Memoirs*. At one point, Hutchinson describes her husband as having been a Gideon-like leader in Nottingham, where the majority of the residents are either tepid during the early stages of the civil wars or actively in opposition to the parliamentary side. John Hutchinson faces opposition even from "the godly themselves, who thought it scarce possible for any one to continue a gentleman and firme to a godly interest"

(89). Rather than working through the conflict between an affirmation of individual conscience, on the one hand, and a belief in inborn class distinctions, on the other, Lucy Hutchinson flatly defends her husband against what she judges to be unjustified class resentment. Later, this same ideological conflict becomes even more pronounced when she explicitly decries those "who endeavour'd the levelling of all estates and quallities" (179). She believes Levellers to be extremists, and declares herself and her husband allied only with the "sober levellers" who were "never guilty of desiring" the eradication of all class hierarchies (179). Her limited sense of egalitarianism applies to religious beliefs, not to inherited property (or to the belief that inborn class privilege is linked to a higher chance of possessing true virtue). This is the republican middle ground that she stakes out through the example of her husband. The affirmation of John Hutchinson's merit as an older brother, husband, and public leader—even in the face of evidence to the contrary—stands in for a more methodical justification of Lucy Hutchinson's particular form of godly republicanism.

Hutchinson's Turtledove

Lucy Hutchinson's description of the wife serving as a mirror for her husband has served as a point of departure for discussions not only of the *Memoirs* but also of her poetry. In the course of introducing Hutchinson's *Elegies*, Norbrook revisits the mirror simile from the *Memoirs* to argue that it is of a piece with the "Christianized version of neoplatonic imagery" that she develops more thoroughly in her poetry.[20] Hutchinson, in Norbrook's estimation, strives to offset both a suspicion of mimesis and the subordinate status of the wife-as-mirror by showing that conjugal love can function as a form of reflection that accommodates an ascent toward the higher truth. Yet Jonathan Goldberg contends that the problems associated with the image and the shadow in Hutchinson's imagination may not be exclusively or even primarily Platonic, but materialist by way of Lucretius.[21] Goldberg revisits the mirror simile to argue that Hutchinson writes of her husband's death and her resulting vanishing into nothingness to advance a materialist poetics, rather than a Christian Neoplatonic view. Only the material act of writing—the physical existence of the *Memoirs*—can preserve the otherwise insubstantial memory of John Hutchinson.

In the terms of my argument, Lucretian materialism poses a distinctive challenge to fixed conjugal love, especially when that love persists after the death of a spouse. When Lucy Hutchinson had, in the 1640s and 1650s, undertaken the task of translating Lucretius's *De rerum natura*, she had avoided the poem's most direct challenge to the fixity of love. Hutchinson refused to translate sections from the fourth book treating erotic desire and sex. Her own marginal note explains, "*The cause and effects of Love which* [Lucretius] *makes a kind of dreame but much here was left out for a midwife to translate whose obsceane art it would better become then a nicer pen.*"[22] Hutchinson's avoidance of lines that are sexually explicit is of a piece with her disapproval of Lucretius's claim that love is merely a dream. Lucretius describes intercourse in detail because he deems it the natural, generative resolution to frustrated desire. *De rerum natura* opens with an invocation to Venus and, in the fourth book, Lucretius explains that erotic desire is the expression of that goddess.[23] Desire only produces wayward effects when it is estranged from consummation: "For if what you love is absent, yet its images are there, and the sweet name sounds in your ears. But it is fitting to flee from images (*simulacra*), to scare away what feeds love, to turn the mind in other directions. . . . nor to cherish care and certain pain for yourself."[24] Insofar as *De rerum natura* still reverberates in Lucy Hutchinson's later imagination, this kind of teaching would deem the fixed love for a deceased husband as a delusional yearning for what no longer exists.

De rerum natura issues an even more basic challenge to the love of an object perceived as singular. Lucretius is willing to voice the idea that something in the world could be absolutely unique, but only as a concession for a thought experiment:

> Sed tamen id quoque uti concedam, quamlubet esto
> unica res quaedam nativo corpore sola,
> cui similis toto terrarium non sit in orbi.[25]
> (But I would grant even this: let there be, as it pleases you, innate to a
>   body something unique and singular, similar to nothing else in the
>   whole world.)

This concession serves to prove the necessity of an infinite number of atomistic particles in the universe. Only an infinite number, Lucretius argues, could produce accidental configurations that are unique—but unique only as temporary arrangements. Lucretius teaches that, ultimately, meaningful degrees of fixity in a world of flux are not exhibited by singular things or persons but rather by species and genera. Even though Lucretius believes in an infinite number of atomistic particles, he believes that the types of particles are limited: "every kind is produced from fixed seeds."[26] This view underlies Lucretius's affirmation of love when it is aligned with procreation—which perpetuates the species—and his critique of frustrated desire as an unproductive error.[27] In this view, the stubbornly fixed love for an individual person—not to mention after that person's death—is susceptible to the charge of error.

In *Order and Disorder*, Hutchinson attempts to show how Christian belief can withstand the atheistical impulses of Lucretian materialism. The opening canto follows *Paradise Lost* in importing an uncreated realm of material chaos into the Genesis narrative. Hutchinson's own arrangement of philosophical and scriptural thinking emphasizes that any sense of material separation from God is temporary.[28] When it comes to the unique identity of persons, the only distinctiveness that will exist for all of eternity is located within the Trinity:

> Distinguished, not divided, so that what
> One person is, the other is not that. (1.87–88)

The three persons of the Godhead work together,

> yet so as every one
> In a peculiar matter suited to
> His person doth the common action do. (1.106–8)

When the opening of *Order and Disorder* accounts for the temporary nature of any distinct material identity apart from God, it does not necessarily question the fixed love between two mortal individuals but rather asks about the poet's artistic ambitions. Hutchinson's own arrangement of words will enjoy some limited distinctiveness until whatever truth it contains is assimilated into the divine word, with any untruths purged away by fire.

At the end of the first canto, however, Hutchinson begins to lay the groundwork for investigating the origins and the postlapsarian realities of faithful love. As she narrates the story of creation, she describes the Spirit of God moving on the deep,

> Brooding the creatures under wings of love,
> As tender birds hatched by a turtle-dove. (1.307–8)

In the *Divine Weeks* (completely translated into English by Joshua Sylvester by 1604), Guillaume du Bartas describes the Spirit "as a Henne that faine would hatch a brood."²⁹ In *Paradise Lost*, Milton turns this imagery into a site of typological reinterpretation: the Spirit "Dovelike satst brooding on the vast abyss," in a way that anticipates the gospel accounts of the Spirit descending like a dove on the scene of Jesus's baptism (1.21). Yet unlike either du Bartas or Milton, Hutchinson likens the Spirit specifically to a turtledove, the bird conventionally associated with lifelong fidelity. *Paradise Lost* contains no mention of the turtledove. Du Bartas invokes the turtledove much later in the narrative to contrast the goodness of creation with the wickedness of fallen humanity:

> O can ye see with vn-relenting eyes,
> The Turtle Dove, sith when her husband dies
> Dies all her ioy; for neuer loves she more.³⁰

Du Bartas explicitly chastens sinful readers who hate their spouses and long for the deaths that would allow them to remarry. This lesson would have had a particular resonance for Hutchinson, who had described herself as a shadow (or nothing) after the death of her husband and would never go on to remarry. In *Order and Disorder*, Hutchinson's comparison of the Spirit to a turtledove locates a fidelity more powerful than death as a principle expressed in the divine act of creation.

This teaching is initially offered as a mere simile rather than as a truth claim. In the second canto, Hutchinson goes on to list some of the actual birds that God has created and then invites us to interpret them as exemplars of love. Instead of referring to turtledoves again, she instructs us to consider the "[c]onjugal kindness of the pairèd swans" (2.297). In book 8, however, turtledoves are the very first birds to emerge from Noah's ark to find a world in the first stages of renewal after the Flood:

> Again the gentle amorous turtle-doves
> Single their mates in solitary groves. (8.207–8)

Turtledoves reemerge to promise a renewed synthesis of divine creativity, the physical world, and human meaning—all under the principle of loving fidelity. These turtledoves "[s]ingle their mates" to manifest their natural and God-given inclination toward what humans experience as strict monogamy. Hutchinson, however, repeatedly uses the subjunctive to describe the lessons that birds like turtledoves might offer us. She signals a disjunction between God's creation and the usefulness of our interpretations of the world. Even if the divine word has created turtledoves, it remains unclear if the comparison of God's creative Spirit to the turtledove is more than a human fabrication. Or, in other words, even if turtledoves reveal that lifelong fidelity is a natural principle reflecting something about divine creation, that principle may still not pertain directly to human experience. This is not a theoretical or idle concern, as Hutchinson will go on to recount multiple stories of polygamy, concubinage, and remarriage found in Genesis.

A meditation concerning the natural world, language, and human experience frames Hutchinson's inquiry into the origins of love. Hutchinson introduces the fifth day of creation—when birds are created with sea animals—with an elaborate conceit likening the sun to "a fresh bridegroom" who rises "to greet his virgin bride" (2.215–17). Yet this simile cannot commemorate a joyous union, both because "no living creatures" exist to witness the sun's splendor and also because the sun never occupies the same space as the moon, "night's pale queen," who grows "sick to shine where she could not be seen" (2.224, 2.239–40). Hutchinson turns nature into the site of a royal epithalamion only to foster a Petrarchan sense of frustrated desire.[31] All of this sets the stage for marriage to become the focal point of the narrative in canto 3. Hutchinson establishes a context in which the union of Adam and Eve will promise to harmonize physical reality with a higher meaning, without lapsing into the kind of disappointment that has been projected onto the sun and the moon.

Such harmonization, if it is to result in an effective Christian rebuttal of Lucretian thinking, requires not only love but also reproduction. The centrality of reproduction leads Hutchinson to challenge the precedent of *Paradise Lost* quite openly. "Whether [Adam] begged a mate it is not known," Hutchinson reminds us, hewing more closely to the letter of Genesis than Milton had in narrating Adam's acute loneliness (3.312). Hutchinson does concede, "Likely his want might send him to the spring" of his own creation, but she elaborates on how Adam's solitude could not have been "a natural, nor a moral ill" because he was in a state of perfection (3.313–19). All of this anticipates Hutchinson's sharpest break from Milton's view of companionate marriage. She concludes that Adam required a wife not to remedy any spiritual deficiency but rather for the sake of reproduction. Yet Hutchinson bypasses the command to fill the earth found in Genesis and—blurring the lines between pre- and postlapsarian realities— looks ahead to the existence of the church. If Adam had not received a reproductive partner, Hutchinson explains,

> The Church, fruit of this union, had not come
> To light, but perished, stifled in the womb. (3.331–32)

Merely populating the earth is not the rationale for the original marriage. Hutchinson looks ahead past the Fall to ask her Christian readers to be grateful that Eve was created so that they could eventually be born as members of the redeemed church. After narrating the creation of Eve and her union with Adam, Hutchinson expands on this earlier suggestion. She links the marriage of Adam and Eve to the marriage of Christ, the second Adam, to his church:

> So from the second Adam's bleeding side
> God formed the Gospel Church, his mystic bride. (3.467–68)

Yet in Hutchinson's poem as in Pauline teaching, the redefinition of Adamic marriage generates practical questions about Christian marriage. Whereas Adam has an obvious, organic reason to join with Eve as his wife, it still remains unclear why any individual Christian husband or would-be husband should love one particular woman in the way that Christ loves the church.[32] Hutchinson goes on to confront this affective problem—and what it means for Christian wives—directly. In canto 5, the twofold curse placed on Eve (submission to her husband and pain in childbirth) occasions a meditation on why any woman would willingly agree to marry any man. Even marriage to a relatively good husband amounts to "golden fetters, soft-lined yokes" that are "curbs of liberty"; marriage to "an unmanly, fickle, froward fool" is obviously far worse (5.141–46). Yet the virtues of a particular husband seem irrelevant when it comes to the pain of childbirth and the difficulties of motherhood, which are, Hutchinson laments, "[u]nrecompensed with love and gratitude" (5.168). To attempt a viable answer to the question of why Christian women should marry, Hutchinson revisits her conflation of physical reproduction and typological thinking. All mothers suffer from Eve's curse, but they can also identify with her in receiving

> a promise that thereby she shall
> Recover all the hurt, of her first fall
> When, in mysterious manner, from her womb
> Her father, brother, husband, son shall come. (5.225–28)

Hutchinson calls for a conflation of past and present, in a way that calls Christian women to align their experiences with a pre-Christian past. Without this imaginative regression, she can offer Christian wives no binding reason to reproduce, as the birth of Christ is an event in the distant past rather than in the promised future. In the previous chapter, I discussed how Milton's promotion of companionate marriage silently affirms the mandates of reproductive futurity as embedded in the *protoevangelium*. Hutchinson is far more attuned than Milton to the gendered asymmetries involved in reproduction and marriage. Yet she, too, relies on a typological inversion to assert (even more explicitly than Milton) that Christian women should embrace their conjugal and maternal destinies as if they were like Eve.[33]

Hutchinson goes on to refine her interpretation of the Pauline alignment of husband and Christ. Whereas she had, in canto 3, celebrated Adam and Eve's original union as the source of the church, in canto 5 she asks any would-be mother to imagine that her "father, brother, husband, son" will emerge from her womb. A fictive anticipation of Christ's birth as a future event has been replaced by a combination of fact and fiction concerning intergenerational replacement. Hutchinson directs a woman to imagine the birth of her son not only as the birth of God's Son but also now as the birth of her other male relatives, including her own father. Hutchinson admits that this kind of motivation can only function "in mysterious manner." Whereas for Paul, the mystery of marriage concerns the untruth of a husband's Christlikeness, Hutchinson teaches that the mystery lies in a rationale for reproduction oscillating between a forward-looking faith in

Christ and the need to perpetuate the family by generating replacements. After announcing this mystery, Hutchinson switches topics from the reasons a woman might agree to bear children back to the question of why she would consent to marry. Hutchinson proposes that "[s]ubjection to the husband's rule" is rendered tolerable because "that yoke with love is lined" (5.229–30). The alignment of husband and Christ does register here insofar as the yoke of marriage is reminiscent of the light and easy yoke that Christ places on his disciples (see Matt. 11:29–30). Yet this solution remains unsatisfying insofar as Hutchinson has previously questioned (or mocked) the desirability of the "soft-lined yokes" of marriage. The difference between Christ's light yoke and the yoke of marriage to an imperfect husband may persist in the reader's awareness.

If Hutchinson's interpretation offers an unstable basis for an affirmation of Christian marriage and childbearing, it initially establishes a more stable basis for a critique of hereditary succession. In canto 6, Hutchinson describes how Eve, after giving birth to Cain, succumbs to the "fond conceit" that her firstborn son will be a "champion" (6.34–35). This will, of course, turn out to be an erroneous belief because Cain will murder his own brother. Hutchinson frames the original fratricide as a reason to question the appeals of both primogeniture and succession:

> alas, from whence
> Doth vain nobility raise its pretence,
> When the first monarch's sons, in slavery born,
> Were taught those trades which upstart nobles scorn:
> The eldest prince to agriculture bred,
> The next white flocks in the cool shadow fed? (6.61–66)

God prefers the sacrifices of the second-born shepherd Abel to that of the firstborn farmer Cain. Cain's murderous reaction confirms that the firstborn is not necessarily more virtuous. To these familiar aspects of the Genesis story, Hutchinson adds her own political and socioeconomic commentary. In lowering the self-regard of the nobility, Hutchinson brings some of her class prejudices (of the sort that she had, in the *Memoirs*, exhibited in referring to Richard Cromwell's peasant nature) to bear on the biblical narrative. She belittles the original princes by reminding us that they were taught agriculture and animal husbandry. What Adam bequeaths to his sons is not prestige but rather the postlapsarian curse of labor. At the same stroke, however, Hutchinson also criticizes the nobility of the present for refusing to apply their heirs to humble forms of labor, of the sort that Adam's own sons practiced. When it comes to the relationship between inborn nobility and labor, Hutchinson positions herself in the ambivalent middle. She decries labor as the result of the Fall even as she criticizes the nobility for shunning hard work by believing, wrongly, that they are born to a higher calling.

This retelling of the Cain and Abel story begins to test the compatibility of Hutchinson's critique of hereditary succession, on the one hand, and her affirmation of Christian marriage and childbearing, on the other. Hutchinson concludes, "Though Abel childless died, yet God's house stood" (6.435). As Goldberg remarks, Abel's typological role "supplies the link between ordinary biology and a regeneration that has no need of biology except as a figure."[34] For this very reason, however, the link between the goodness of reproduction and Christian typology threatens to come undone within Hutchinson's rationale for marriage. For Cain, reproduction functions as a morally corrupt instrument of power in the fallen world: "Cain got sons and did a city build" although he "continued cursed and desolate" (6.401–4). The original firstborn son has survived to practice a debased form of reproduction for the sake of dominion rather than love. "Such the bright slaves of Satan's empire be," Hutchinson comments about Cain's progeny (6.413).[35] Hutchinson then interprets the biblical story of the sons of God marrying the daughters of men as the story of the sons of Seth marrying the wicked daughters of Cain. She laments how

> these mixed marriages produced a brood
> That stained the earth with violence and blood. (6.541–42)

In the *Memoirs*, as we have seen, Hutchinson decries the marriage between Protestants and Catholics as necessarily leading to debasement; in her autobiographical preface, however, she suggests that some forms of intermarriage—between the Normans and Saxons—could be beneficial for national history. In *Order and Disorder*, she hews toward the more pessimistic view. The union of the offspring of Seth and of Cain furnishes the mythic origins of mixed marriage in the postlapsarian world. This is the original, transgressive intermarriage that makes it so difficult to disentangle conjugal love from the demands of succession in the name of power.

Only the biblical Flood promises to usher in a happier era of familial relationships. As we have seen, the reemergence of turtledoves after the Flood signals that conjugal fidelity has been restored in the natural world. Yet as Hutchinson retells the story of the Flood, she continues to remind us of the distinction between human experience and natural reality. She devotes multiple cantos to detailing Noah's drunkenness, Ham's transgression, and the intergenerational curse that returns to the postdiluvian world. Here, too, she is able to make the unhappy realities of familial life the basis of her attack on hereditary rule. At the opening of canto 8, Hutchinson likens the mountains reappearing after the Flood to

> a prince who, long in prison bound,
> Comes squalid forth at first, untrimmed, uncrowned. (8.35–36)

This might seem to be a surprisingly royalist simile. Yet Hutchinson prefaces it by inviting us to compare the restoration after the Flood to the final cleansing at the end of the world:

> What will full Restoration be, if this
> But the first daybreak of God's favour is? (8.27–28)

This seemingly happy comparison between the postdiluvian restoration and the final redemption then turns into grounds for a prophetic warning: "But curb, fair hills; O curb, your growing pride" (8.45). Hutchinson goes on to remind us that the final restoration will involve not cleansing but a fiery purification:

> Your new-restorèd glory shall expire,
> To ashes turned in the world's funeral fire.
> And you, great Lords, who on the mountains reign,
> With them shall once more be destroyed again. (8.51–54)

Hutchinson suddenly addresses great lords who rule on the mountains rather than the mountains personified as restored princes. At the moment when her prophecy against pride gains fervor, she redirects her animus from a metaphorical form of royal pride projected onto the landscape and toward the people who have reintroduced unjust dominion into a world once cleansed by the Flood.

When, in canto 9, Noah's drunkenness unleashes corruption back into the world, Hutchinson seizes the opportunity to renew her attack on the restored monarchy. She declares that Noah perverts natural goodness of wine with the "vile abuse" of excess (9.40). She describes Noah's drunkenness as removing "sovereign reason," which had properly "ruled as monarch in the breast," from its metaphorical throne; she also describes drunkenness as undoing the "great distinction between man and beast" (9.46–48). As Noah becomes beastly in drunkenness, the sovereignty of reason gives way to the reemergence of kingship—somewhere between metaphorical and real—in the world. Hutchinson mocks Noah as "the new world's monarch" in his shameful drunkenness (9.187). Noah the monarch

> here lies drunk
> His awful dread is with his temperance sunk;
> And Ham, finding him naked on the earth,
> Dares make him thus the subject of his mirth. (9.188–191)

This canto had opened with Noah and his sons applying

> all their thoughts and busy cares
> To plant and build for their succeeding heirs. (9.7–8)

This kind of concern for patriarchal succession becomes more recognizable as the basis of hereditary monarchy just as familial relations become corrupted again so soon after the Flood.

Hutchinson's treatment of Noah's drunkenness rebuts royalist depictions of Noah as the first legitimate monarch after the Flood. As Norbrook points out, this critique acquires a topical edge as it mocks "the notorious drunkenness of the Restoration court."[36] Noah's corruption after the Flood offers Hutchinson an occasion to embed topical commentary within her much broader exploration of the mythic foundations of succession. Whereas Charles I had exhibited the danger of an excessive love for his wife, Charles II's court reveals how monarchy threatens to turn the family into a site of debauchery. The poem repeatedly depicts, as Shannon Miller observes, how "the inheritance structure validated by the narrative of biblical events" relies on "faulty, even parodic modes of power transfer."[37] Yet even as Hutchinson laments the politics of succession, she strives to mend the appeal of marriage and reproduction to the Christian reader, and to Christian women in particular. In contrast to the way that the *Memoirs* had sidestepped the Pauline definition of marriage and the instruction to regard husbands as Christlike, *Order and Disorder* aims to explain how that fictive core of Christian marriage can nonetheless be felt as true, even by women who have a critical view of the patriarchal demands of succession.

But to Let Dreams Pass

Abraham emerges as the hero whose status as patriarch should advance rather than hinder a spiritual narrative pointing to Christian love. The conjugal narratives of Abraham and Sarah (and Hagar)—and, subsequently, of Isaac and Rebecca and of Jacob, Leah, and Rachel—offer exemplary cases of fixed love existing in tension with interlinked economies of substitution. These economies include intergenerational succession, sacrifice, as well as exchanges of property. To affirm loving Christian monogamy, Hutchinson needs to render the stories of marriage in Genesis compatible with a typological redefinition. This work of interpretation matters for Hutchinson's highly personal understanding of her marriage. A crucial difference emerges between the marriage of Abraham and Sarah and that of the Hutchinsons: Abraham remarries after Sarah dies, whereas Lucy Hutchinson remains attached to the memory of her deceased husband. Abraham may be both Israel's patriarch and a hero of faith celebrated in the New Testament, but he does not exhibit the permanent fixity in love that Lucy Hutchinson displays.

At the very end of canto 15 of *Order and Disorder*, Hutchinson surprises the reader with an abrupt reminder of Abraham's remarriage after Sarah's death:

And then again the comforts sought of life,
And to his bosom took a second wife. (15.387–88)

Before this concluding couplet, Hutchinson had been narrating the negotiations involved in the purchase of Sarah's burial plot. Around the question of marriage and remarriage, Hutchinson breaks from the biblical order of events. In Genesis 24, the widower Abraham has been blessed by God with prosperity and commissions a servant to help Isaac find a wife from among his father's kin. In Genesis 25, after Isaac finds his wife Rebecca, we learn of Abraham marrying Keturah in his old age. By contrast, at the outset of canto 16, Hutchinson describes the aged Abraham, near death,

> Recounting how the Lord had blessed his cares
> And made him prosperous in all affairs,
> How he in wealth and plenty did abound,
> That no room now for more desire was found,
> He piously his latest thoughts employed
> Successors for his family to provide. (16.3–8)

After canto 15 had prematurely announced Abraham's remarriage, a delicate negotiation now ensues over his affective, erotic, and economic investments. Hutchinson suggests (without explicitly claiming) that Abraham in his old age replaced a concern for personal love with a concern for legacy. In the *Memoirs*, I have argued, Lucy Hutchinson's fixation on the life of her husband licenses the open and repeated articulation of her economic concerns. The insistence on John Hutchinson's singular worth prevents him from being a mere economic resource (or liability) in his wife's eyes. In *Order and Disorder*, Lucy Hutchinson reminds us that Abraham did replace Sarah in remarriage after her death. Yet in Abraham's experience, prosperity and wealth—and not just old age—have the effect of precluding erotic desires. Hutchinson tries to have it both ways, surprising the reader with an abrupt reminder of Abraham's remarriage but then affirming Abraham's pious concern for his familial legacy. She announces how Abraham's love did seek a substitute for Sarah only to shift our focus to the necessity of intergenerational substitution for preserving the prosperity that God confers.

In Hutchinson's retelling of Genesis, the recurring emblem of lifelong fidelity becomes literally sacrificed within the contestation between succession and love that takes place within Abraham and Sarah's marriage. When God visits Abraham to reaffirm his intergenerational blessing, Abraham asks for confirmation. God demands sacrifices including a "turtle-dove and a young pigeon" (12.37). Hutchinson follows scriptural precedent when she describes how Abraham had lain all the animal sacrifices demanded by God on the altar, "[b]ut the two lifeless birds did not divide". (12.42; cf. Genesis 15:9–10). Yet Hutchinson's earlier appeals to the turtledove make this detail especially meaningful. Monogamous love is at once preserved and sacrificed to reaffirm Abraham's status as patriarch. Immediately after this encounter, Sarah encourages Abraham to take a concubine because she still doubts her own ability to bear children. She encourages Abraham to father children with her Egyptian maid, Hagar. When Abraham and Sarah's marriage produces the male heir Isaac, the belated son inherits not just God's blessing but also the conflict between conjugal love and the demands of succession.

Hutchinson emphasizes how those demands of patriarchal succession thwart a simple affirmation of proto-Christian monogamy. After Isaac marries Rebecca, Hutchinson underscores how he inherits from his own parents—to the point of farcical repetition—the tensions between marriage as an expression of personal love and as a vehicle of intratribal and nearly incestuous filiation. Isaac also faces the existential dilemma (albeit less acutely than his father) of being a would-be patriarch who has no heirs. Canto 17 opens by reminding us,

> At forty years the patriarch Isaac wed,
> For twenty more enjoyed a fruitless bed,
> O the unperfect state of human bliss! (17.1–3)

If it seems that the reader is led to sympathize with Isaac, Hutchinson immediately redirects our affective response. The poet decries "man's wayward nature," which,

>   one
> Felicity denied,

forgets all other forms of happiness (17.5–6). We are, presumably, led to find fault with Isaac for being too concerned with his status as a patriarch rather than enjoying the blessings of marriage apart from reproduction.

To mediate between love and succession more helpfully, *Order and Disorder* elevates Rebecca as the poem's central heroine. Rebecca agrees to marry Isaac to accommodate a proper intergenerational transfer—not just of property but also of affections. Hutchinson dramatizes how Rebecca's parents, Bethuel and Milcah, had felt compelled to marry their daughter to Isaac. When Milcah seeks to delay the marriage, Rebecca expresses her willingness to marry immediately because

> [a] short stay might her pious griefs augment,
> And make her virtuous courage to relent,
> Softened with her fond mother's melting tears. (16.187–89)

Despite her own reservations, Rebecca not only accepts but also hastens marriage. She allows the original rationale for marriage expressed in Genesis ("Therefore shall a man leave his father and his mother, and shall cleave unto his wife") to take hold in the postlapsarian world. When Hutchinson narrates the night of Isaac and Rebecca's wedding, she makes Rebecca the object of desire motivating Isaac finally to leave behind the love of his mother. Isaac leads his new bride "[i]nto his mother's tent," where Rebecca's "unveilèd beauty" fills his soul with a "loving ardour" that

> banished out of it that pious grief
> Which since his mother's death found no relief. (16.258–62)

The story of Rebecca and Isaac's union occasions another affirmation of love, one that shapes Hutchinson's response to Lucretius into a political allegory. Hutchinson concedes that Love personified can banish all other cares while bringing "[i]n its own swarm too many smarting stings" (16.270). When Love proves to be this kind of "imperious guest," it undoes the "temper which makes Reason sovereign" and threatens to expel Reason from its seat as ruler (16.278–80). Yet somewhat surprisingly, after Reason is expelled in this manner, it "[g]ood correspondence hath with chaste Love" (16.282). Hutchinson celebrates this renewed alliance of reason, love, and chastity that takes hold precisely in the aftermath of disruption. She concludes that this is just the kind of "pure legitimate flame" that reigned in "Isaac's virtuous bosom" (16.286–87). At the level of intergenerational affect, Hutchinson can construct a politicized allegory in which a disruptive civil war or usurpation can lead to a real restoration—a new form of legitimacy that harmonizes the previously warring factions. Yet in terms of the ongoing investigation about biblical marriage, the problem is that

Isaac's story does not conform to the allegory that Hutchinson imposes on it. Isaac had not previously exhibited irrational lust for another woman before marrying the chaste Rebecca. Hutchinson can only imply that Isaac's grief for his mother is analogous to the irrational form of frustrated desire that Lucretius decries as delusion. The replacement of a deceased mother by a new wife expresses in practical form the alliance of reason, erotic love, and chastity within marriage. This is not, however, the quasi-incestuous rationale that Hutchinson wants to pursue at greater length as a basis of Christian (or, at least, proto-Christian) marriage.

Hutchinson goes on to promote Rebecca's role in the key twist that should make marriage not only a vehicle of intergenerational replacement but also a site of Christian truth—and in a way that might accommodate a critique of hereditary succession. *Order and Disorder* follows Genesis in describing Rebecca's preference for her younger son, Jacob, as well as her active plotting in having Jacob receive his father's blessing in the place of the older Esau. Hutchinson's promotion of Rebecca's underhanded dealings above Isaac's patriarchal prerogative receives justification from the New Testament. Hutchinson attributes Isaac's love for his older son, Esau, to "partial blind affection" which "was not God's election" (18.77–78). She refers to Paul's reinterpretation of the Jacob and Esau story in the ninth chapter of Romans, whereby God's election of the younger Jacob foreshadows God calling more Gentiles than Jews to be members of the spiritual Israel (see Rom. 9:7–16). This Pauline teaching promises to transform the "pious fraud" that Hutchinson's Rebecca undertakes out of maternal preference into an expression of God's mysterious choice (18.75). This paradox offers a meaningful point of contact between *Order and Disorder* and the *Memoirs*. In the *Memoirs*, Hutchinson had described her own seemingly dishonest dealings—disobeying her husband and forging his name in a letter—as an expression of God's plan to save his life.

Hutchinson's earlier composition of the *Memoirs* also helps to explain what it means for *Order and Disorder* to stop abruptly where it does. In retelling the story of the younger brother Jacob becoming the next patriarch of Israel and also setting a pattern for the emergence of the church, Hutchinson could have reinforced the link between her critique of succession and her typological interpretation. Yet as we have seen, the *Memoirs* works to affirm John Hutchinson's worth not just as a husband, military leader, and governor, but also as an older brother. The claim that Lucy

Hutchinson presents her husband's individual merits accurately licenses her to be candid about her economic stake in his familial property. I do not want to propose a strong causal claim whereby Lucy Hutchinson could not advance beyond the Jacob and Esau narrative because she could not bring herself to complete the story of the younger son prevailing over the older through trickery. Yet I do want to argue that the point at which *Order and Disorder* stops emphasizes an ideological impasse in Hutchinson's political and religious imagination.[38]

This impasse helps us to understand why the political critiques offered by *Order and Disorder* become less coherent in the late portions of the extant narrative. Hutchinson's views about hereditary monarchy become muddled precisely as Isaac assumes his role as an expectant patriarch. Like his father before him, Isaac lies to the Philistine king Abimelech by telling him that his wife is his sister. "Philistia's monarch" is angered when he discovers by chance that he has been deceived (17.249). Isaac and Abimelech do reconcile, but only until the monarch grows suspicious of the extent of Isaac's prosperity. Isaac's eventual banishment leads Hutchinson to lament the fickleness of human fortune. Hutchinson concludes, "Thus did Abimelech the patriarch chase," or drive away (17.327). The line initially seems to crystallize an antagonism between Philistine monarchy and Israelite patriarchy, as one chases the other away in a state of competition. Yet at the conceptual level, this "chase" between kingship and patriarchy proves to be more of a pursuit than an expulsion and separation. Hutchinson immediately begins a meditation on the way chance governs "the tides of princes' grace" (17.328). Hutchinson has reshaped the story of the would-be patriarch Isaac suffering from the whims of a monarch into a lesson about chance ruling over kings:

> Behold the state of kings, they would despise
> What now, regarding with unsteady view,
> The general wishes of mankind pursue. (17.334–36)

This meditation ends up marking a significant change in Hutchinson's mythopoetic critique of monarchy. Hutchinson laments that kingship is a widespread object of desire among many men. She describes how the competition for the "high throne" involves "blood and strife" (17.338–39). Out of the seeming antagonism between Philistine monarchy and Hebraic patriarchy, Hutchinson's critique of hereditary succession has given way to a diffuse attack on ambition.

Hutchinson resumes this line of thinking in the penultimate canto of *Order and Disorder*. This time, the denunciation of ambition is framed by the story of Jacob, the younger son who actively usurps the place of the firstborn. When Jacob sets out to find a wife, he finds himself sleeping at Bethel with a hard rock for a pillow. This occasions Hutchinson's commentary:

> O how are mean men, if they know it, blessed!
> They on the hard earth can find pleasant rest
> When princes, rolling in their beds of plume,
> With waking cares the tedious night consume. (19.9–12)

This is reminiscent of the contrast between kingly insomnia and the restful sleep of the commoners found in Shakespeare's *Henry IV, Part 2* (see 3.1.4–31) and again in *Henry V* (see 4.1.230–84). Hutchinson may not have had these Shakespearean speeches specifically in mind; the sentiment about the difficulties of being a king is commonplace. Yet the Shakespearean precedents are useful reminders of how disingenuous this rhetorical lament can be. Shakespeare's Henry IV waxes on about his anxious nights after having usurped the throne and having worked to secure it. Henry V echoes his father's sentiments while he is waging a war that promises to consolidate his legitimacy. A parallel irony obtains in Hutchinson's poem: Jacob has practiced deception to displace his brother, and he now seeks a wife so that he can become the next patriarch. He has not been unambitious. Hutchinson seems to understand that her political critique has become much more diffuse now that its direct and primary target is not hereditary monarchy. Her lament about ambition shifts from the uncertainty that princes confront to the anxieties of the ploughman who dreams of his crops, the usurer who dreams of his profit, the

> labourer of his toil, the awful slave
> Of the last harsh commands his stern lord gave

—as well as the anxious dreams of the scholar, young lovers, courtiers, and seamen (19.39–40). The attack on political ambition, in other words, has given way to a complaint about the uncertainties that beset many or most human endeavors. Kingship now only seems as unblessed as any other postlapsarian mode of life.

In the *Memoirs*, Hutchinson is willing to negotiate her political thinking against her economic interests. In place of an explanation of how a commitment to individual conscience is fully compatible with primogeniture and innate class distinctions, she can only uphold the singular example of her husband as a deserving older brother and republican hero. When the *Memoirs* cannot offer straightforwardly positive evidence of John Hutchinson's merit, the text resorts to foils that make him look virtuous by contrast. Lucy Hutchinson appeals to a similar form of nonlogic in *Order and Disorder*. The poem does not perfect the calibration of conjugal love and hereditary succession found in Genesis through a typological redefinition. Instead, it offers counterexamples to help the reader feel that the biblical heroes in question have arrived at a superior form of marital and familial life. The displaced older brother, Esau, emerges as the key negative example.[39] Yet the stories of Esau and Jacob contain as many similarities as they do clear-cut differences. Jacob, like Esau, ends up practicing polygamy owing to a combination of sexual desire and politic considerations. Hutchinson devotes many lines to Rachel's beauty, which enchants Jacob; the distinction between Esau's lust and Jacob's desire lies not so much in their intrinsic qualities but rather in the fact that the latter is an expression of God's mysterious will. Jacob, however, comes to be duped by his own desires. The Genesis narrative only offers a terse description of how Laban "took Leah his daughter, and brought her to him" in Rachel's stead on the night of their wedding (Gen 29:23). Hutchinson elaborates on Laban's fraud—which is another dubious manifestation of divine will but must not be deemed pious in the same way Rebecca's trickery had been. Hutchinson offers an epic simile likening Jacob's shock upon discovering Leah the next morning to "some brave chief" who thought himself a successful conqueror of "an enemy's town" until he ends up becoming a captive in the "fort he thought his prize" (19.339–46).

Yet this extended simile—which casts blame not on the hubris of the chief but instead on his false troops—cannot undo the impression that the bed trick Laban has effected results in a farce of substitution rather than a heroic twist of events. Jacob's shock upon discovering Leah leads immediately to "such a hate" that makes her "uglier by her impudence" in his eyes (19.351–53). Hutchinson skips quickly past the seven years of labor that Jacob endures to secure his second marriage to Rachel. The narrative of *Order and Disorder* ends very soon after the revelation that Jacob's polygamous unions are—like Esau's—marked by idolatry. In the case of Jacob's marriage, however, the source of idolatry cannot be identified as foreign. When Jacob seeks to depart from Laban with his new, fractious household, Rachel steals some of her father's idols because "her mind" was

> [u]ntil her youth's idolatry inclined,
> Or to the idol-maker's art at best. (20.83–85)

Hutchinson's qualification about Rachel's idolatry proves meaningful. At first, it may seem that Hutchinson is simply mitigating the idolatrous tendencies of one of Israel's matriarchs by suggesting that Rachel may have appreciated idolatrous artwork rather than the outright worship of false gods. Yet this brief suggestion about idolatry in relation to artistic representation directs us to larger questions about interpretation raised by *Order and Disorder*. Earlier in the poem, Hutchinson announces an emphatic break between her Christian interpretation and the Hebraic understanding it claims to supersede. After describing the rainbow that God shows Noah, she gestures toward a rabbinical tradition ("The Hebrews say") of interpreting this sign in the natural world (8.355). She criticizes this tradition by commenting:

> These Jews, to superstition still inclined
> Would in the several colours mystery find. (8.369–70)

According to these supposedly superstitious teachings, the blue of the rainbow should

> present those swelling waves
> Wherein the old world's sinners found their graves. (8.371–72)

Hutchinson claims that Christians should exhibit a superior understanding than the Jews and "pass by their fictions" (8.389). Yet she immediately reveals how the supposedly superstitious (or fictional) alignment of natural reality and moral allegory is not truly distinct from her Christian understanding. Hutchinson admits that

> even we
> When this [rainbow] amidst the blackened clouds we see
> With humble gratitude should call to mind
> God's past and present mercies to mankind. (8.389–92)

Even while Hutchinson appeals to a Christian feeling of grace as superior to a Hebraic one, she registers how the distinction is insufficient to shore up her claim that Hebraic interpretations are clearly inferior in kind. In an act of overcompensation, Hutchinson has already aligned the rabbinical interpretations of the rainbow with "the pagans" who imagined the rainbow as the "female deity" Isis (9.383–84). When, in the final canto of the poem, Hutchinson adds that Rachel's idolatry may have been aesthetically motivated from her youth, she is attempting to identify an internal, hereditary source of a supposedly Jewish tendency toward misinterpretation—of a sort that imposes overly allegorical or even fictive meanings onto God's creation.

When Hutchinson concedes that "even we" cannot help but engage with a mode of thinking that she has labeled as superstition and as fiction, she reveals how much she strains to insist on the superiority of Christian thinking. This pattern of self-exposure and concealment also reminds us of aspects of her writing in the *Memoirs*. In the earlier text, Hutchinson exhibits self-consciousness about manipulating fictions for her own purposes. One late episode makes it especially clear how the question of literary interpretation is bound up with claims to religious truth or superstitions. Hutchinson relates that her husband had dreamt of being a passenger on a boat on the Thames. When the boat becomes stuck, he alone proves able to dislodge and to guide it. Upon arriving safely at Southwark, John Hutchinson meets his father, who hands to him laurel leaves that he cannot decipher. Lucy Hutchinson remarks that she does not know if her husband's dream had been genuinely inspired by God. Yet she still elaborates an allegorical interpretation, with "the boate representing the commonwealth" (242). Her allegorizing of the dream turns hesitant, describing how her husband's actions in rescuing the boat "might signifie the advancement of the Cause by the patient suffering of the Martyrs"

(242). Lucy Hutchinson finds firmer footing in her belief that his arrival at Southwark within the dream signifies his impending death and entry "into walkes of everlasting pleasure" (242). The laurel leaves, however, remain indecipherable (both within the dream and to her understanding) because they foretell "those triumphs which he could not read in his mortall estate" (242). Lucy Hutchinson abruptly concludes, "But to let dreams pass—" (242). In this abrupt gesture, an acknowledgment of the dubious provenance and truth status of this dream coexists with a call for faith in the republican cause prevailing after martyrdom. Hutchinson knows how to admit that her own allegorical constructions might be fictions—in this case, a pastiche of English, biblical, and pagan imagery—while still working to make them feel like prophecy.[40] In *Order and Disorder*, Hutchinson eventually arrives at an impasse in showing how a Christian understanding of marriage elevates lifelong monogamy while drawing forth a higher truth from the Old Testament's stories of patriarchal succession, polygamy, and concubinage. She stops just when the triumph of the younger son offers one way to link the Genesis narrative to its Christian reinterpretation. In the face of this impasse, she can only insist on the superiority of her Christian understanding of love over that of the Jews.

* * *

In the *Elegies*, the death of John Hutchinson generates different mythopoetic resources for showing that Christian belief accommodates the permanent fixity of married love. In "On the Spring 1668," Hutchinson may

> heare The Chastly Amarous Dove
> Answerd againe by her kind mate,

but that voice of monogamy in the natural world only reminds her of her sad mateless condition.[41] As a widow enduring grief, Hutchinson has no need to harmonize her conjugal love with the physical world but can rather announce a break from it. As she declares testily, if the sun proves to be both a literal source of unwanted illumination and a metaphor of monarchical splendor, she can simply reject it by preferring the darkness. Hutchinson will look ahead to a future when Christ will return as the true illuminating king and render the sun itself unnecessary. As *Order and Disorder* has already signaled, the resurrection offers a decisive Christian solution to the challenges of Lucretian materialism—including the teaching that the fixed love for an absent object is delusion. As the fifteenth elegy, "An Epitaph," puts it, John Hutchinson's tomb contains his "Consecreated Attomes," but those atoms will be recomposed in the resurrection in a fashion that Lucretius could never have understood.[42]

As a defiant widow, Lucy Hutchinson can remember her husband as a republican hero while downplaying political defeat: "So fell ye Victime who a Victor died."[43] Within the context of elegiac mourning, the awareness that John Hutchinson can, at best, resemble Christ imperfectly does not preclude Lucy Hutchinson's elevation of her husband:

Nor yett can his descendants wholly fall
Exalted Still in Their Originall.[44]

In contrast to her warning to her children (offered in the preface added to the *Memoirs*) of idolizing John Hutchinson, "An Epitaph" concludes by suggesting that his virtues have partially offset the Fall—not through Christlike salvation but instead through something resembling an Adamic institution of a blessed lineage. This promotion can only take place insofar as Lucy Hutchinson insists on John Hutchinson's irreplaceability. "Leaue of[f] yee pittying friends," she apostrophizes those who advise her to remarry; these friends might as well "perswade ye dead to liue againe," because, in fact, the only remarriage that Lucy Hutchinson will accept is a reunion with her one and only husband after the resurrection.[45] If her grief exceeds the demands of Christian teaching or of Protestant practice, she insists on it as the right way to uphold a fixed conjugal love that she could not secure within biblical teaching itself.

6

From Remarriage to Tragic Fungibility
Behn's The Forc'd Marriage and Oroonoko

Little about Aphra Behn's writings and life suggests a deep investment in Christian marriage. Even though she identified herself as Mrs. Behn, we do not have records of her marriage to Johann Behn, which seems to have taken place in or around 1664. It is unclear whether the couple separated or whether Johann Behn died soon after they married. Despite the scarcity of concrete evidence, Behn's biographer Janet Todd speculates that the tragicomic escapes from unhappy marriages dramatized in *The Forc'd Marriage, or The Jealous Bridegroom*, (the first of Behn's plays to be performed, in 1670) and in *The Luckey Chance* (the last of her plays to be performed during her lifetime, in 1686) reveal something about the playwright's personal experiences in marriage. "Preceding many of her characters," Todd ventures, "Aphra probably married partly for money. Her irritation when she discovered there was not as much as she had hoped . . . may have fueled her contemptuous descriptions of wedded sex."[1] Even if we are skeptical of drawing such connections between life and art, we do know that Behn writes in a cynical, sometimes profane manner regarding marriage, sex, and love. It is unsurprising that Behn's disposition toward marriage partially resembles that of the royalist poet and playwright William Davenant. Behn, too, displays a cynical awareness of fixed love as a literary ruse. Yet Behn has far less of a stake than Davenant in deploying poetic resources to prop up some version of the Christlike superiority of a husband.

This chapter examines how Behn experiments with the vocabulary of conjugal love established earlier in the century as she shapes her various literary endeavors in the late 1600s. I begin with *The Forc'd Marriage*, which relies on the precedents of Shakespeare's plays of jealousy to offer a different tragicomic twist. As readers have noted, the descent into jealous violence in *The Forc'd Marriage* clearly recalls that of *Othello*.[2] Yet at the end of the play, Behn reimagines the conclusion of *The Winter's Tale*—and the trope of the resurrection of the wronged wife—to propose remarriage as a tragicomic solution. Her play does not conclude with the reconciliation of a jealous husband and the wife who has returned to life after her victimization. Instead, the play ends with the husband and wife of the forced marriage separating so that they can marry other people. By recalibrating personal love and replacement in this way, Behn works to restore the king's prerogative. At the play's outset, the king unwittingly orders the deeply unhappy marriage to take place and unleashes the antisocial effects of jealousy. By the end of the play, orchestrating happier remarriages provides a way for the king to reassert control. *The Forc'd Marriage* expresses Behn's early royalist views in a broad sense, but it remains unclear whether it offers narrowly topical commentary—about, for example, the secret marriage of James, Duke of York, to Anne Hyde a decade earlier.[3] In this chapter, I read the play as primarily interested in the fictiveness of husbandly superiority in the eyes of a future wife—a familiar Pauline problem that Behn translates into a less religious register of drama than Shakespeare had before her.[4] By the end of the play, it is not just the king who has gained the upper hand. Princess Galatea's persistent love for Alcippus—who has committed jealous and nearly lethal violence against his first wife—furnishes him with a redemptive remarriage he does not deserve. Behn's epilogue concludes that if the play's tragicomic resolution has not been particularly convincing in announcing the superiority of wives over undeserving husbands, that artistic failure might still promote the compromise of increased gender parity.

In the second half of this chapter, I pair *The Forc'd Marriage* not with *The Luckey Chance* but instead with the 1688 prose fiction *Oroonoko, or The Royal Slave*. In *Oroonoko*, Behn turns fictional incidents set in the 1660s into the basis of urgent political commentary on the unfolding events that would culminate in the Glorious Revolution. She does so by revisiting the vocabulary that defines fixed love against substitution. The African prince Oroonoko's insistence on monogamy is described as an anomalous expression of his inborn nobility. His love for Imoinda rises above the economies of human replacement at play in Behn's exoticized romance set in Coramantien. Initially, jealous delusion does not seem to characterize Oroonoko's predicament; his descent into conjugal tragedy begins when the king, his grandfather, seeks to make a mistress of Imoinda. Neither is jealousy a central problem when both Imoinda and Oroonoko are sold off into slavery and find themselves in the English colony of Surinam. Yet we do realize that Behn's African hero has been modeled partly on Othello when he eventually resorts to killing his wife. In this gruesome scene, Behn's narrator directs the reader to understand the killing of Imoinda in the name of love as possibly tragicomic in and of itself. Far from exhibiting the deluded violence that Othello had exhibited, Oroonoko kills his pregnant wife (Behn's narrator insists) in a loving, honorable fashion, with Imoinda paying him reverence. Yet this appeal to a tragicomic killing proves utterly discordant, and it cannot provide even a provisional form of narrative closure. The actual conclusion of *Oroonoko* confirms Behn's aim in telling a story of human commodification undermining a royal, loving marriage. Behn does not decry slavery in general but only as it is administrated by a corrupt form of English authority in Surinam. Oroonoko's execution at the hands of the wicked deputy Byam is reminiscent of Charles I's execution in 1649, but only as a farcical reiteration. Behn's story recalls the events of 1649 and also appeals to the realities of transatlantic slavery to present a conjugal tragedy that is designed to decry the imminent ouster of James II. In *Oroonoko*, Behn sets the fixity of love against the condition of enslavement as a way to register a royalist lament over the latest threat to the Stuart monarchy.

As an author working across many genres, Behn proves especially adept at rearranging the vocabulary of married love developed earlier in the century. This is one reason why I turn to her as the culminating author studied in this book. I have found it even more important to conclude with *Oroonoko* because it deals with the slave trade. Behn's story, as Laura Brown puts it, has proven to be "a seminal work in the tradition of antislavery writings from the time of its publication down to our own period."[5] Yet as Brown also notes, *Oroonoko* has never fit easily or neatly into the category of antislavery literature; Behn's story clearly announces that "the trade in slaves is unjust only if and when slaves are not honorably conquered in battle."[6] Behn turns to a depiction of slavery to decry human fungibility, but only to the extent that that reality prevents the proper restoration of a prince's singular status—as well as the capacity of loving marriage to affirm that status while also legitimizing his hereditary replacement. This royalist view of innate nobility and love requires other, ignoble subjects to be viewed as lacking in unique individuality. Oroonoko himself comes to deem that the other slaves around him have merited their condition because they are not heroic in the way that he is.

Behn promotes the lasting impressions that Oroonoko and Imoinda can make on readers. These impressions promise to confer on these characters a form of permanent singularity that the condition of enslavement had denied them. Yet *Oroonoko*'s final note of optimism about a literary future aims to link Behn's own reputation to the royal slaves that she has imagined into a tragic existence. The most famous remark about her role in literary history remains Virginia Woolf's proclamation, "All women ought to let flowers fall upon the tomb of Aphra Behn, for it was she who earned them the right to speak their minds."[7] In Woolf's esteem, Behn should not only be celebrated for achieving this right for all women but also for showing them "that money could be made by writing" because women's writing could also be "of practical importance."[8] At the end of *Oroonoko*, Behn links hopes of her fame specifically with the lasting memory of Imoinda. Yet that conclusion should still alert us to how and to what end, exactly, Behn seeks to elevate Imoinda above the fictionalized version of the realities of human commodification. By relocating the patterns of inclusion and exclusion contained within conjugal love to the slave economy of Surinam, Behn negotiates to her own advantage appeals to gender parity with a romance fantasy of inborn inequality.

Behn's Tragicomedy of Remarriage

The Forc'd Marriage opens with a conflict between valor and authority. The nominal setting is the French court, but the play offers little detail about the specific historical backdrop of the action. In the aftermath of a recent military campaign, Prince Phillander declares to his father, the king, that Alcippus has served on the battlefield with distinction. When Alcippus modestly rejects the king's offers of rewards, the king deems this to be an affront. The prince intervenes and asks his father, "Permit me, Sir, to recompence his valour."[9] The king responds,

> I like it well, and till thou hast perform'd it,
> I will divest my self of all my power,
> And give it thee, till thou hast made him great. (1.1.52–54)

This is a restricted and temporary abdication. Yet the king's inability to reward Alcippus points to his dependence on others to uphold his power, and to a tension between the young and the old. Once in possession of royal prerogative, Prince Phillander names Alcippus as the new general. Yet the old general, Orgulius, is present. When the king steps in to ask, "*Orgulius*, are you willing to resign it?" Orgulius responds graciously and admits that his old age has left him "uncapable" (1.1.63–66). Unlike kingship, the title of general is one that can be handed over voluntarily and without tragic consequences. Orgulius's willingness to surrender his office should, in turn, allow the king to reclaim the authority only temporarily invested in his son. If this were the end of the matter, the reversal of king and prince would have run its course. Yet it turns out that Alcippus's desire has not been for Orgulius's office but rather for his daughter, Erminia. The king seizes the opportunity to outdo his son in granting honors. Alcippus barely has the chance to mention the name of Erminia before the king interrupts, "*Alcippus*, with her fathers leave, she's thine" (1.1.118). The king, however, has generated a new problem: unbeknownst both to him and to Alcippus, Erminia and Prince Phillander are in love and have exchanged a private oath to marry. At first, the forced marriage of the play's title seems to allow the king and Orgulius to reassert their prerogative at the expense of their children's desires. Whereas the king remains ignorant of his son's love for Erminia, Orgulius learns of Erminia's affections but still commands her to marry Alcippus. Erminia complains that her father's words "half [her] love to duty does convert," but concludes that she must submit to his authority. (1.3.78).

The opening premise of *The Forc'd Marriage* is reminiscent of some aspects of *Othello*'s opening. Behn turns the question of heroic merit—leading to the title of general—into the grounds of a conjugal narrative. Yet at first, the differences between Behn's and Shakespeare's plays of jealousy are more conspicuous than their similarities. The absence of racial difference is the most obvious contrast, but also striking is the fact that Erminia does not love Alcippus for his valor. Whereas *Othello* opens by describing how stories of the protagonist's adventures had attracted Desdemona to him, the opening of Behn's play sunders the link between heroism and esteem in the eyes of a would-be wife. Even if Alcippus wins the title of general and the object of his desire, the two triumphs are disconnected. When Erminia complains to her father before obeying him, her language of duty may faintly echo Shakespeare's Desdemona. "My noble father," Desdemona declares before the Venetian senate, "I do perceive here a divided duty" (1.3.180–81). In contrast to Erminia, however, Desdemona has made her choice in a secret marriage and will honor her new husband above her father.

Yet the relevance of *Othello* becomes unmistakable in the fourth act. By this point, Alcippus is not only jealous but also sexually frustrated. We recall that the question of whether Othello and Desdemona consummated their marriage remains unresolved; if they have not, then Desdemona's death on her wedding sheets stands in for that consummation. Alcippus's situation is far less mysterious. On the night of their wedding, Alcippus confronts Erminia with a rumor that Phillander has been claiming her as his own. Erminia confesses that her heart does not belong to her new husband. She proposes to honor their marriage as a bond of duty even though it would not be a bond of love. This solution involves her refusal ever to have sex with her husband. Alcippus reveals his propensity for domestic violence on that first night; he draws his dagger but finds himself "disarm'd" by Erminia and by "shame and softer passions" (2.3.88–89). In act 4, however, Alcippus fully commits to jealous violence after he discovers Prince Phillander in Erminia's bedchamber. After Phillander departs the room, Alcippus attempts to kill Erminia—and thinks he has succeeded—even as she continues to uphold her innocence. As Todd notes, "The influence of *Othello* was here so strong that Behn even gave the option of suffocating in the first printed edition of the play."[10] Like Othello, Alcippus expresses a concern for his wife's soul even as he prepares to murder her:

> Preserve thy soul if thou hast any sense
> Of future joys, after this damned action. (4.6.73–74)

When Erminia responds, "Ah, what have I done?" the question seems strained (4.6.75). Erminia can only insist that she has not had sex with Phillander even though he has been caught in her bedchamber. By contrast, Desdemona is sincere in asserting both her innocence and her confusion about Othello's accusations of infidelity.

Before making the relevance of *Othello*'s precedent so clear, Behn's play initially proposes jealousy as a possible solution to the problem of a forced marriage rather than a source of tragedy. This is, at least, what Phillander's sister, Princess Galatea, proposes. Galatea is not merely motivated by her desire to see her brother united with Erminia. She has a stake in undermining Alcippus's recent marriage because she desires him for herself. When Phillander reveals his suicidal despair after Erminia marries Alcippus, Galatea proposes a plan of action that involves deliberately provoking Alcippus's jealousy. Because Galatea is gnomic ("let the rest be carried on by me," she instructs her brother without revealing more), we do not know what she thinks the outcome of inciting jealousy will be (2.1.103). If Galatea hopes that Alcippus will simply reject his marriage because his new wife loves another, those hopes prove entirely misguided. Long before Alcippus tries to kill Erminia, he gets into a confrontation with Phillander. The prince follows his sister's advice and hires musicians to serenade Erminia, and this affront is enough to spark jealous violence. Phillander gets the upper hand in this fight as Erminia watches, startled, from her window. Yet this triumph over Alcippus does not seem to achieve anything. It does not alter Erminia's affections, which never properly belonged to Alcippus in the first place. Erminia, in fact, begs Phillander not to harm her husband any further; Phillander heeds her request, calling her "too great a Tyrant" over his feelings and behavior (2.7.70). By inciting jealousy as Galatea had advised, Phillander ends up merely reinforcing the marital bond—based on duty without reciprocal love—between Erminia and Alcippus.

In the aftermath of this scene, Phillander speaks to the way that the forced marriage orchestrated by his father has generated a confusion that is not just a personal crisis but also a crisis of authority. Phillander expresses exasperation that he has allowed Alcippus and Erminia to reunite. Phillander asks, "Is not she my wife, and I his Prince?" (2.7.79). Even though this is asked rhetorically, the two-part question reveals how the problem of marriage and the problem of authority have become intertwined in a way that offers no easy resolution. Nobody in the play raises the possibility that Phillander and Erminia's private oath to marry was, in fact, a binding contract that should nullify her marriage with Alcippus.[11] As a result, Phillander's claim that Erminia is his wife seems only to be a frustrated outburst rather than a legitimate claim. By contrast, Phillander is certainly Alcippus's prince. Yet we eventually witness how tenuous his princely authority is. When, in the fourth act, Alcippus enters Erminia's bedchamber and discovers Phillander there, he proclaims,

> You merit death for this base injury.
> But you're my Prince, and that I own you so,
> Is all remains in me of sence or justice. (4.6.48–50)

The use of the word "own" for "acknowledge" seems especially apt as Alcippus has the life of his prince at his disposal.

Alcippus, in turn, is aware that his passions threaten the reign of reason. He refers to love as "a surly and lawless Divel" who "will not answer reason" (4.2.39–40). In an ensuing soliloquy, Alcippus deploys the conceit of reason as a legitimate but beleaguered sovereign. He reflects on the rage that recently "strove to dispossess the Monarch" reason from his mind (4.5.4). His wilder passions continue to clamor

> for liberty
> And nothing but a common-wealth within
> Will satisfie their appetites of freedom. (4.5.12–14)

Even in Alcippus's own mind, this political allegory does not suggest the desirability of a commonwealth or democracy ruled by the lower passions in the absence of reason. Instead, Alcippus refers to a "Tyrant" in his soul who, like a usurping demagogue, threatens to unleash these lower passions for his own ends (4.5.16). Alcippus does not explicitly identify this usurper tyrant, but jealousy is the obvious candidate. After this soliloquy, Alcippus breaks into Erminia's bedchamber, and his discovery of Phillander tests the limits not only of his commitment to the reign of reason but also to his prince. Alcippus refrains from killing him with some difficulty. After escaping, Phillander recognizes how fragile his authority has become:

> Gods, am I tame, and hear the Traytor brave me,
> I have resentment left though nothing else. (4.6.54–55)

If the play is to achieve a comic conclusion, it must restore personal love and marriage under the proper auspices of kingly authority. Behn's solution lies in remarriage, which makes sanctioned replacement—of an unwanted spouse for a wanted one—the way to allow Erminia, Phillander, and Galatea to obtain the objects of their respective desires. Yet this is a solution that Alcippus accepts only after much resistance. For Alcippus, remarriage is not an expression of his love but a practical form of redemption that he should accept after his treatment of his first wife.

It may be useful to situate Behn's attempt at a tragicomedy of remarriage within a very broad trajectory of conjugal narratives. I have in mind the way Stanley Cavell looks back to seventeenth-century England while identifying a subgenre of films from the 1930s and 1940s as the Hollywood comedy of remarriage. Yet by remarriage, Cavell mostly means reconciliation; the general pattern of this subgenre involves engagements or recent marriages that are badly frayed before they are comically restored. It makes sense, then, that Cavell cites *The Winter's Tale* as a key precedent. He asks at the outset of his study "why the film comedies of remarriage took as their Shakespearean equivalent, so to speak, the topic of divorce, which raises in a particular form the question of the legitimacy of remarriage."[12] For Shakespeare's Leontes, remarriage after the death of Hermione must not be the solution; in the comedies that Cavell considers, divorce followed by marriage to other people should generally be avoided, either as tacit or as explicit possibilities. Yet Shakespeare does not provide the only seventeenth-century precedent for the Hollywood comedy of remarriage. Cavell also cites Milton's divorce tracts as forecasting a cultural shift whereby marriage is not so much about reproduction as it is about enriching conversations.[13] Cavell cites Milton's rationale for divorce even while studying Hollywood comedies designed to foreclose the possibility of remarriage. If this seems paradoxical, it may be justifiable—although Cavell does not put it this way—because Milton emerged from being a vilified advocate of divorce to become a poet who promotes fixed love and reconciliation as heroic virtues in *Paradise Lost*.[14]

As Cavell discusses at length, *It Happened One Night* is the exceptional test case for the subgenre he proposes.[15] This 1934 film comes closest to being a comedy of remarriage after divorce or annulment. The film opens after Ellie Andrews has eloped in defiance of her wealthy, controlling father. In her madcap quest to unite with her new husband, who happens to be named King Westley, Ellie ends up falling in love with another man. This other man, Peter Warne, proves himself worthy of love—especially in the eyes of Ellie's father—because he is not interested in her money. The plot device of a formal wedding ceremony, in which Ellie will not or cannot utter "I do" to King, reinforces the impression that her rash elopement should never have been considered legitimate to begin with. (The movie begins with Ellie insisting to her father that her vows were legally binding, but we do not see the elopement itself.) When King Westley accepts a financial settlement to allow an annulment, Ellie becomes free to marry (or remarry) properly—and under the auspices of her father's wishes.

If *The Winter's Tale* establishes the main precedent for Cavell's subgenre of twentieth-century comedy, *The Forc'd Marriage* partially anticipates the exceptional case. In Behn's play, Erminia (whose name, of course, is a variation of Hermione's) has been forced by her king and her father into an unhappy and unconsummated marriage. Actual remarriage will be the tragicomic conclusion after she is subjected to domestic violence. Before this violence occurs, the stakes of remarriage are discussed openly in act 3, when Alcippus learns from his friend Pisaro that he has been desired all along by the Princess Galatea. Pisaro discloses this information against his own self-interest; he has previously desired the hand of Galatea for himself. Alcippus is initially "amaz'd," and he tries to process how he should now think about unrequited love, marriage, and political advantage (3.1.61). "I have a kind of war within my soul," he declares (3.1.117). Alcippus does not bring himself to assert that he should have originally asked the king for Galatea's hand, or that he should now seek to annul his unconsummated marriage. Yet Alcippus does describe an inner conflict between love and public glory. Before accepting an expedient remarriage to the princess, Alcippus will first be swayed by extreme jealousy. His jealousy amounts to a violent insistence that marriage should be an expression of love—even in the form of frustrated, unrequited desire. Eventually, however, Alcippus must accept remarriage so that Erminia can happily marry (or remarry) Phillander. The resolution of a double remarriage will finally render it unclear whether the jealous bridegroom of the play's title truly refers to Alcippus or to Phillander. Both husbands, after all, jealously claim to be the rightful husbands of Erminia. This oscillation points to the way that Behn's tragicomedy promotes jealousy from an irrational passion to an ennobling insistence on a fixed love—even at the expense of fidelity to a first marriage.

Behn attempts this renegotiation of jealousy by divvying up the roles that Shakespeare's Leontes occupies. Leontes has sinned against Hermione, and her inexplicable resurrection transforms his guilt into a new form of belief in her. In *The Forc'd Marriage*, Erminia—pretending to be raised from the dead—revisits both Phillander and Alcippus. When Erminia visits her future husband, she is trying to instill in him a kind of faith in her. When she subsequently tries to render Alcippus more remorseful, her aim is not to reconcile with him but rather to convince him to marry the princess. When it comes to the return of the wronged wife, *The Winter's Tale* and *The Forc'd Marriage* present very different adaptations of the Alcestis myth. Erminia returns in a farcical rather than miraculous scene. She initially appears "*veil'd with a thin Tiffany*" and terrifies the coward Falatius, who takes her for an avenging ghost.[16] Only in the next scene does Erminia appear to Phillander and declare herself to be a "soul that from *Elizium* made escape" (4.9.30). She exits the scene just to give Phillander enough time to articulate his bewilderment to his friend Alcander. Phillander—perhaps like the audience—cannot decide whether the apparition was truly Erminia in the flesh or a ghost. When Erminia reenters, she invites both men to clear up their doubts about her. "You cannot think *Alcander*, there be Ghosts," she chides. "No, give me your hand & prove mine flesh and blood" (4.9.74–75). It may seem odd that Erminia specifically addresses Alcander rather than her beloved Phillander, yet this targeted address helps to downplay the impression that Phillander has displayed the same cowardice that Falatius had previously shown. The stage directions instruct both Phillander and Alcander to refuse to touch Erminia's hand at first. Yet Phillander, not Alcander, will dare to believe in Erminia first. Erminia is not seeking to instill in her future husband a Christian belief in the resurrection of the body as well as of the soul. She will soon give up the entire ruse of a resurrection by explaining that she has simply survived Alcippus's assault. Yet even as Behn deflates the miraculous nature of this staged resurrection, she still experiments with the possibilities of redirecting religious forms of faith into an increasingly secular drama. Phillander—like Shakespeare's Leontes before him—ends up occupying a role analogous to that of doubting Thomas before the resurrected Christ. Yet Behn makes Phillander much more of a doubter than Leontes; she also makes Erminia a mischievous instigator of that doubt even as she becomes the flesh-and-blood object of his faith.

The final act shows us why Behn makes all these alterations. After the mock-resurrected Erminia teaches her future husband to believe in her, she must visit the husband who has wronged her. Alcippus must display the more decisive form of belief and guilt so that he can free Erminia to remarry. Act 5 begins with Pisaro reporting that he has observed Alcippus exhibiting remorse for his treatment of Erminia. "I found him sitting by a fountain side," Pisaro tells Galatea,

> Whose tears had power to swell the little tide,
> Which from the Marble Statues breasts still flows. (5.1.3–5)

The setting signals the importance of the blurred relationship between reality and mimesis in Alcippus's guilty mind. Alcippus's remorse makes him "almost frantick" until

> [t]he Marble Statue *Venus*, he mistook
> For fair *Erminia*. (5.1.13–20)

We might remember that Othello imagines that he will admire Desdemona as an alabaster statue once he has finished killing her. Alcippus has also tried to justify jealous murder as appropriately sacrificial, but his remorse registers the perversity of that kind of thinking.[17] In the next scene, Erminia attempts to intensify Alcippus's existing remorse by appearing as a spirit, "*drest like an Angel with wings*."[18] She does not appear directly before Alcippus but rather in the mirror that he has been using to reproach himself as a murderer. This configuration signals how many layers of artifice are involved in fostering the false impression that Erminia has returned from the dead. When Alcippus turns to confront his late wife, she reframes his violence against her as an effective apotheosis:

> *I am thus Deifi'd by you;*
> *To you I owe this blest abode,*
> *For I am happy as a God.* (5.2.72–74)

If this remark is a gracious reframing of attempted murder, it is at the same time an inducement to feel guilt. Yet Behn's audience knows by this point that Erminia is misleading Alcippus to manufacture a sense of wonder. Previously, the question of whether Erminia might be a ghost had been comical but still genuinely uncertain, at least until we discover alongside Phillander that Erminia has returned in the flesh. All of this is in direct contrast to the resurrection scene in *The Winter's Tale*, in which the audience is stunned, along with Leontes, by Hermione's statue coming to life.

In further contrast to the end of Shakespeare's tragicomedy, Erminia's attempt to manipulate Alcippus's feelings backfires. We witness this failure unfold when Erminia relies on even more artifice to persuade Alcippus to marry Galatea. The princess herself enters "*over the Stage as a spirit*" to initiate an allegorical masque.[19] Glory and Honour join Mars, Pallas Athena, and Cupid to entice Alcippus into accepting his new conjugal destiny. Erminia has the only speaking part in this masque, and she directs Alcippus's attention to his future royal bride:

> 'tis she you must possess,
> 'Tis she must make your happiness. (5.2.97–98)

This masque is designed to intensify Alcippus's existing feelings through a combination of allegory and myth, with the goal of reshaping his remorse into an inducement to remarry. Yet the masque has the opposite effect, leaving Alcippus defiant again. His final change of heart only occurs through the interventions of Phillander, Galatea, and the king himself. In this play, the conflation of resurrection and art punctures any compelling belief in spectacle. Behn shifts the ruse of a mock resurrection to a play within a play only to render it ineffective in achieving tragicomic closure. That closure will be achieved instead by Behn's own plot of remarriage as the desirable means of restoring political stability.

Variety Enough

Alcippus ultimately finds Erminia's human forgiveness more liberating than her visitation as a supposed spirit. Forgiveness sanctions his remarriage to Galatea even though his first marriage has been nullified neither by divorce nor by death. Behn downplays belief in a spectacle that blurs the lines between religious iconography and dramatic entertainment. *The Forc'd Marriage* asks us to put less faith in a stage resurrection felt as miraculous and more faith in Galatea's fixed love for Alcippus—as well as in the king's return to control over his subject's lives. Yet Pauline marriage still matters for Behn's play insofar as it frames (largely through the mediation of *Othello* and *The Winter's Tale*) the question of genuine versus imputed forms of husbandly merit. Princess Galatea wants to marry Alcippus even though he has attempted to kill his first wife. The play does not dwell at length on the religious and legal question of why Alcippus can remarry—whether because he has never consummated his marriage with Erminia, or because his attempted killing stands in for a formal annulment. The play does, however, register the problem of Alcippus's lack of merit as a would-be husband for the princess. As Alcippus declares to her,

> Yet I had liv'd and hop'd, and aim'd to merit you
> But since all hopes of that are taken from me,
> My life is but too poor a sacrifice
> To make attonement for my sins to you. (5.5.68–71)

By this point in the play, the king has already declared that Alcippus's death must serve as "a sacrifice to *Erminia's* Ghost" and as the repayment of a "debt" to her father Orgulius (4.7.46–47). Because Erminia lives, however, Alcippus will not have to offer his life as recompense. He avoids being executed by the king, and his willingness to marry Galatea should suffice in and of itself as atonement. Yet we also know that this conclusion is underwritten by an uneasy compromise between love and political considerations: Alcippus accepts his second marriage out of a combination of guilt, relief, and a desire for glory rather than out of any existing love for Galatea.

Intertwined with the drama of Alcippus's jealousy giving way to remarriage is a subplot that brings into sharper focus the tension between fixity and substitution within comic marriage. In contrast to the main plot, jealousy does function effectively in the lower plot as a device for bringing desire under the auspices of monogamous marriage. Phillander's follower Alcander competes with the coward Falatius for the affections of Aminta, one of Princess Galatea's waiting women. Falatius does not pose a serious challenge. Alcander's primary obstacle lies in Aminta's disillusioned view of love and sex. She enters the play trying to impart her cynicism to Galatea, who remains steadfast in her love for Alcippus. Galatea agrees with Aminta that "the World's inconstant," but she insists on the qualification, "in every thing but Love" (1.2.11–12). Aminta, however, reveals that she has loved "half a score" times (1.2.41). She goes on to provide a playfully lewd description of how, after Cupid's dart initially penetrated her heart,

> he'as got the knack on't, 'tis with ease,
> He domineers and enters when he please. (1.2.47–48)

Much later, we learn that Alcander's philandering may have mirrored or even motivated Aminta's blasé attitude toward love and sex. Aminta reminds Alcander that he has professed love for many women before her. Yet she then suggests the way for Alcander to win her over:

> could you be
> Content to dismiss these petty sharers in your heart,
> And give it all to me, on these conditions
> I may do much. (4.1.67–70)

Aminta's jealous desire promises to reform promiscuity into monogamy.

Pisaro, who is Aminta's brother and Alcippus's follower, shuttles the lessons of the lower subplot into the main plot. Pisaro, too, takes part in a ruse of mock resurrection. Unlike Erminia, however, his mock resurrection is only designed to facilitate the marriages of others; he has given up his desire for Galatea to assist Alcippus. At one point in the narrative, Alcander mistakenly believes that he has killed Pisaro as part of the fight that takes place when Phillander incites Alcippus's jealousy. This belief leads a chastened Alcander to present a sword to Aminta so that she can avenge the death of her brother. Aminta initially believes Alcander but does not pursue vengeance directly. Instead, she commissions Alcander's rival suitor Falatius to carry out the retribution for her. There is never any real danger of this retribution taking place. Falatius is a coward and, at any rate, Aminta quickly learns that Pisaro is alive. Yet she devises a plan to keep Alcander believing that he has killed Pisaro. Pisaro is privy to his sister's ruse and consents to it out of the belief that "time and management will joyn us all" (3.2.159). Whereas the play's main plot is indebted to *Othello* and *The Winter's Tale*, this comic subplot is reminiscent of *Much Ado about Nothing*—another precedent in which a mock resurrection facilitates marriage. Behn farcically duplicates the motif of the stage resurrection. Pisaro's mock resurrection makes Alcander experience a lesser version of Claudio's guilt in *Much Ado* so that he can assume a husbandly role analogous to Benedick's.

Pisaro's ruse ends anticlimactically, with no meaningful moment of discovery. At the end of the play, however, he is present to comment on Alcander and Aminta's union. Pisaro reminds us of the logic behind his sister's plan to draw out Alcander's mistaken sense of guilt:

> Give him your hand, *Aminta*, and conclude,
> 'Tis time this haughty Humour were subdu'd
> By your submission, whatsoe're he seem,
> In time you'll make the greater slave of him. (5.5.243–46)

Aminta agrees to this rationale for marriage and concludes,

> Take me, *Alcander*,
> Whilst to Inconstancy I bid adieu,
> I find variety enough in you. (5.5.249–51)

This exchange confirms that Pisaro's death and resurrection had been fabricated to give the seemingly submissive wife the upper hand in her future marriage. Even if Alcander's guilt is revealed as groundless, his relief upon discovering he has not actually killed Pisaro should still render him grateful enough to make him a "slave" to his wife. This manipulated sense of relief papers over questions that remain unanswered: In what way has the philandering Alcander been reformed? In what way has he come to merit Aminta's fixed love? What we do know is that Aminta accepts Alcander as embodying a desirable combination of singular personhood and variability in matters of love.

At the same time, Pisaro's commentary about marriage retroactively informs our understanding of the main plot's conclusion. When it comes to the union of Princess Galatea and Alcippus, the king offers a tactful negotiation of Alcippus's lack of husbandly merit. "Then to compleat thy happiness," the king tells Alcippus,

> Take *Galatea*, since her passion merits thee,
> As do thy Vertues her. (5.5.215–17)

This contains the hint of a rebuke directed toward the irrational nature of Galatea's fixed desire for the violent Alcippus. Yet the king's overt meaning is that the princess deserves Alcippus's hand. The truth is, of course, far more lopsided than this: when it comes to domestic matters, Galatea's affection has effectively imputed merit on an undeserving Alcippus. Yet the king is invested in reminding us that Alcippus does possess virtues—not in matters of love, but on the battlefield, where he has served the king well.

Around the role of Pisaro, we can observe one final contrast between Behn's tragicomedy and *The Winter's Tale*. At the very end of Shakespeare's play, Leontes exercises his renewed roles as king and husband to urge Camillo to take the hand of the widow Paulina. This is jarring insofar as nothing has suggested that these two characters have any interest in each other. Pisaro, by contrast, is offered no compensation for his losses. He seems to have surrendered any conjugal future of his own; the king has nothing to say or do for him in the final scene. This helps to explain why Pisaro is free to comment so candidly about the advantages that a wife may claim over an undeserving husband. Pisaro's commentary threatens to unsettle the political harmony that the play has tried to achieve through the orchestration of two remarriages. Even though *The Forc'd Marriage* does celebrate the king's power to render marriage and substitution compatible in a new way, the play has struck readers as a muddled expression of Behn's royalist values. When, for example, Todd suggests that the play may offer a belated compliment to the Duke of York's marriage to Anne Hyde, she still notes that the resolution that the play offers is not stable: the "kingdom in which Erminia and Alcippus exist can have no very great hope of peace."[20] As Todd goes on to observe, Behn's earlier plays (especially the ones composed before the Exclusion Crisis) differ from her later writings in their willingness to question the limits of monarchical authority.[21] Despite promoting remarriage as its own form of atonement, *The Forc'd Marriage* leaves it unclear whether the prince and his new brother-in-law can put aside their previous jealousies to avoid future political strife.

The prologue and the epilogue to *The Forc'd Marriage* articulate what may have been more pressing to Behn at the time of the play's composition than topical political commentary. The prologue begins by warning that the female playwright may be leagued with the wily women in the audience who will deploy not just beauty but also wit to cheat men. It ends with an actress entering to chide the male actor delivering the prologue. The actress admits that beauty and wit are powerful weapons but then claims that the aim of this campaign is "*nought but constancie in love*" (line 58). "*That's all our Aim,*" she concludes,

> and when we have it too,
> We'll sacrifice it all to pleasure you. (59–60)

Even as the play moves further toward a secular drama than its Shakespearean precedents, it amplifies the kernel of untruth that persists within a Pauline understanding of marriage, whereby husbands need to lay claim to a Christlike status in the eyes of their wives. If *The Forc'd Marriage* concludes with Pisaro's observation that his sister Aminta can make a "slave" out of her new husband, the prologue insists that women will sacrifice any advantage that they might enjoy to promote love. After the play's conclusion, the epilogue claims modestly that "we" (speaking again on behalf of the playwright, the actresses, as well as the women in the audience) did not manage to conquer the men in the audience through the resource of wit. The epilogue turns the failings of the tragicomedy as evidence that women, too, have something to be forgiven for: "*A fault, methinks, might be forgiven too*" (14). The need for forgiveness allows for a bid for "*equal treatment*" based on the awareness of asymmetrical but shared weakness:

For neither Conquer, since we both submit;
You, to our Beauty, bow; We, to your Wit. (17–18)

Even if the tragicomedy fails to sway the audience, that failure should still form the grounds of a certain kind of gender parity—especially when it comes to judging the work of a female writer. If, on the other hand, this work of the female playwright succeeds, then the play effectively teaches that loving wives have the grounds to lord over their underserving husbands even while claiming to submit.

The Greater Slave of Him

By the time Behn published *Oroonoko* in 1688, the situation in England demanded a different kind of engagement with urgent matters in national politics. *Oroonoko*, as Richard Kroll reminds us, "was almost certainly published on 27 June or 4 July 1688," and "its meaning is infused with a political melodrama that had been unfolding since April of that year"—and would soon culminate in the Glorious Revolution.[22] Kroll reads *Oroonoko* as "Behn's desperate attempt between 10 and 29 June 1688 to warn James II that if he continues on the path he has described since his accession, he risks suffering the same fate as his father."[23] By describing the topical significance of Behn's composition, Kroll advances two claims about how we should read the story: "*Oroonoko* is therefore not a novel; nor it is [*sic*] a quasi-sociological account of the conditions of slavery or emerging colonialism."[24] I agree that *Oroonoko* comments on a moment of rapidly developing political crisis. It does so by looking back not only to earlier decades when Surinam remained an English colony but also to the execution of James II's father in 1649. Yet I believe that Kroll overstates the case in qualifying the importance of slavery and colonialism—not to mention race—in *Oroonoko*.

Behn fictionalizes the realities of transatlantic slavery to depict human replaceability in its most extreme form. In *Oroonoko*, she does not necessarily lament the basic fact that the transatlantic slave trade has turned African people into fungible commodities. Near the end of the story, when the slave revolt that Oroonoko has incited has failed, he regrets having endeavored "to make those Free, who were by Nature *Slaves* . . . fit to be us'd as *Christian* Tools."[25] It is ironic that the slaves whom Oroonoko deems innately fit for their condition had been hesitant to join his insurrection out of concern for their own wives and children. Their choice to surrender at last has been similarly motivated. Oroonoko is convinced that the liberation of his own royal family is of supreme importance, and that it is more honorable for any husband to lead his family to death than to remain in bondage. As a result, the protagonist's heroic sense of his own nobility ends up undermining any general renunciation of slavery. Behn's story narrowly identifies the commodification of Oroonoko, Imoinda, and their unborn heir as the real travesty to be lamented.

Attending to the logic of substitution in its varied forms gives us a way to understand how Behn's depiction of Oroonoko and Imoinda's predicament speaks to the imminent disruption of the Stuart monarchy in 1688—without downplaying the centrality of slavery and race in the narrative. In Behn's view, the tragic paradox of the royal slave can only exist because the proper chain of authority, stretching from the king to the colony of Surinam, has been disrupted. This is why the deputy governor William Byam ("a Fellow, whose Character is not fit to be mention'd with the worst of the *Slaves*") is able to thwart Oroonoko's promised liberation and then to exact a cruel revenge on him (54). The debasement of political and moral authority in Surinam prevents the unique status of a prince, his wife, and their unborn child from being elevated above the condition of commodification. After Oroonoko's attempt to liberate his family fails, he ends up reprising a version of the tragic fate of Charles I. As Behn tells us early on, Oroonoko had heard of "the late Civil Wars in England, and the deplorable Death of our great Monarch, and would' discourse of it with all the Sense, and Abhorrence of the Injustice imaginable" (13). Because Oroonoko rejects Christian teaching, however, he denies the religious logic whereby his own death might be aligned fully with kingly martyrdom. Through this pattern of debased repetition, Behn works to turn a fictional story of a royal slave and reminders of 1649 into a warning against overthrowing yet another Stuart monarch. Oroonoko's downfall is unredemptive and final; he and his unborn child die as the very last survivors of a dynasty. Yet Behn does not dwell on the uncertain political future of Coramantien at the conclusion of her story. Instead, she generates a sense of irretrievable loss concerning Surinam as a former English colony. She repeatedly claims that England has lost control of what could have been a new paradise. This pervasive sense of loss confirms that the demise of Oroonoko's royal lineage is meant to warn the English about suffering the consequences of their own political behavior.

Oroonoko does not only investigate the logic of substitution by pitting the commodification of humans against hereditary succession as a vehicle of continuity. The key third term that mediates between these two is conjugal love, in a form that insists on personal uniqueness. The literary vocabulary pitting conjugal love against substitution shapes how Behn's fictionalized version of past events aims to comment on the developments of 1688. By the time Behn was writing *Oroonoko*, she had experimented not only with the dramatic meanings of marriage but also with a poetry of love that negotiates the controversies surrounding James II. Behn's "Pindarick Poem on the Coronation" registers the dangers posed by James's second marriage to Mary of Modena. James's first marriage to Anne Hyde had already been a source of potential conflict; his second marriage, in 1673, to a foreign, Roman Catholic princess threatened to make the next heir to the English throne even more ominously like Charles I. Behn's poem on the 1685 coronation celebrates James and Mary but nonetheless invokes the new queen repeatedly as Laura, casting her as the potentially recalcitrant object of the newly crowned king's love. Behn is not, of course, suggesting that James is a frustrated Petrarchan lover. Yet the legacy of Petrarchism matters for the way Behn celebrates the new, Roman Catholic king and queen. This legacy includes Petrarch's own renunciation of Laura for the Virgin Mary and Spenser's project to redirect Petrarchan desire for a Protestant celebration of marriage. Behn celebrates the royal couple in a poem that is partly reminiscent of an epithalamion, as if the new king and queen were something like a new husband and wife. "Awake, Oh *Royal Sir*! Oh *Queen*, ador'd, awake!" Behn pleads.[26] She banishes from this conjugal coronation those who would gaze on the "bright *Goddess* of the Day" with envy and "raging **Malice** even to **Madness** wrought" (lines 106, 134–35). Behn imagines a negative overreaction to the idolatrous form of admiration that Mary inspires; Behn seeks to reject anyone who would harbor such feelings about the new queen.

Within these poetic and religious coordinates, the latter half of Behn's poem works to stabilize the mythic status of Mary of Modena in relation to her husband. After describing Mary, ominously, as "the fair *INCHANT-RESS*" (534), Behn compares her emergence to the

> *wonder* that the *Prophet* did unfold,
> When Heav'n in Revelation he survey'd
> And the Bright *Woman* did behold. (548–50)

Behn aligns the new queen with the "woman clothed with the sun," who is described in Revelation as being persecuted by the dragon as she gives birth to "a man child, who was to rule all nations with a rod of iron" (Rev. 12:1–5). If we were to follow the Roman Catholic line of interpretation that identifies this woman with the Virgin Mary, then Mary of Modena would be compared to her biblical namesake. This identification would elevate Mary's maternal status as the mother of a divine (or, at least, godlike) son. Yet in 1685, it remained very unclear whether Mary of Modena would or could, in fact, bear a viable male heir. All of the royal couple's children had been stillborn or died early. It may be useful to the poem, then, that Protestant interpretations of Revelation tend to interpret the woman clothed with the sun as the church. This identification would reinforce the celebration of James emerging not only as a "*Godlike King*" but specifically as a Christlike bridegroom on the day of his coronation (line 25). Because Behn describes Mary as an enchantress, however, the underlying presence of that other woman of the apocalypse—the whore of Babylon—cannot be fully banished. Yet Behn, I argue, takes advantage of sectarian controversy by optimistically splitting the difference between Catholic and

Protestant understandings of the woman clothed with the sun—as either the mother of the Son of God or as the metaphorical bride of Christ. Behn can hail Mary simultaneously as a potential mother of a future godlike prince and as the wife of a new, godlike king without specifying which register of praise—maternal or conjugal—should be preferred.

In *Oroonoko*, the intensifying controversy surrounding James II's Catholicism registers far more obliquely. It is possible that Catholicism—and the question of Behn's own sectarian identification—is relevant to Oroonoko's rejection of Christianity. As a character in the story, Behn attempts to convert Oroonoko by offering lessons that include "Stories of Nuns" (41). Yet Oroonoko's key complaint does not concern celibacy but rather "our Notions of the Trinity, of which he ever made a Jest; it was a Riddle, he said, wou'd turn his Brain to conceive" (41). Behn dedicated *Oroonoko* to the Jacobite and Roman Catholic Richard, Lord Maitland. In the Epistle Dedicatory, Behn praises Maitland as a "Champion for the Catholic Church," one who is able to clear "all these Intricacies in Religion, which even the Gown-men have left Dark and Difficult!" (6). Yet the sentences containing this praise were excised from the 1688 publication. Perhaps Behn initially meant for the reader to understand that if Lord Maitland had been present in Surinam, he could have taught Oroonoko more persuasively. The published version of the dedication does liken Maitland to St. Augustine, "Teaching the World divine Precepts, true Notions of Faith"; perhaps he would have had more success in teaching Oroonoko about the Trinity (6). The expurgated form of Behn's dedication leaves it unclear whether Maitland would have triumphed as an expositor of Christian doctrine in general or as a specifically Roman Catholic instructor. Far from staking out a sectarian position, the ensuing story of *Oroonoko* investigates the utility of Christian belief or of religion in general and the potentially greater appeal of a nonsectarian code of honor.[27] Early on, Behn describes Surinam as nearly Edenic; she opines that "Religion wou'd here but destroy that Tranquillity, they possess by Ignorance" (10).

An elevation of conjugal love lies at the center of this crossover between Christian belief and a potentially universal view of honor. We learn that Oroonoko's honorable insistence on monogamy is anomalous in his native Coramantien: "contrary to the Custom of his Country, he made [Imoinda] Vows, she shou'd be the only woman he wou'd possess while he liv'd; that no Age or Wrinkles shou'd incline him to change, for her

Soul wou'd be always fine, and always young" (15). This propensity toward monogamy displays Oroonoko's innate nobility, which distinguishes him not only from his lesser-born compatriots but also from the natives of Surinam. In describing the "State of Innocence" that prevailed among the local people, Behn mentions, "They have Plurality of Wives, which, when they grow old, they serve those that succeed 'em" (10). In this story, an inclination toward monogamy may play a more decisive role in displaying royal honor than Christian belief. Oroonoko's insistence on fixed love promises to make his sense of honor compatible with the demands of hereditary succession—and compatible enough with a Christian sensibility. To test this dual compatibility, Behn situates the origins of Oroonoko's love within overlapping logics of human substitution: office-based, intergenerational, and sacrificial. Oroonoko's love for Imoinda originates in a heroic act of self-sacrifice. In battle, Imoinda's father, the general, "was kill'd with an Arrow in his Eye, which the Prince *Oroonoko* . . . very narrowly avoided; nor had he, if the General, who saw the Arrow shot, and perceiving it aim'd at the Prince, had not bow'd his Head between, on purpose to receive it in his own Body rather than it shou'd touch that of the Prince, and so saved him" (12). The detail about the eye emphasizes the exact, eye-for-eye logic of the general's substitutionary sacrifice. Military valor turns into a form of martyrdom when the general bows his head. Oroonoko subsequently visits Imoinda to make amends for her father's death with a gift of slaves.

In Behn's royalist romance, distinctively noble love remains fixed even as it rises out of economies of substitution. In the aftermath of the general's sacrifice, Oroonoko's sense of nobility underwrites an implied exchange rate between a heroic life and the lives of the captives of war. He presents Imoinda with 150 captive slaves to compensate for her father's death. Yet in a twist, this encounter is when Imoinda's beauty and comportment gain "a perfect Conquest" over Oroonoko's "fierce heart" (14). The general's eye-for-eye sacrifice ends up giving rise to the eye language of new lovers: "he told her with his Eyes, that he was not insensible of her Charms" (15).[28] The new love between Oroonoko and Imoinda does not amount to a blanket rejection of the notion of human replaceability. Only Oroonoko's love for Imoinda remains permanently fixed. When it comes to followers or confidants, Oroonoko is amenable to numerous replacements within his affections. An unnamed French tutor, Aboan, Jamoan, Trefry, and Tuscan are all esteemed by Oroonoko but exit his story (often with one taking the place of another) without leaving an affective trace—in contrast to the permanence of his love for Imoinda.

Yet Oroonoko's grandfather, the aged king, jeopardizes Oroonoko and Imoinda's union by sending her the royal veil—"that is, the Ceremony of Invitation" (16). Neither Imoinda nor Oroonoko knows how to respond when obedience to the king clashes with their mutual vows of fidelity. The only reprieve from this crisis arises from the king's impotence and from the opportunity for Oroonoko and Imoinda to consummate their union secretly. Because Oroonoko and Imoinda are discovered, however, their union is once again jeopardized. Imoinda is sold into slavery in another act of the king's duplicity; Oroonoko is sold into slavery as a victim of a corrupt English trader. At first, Behn gives us the grounds to believe that the deplorable condition of enslavement might still accommodate the restoration of royal marriage. In Surinam, Oroonoko and Imoinda are reunited and promised liberation; the couple seek to return to Coramantien to claim their rightful place. What thwarts this restoration is not merely the condition of slavery but rather the condition of slavery as administered by a corrupt form of English authority. The slave trade reveals the possibility of human replaceability in its most extreme form. Only an unbroken chain of authority by proxy, spanning across the Atlantic, could properly contain the realities of human fungibility while also respecting and safeguarding royal uniqueness. All the virtuous English characters, including Trefry and Behn herself, agree that Oroonoko and Imoinda should be freed. Yet Byam is able to delay this emancipation until the paradox of royal slavery becomes intolerable. He prevails because of the absence of the governor, Francis, Lord Willoughby of Parham—who, we eventually learn, will never arrive to restore order in Surinam because he has drowned in transit.

In my chapter on Shakespeare, I discussed how the sea in *Othello* is a mythopoetic construct as much as it is a geographic reality. Through the interplay between these registers, the play widens the affective gap between a highly personal experience of tragedy and the political triumphs of the Venetian state. In *Oroonoko*, the perilous ocean furnishes Behn's story with a source of causation—both historical and fictive—for the disruption in proper English authority. The historical Willoughby was, in fact, "drown'd in a Hurricane" (as Behn puts it) in 1666, off the coast of Guadalupe (51). Yet it makes sense for Behn to avoid any details concerning the real person of Willoughby. During the midcentury civil wars, Willoughby had been a parliamentary military leader but switched allegiances. His embattled term as the governor of Barbados, starting in 1650, demonstrated how the strife in England spilled over into colonial affairs. He was pressured to demonstrate his allegiance to the exiled Charles Stuart and clashed with Parliament's attempts to impose control over Barbados.[29] Willoughby was ousted (although he did manage to have a small colony in Surinam named after him) and regained a position of power in the Americas only after the Restoration. Charles II restored Willoughby's coproprietorship of Surinam in 1663. Yet Willoughby's record of promoting stability in the colonies continued to be spotty at best. He survived an assassination attempt in 1665 and led a disastrous naval expedition against the French before drowning. Behn's wistful claim that Willoughby would have represented the king's person effectively in Surinam makes more sense if he remains somewhat of a cipher.

The drowning of Willoughby is particularly convenient for Behn's fiction because it tends to deflects the reader's possible awareness, in 1688, of the active involvement of James, Duke of York, in the slave trade and in Anglo-Dutch conflict. James, admiral of the Royal Navy, became the governor of the Royal African Company by royal charter in 1660, and of the reconstituted company in 1672. He was the company's largest shareholder and a key proponent of its activities. Controversies surrounding the crown's monopoly on the slave trade would become intertwined with the political and religious strife that would lead to James's ouster from the throne. As William Pettigrew notes, even before the Glorious Revolution, the Royal African Company "began to appreciate the precariousness of James's hold on power owing to his increasingly reckless attitude toward England's Anglican Church and markedly heavy-handed treatment of venerable institutions like the City of London corporation."[30] In *Oroonoko*, Behn is able to lament the corrupt and venal administration of a slave-based colonial economy as well as the eventual loss of Surinam even while affirming her unflagging support for James II's legitimacy. (Behn certainly does not note that, in the 1667 Treaty of Breda, the Dutch were willing to cede New Netherland—including the city that the English had renamed New York in the Duke of York's honor—in exchange for territory including Surinam.) Behn can do this, in part, by turning the historical fact of Willoughby's drowning into a source of fictive causation that is meant to explain why injustices and travesties took place under a debased form of English authority.

In place of any real details about Willoughby, Behn inserts a fabricated story about her own family within the larger breakdown of authority in Surinam. This fabrication reinforces the links among the forms of substitution (office-based, familial, and sacrificial) operating within her story. Behn claims that she was present at the colony because her father was to be "Lieutenant-General of Six and thirty Islands" (43). Yet Behn's father, like Willoughby, has died at sea before assuming his position as a proxy of the English crown. The wicked Byam occupies the position of authority that both Willoughby and Behn's father have been rendered unable to fill because of lethal sea crossings. Behn does claim to be a stand-in for her absent father, at the level of the family if not of English colonial governance. The story about Behn's father, in turn, might be standing in place of an account of her real-life marriage and its relevance for the plot of *Oroonoko*. Behn's meeting with her future husband, Johann, may have been occasioned by her travel to Surinam in 1644; it is possible that Johann Behn was in Surinam as a slave trader.[31] In *Oroonoko*, the historical fact of Willoughby's drowning gives rise to a chain of replacements that functions as a fictive source of causation—not only for the corrupt nature of English rule in Surinam but also for the conditions of Behn's authorship of this story.

By configuring history and fiction around this network of replacements across the ocean, Behn attempts to render her story of Surinam in the 1660s fit to speak to urgent events in England in 1688. When Trefry, who serves as the overseer of Lord Willoughby's estate, attempts to protect Oroonoko from the deputy Byam's vengeance, he makes the case that the servants of Parham represent Willoughby directly, bypassing Byam's twice-removed authority. Trefy argues that Byam's men "ought no more to touch the Servants of the Lord [Willoughby] (who there represented the King's Person) than they cou'd those about the King himself" (59). Geographic distance produces a cleavage between sovereignty and management, but Trefry attempts to conjoin the two. Trefry insists that monarchical presence is infused even in Willoughby's servants. Yet Trefry's argument fails. Ironically, his speech only works to underscore the infelicitous connections between Oroonoko's and Charles I's fates by explicitly likening the plantation to Whitehall. A breakdown in hierarchy will lead to the lamentable execution of a prince in a site reminiscent of the palace where Charles's execution had become a public spectacle.

Willoughby's absence not only delays Oroonoko's and Imoinda's liberation to the point of catastrophe but also provides Behn's narrative the opportunity to expand on the different logics of substitution—religious and economic—that underlie the climactic conjugal tragedy. Behn does this in a series of romance dilations. The narrator and her crew are enlisted to accompany Oroonoko on a series of diversions to distract him while he waits for freedom. Through these episodes, Behn signals a generic shift in the relationship between romance and epic within her prose fiction. Earlier, in the backstory set in Coramantien, Oroonoko responds to the loss of Imoinda by devoting "the small Remains of his Life to Sighs and Tears" and refusing to engage in any more warfare despite being camped on the battlefield (28). His soldiers, "wondring at the Delay," try but fail to convince their prince to lead the campaign against the enemy (28). Yet this form of delay aligns Oroonoko with Achilles. Motivated by the bravery of his follower Aboan, who attempts to "command as General," Oroonoko finally "suffer'd his People to dress him for the Field" (28–29). Oroonoko's valor affiliates Behn's exotic romance with a recognizably Homeric pattern. In contrast to the story of Achilles, however, Oroonoko's delayed display of epic heroism does not result in a tragic conclusion. Aboan (who plays a role analogous to Patroclus) does not have die to rekindle Oroonoko's heroism. Oroonoko's conquered opponent, Jamoan, is neither killed nor displayed cruelly in triumph, as Hector is, but rather becomes Oroonoko's close friend even in defeat.

In Surinam, by contrast, the dilations of romance are designed to contain Oroonoko's valor. The English colonists want to suppress the heroism that Oroonoko eventually exhibits when he can no longer endure the delay of promised liberation. Even when Oroonoko does resort to violence, his heroism is undercut by the condition of enslavement. When he becomes the victim of Byam's cruelty, Oroonoko's death will prove to be gruesomely farcical. The romance episodes in the middle of *Oroonoko* are designed to defer this debased conclusion for a while. At the same time, these episodes establish the literary and religious logics through which Oroonoko will come to suffer a fate somewhere between tragedy and farce. In the episodes of Oroonoko's diversions, Behn expands on the forms of dangerous doubling and replacing that are internal to romance. One of these episodes offers a hint about the religious beliefs and practices that have been travestied by literal human commodification. When Oroonoko takes up fishing in Surinam, an electric eel paralyzes him. Oroonoko is rescued from the river, and the entire episode ends in a curious celebration: "we had the *Eel* at Supper; which was a quarter of an Ell about, and most delicate Meat; and was of the more Value, since it cost so Dear, as almost the Life of so gallant a Man" (47). I suggest that this description offers a transgressive parody of the Eucharist. Eating the eel's "delicate Meat" will be as close as these characters get to eating the flesh of Oroonoko. This is a secular communion that imparts nothing more (but also nothing less) than nearly cannibalistic delight. Here, too, Behn does not want to make possible sectarian questions—about, for example, a belief in transubstantiation—very explicit. Instead, Behn makes this episode an opportunity to think about substitution in relation to fungible value. Oroonoko's near death has become a source of added value for the eel as a consumed good. Behn does not specify whether Oroonoko himself eats the eel that has almost killed him. If he does, the sign and signified of this mock Eucharist would be linked in a vacuously circular economy of enjoyment.

When romance dilations can no longer defer an unhappy conclusion, Behn turns to different literary modes to resituate the disparate forms of substitution at play (succession, commodification, and sacrifice) within the central narrative. She turns to the resources that she had experimented with from the outset of her career as a playwright—that of conjugal tragedy and the possibility of tragicomedy. In an expansive study of Restoration tragicomedy, Kroll explores the genre as a site of different forms of circulation, including foreign trade, physiological circulation, and the transmission of print materials. Tragicomedy, according to Kroll, allows royalists to embed politically complex advice into their plays. Mixed plots accommodate representations of a mixed monarchy, and the trope of circulation allows disparate, even opposed ideas and elements to coexist without any simple claims to unity and coherence.[32] Pairing *Oroonoko* with Behn's *The Forc'd Marriage* allows us to discern the development of her literary and political thinking across two momentous decades and across multiple genres of writing. The conflict between conjugal love and substitution functions as a unifying link. *The Forc'd Marriage* plunges us into the tragedy of jealousy and then pushes toward the comic resolution of remarriage to test the king's ability to harmonize love with replacement through marriage. *Oroonoko* communicates Behn's awareness of the realities of human commodification. The hero and heroine are circulated as goods, and the corruption of English authority makes it impossible for the supposedly desired configuration of replaceability and singularity—for the distinction between all the other enslaved Africans and the royal subjects whose identities should never be rendered negotiable—to emerge. Oroonoko's situation proves untenable because he knows that his heir will be born as a slave. Within Imoinda's womb, the economy of the slave trade collides with that of royal succession.[33] Oroonoko feels that the condition of fungibility must not imperil the loving form of intergenerational substitution that can give rise to a succession of singular royal subjects.

In the aftermath of Oroonoko's failed revolt, it becomes clear that Behn's presentation of her African hero has, in fact, been informed by the tragedy of *Othello*. In Oroonoko's backstory, Behn tests the question of personal merit as it applies to the titles of king, of general, and of husband—just as she had at the outset of *The Forc'd Marriage*. In contrast to the way Alcippus gains the title of general and the hand of Erminia separately, Oroonoko takes the place of the aged general and also wins the love of his daughter; the general is sacrificed in this intergenerational crossover from valor to love. Yet the similarities between Oroonoko and Othello have been occluded because jealousy does not take root as a problem internal to married love. Oroonoko's and Imoinda's insistence on each other as fixed objects of desire has not lapsed into a tragic problem but rather serves as a consistent expression of their character. In the absence of jealous delusion, race has been the most conspicuous link between Oroonoko and Othello. Yet in the early portions of *Oroonoko*, race is insufficient to bring about a tragic outcome. Oroonoko's African identity is qualified by the European and Roman (and thus supposedly superior) traits that serve to distinguish him. From Oroonoko's and Imoinda's perspective, enslavement remains an external imposition rather than a contradiction internal to their love. In my second chapter, I detailed how jealousy arises out of the contradictions within Christian marriage to unravel the incorporation that Othello could have achieved in Venice. Oroonoko, by contrast, has no desire to assimilate to English society and rejects Christianity as unreasonable. His desire is to leave Surinam and return home to take his rightful place. As a result, Behn's story inverts an existing pattern relating literal enslavement to metaphors of fixed love as a kind of unfreedom. At the end of *The Forc'd*

Marriage, when Pisaro remarks on his sister's ability to make a so-called slave out of her undeserving husband, he appeals to domestic enslavement to a domineering wife in a bit of hyperbole. In *Othello*, by contrast, after the hero remarks that,

> But that I love the gentle Desdemona,
> I would not my unhoused free condition
> Put into circumscription and confine,

he goes on to describe himself as once having been sold into literal slavery and then liberated (1.2.25–27). The Shakespearean precedent links a metaphor of domestic bondage to the reality of enslavement. Yet the exact nature of Othello's literal enslavement—and the degree to which racial as well as religious difference set its conditions—remain unspoken. For Oroonoko and Imoinda, by contrast, faithful monogamy is never felt as potential bondage. It is only literal enslavement, in an unambiguously racial form, that prevents them from making the fixity of their love the vehicle of legitimate succession.

In *The Forc'd Marriage*, jealousy is initially proposed as a solution to an unhappy marriage only to be realized as a dangerous passion. The play must neutralize the threat of jealousy through a mock resurrection that facilitates remarriage as a superior expression of loving jealousy. *Oroonoko* inverts this pattern as well. Something resembling a mock resurrection does take place, but halfway through the story rather than at the end: Oroonoko realizes that Imoinda has not been killed, after all, but sold off into slavery. The improbable and marvelous restoration of the original union promises a comic conclusion. Yet later in the story, in the absence of a tenable tragicomic solution, Oroonoko comes to resemble Othello after all by killing his wife in the name of exclusive love. Oroonoko cannot leave "his lovely *Imoinda* a Prey, or at best a *Slave*, to the inrag'd Multitude" (60). Sexual violation and the loss of personal singularity that enslavement entails have now become indistinguishable: "*Perhaps*, sad he, *she may be first Ravished by every Brute; exposed first to their nasty Lusts, and then a shameful Death*" (60). Oroonoko concludes that killing Imoinda is the only solution, and she willingly consents, "for Wives have a respect for their Husbands equal to what any other People pay a Deity" (60). *Oroonoko* repeatedly asks whether Christian belief is any better at promoting virtuous action than a nonreligious sense of nobility. In a cruel irony, Imoinda outdoes Christian wives in revering her husband as godlike, but only to assent to her own killing.

In this instance, jealous violence is provisionally—and improbably—called on to register as tragicomic in and of itself. Behn's narrator goes to great lengths to insist that this violence is noble rather than debased, but this ends up producing a remarkably discordant effect. Oroonoko is described as "first, cutting her Throat, and then severing her yet Smiling Face from that Delicate Body, pregnant as it was with Fruits of tend'rest Love" (61). The narrator's insistence that this violence is loving may only heighten the reader's inability to accept the claim. Both the detail of the "yet Smiling face" and the reminder that Imoinda is pregnant render this scene unacceptably gruesome. The ensuing action confirms that Oroonoko's killing of Imoinda cannot truly harmonize tragic and comic impulses. Oroonoko has not killed his wife out of jealous delusion, but like Othello before him, he finds himself stripped of his heroic strength after the act. "*No*," Oroonoko laments, "*since I have sacrificed* Imoinda *to my Revenge, shall I lose that Glory which I have purchas'd so dear, as at the Price of the fairest, dearest, softest Creature that ever Nature made? No, no!*" (61). Oroonoko's rhetorical question contains its own answer as to why killing Imoinda cannot register as a fully heroic act. Oroonoko has thought of that killing as transactional, with Imoinda's death being the price to pay to secure the possibility of revenge. He has compromised his insistence on Imoinda's singularity by making her life negotiable within an affective exchange. In the aftermath, Oroonoko finds himself incapable of obtaining the revenge he thought he had purchased because his heroic strength is depleted.

In *Othello*, the tragic hero finally musters enough strength to kill himself in a way that reveals his divided sense of self. He commits one last act of service to Christian Venice by identifying himself as the enemy to be killed. Oroonoko's split identity—as both the rightful prince of Coramantien and a slave given the ironic name of Caesar—is not something he has to discover in a parallel moment of anagnorisis. This tragic knowledge has been foisted on him. Even in defeat, Oroonoko initially rejects suicide: "*No, I wou'd not kill my self, even after a Whipping, but will be content to live with that Infamy . . . till I have completed my Revenge; and then you shall see that* Oroonoko *scorns to live with the Indignity that was put on* Caesar" (58). Eventually, however, Oroonoko does try to commit self-harm, but in a way that communicates his defiance. Surrounded by Byam's men, Oroonoko "cut a piece of Flesh from his own Throat, and threw it at 'em" (62–63). Oroonoko mimics the heroic self-mutilation of the Indian warriors he had witnessed earlier. Through this mimicry, he declares himself to be resolutely non-Christian, willing to adopt a manner of self-violence that is foreign to him but perhaps even more foreign to the English. Yet even this bit of agency is denied him. Oroonoko's friend Tuscan saves him out of love, but Byam and his men wrest control of Oroonoko's life so that they can dictate the meaning of his death.

Equal Force

The result is a spectacle "of a mangl'd King" that is neither entirely tragic nor farcical (65). Oroonoko dies in a manner partially reminiscent of Christ's crucifixion and of the political martyrdom Charles I had endured in 1649. Behn reminds us that this repetition will not be redemptive—not only because the victim refuses the religious logic of Christian sacrifice but also because he remains a slave. When Oroonoko ironizes his own death by smoking a pipe, he presents a new form of subversive mimicry. In this case, he mocks the habits that English gentlemen have come to adopt as a result of new-world commerce. As Stephanie Athey and Daniel Cooper Alarcón remind us, "Orinoco" was the name of a strain of tobacco. As a result, "the arresting image of Oroonoko taking tobacco while his own body burns makes literal the analogy between enslaved slave trader and the commodity for which he is named."[34] As Oroonoko parodies his own martyrdom, he reminds us of his debased status in a world of commodities. I have argued that the earlier episode of the electric eel culminates in a parodic version of the Eucharist, in which Behn and those around her partake of the eel as a proxy for Oroonoko. His near death adds value to the eel in the form of the pleasure it imparts when it is consumed. At the end of *Oroonoko*, this same kind of circulation recurs in a way that hollows out the possibility of religious significance more explicitly. Oroonoko reminds us that he is not a royal Christian martyr but an enslaved African who will, at the moment of his own death, consume a new-world commodity with whom he shares a name.

After ordering the vengeful killing, Byam attempts to reassert control over the meaning of Oroonoko's body: "They cut *Caesar* in Quarters, and sent them to several of the chief *Plantations*. One quarter was sent to

Colonel *Martin*, who refus'd it; and swore, he had rather see the Quarters of *Banister*, and the *Governor* himself, than those of *Caesar*" (64–65). By ordering the quartering of Oroonoko's body, Byam is marking him as a traitor. At the same time, the tactic of sending his quartered remains to different locations follows biblical precedent. The Book of Judges recounts how a Levite takes his new concubine into Benjamite territory. In Gibeah, "certain sons of Belial" seek to sleep with the Levite; his host offers instead both his own maiden daughter and the Levite's concubine (Judg. 19:22). The next morning, the Levite finds his concubine defiled and "fallen down at the door of the house" (Judg. 19:27) Once home, the Levite kills his concubine, divides her body into twelve pieces, and sends them to "all the coasts of Israel" (Judg. 19:29). Israel responds by waging a divinely sanctioned war against the Benjamites, killing twenty-five thousand and setting fire to their cities.

This biblical echo connects the unhappy conclusion of *Oroonoko* to the topical realities of 1688. The story of the Levite and his concubine occurs in "those days, when there was no king in Israel" (Judg. 19:1) and takes part in the leitmotif of the entire book: "In those days there was no king in Israel: every man did that which was right in his own eyes" (21:25). Through much of the 1680s, references to the book of Judges play a role in commenting on shifting challenges to the monarchy. Committed royalists could turn to Judges to illustrate the moral chaos that arises in the absence of monarchy; conversely, the retribution against the Benjamites for their corruption could be seen as authorizing the active defense of Christian values, including the Glorious Revolution.[35] In this context, the contestation over the meaning of Oroonoko's quartered body proves especially significant. Oroonoko preempts the violation of his beloved wife by killing her, yet this means that he ends up suffering the fate of the concubine in the biblical story. His body is dismembered and scattered as a warning. Byam intends to warn against future slave uprisings, but for the more virtuous interpreter, Oroonoko's victimization might serve as a warning against the kind of corrupt authority that Byam himself represents. When, however, Colonel Martin refuses the quartered remains of Oroonoko's body, he does not fully articulate his superior understanding of the situation. Instead, he flatly rejects this gruesome occasion for interpretation as intolerable—as devoid of any meaning he wants to consider. Because Behn affirms Martin's moral character, we might read his refusal of Oroonoko's remains as a defiant message in and of itself—one that declares that the relationship between the English crown and colonial authority is utterly broken. The ambivalences surrounding Colonel Martin's refusal are amplified because Behn has already reminded us that George Martin (or Marten) was "Brother to *Harry Martin*, the great *Oliverian*"—or, at least, a signatory to Charles I's death warrant (45). Here, too, the breakdown of English authority in Surinam recalls the turmoil of 1649 even as it forms the basis of a warning about the events of 1688. Yet it remains unclear whether Behn's story can pair its dire warning about political debasement with any practical advice. When it comes to the future of Surinam, we know that English authority was not reformed but instead withdrew entirely.

As a result, *Oroonoko*'s final warning is reminiscent not only of the Gibeah episode in Judges—in which the people cooperate with God to right an injustice—but also of the older narrative of Sodom and Gomorrah's destruction. Lot successfully defends his family from the lust of the residents at Sodom and flees as God brings destruction on the wicked city. The spectacle of injustice may not induce political action on the part of the people, but God himself strikes down corruption. Behn's story reminds the reader repeatedly that the English have already allowed a colonial paradise to turn into a site of destruction. After taking control of Surinam, the Dutch have treated the natives "not so civilly as the *English*; so that they cut in pieces all they cou'd take, getting into Houses, and hanging up the Mother, and all her Children about her; and cut a Footman, I left behind me, all in Joynts, and nail'd him to Trees" (47). This might offer some vicarious satisfaction of a longing for retribution against the Dutch, yet it is important for Behn to specify that her own footman has also suffered ritualistic violence. Behn's laments about the fate of English Surinam may link the stories of Gibeah and of Sodom only to emphasize that the dire consequences of the earlier Genesis narrative have already occurred. In Behn's outlook, more recent developments leading up to 1688 suggest that the warnings of Sodom or Gibeah might apply to England itself rather than to its overseas colonies.[36] Whether England will succumb to more civil war or to divine judgment remains unclear, but no obvious way of avoiding some tragic conclusion presents itself. Behn's story concludes not with a practical exhortation to James II or to English subjects, but instead with a warning of impending and likely unavoidable destruction.

In the last sentence of *Oroonoko*, however, Behn strikes a note of cautious optimism. This optimism is not directed toward the future of English authority at home or abroad, but rather toward the literary future. This future specifically concerns the female author and Imoinda: "yet, I hope, the Reputation of my Pen is considerable enough to make his Glorious Name to survive to all Ages; with that of the Brave, the Beautiful, and the Constant *Imoinda*" (65). In describing the fraught identification between author and heroine, Margaret Ferguson refers to the text of *Oroonoko* itself as "a safe-sex substitute for the potentially mutinous but also economically valuable black slave-child Oroonoko might have had with Imoinda."[37] We might also refer to this literary changeling as a safe-race substitute for the Black heir who has been killed before he could be born.[38] The last sentence of *Oroonoko* suggests that the clash between love and substitution may be harmonized in the relationship between character and text, between heroine and author. Behn's writing might perform some of the functions that conjugal love has been unable to achieve within the plot: redeeming some sense of Imoinda's uniqueness out of the various economies of substitution—intergenerational and sacrificial as well as commercial—from which her story arose and then ended.

Insofar as Behn's optimism in linking her reputation with the lasting memory of Imoinda's name has proven correct, the enabling fiction of personal singularity within economies of substitution may have taken hold within literary history. Oroonoko and Imoinda are neither real nor unique. As Behn's literary creations, they partially figure forth various persons and personae: Adam and Eve, Aeneas and Dido, Othello and Desdemona, Charles I and Henrietta Maria, James II and Mary of Modena. Yet readers may still confirm the author's hope that this pair retains enough singularity to produce a lasting impression. The capacity of literary writing to mediate between love and replacement may, in fact, prove more necessary as a royalist ideology of hereditary succession is challenged once again. The political message of *Oroonoko* had no chance of helping James II avoid his own ouster. Yet Behn's last word directs our attention to a fictional wife and princess who, despite obeying her husband to the point of death, might be remembered as a heroine in her own right.

After the Glorious Revolution, Behn declined to praise William of Orange as the new English monarch.[39] She would remain a Jacobite until her death in April 1689. Yet she did seize an opportunity to couple her Tory values with her gender politics by praising the new Queen Mary in "A Congratulatory Poem to Her Sacred Majesty." Four years earlier, Behn had celebrated this queen's father and stepmother in a Pindaric ode reminiscent of an epithalamion. Yet Behn's earlier poem, as we have seen, had to negotiate uncertainties about whether Mary of Modena should be celebrated as a royal mother or royal wife. In "A Congratulatory Poem," Behn praises a greater Mary, one who can be celebrated in distinction from her kingly husband. Whereas Behn had dangerously associated Mary of Modena with the woman clothed with the sun, she now writes, "*Maria* with the Sun hath equal Force" (line 45). The poem revives the tired pun on "sun" and "son" to declare that Mary has emerged as radiant as any male heir. Mary's "Lovely Face" reveals her "great Father's Trace" (89–90), and her mind more fully displays James's "God-like Attributes" (95). Behn finds herself able to compose a poem of unambivalent adoration for a royal woman. Mary is the subject and object of both love and substitution, the proper heir of a godlike father whose status as a wife seems hardly to matter. In the aftermath of the revolution that Behn decries, she finds a queen who might authorize her desire to be irreplaceable within but also apart from the economy of marriage.

Epilogue

My book's argument looks forward to the novel as the form in which married love and domestic life would become privileged topics of literary representation. The novel is a key site where the enabling fictions of love and personal uniqueness take a heteronormative shape. My aim in this book has been to detail an earlier literary vocabulary of conjugal love that spans numerous genres and reimagines the meaning of Christian marriage. It would be far beyond the scope of my project to trace the crossover from the seventeenth-century vocabulary of love against substitution to a bourgeois, novelistic view of domesticity. Yet I do want to conclude by pointing, however briefly, to Mary Shelley's *Frankenstein* (1818) and George Eliot's *Daniel Deronda* (1876) as two nineteenth-century novels that engage closely with seventeenth-century writings about marriage. Although in remarkably different ways, Shelley and Eliot both consider how a recognizably Christian logic of marriage continues to shape and to constrain the desire for singularity within affective attachments—with results that are unhappy and even lethal. Both *Frankenstein* and *Daniel Deronda* identify seventeenth-century writings as channels through which the volatile combination of Christian teaching and literary affirmations of uniqueness within love remains active.

In Shelley's novel, the scientific discovery of the principles of life hold out for Victor the allure of personal singularity apart from marriage. Victor hopes to enjoy a new form of patriarchal prestige: "No father could claim the gratitude of his child so completely."[1] Even if Victor remains in denial about his own feelings, we know that this new mode of generating life offers him an alluring alternative to the family structure formed by his father. Alphonse Frankenstein started his family by rescuing the wretched orphan of his destitute friend. "When my father became a husband and a parent," Victor recalls to Robert Walton, "he found his time so occupied by the duties of his new situation, that he relinquished many of his public employments" (19). The phrase "husband and a parent" momentarily leads us to think that Alphonse Frankenstein is both a father and a husband to Caroline Beaufort; this is not what Victor means, but it still contains a degree of truth. Victor subsequently seeks to outdo his father as a singular patriarch (one who does not need a wife or any woman to generate life) whose prestige might eventually transcend the division between familial affairs and public employments. The catalyst for this ambition is not just the fact of his mother's death due to illness. Victor registers how his mother's death gives rise to a proliferation of proxies and replacements—his cousin and future wife, Elizabeth Lavenza, the innocent servant Justine Moritz, even the miniature portrait of the mother bound up in William Frankenstein's killing. Victor's discovery of the principle of life promises to stop (or, at least, reshape) the cycle of substitution after the death of his mother. When, however, Victor resolves to marry Elizabeth despite numerous misgivings, his father explicitly affirms that the consolation of intergenerational replacement is one rationale for marriage: "new and dear objects of care will be born to replace those of whom we have been so cruelly deprived" (132).

Despite creating new life, Victor finds that he cannot avoid entanglements in marriage. This is due not only to his blindness about his own desires but also to the fact that his creature goes off on his own and reads a version of *Paradise Lost*. Whatever unidentified French translation of Milton's poem that the daemon reads, he comes away impressed by a *felix culpa* logic that downplays the problems within the original marriage and elevates conjugal love as a site of redemption.[2] If Victor were also a student of *Paradise Lost*, he might recognize in the poem some versions of his own ambitions. After the Fall, Milton's Adam bitterly regrets that God created Eve to populate his latest creation, and wishes that humanity could have been exclusively masculine, like the angels. Adam must be trained away from misogyny and toward grace. Yet the angel Michael does inform him that had he not fallen, he would have been revered by "[a]ll generations" as "their great progenitor" (11.343–46). To accept the conclusion that a happier Eden is possible after the Fall, Adam should prefer redeemed conjugal love over patriarchal prestige. Victor does not accept any version of these Miltonic lessons but, instead, withholds a wife from the daemon. This act unleashes a profoundly unhappy way to promote Victor's desire for singularity apart from marriage. Victor's decision motivates the daemon to kill Victor's new wife and most of the others whom he ostensibly loves.

In Eliot's novel, Gwendolen Harleth confronts a basic dilemma regarding marriage: "The questioning then, was whether she should take a particular man as a husband."[3] Marriage is a form in which Gwendolen can negotiate her desire for personal distinctiveness against various realities of replacement. She chooses to marry Henleigh Grandourt, despite her guilty awareness that she is taking the place of Lydia Glasher—Grandcourt's previous lover and the mother of his son. If Gwendolen has any hopes about coming to love Grandcourt in particular, those hopes are framed on a gambler's calculation of probabilities. Gwendolen's decision to marry Grandcourt is based on negative constructions rather than any positive affirmation: "it was not likely she could ever have loved another man better than this one" (274). Or, more simply, "He really is not disgusting" (261). Grandcourt does, however, prove to be disgusting, and Gwendolen's choice in marriage proves to be tragic. In *Daniel Deronda*, no single seventeenth-century work emerges as the central text that clarifies the purchase of a religious past on nineteenth-century notions of marriage. Eliot presents instead a dizzying network of allusions spanning from classical antiquity to her present. Whereas *Frankenstein* announces its engagement with *Paradise Lost* near the center of its narrative (and, in the 1818 publication, on the title page), Eliot reserves her most important citation of Milton for the very end of *Daniel Deronda*.[4] Lines from the biblical tragedy *Samson Agonistes* culminate the novel's attempt to recalibrate tragic catharsis around a latter-day fiction of Jews and Christian marriage that might reach some tragicomic conclusion.

Early on in *Daniel Deronda*, *The Winter's Tale* seems to be the seventeenth-century work most relevant for the story of Gwendolen Harleth.[5] When she participates in a staged tableau of the play's final scene, her attempt to portray Hermione's statue is marred when a memento mori that happens to be in the house refuses to remain hidden. This entire scene seems designed to signal the difference between Gwendolen's story and Hermione's. Leontes is being performed by Rex Gascoigne. Despite his name, Rex is no king but rather Gwendolen's cousin and hapless suitor. It will be Gwendolen's destiny, not Rex's, to become a penitent spouse in a lethally unhappy marriage. Unlike the faithful Hermione, Gwendolen will knowingly choose to be a kind of replacement in marriage—a choice that causes her intense guilt even though Lydia Glasher had never been married to Grandcourt. The subsequent use of lines from *The Winter's Tale* as the epigraph of chapter 31 further underscores the incongruity between Shakespeare's tragicomic precedent and the present narrative. To begin the chapter that narrates Gwendolen and Grandcourt's wedding day, Eliot quotes Camillo directing Florizel and Perdita to a wiser course of action than a

> wild dedication of yourselves
> To unpath'd waters, undream'd shores. (295; cf. *The Winter's Tale*, 4.4.566–67)

Gwendolen will prove to be unlike the lost daughter Perdita, who gains both a loving husband and a familial restoration that she could not have imagined. Gwendolen eventually feels that her unloving marriage to Grandcourt has merely replicated some version of her mother's unhappiness, which involved her second marriage to an unworthy husband.

Yet the allusions to *The Winter's Tale* end up proving increasingly apt insofar as jealousy develops as a key motif in the novel. Around jealousy, the typological patterns of Christian marriage come into clearer view even though the English society depicted in the novel seems far more interested in prosperity and decorum than in religious doctrine. (Eliot makes this the basis of a joking allusion to sixteenth-century English history when she reveals that Lush, Grandcourt's go-between in unsavory matters concerning Mrs. Glasher and Gwendolen, is named Thomas Cranmer Lush.) In establishing the importance of jealousy, the novel pairs the allusions to *The Winter's Tale* with briefer but still revealing allusions to *Othello*. "Perdition catch my soul if I love *him*," Gwendolen remarks about a hapless suitor of little significance (45). When Grandcourt desires to marry Gwendolen and encounters coy resistance, he thinks to herself, "Damn her!" (109). It is possible that Grandcourt is echoing Othello's jealous outburst, "Damn her, lewd minx!" (see *Othello*, 3.3.476). We find a more conspicuous but still roundabout allusion to *Othello* in Daniel Deronda's story. He is unconsciously humming to himself a song from Rossini's *Otello* (with lines that are taken from Dante rather than translated from Shakespeare) as he is rowing on the Thames when he ends up saving Mirah Lapidoth, his future wife, from suicide.

Operating alongside the allusions to *The Winter's Tale*, the echoes of *Othello* suggest the ways that the relationships among the four main characters—Gwendolen, Grandcourt, Daniel, and Mirah—will eventually be structured by jealousy. My chapter on Shakespearean jealousy detailed how that affect channels into a dramatic form the unresolved contradictions between inclusivity and exclusivity within the typological redefinition of Christian marriage. *Daniel Deronda* relies on a kind of typological inversion as its solution: jealousy will drive the central Christian marriage in the plot to tragedy before the novel promises redemption through the culminating story of Jewish marriage. At one point, Grandcourt explicitly asks himself, "Was he going to be a jealous husband?" (347). Initially, the answer seems to be no. His marriage is not centrally defined by personal love (although Grandcourt does experience some form of it, to his surprise) of the sort that might occasion intense jealousy. Deronda does not seem to be a suitable object of Grandcourt's suspicion. Regarding Deronda, Grandcourt flatly tells his wife, "You may talk to him as much as you like. He is not going to take my place" (378). Yet jealousy does take hold. Grandcourt turns increasingly tyrannical in general, and more specifically in his suspicions about Gwendolen and Deronda. By the time Gwendolen goes yachting in the Mediterranean with her husband, she recalls her earlier fear of "his throttling fingers on her neck" (512, cf. 477). Yet the narrator steps in to inform us that—this story being neither *The Winter's Tale* nor *Othello*—Gwendolen will not suffer violence from her jealous husband. Instead, Grandcourt drowns in the sea when Gwendolen commits a kind of passive murder, by not attempting to save his life, to leave a marriage without resorting to divorce.

Eliot calls on her Jewish characters to redeem jealousy as an appropriate insistence on fixity and particularity within love. Before Deronda realizes that he is Jewish but begins to feel the stirrings of a particular identity, he feels within himself a tension between "the blending of a complete personal love in one current with a larger duty" and "a mood of rebellion (what human creature escapes it?) against things in general" (524). In this mood, he suddenly thinks of Gwendolen in particular—in a way that makes the possibility of loving her dimly possible. Yet if Gwendolen's status as a widow should make her newly marriageable, her remarriage to Deronda is never a tenable reality but merely the pretext for misguided jealousy. This feeling of jealousy is useful, however, because it leads Mirah to a realization: "this that I am feeling is the love that makes jealousy" (616). Deronda, for his part, recognizes the extent of his feelings for Mirah when he feels pangs of jealousy toward his friend Hans Meyrick. Deronda can fully recognize himself as the only fitting husband for Mirah when he discovers his own Jewish identity. After the novel's central Christian marriage has lapsed into tragedy, Deronda and Mirah recuperate jealousy as the expression of appropriately exclusive love among the Jewish characters. The novel presents the hope that the work of typological redefinition—of the sort found within biblical marriage—might be carried out again at the registers of art, culture, and national politics.

It is possible that a late allusion to *The Winter's Tale* operates tacitly in this tragicomic culmination. The chest that Deronda's grandfather has left behind, containing evidence of his Jewish heritage, may be reminiscent of the fardel that preserves evidence of Perdita's identity. Deronda, not Gwendolen, is the found child whose restoration anchors some hope of a renewed future. Yet the chest may simply be a generic trope of romance rather than a recognizably Shakespearean device of tragicomic restoration. Around this chest, in fact, Eliot emphasizes the special importance of Milton's writings for the novel's conclusion—and for the calibration of Jewish and Christian love that it attempts. In Deronda's mind, that chest contains "[t]hose written memorials which, says Milton, 'contain a potency of life in them as to be active as that soul whose progeny they are'" (605). Earlier, this same sentiment from *Areopagitica* had been echoed briefly by Hans to Deronda. Yet Hans cites Milton in passing to defend his project of painting Mirah as Berenice; Hans's art—which is a basis of his vain hope to marry Mirah—comes to be gently mocked as second-rate. A specifically Jewish configuration of writing and familial legacy must provide the real affirmation of Milton's remarks about living art.

Prior to this allusion to *Areopagitica*, Eliot provides some suggestive but glancing echoes of Milton. Earlier in the novel, Eliot provides a visual emblem of Gwendolen trying to make the best of her marriage: "she turned his gentle seizure of her hand into a grasp of his and by both hers" (298). This is likely an echo of Milton's Eve recalling how Adam's

      gentle hand

Seized

hers in an act of involuntary possession that she has come to accept (4.488–89). The same echo may be present in Gwendolen's later reflection that Deronda "might have seized her arm with warning to hinder her" from her unwise decision (494). Yet it facilitates Eliot's engagement with Milton to keep these potential allusions to *Paradise Lost* fleeting.[6] Eliot does not elevate Milton as a great poet of Christian conjugal love—or, for that matter, as an advocate of divorce and remarriage on the grounds of incompatibility. Eliot alludes to *Paradise Lost* unambiguously only when she describes how Mirah, in the grip of loving jealousy, responds to Hans's joking about Deronda's seeking to marry the newly widowed Gwendolen. Mirah gives Hans "a look of anger that might have suited Ithuriel" (612). In *Paradise Lost*, Ithuriel is the angel who forces Satan to change back into his shape from his disguise as a toad, as he insinuates a wicked dream into the mind of sleeping Eve. This moment, in other words, identifies Hans (and his hope to turn Mirah into a converted wife) as a hidden enemy who should be exposed. For the purposes of *Daniel Deronda*, Milton serves chiefly as a Christian poet who leaves the typological redefinition of marriage incomplete while focusing on the tragic inheritances of the past.

All of this helps to explains why *Daniel Deronda* concludes with a quotation of *Samson Agonistes*. In Milton's retelling, Samson's repeated marriages to Philistine women have been in bad faith and the occasions for tribal violence rather than incorporation. When Eliot quotes Milton's chorus describing the catharsis experienced after Samson's violent death, she signals that she has renegotiated the tragic or tragicomic possibilities of Christian marriage through a new narrative of Jewish exclusivity. Mordecai's death is acceptable because Mirah's and Deronda's fixed love for one another will carry on a Jewish legacy. Mordecai has given emphatic voice to his beliefs that Jews should neither marry Christians nor assimilate but instead seek to restore a holy nation. For Mordecai, only Jewish particularity can anchor a desirable form of internationalism. Or else, as Deronda's own grandfather is reported to have concluded, "It's no better . . . than the many sorts of grain going back from their variety into sameness" (608). Deronda, for his part, promises to negotiate his newfound Jewishness and his Englishness in some new way. "'The Christian sympathies in which my mind was reared can never die out of me,'" he explains to announce why he will not merely replicate the Jewishness of his grandfather (557).

It may seem absurd to view Deronda as a kind of latter-day Christ who promises to perfect marriage in a newly tenable form. Yet Deronda grows willing to entertain Mordecai's messianic anticipation of him. Deronda does remain absolutely unlike Christ insofar as he brings the redemptive core of marriage into the practical plane—by becoming a literal Jewish husband. Within the exclusive form of loving marriage, the novel's grandly sweeping claims about reconfiguring the particular with the general or universal can assume a more concrete form. It is too late for Gwendolen's own conjugal destiny to be perfected. Deronda begins the novel as the redeemer of her turquoise necklace, but he cannot be the moral redeemer that she has desired him to be. Yet Gwendolen writes to Deronda on his wedding day to articulate an open-ended optimism: "*it shall be better with me because I have known you*" (682). As a result of all this, Eliot's revision of the tragic catharsis found in *Samson Agonistes* may also recuperate a Shakespearean form of jealousy. We recall that in Rossini's *Otello* (the work that was on Deronda's mind on the day he saves his future wife), Desdemona happens to survive while Othello kills himself after his anagnorisis. In Eliot's narrative, the wickedly jealous husband Grandcourt dies, but Gwendolen is allowed some promise of a future even if she is almost guilty of killing him. The appropriately jealous husband Deronda, by contrast, has redeemed his own future wife from suicide.

In *Frankenstein* and *Daniel Deronda*, the religious and theological meanings of marriage are channeled into aesthetic and affective registers of experience. I call attention to the most rudimentary appeals to aesthetic sensibilities in these novels—namely, how claims about a character's remarkable beauty or ugliness generate a fictive sense of singularity. Shelley's novel relies on the fact of the daemon's extreme ugliness as a central explanatory device. Ugliness explains his estrangement from his creator and from society, as well as the gendered identifications (either with Adam or with Satan) that he forms as he reads *Paradise Lost*. Ugliness also underlies the rationale whereby Victor denies him a wife. Eliot's novel begins by asking if Gwendolen was or was not beautiful—specifically, it turns out, in Deronda's eyes. If the entirety of the novel confirms that Gwendolen could be little other than beautiful, Deronda's initial fascination signals the importance of Gwendolen's needing to be something other than conventionally beautiful. Her appearance is her way of achieving some fictive degree of singularity. This would seem to conform entirely to Nancy Armstrong's observation that "Victorian fiction took the task of retailoring the representation of women to indicate that each individual had slightly different desires; no two women could be right for the same man, nor any two men for the same woman."[7] Yet Deronda will not affirm Gwendolen's singularity by marrying her, because his calling is to recalibrate particularity and love through Jewish marriage. Deronda's own good looks, in turn, distinguish him even when—in his ignorance of his Jewishness—he remains somewhat of a pleasing and likeable cipher of a character, existing uncomfortably between Christian typology and a full simulacrum of personhood.

In both novels, the translation of religious patterns into the aesthetic register around the question of loving marriage results in a confusion about political values—a confusion that persists even though overt political statements are made. In *Frankenstein*, we know that the daemon feels sympathy for the colonized and the dispossessed, weeping when he learns of America and "the hapless fate of its original inhabitants" (80). Yet when the daemon requests a wife, he promises to Victor that he will depart "the vast wilds of South America," where no human being will ever see him again (99). The daemon can only think of South America as a *terra nullius*—not for conquest, necessarily, but as the new grounds of a domestic future with his wife.[8] At the center of the novel, the daemon's desire for a wife is sparked not just by his encounter of *Paradise Lost* but also by witnessing the union of Felix and Safie. The daemon is prepared to accept the superiority of a specifically Christian understanding of marriage by witnessing a stock romance fantasy that involves Safie receiving virtue from her Christian mother while being oppressed by her Turkish, Muslim father. What ends up sundering the identification between the daemon and Safie is not just gender, but the fact that Safie is beautiful and desirable—and thus assimilable through marriage to Felix.

In recent decades, Eliot's expression of nascent or proto-Zionism in *Daniel Deronda* has been a topic of much critical discussion.[9] By attending to Eliot's renegotiation of jealousy, fixed love, and replacement within a typological framework of marriage, we can discern how her novel affectively links a resistance to antisemitism to an affirmation of a Jewish nation. Eliot leverages a literary form of conjugal love to promote Mordecai's Zionism over the opinions of the more rationally minded Jews in his conversational circle. Pash and Gideon look forward to an enlightened universalism without nations. They openly criticize the longing for a Jewish nation while also deeming intermarriage and assimilation to be acceptable. In the story of Herr Klesmer and Catherine Arrowpoint, in fact, *Daniel Deronda* presents a case of Jewish-Christian marriage accommodating genuine, mutual love that is grounded in a shared appreciation of art. Yet if the novel leads us to feel that Mordecai's prophetic convictions are somehow more profound than the enlightened views of his acquaintances, then the marriage of Klesmer and Arrowpoint must be felt to be somehow less relevant. This is not because Klesmer and Arrowpoint are jointly less interesting (or less affluent) than the four protagonists whose marriages hew toward sectarian lines. Eliot simply presents Klesmer and Arrowpoint, especially the latter, as being less charmingly beautiful, in a way that marks the couple as minor characters despite their importance in the novel.

Yet as Mordecai's defense of Jewish particularity anchors the novel's conjugal narratives, it reveals the limitations of his—and the novel's—political vision. These limitations have to do with race and the legacies of slavery. At one point in the novel, Eliot presents the moral difference between Grandcourt and Deronda by staging a discussion of the 1865 rebellion in Jamaica: "Grandcourt held that the Jamaican negro was a beastly sort of Baptist Caliban; Deronda said he had always felt a little with Caliban, who naturally had his own point of view and could sing a good song" (276). Elsewhere in the novel, Eliot provides brief reminders of the American Civil War, which is taking place during the time of the novel's action. Mordecai provides us some clues about how the question of Black slavery needs to be kept in the margins to announce the central story of Christians and Jews, of distinctiveness anchoring a new possibility of loving unity. As part of his case for a Jewish nation, Mordecai remarks that "Baruch Spinoza had not a faithful Jewish heart" and that he "laid bare his father's nakedness" (452). Momentarily, Mordecai aligns Spinoza with Noah's transgressive son Ham. Mordecai might be implying that the curse of Ham—which served as a long-standing racist myth of why Black Africans came to be cursed and thus fated to slavery—could, in his eyes, fall on faithless Jews.[10] Yet immediately, Mordecai qualifies his judgment by reminding his listeners that "Spinoza confessed, he saw not why Israel should not again be a chosen nation" (452). Even this weak confession seems to suffice, in Mordecai's mind, for the excommunicated Spinoza to be recuperated from the curse of Ham. When Mordecai then promotes the reconstitution of the Jewish nation by reminding us that it has been "only two centuries since a vessel carried over the ocean the beginning of the great North American nation," that nation would very much seem to be White rather than indigenous or Black (453). We know why Mordecai would quickly foreclose the possibility of a faithless Jew being cursed in a way that would make him partially akin to the enslaved African, and why he would promote instead a comparison between Jewish nationalism and the construction of a tacitly White American nation. Mordecai emphasizes "human choice," and the choice that Jews can make so "that God may again choose them" (453). Mordecai insists on the freedom of self-reconstitution as belonging to Jews and the Jewish nation.

It remains theoretically possible that the new configuration of Jewish particularity and Christian universality that Deronda attempts would accommodate his earlier sympathy with the so-called Calibans. This could be an important facet of Deronda's calling to make Jewishness—in a form defined not by aggrievement but by love, as Mordecai teaches—the basis of a renewed humanism. Deronda must live up to this calling within a conjugal narrative that demands that he renegotiate exclusive jealousy with inclusive love. It remains uncertain, at best, how far Eliot's protagonist could go in refining Mordecai's vision of unity through particularity when he must work through the affective medium of a love that is jealousy fixed, so that it can revive a recognizably typological structure of the singular and the universal.

Notes

INTRODUCTION

1. John Donne, *The Variorum Edition of the Poetry of John Donne: The Holy Sonnets*, ed. Paul A. Parrish, vol. 7, part 1 (Bloomington: Indiana University Press, 2005), 19; line 1. Helen Gardner, in *John Donne: The Divine Poems*, corrected 2nd ed. (Oxford: Oxford University Press, 1978), 77–78, established the conclusion that *Holy Sonnet* 18 was composed after Donne's ordination. Gardner is among the scholars who have downplayed this sonnet's indecorousness. For a reconsideration of this sonnet's textual and critical histories as they relate to Donne's desire for ecumenism, see Lukas Erne, "Donne and Christ's Spouse," *Essays in Criticism* 51, no. 2 (April 2001): 208–29.

2. Donne, *Variorum Edition*, 19; lines 13–14.

3. Unless otherwise noted, quotations from the Bible throughout this book are taken from the Authorized 1611 Version.

4. The Epistle to the Romans also strains gender-specific identification to describe the corporate experience of marriage to Christ. Paul turns remarriage after the death of a spouse into a metaphor for the condition of being redeemed: "if her husband be dead, she is free from that law; so that she is no adulteress, though she be married to another man. Wherefore, my brethren, ye also are become dead to the law by the body of Christ; that ye should be married to another, even to him who is raised from the dead" (7:3–4). Paul exhorts all Christians—with *adelphoi*, translated here as "brethren," functioning as an inclusive term—to identify with the hypothetical widow.

5. See Will Stockton, *Members of His Body: Shakespeare, Paul, and a Theology of Nonmonogamy* (New York: Fordham University Press, 2017); and Melissa E. Sanchez, *Queer Faith: Reading Promiscuity and Race in the Secular Love Tradition* (New York: New York University Press, 2019). Stockton studies how the dynamism between plural love and the couple found in Paul's definition of marriage informs Shakespearean drama. Sanchez pairs Pauline theology with Renaissance love poetry. Turning to *Holy Sonnet* 18, she concludes that Donne recognizes how religious fidelity, as the New Testament describes it, "unfixes and dematerializes the positions of gender and agency on which its accommodatory logic relies" (33–34).

Both Stockton and Sanchez discern the queerness of Paul's unstable definition of marriage. Stockton finds the use of this label to be strategic because it "locates the ostensibly anti-Christian institution of plural marriage" within biblical marriage itself (5).

6. The pattern of male desire for a woman serving to reinforce a homosocial bond has been described influentially by Eve Kosofsky Sedgwick, in *Between Men: English Literature and Male Homosocial Desire* (New York: Columbia University Press, 1985). As Sedgwick explains, the primacy of homosocial and homoerotic bonds between men reinforces gender hierarchy in a patriarchal culture.

7. Walton reports, in *The Life of John Donne* (London, 1658), 52, that after Ann Donne died, John gave their seven surviving children "a voluntary assurance never to bring them under the subjection of a step-mother, which promise he kept most faithfully" until his own death at the age of forty-four. Scholars remain uncertain about the accuracy of this account and the meaning of Donne's reported vow. For the claim that Donne eventually turned away from earthly love in favor of spiritual concerns, see Ramie Targoff, *John Donne, Body and Soul* (Chicago: University of Chicago Press, 2008), 76–78; and *Posthumous Love: Eros and the Afterlife in Renaissance England* (Chicago: University of Chicago Press, 2014), 22–23. For a discussion of Walton's description within a broader case for the importance of asceticism in Donne's religious imagination, see Patrick J. McGrath, *Early Modern Asceticism: Literature, Religion, and Austerity in the English Renaissance* (Toronto: University of Toronto Press, 2020), 34–48.

8. Martin Luther, *Luther's Works,* vol. 1, *Lectures on Genesis: Chapters 1–5,* ed. Jaroslav Pelikan (Saint Louis: Concordia, 1958), 139.

9. Judith M. Lieu, *Marcion and the Making of a Heretic: God and Scripture in the Second Century* (Cambridge: Cambridge University Press, 2015), 142.

10. For some examples, see E. M. W. Tillyard, *Milton*, rev. ed. (London: Macmillan, 1966), 318–26; David Quint, "Expectation and Prematurity in Milton's Nativity Ode," *Modern Philology* 97, no. 2 (November 1999): 195–219; and Brooke Conti, "Milton, Jerome, and Apocalyptic Virginity," *Renaissance Quarterly* 72, no. 1 (Spring 2019): 194–230.

11. Anselm of Canterbury, *Anselm of Canterbury: The Major Works*, ed. Brian Davies and G. R. Evans (Oxford: Oxford University Press, 1998), 282.

12. On Anselm's theory of atonement and the penal doctrine developed by Protestant theologians such as Martin Luther and Philip Melanchthon, see Jaroslav Pelikan, *The Christian Tradition: A History of the Development of Doctrine*, vol. 4, *Reformation of Church and Dogma (1300–1700)* (Chicago: University of Chicago Press, 1985), 155–67. Pelikan notes that it is accurate to describe Luther's doctrine as an extension of Anselm's. Yet Pelikan also cautions against conflating the two, given the meaningful differences between the payment of a debt of honor, as described by Anselm, and the displaced form of divine punishment that the penal doctrine describes.

13. For feminist scholarship that has recuperated the importance of Speght's writings and the *querelle des femmes* in England more generally, see Ann Rosalind Jones, "Counterattacks on 'the Bayter of Women': Three Pamphleteers of the Early Seventeenth Century," in *The Renaissance Englishwoman in Print: Counterbalancing the Canon*, ed. Anne M. Haselkorn and Betty S. Travitsky (Amherst: University of Massachusetts Press, 1990), 45–62; Diane Purkiss, "Material Girls: The Seventeenth-Century Woman Debate," in *Women, Texts, and Histories: 1575–1760*, ed. Clare Brant and Purkiss (London: Routledge, 1992), 69–101; Barbara Kiefer Lewalski, *Writing Women in Jacobean England* (Cambridge, MA: Harvard University Press, 1993), esp. 153–75; Helen Speight, "Rachel Speght's Polemical Life," *Huntington Library Quarterly* 65, nos. 3–4 (2002): 449–63; Christina Luckyj, "Rachel Speght and the 'Criticall Reader,'" *English Literary Renaissance* 36, no. 2 (Spring 2006): 227–49; and "*A Mouzell for Melastomus* in Context: Rereading the Swetnam-Speght Debate," *English Literary Renaissance* 40, no. 1 (Winter 2010): 113–31.

14. For accounts of Speght's reading of Genesis in relation to the gendered thinking of *Paradise Lost*, see Mary Nyquist, "The Genesis of Gendered Subjectivity in the Divorce Tracts and in *Paradise Lost*," in *Re-membering Milton*, ed. Mary Nyquist and Margaret W. Ferguson (New York: Methuen, 1987), 99–127; and Shannon Miller, *Engendering the Fall: John Milton and Seventeenth-Century Women Writers* (Philadelphia: University of Pennsylvania Press, 2008), 21–47.

15. Rachel Speght, *The Polemics and Poems of Rachel Speght*, ed. Barbara Kiefer Lewalski (New York: Oxford University Press, 1996), 18.

16. Ibid., 23.

17. Ibid.

18. William Gouge, *Of Domesticall Duties: Eight Treatises* (London, 1622), 44.

19. Ibid., 125.

20. Ibid., 344.

21. John Calvin, *The Institution of the Christian Religion*, trans. Thomas Norton (London, 1561), 2:51^r.

22. C. S. Lewis was deliberately overstating the case when he declared, in *The Allegory of Love: A Study in Medieval Tradition* (Oxford: Oxford University Press, 1936), 13, that medieval marriage "had nothing to do with love, and no 'nonsense' about marriage was tolerated. All matches were matches of interest." I do not seek to make overly emphatic claims about historical periods to describe meaningful cultural changes.

23. Northrop Frye's schematization of comedy has become so influential that his ideas are sometimes referred to without being cited. See "The Argument of Comedy," in *English Institute Essays*, ed. D. A. Robertson, Jr. (New York: Columbia University Press, 1949), 58–73; this argument was subsequently incorporated into the "Third Essay" of *The Anatomy of Criticism* (Princeton, NJ: Princeton University Press, 1957), 163–86.

24. Frances E. Dolan, *Marriage and Violence: The Early Modern Legacy* (Philadelphia: University of Pennsylvania Press, 2008), 4. For discussions of how classical ideals of friendship present a partial alternative (often, but not always, a same-sex alternative) to the inequality that persists within companionate marriage, see Laurie Shannon, *Sovereign Amity: Figures of Friendship in Shakespearean Contexts* (Chicago: University of Chicago Press, 2002); Thomas H. Luxon, *Single Imperfection: Milton, Marriage and Friendship* (Pittsburgh: Duquesne University Press, 2005); and Penelope Anderson, *Friendship's Shadows: Women's Friendship and the Politics of Betrayal in England, 1640–1705* (Edinburgh: Edinburgh University Press, 2012).

25. Lawrence Stone's work on the nature of attachments within families has been important for this body of scholarship. See *The Crisis of the Aristocracy, 1558–1641* (Oxford: Clarendon, 1965); *The Family, Sex and Marriage in England, 1500–1800* (New York: Harper and Row, 1977); and *The Road to Divorce: England, 1530–1987* (Oxford: Oxford University Press, 1990). Most relevant to my argument is Stone's account of the rise of affective individualism, which is described as taking hold at the end of the seventeenth century and more firmly in the eighteenth. Stone's claims have been the object of much scrutiny and disagreement. As Christopher Hill remarks in an early review of *The Family, Sex and Marriage* in *The Economic History Review* 31, no. 3 (August 1978): 457, "Much of what Prof. Stone has to say about the upper 10 per cent of the population is fascinating and convincing. . . . For classes below that level it is difficult to find evidence." It has become common to cite Stone primarily to question his findings. In the introduction to *The Family in Early Modern England* (Cambridge: Cambridge University Press, 2007), 16, Helen Berry and Elizabeth Foyster ask, "Overall, was Stone right?" They conclude that recent work shows that "the answer must be no" in part because "the pattern of gender relations was neither as straightforward as he suggested, nor the sole axis of power at play between family members." Historians have provided more detailed views of early modern domestic life in part by reexamining archival records. See, for example, Amy Louise Erickson, *Women and Property in Early Modern England* (London: Routledge, 1993); and David Cressy, *Birth, Marriage, and Death: Ritual, Religion, and the Life Cycle in Tudor and Stuart England* (Oxford: Oxford University Press, 1997). Cressy, 261, remarks that "the notion, recklessly set forth by Lawrence Stone, that early modern marriage was barren of love, has been thoroughly rejected by studies of diaries, letters, and church court cases."

26. Hill uses this phrase in *Milton and the English Revolution* (1977), paperback ed., (London: Verso, 2020), 359, and, subsequently, in "God and the English Revolution," *History Workshop* 17, no. 1 (Spring 1984): 26.

27. An important line of thinking about marriage in seventeenth-century England concerns the coexistence of consensual contract and gender inequality.

As the marriage contract becomes deployed as a metaphor for political contracts and obligations, this coexistence furnishes a basis of heated debate. For a brief but influential consideration of this topic, see Mary Lyndon Shanley, "Marriage Contract and Social Contract in Seventeenth Century English Political Thought," *Western Political Quarterly* 32, no. 1 (March 1979): 79–91. In *Wayward Contracts: The Crisis of Political Obligation in England, 1640–1674* (Princeton, NJ: Princeton University Press, 2004), Victoria Kahn provides an authoritative account of contractual thinking within the upheavals of the seventeenth century. Kahn frequently mentions marriage as a metaphor for political obligation; see 149–69 for sustained discussion.

28. We can find evidence of the lasting importance of marriage in the prominence that advocating for same-sex marriage has assumed within the contest for queer rights. In the United States, arguments that the right to same-sex marriage should not be an objective because queer desire promises different forms of sociability and desire have circulated both in theoretical discussions as well as arguments aimed at a more general readership. At the broad level of national politics and popular sentiment, however, such arguments have not tended to prevail over the impulse to secure the right to marry (and the range of benefits that comes with it) for same-sex couples.

29. See, for example, Uma Narayan, "'Male-Order Brides': Immigrant Women, Domestic Violence and Immigration Law," *Hypatia* 10, no. 1 (Winter 1995): 104–19; Helena Wray, "An Ideal Husband? Marriages of Convenience, Moral Gate-Keeping and Immigration to the UK," *European Journal of Migration and Law* 8, nos. 3–4 (January 2006): 303–20; and Catherine Dauvergne, "Gendering Islamophobia to Better Understand Immigration Laws," *Journal of Ethnic and Migration Studies* 46, no. 12 (2020): 2569–84.

30. See Anne-Marie D'Aoust, "In the Name of Love: Marriage, Migration, Governmentality, and Technologies of Love," *International Political Sociology* 7, no. 3 (September 2013): 258–74; and Mons Bissenbakker, "Attachment Required: The Affective Governmentality of Marriage Migration in the Danish Aliens Act 2000—2018," *International Political Sociology* 13, no. 2 (June 2019): 181–97.

31. See *Biao v. Denmark*, no. 38590/10 (ECHR), May 24, 2016. The case in question involved a Ghanaian-born Danish citizen seeking a residence permit for his Ghanaian wife. The attachment requirement was in effect as a rising number of asylum seekers—from countries including Afghanistan, Eritrea, Iraq, and Somalia—led to a surge in nationalism in Danish politics. In July 2019 the European Court of Justice found that provisions of the attachment requirement violated the 1980 Association Agreement between the EU and Turkey by restricting the movement of people. Bissenbakker, in "Attachment Required," discusses how the so-called ghetto clause of the Danish Aliens Act continues to do the work of the attachment requirement; this clause denies the right of anyone living in

a "problematic" or "vulnerable" neighborhood to apply for spousal reunification (193–94).

32. Saidiya Hartman, in *Scenes of Subjection: Terror, Slavery, and Self-Making in Nineteenth-Century America* (New York: Oxford University Press, 1997), esp. 17–32, 52–54, 61–65, and 115–24, describes fungibility as shaping not only the experiences of slaves but also the lives of emancipated Black Americans. In *Investing in Life: Insurance in Antebellum America* (Baltimore: Johns Hopkins University Press, 2010), Sharon Ann Murphy recounts how, in the early nineteenth century, life insurance was a new practice that many White Americans deemed distasteful because it asked them to calculate the worth of their loved ones. Murphy presents case studies such as the history of the Baltimore Life Insurance Company, which initially aimed to sell life insurance to White Americans but ended up finding greater demand for slave insurance. C. Riley Snorton, in *Black on Both Sides: A Racial History of Trans Identity* (Minneapolis: University of Minnesota Press, 2017), 55, reminds us that the first recorded use of the English word "fungible" lies an 1818 statement that anxiously denies that slaves are actually fungible even while admitting at they may be (like cattle and horses) "subjects of *compensation*."

33. Throughout this book, I capitalize both Black and White when referring to racial categories. I find convincing the arguments set forth by Kwame Anthony Appiah, in "The Case for Capitalizing the B in Black," *Atlantic*, June 18, 2020, and by Eve L. Ewing, in "I'm a Black Scholar Who Studies Race. Here's Why I Capitalize 'White,'" *Zora*, July 2, 2020, https://zora.medium.com/im-a-black-scholar-who-studies-race-here-s-why-i-capitalize-white-f94883aa2dd3.

34. Othello's remark that he had been enslaved and then liberated is brief and leaves it unclear how his racial and religious identities figured into this experience. See William Shakespeare, *Othello*, in *The Riverside Shakespeare*, ed. G. Blakemore Evans and J. J. M. Tobin, 2nd ed. (Boston: Houghton Mifflin, 1996), 1256; act 1, scene 3, lines 71–75. Unless otherwise noted, all quotations from Shakespeare's plays are taken from the *Riverside* and will be cited parenthetically by act, scene, and line numbers. As Daniel Vitkus observes, in *Turning Turk: English Theater and the Multicultural Mediterranean, 1570–1630* (Houndmills, UK: Palgrave / St. Martin's Press, 2003), 92, Othello may have been abducted as a Christian Moor by Muslim corsairs or he might have been enslaved as a Muslim Moor but then later redeemed physically and also spiritually through religious conversion.

35. Ernst Kantorowicz, *The King's Two Bodies: A Study in Mediaeval Political Theology*, reprint ed. (Princeton, NJ: Princeton University Press, 1997), 20.

36. Ibid., 223. Constance Jordan, in "The Household and the State: Transformations in the Representation of an Analogy from Aristotle to James I," *Modern Language Quarterly* 54, no. 3 (September 1993): 307–26, revisits James's declaration within a broad survey of the analogy between marriage and monarchical rule, and the incoherence it contains.

37. Kantorowicz, *King's Two Bodies*, 223.

38. Ibid., xviii.

39. Ibid. For a discussion of what may be lurking behind this disavowal, see David Norbrook, "The Emperor's New Body? *Richard II*, Ernst Kantorowicz, and the Politics of Shakespeare Criticism," *Textual Practice* 10, no. 2 (1996): 329–57. Norbrook reminds us that even in the 1640s, appeals to the logic of the king's two bodies were not nearly as pervasive as Kantorowicz suggests. Norbrook's critique of Kantorowicz on the grounds of accuracy is framed by a pointed biographical argument. Kantorowicz composed *The King's Two Bodies* in the United States as a Jewish emigré who had fled Germany in 1938. Yet in his earlier scholarship, Kantorowicz had taken part in a spirit of German nationalism. In 1927, Norbrook reminds us, he had published a romanticized biography of the thirteenth-century Holy Roman emperor Frederick II. Norbrook argues that *The King's Two Bodies* exhibits the residual sway of that tendency toward political mythmaking.

40. See Michel Foucault, *Discipline and Punish: The Birth of the Prison*, trans. Alan Sheridan, 2nd ed. (New York: Vintage, 1995), 28–30.

41. Graham Hammill and Julia Reinhard Lupton, introduction to *Political Theology and Early Modernity* (Chicago: University of Chicago Press, 2012), 1.

42. Carl Schmitt, *Political Theology: Four Chapters on the Concept of Sovereignty*, trans. George Schwab (Chicago: University of Chicago Press, 2005), 36.

43. Hammill and Lupton, introduction, 3.

44. See Anselm Haverkamp, "*Richard II*, Bracton, and the End of Political Theology," *Law and Literature* 16, no. 3 (Fall 2004): 313–26; and Jennifer R. Rust, "Political Theology and Shakespeare Studies," *Literature Compass* 6, no. 1 (January 2009): 175–90.

45. For an important work in this recuperation, see Joseph W. Bendersky, *Carl Schmitt: Theorist for the Reich* (Princeton, NJ: Princeton University Press, 1983). Bendersky regularly blurs the line between explanations of and excuses for Schmitt's work on behalf of Nazism. For an example of the later tendency to single out Schmitt's brilliance, see Chantal Mouffe's opening statement, in introducing the volume *The Challenge of Carl Schmitt* (London: Verso, 1999), 1: "That Schmitt is one of the great political and legal theorists of this century is now widely recognized." The inverted syntax subordinates the awareness that Schmitt is thought of in this way only now—that is, after a project of recuperation—to the proclamation of his intellectual greatness. For a very different example, see Jacob Taubes's autobiographical reminiscence of visiting Schmitt after some correspondence in *The Political Theology of Paul*, ed. Aleida Assmann et al., trans. Dana Hollander (Stanford: Stanford University Press, 2004), 1–5. Taubes's vignette is barbed insofar as it is the story of a Jewish scholar teaching Schmitt something new about Paul's Epistle to the Romans. Yet Taubes still begins by narrating his exciting encounter with Schmitt, "the greatest state law theorist [*Staatsrechtler*] of our time" (2).

46. The use of this chant was discussed in numerous media and commentary outlets. For examples, see Yair Rosenberg, "'Jews Will Not Replace Us': Why White Supremacists Go After Jews," *Washington Post*, August 14, 2017; and Emma Green, "Why Charlottesville Marchers Were Obsessed with Jews," *Atlantic*, August 15, 2017. The chant reveals how the connection between antisemitism and racist nationalism operates within paranoia about demographic replacement. Insofar as these protestors were rallying in support of Confederate iconography, their motives would have been anti-Black racism. Insofar as their racism reacts to shifting demographics in the United States, their fear of being replaced (a key feature of White nationalist discourse) could have centered explicitly on Asian and Latin Americans. Yet antisemitism provides the long-established form in which racist fears continue to find expression.

47. Reminders of the way Schmitt's thinking has informed far-right-wing thinking in the United States have circulated in public-oriented commentary outlets. See, for example, Andrew Kolin, "Politics above Law: How Trump Channels Far Right Icon Carl Schmitt, without Knowing It," *Informed Comment*, September 9, 2017; Joseph Owen, "Why Journalists Reviving Carl Schmitt Are Playing a Precarious Game," *Prospect Magazine*, September 11, 2019; and Tamsin Shaw, "William Barr: The Carl Schmitt of Our Time," *New York Review of Books*, January 15, 2020.

48. Eric L. Santner, *The Royal Remains: The People's Two Bodies and the Endgames of Sovereignty* (Chicago: University of Chicago Press, 2011), 46.

49. Ibid., 34.

50. See Sianne Ngai, *Ugly Feelings* (Cambridge, MA: Harvard University Press, 2005), 38–77. We can also recall that the first volume of Lauren Berlant's national sentimentality trilogy, *The Anatomy of Fantasy: Hawthorne, Utopia, and Everyday Life* (Chicago: University of Chicago Press, 1991), details how Nathaniel Hawthorne examines and works against patterns of nineteenth-century American belonging. Berlant's approach to gender, the body, the law, and citizenship draws on theoretical accounts relating the discursive possibilities of the modern nation to capitalism. It would become clearer what affect theory could do in Berlant's handling in the subsequent installments of her trilogy and then in *Cruel Optimism* (Durham, NC: Duke University Press, 2011). These later works attend to contemporary American society, and Berlant increasingly focuses on the affective and aesthetic constitution of the present as such.

51. Sigmund Freud, "On Narcissism," in *The Standard Edition of the Complete Psychological Works of Sigmund Freud*, trans. and ed. James Strachey (London: Hogarth Press, 1957), 14:88.

52. Ibid.

53. Ibid., 90.

54. Ibid., 89.

55. Ibid., 91.

56. Ibid., 101.

57. On the confusion involved in Freud's assumption that attachment to the same gender is tantamount to an attachment to the same self, see Michael Warner, "Homo-Narcissism; or, Heterosexuality," in *Engendering Men: The Question of Male Feminist Criticism*, ed. Joseph A. Boone and Michael Cadden (New York: Routledge, 1990), 190–206. Warner shows how Freudian psychoanalysis transmits that homophobic confusion in a modern form. Yet Warner still finds value in Freud's alignment of homosexual libidinal attachment with the positive, progressive impulses of liberal values.

58. Victoria Kahn, *The Future of Illusion: Political Theology and Early Modern Texts* (Chicago: University of Chicago Press, 2014), 177.

59. I have completed this book as the mishandling of the COVID-19 pandemic contributed to over half a million deaths in the United States. The Trump administration stoked a widespread denial of sound public policy (and even basic medical advice) in the name of economic activity and personal freedom. Not just in the United States but also in other places around the world—including Brazil, Hungary, India, and the United Kingdom—the willful mismanagement of the pandemic has been of a piece with reactionary and nationalistic forms of political leadership.

CHAPTER 1

1. John Haringto[n], trans., *Orlando Furioso in English Heroical Verse* (London, 1591), 404.

2. Ibid., 405.

3. Ibid., ii^r.

4. Edmund Spenser, *The Faerie Queene*, ed. A.C. Hamilton, rev. 2nd ed. (Harlow, UK: Longman, 2007), 29; book 1, canto 1, stanza 1, line 9. All quotations from *The Faerie Queene* are taken from this edition and will be cited parenthetically by book, canto, stanza, and line numbers.

5. Christopher Warley, *Sonnet Sequences and Social Distinction in Renaissance England* (Cambridge: Cambridge University Press, 2005), 101.

6. Louis Adrian Montrose, "'Shaping Fantasies': Figurations of Gender and Power in Elizabethan Culture," *Representations* 1, no. 2 (Spring 1983): 64. Montrose's work has detailed how the erotics of Elizabethan sovereignty permeated the period and its aesthetic productions. See "The Elizabethan Subject and the Spenserian Text," in *Literary Theory / Renaissance Texts*, ed. Patricia Parker and David Quint (Baltimore: Johns Hopkins University Press, 1986), 303–40; "Spenser and the Elizabethan Political Imaginary," *ELH* 69, no. 4 (Winter 2002): 907–46; and *The Subject of Elizabeth: Authority, Gender, and Representation* (Chicago: University of Chicago Press, 2006).

7. For a discussion of this, see Gordon Braden, *Petrarchan Love and the Continental Renaissance* (New Haven, CT: Yale University Press, 1999), 15–20.

8. Petrarch, *Petrarch's Lyric Poems: The Rime sparse and Other Lyrics*, trans. and ed. Robert M. Durling (Cambridge, MA: Harvard University Press, 1976), 578; *Canzoniere* 366, lines 45–48. All quotations from the *Canzoniere* are from this edition and will be cited parenthetically by poem and line numbers.

9. John Freccero's influential essay, "The Fig Tree and the Laurel: Petrarch's Poetics," *Diacritics* 5, no. 1 (Spring 1975): 34–40, describes how the circularity between Laura and the laurel—the putative object of desire pointing to the symbol of poetic fame and vice versa—establishes a language that is idolatrously self-enclosed rather than pointing to God.

10. Edmund Spenser, *Edmund Spenser's Poetry*, ed. Hugh Maclean and Anne Lake Prescott, 3rd ed. (New York: Norton, 1993), 617; line 2. All quotations from the *Amoretti* are taken from this edition and will be cited parenthetically by sonnet and line numbers.

11. See Carol V. Kaske, "Another Liturgical Dimension of *Amoretti* 68," *Notes and Queries* 24, no. 6 (December 1977): 518–19.

12. On this, see Russ Leo, "Jean Calvin, Christ's Despair, and the Reformation *Descensus ad Inferos*," *Reformation* 23, no. 1 (May 2018): 53–78. Leo traces how Calvin breaks from Desiderius Erasmus's questioning of whether Christ's descent should even remain an item of faith and proceeds to develop a less literal account of Christ descending into despair—without, it seems, having read Luther's writings on the topic.

13. Ovid, *Metamorphoses: Books I–VIII*, trans. Frank Justus Miller, rev. G. P. Goold, 3rd ed. (Cambridge, MA: Harvard University Press, 2004), 148; book 3, line 348. Unless otherwise noted, translations from foreign works are my own.

14. Petrarch's most elaborate Ovidian pastiche, *Canzoniere* 23, contains a fleeting allusion to the Narcissus story, suggesting that the frustrated male lover is akin to Echo (see lines 137–38). More emphatic is the allusion to Actaeon near the poem's conclusion. As punishment for gazing on Laura, the speaker is transformed into a stag and hunted by his hounds. When Petrarch describes himself as fleeing the sound of his hounds ("et ancor de' miei can fuggo lo stormo") an echo between *can* and *canto* or *canzone* confirms the suggestion made in the opening of the poem—that the speaker has become the pursued object of his own poetry (line 160).

15. Calvin R. Edwards, "The Narcissus Myth in Spenser's Poetry," *Studies in Philology* 74, no. 1 (January 1977): 72.

16. Warner, "Homo-Narcissism," 200.

17. Britomart, the heroine of book 3 of *The Faerie Queene*, precedes the speaker of the *Amoretti* as a Narcissus figure who finds in a mirror the grounds of genuine love for another of another sex. She finds Artegall partly by becoming like him.

Linda Gregerson traces the role of mirroring in Spenserian subject formation, contrasting the success of Britomart's case with the failure of Malbecco's. In *The Reformation of the Subject: Spenser, Milton, and the English Protestant Epic* (Cambridge: Cambridge University Press, 2006), 54, Gregerson observes that what is missing "from the cuckold's [Malbecco's] tale *and also from Spenser's poem* is the notion of symmetrical reciprocity as the ground and standard of erotic love. . . . The mutual love of equals is not only missing . . . it is not meant to *register* as missing." My discussion details how, in the *Amoretti*, Spenser develops what is missing in *The Faerie Queene*.

18. See *Oxford English Dictionary*, s.v. "will" n.1, def. 2. Hereafter referred to as *OED*.

19. Ovidian precedent informs Spenser's deictic experiments. Both Actaeon and Narcissus have deictic troubles in the midst of their identity crises. "*Iste ego sum*" Narcissus cries out, and his predicament is to be right and wrong at the same time (Ovid, *Metamorphoses*, 156; 3.463). The "*ego*" does confront itself as a reflected "*iste*," but an "*ego*" can never also be in the place of an "*iste*" for itself. Actaeon's utterance, "*Actaeon ego sum!*" seems more useful, breaking the tautology of "*ego sum*" with a proper name (Ovid 140; 3.230). Yet Actaeon cannot utter these words to his hounds because his body has altered and only his mind remains unchanged.

20. Sanchez, *Queer Faith*, 152, suggests that the *Amoretti*'s supposedly happy conclusion provides one occasion for us not only to recall but also to historicize the legal feminist scholar Catherine MacKinnon's critique of consent within heterosexuality.

21. Qtd. from Leonard Barkan, "Diana and Actaeon: The Myth as Synthesis," *English Literary Renaissance* 10, no. 3 (Autumn 1980): 327.

22. Qtd. from Thomas P. Roche, Jr., *The Kindly Flame: A Study of the Third and Fourth Books of Spenser's* Faerie Queene (Princeton, NJ: Princeton University Press), 112.

23. Barkan, "Diana and Actaeon," 329–30.

24. Ibid., 330.

25. William Langland, *Piers Plowman, Piers Plowman Electronic Archive*, vol 7: British Library MS Lansdowne 398 and Bodleian Library MS Rawlinson Poetry 38, http://piers.chass.ncsu.edu/texts/R; passus 18, line 154. All quotations of *Piers Plowman* are taken from the R-text in this electronic edition and will be cited parenthetically by passus and line number.

26. Gregory Nazianzen, "The Second Oration on Easter," in *A Select Library of Nicene and Post-Nicene Fathers*, vol. 7, *S. Cyril of Jerusalem, S. Gregory Nazianzen*, ed. Philip Schaff and Henry Wace, 2nd series (New York: Christian Literature Company), 431.

27. Devin Singh, in *Divine Currency: The Theological Power of Money in the West* (Stanford: Stanford University Press, 2018), 132–65, argues that despite

seeming to be obsolete, the ransom theory continues to be relevant long past early Church history. Singh describes how, "[u]sing language of ownership, property, and exchange, Irenaeus separates out discourse on evil and falleness from a creator God" (140). In Singh's account, the usefulness of this distinction—and its capacity to shield the supposed goodness of sovereignty from the moral dubiousness of management—persists into early modernity.

28. See John N. King, *Spenser's Poetry and the Reformation Tradition* (Princeton, NJ: Princeton University Press, 1990), 169–170.

29. Thomas Wyatt, *Sir Thomas Wyatt: The Complete Poems*, ed. R. A. Rebholz (New Haven, CT: Yale University Press, 1978), 77; line 13.

30. For some discussions of this possible identification, see Retha M. Warnicke, "The Eternal Triangle and Court Politics: Henry VIII, Anne Boleyn, and Sir Thomas Wyatt," *Albion* 18, no. 4 (Winter 1986): 565–79; Jason Powell, "'For Caesar's I Am': Henrician Diplomacy and Representations of King and Country in Thomas Wyatt's Poetry," *Sixteenth Century Journal* 36, no. 2 (Summer 2005): 415–31; and Greg Walker, *Writing under Tyranny: English Literature and the Henrician Reformation* (Oxford: Oxford University Press, 2005), 287–88.

31. In the second installment of *The Faerie Queene,* Spenser makes an overt reference to his marriage to Elizabeth Boyle. In book 6, canto 10, the poet's pastoral persona Colin Clout emerges on Mount Acidale, singing of his own love as she stands out amid a circle of Graces. The poet's voice then interrupts this already intrusive episode, imploring "Great *Gloriana*, greatest Maiesty" to pardon the shepherd who has taken the time to "make one minime of thy poore handmaid" (6.10.28.3–6). He has done so, the poet explains, to embed her praise within the queen's greater poetic glory.

32. In *The Allegory of Love*, 344–45, C. S. Lewis worries that "some stupid person will ask us, 'Who, then, is Scudamour? And if Chastity means (for Spenser) married love, and that is Britomart, then what is the difference between Britomart and Amoret?'" This dismissal of certain questions as "stupid" has proven to be unwarranted. Critics have shown the value of engaging with questions about compatibility in marriage, in a way that that treats Spenser's characters as something resembling persons. See, for example, Richard A. Levin, "The Legende of the Redcrosse Knight and Una, or of the Love of a Good Woman," *SEL* 31, no. 1 (Winter 1991): 1–24; and Andrew Hadfield, "Spenser and Religion—Yet Again," *SEL* 51, no. 1 (Winter 2011): 21–46.

33. Spenser, *Faerie Queene*, 717.

34. Darryl J. Gless, *Interpretation and Theology in Spenser* (Cambridge: Cambridge University Press, 1994), 52.

35. James Nohrnberg, in *The Analogy of* The Faerie Queene, rev. ed. (Princeton: Princeton University Press, 1980), 35–58, discusses the relationship between Arthur's all-encompassing virtue and the individual knights with their respective

virtues. Arthur, as a type of Christ, confronts the problems besetting Christian typology, whereby all partial types of Christ must be rendered obsolete.

36. As Hamilton notes, Redcrosse's birth as a Saxon makes would make him a fourth-century character, whereas Arthur and the Britons belong to the sixth century. See Spenser, *Faerie Queene*, 1.10.65.1–5n.

37. In "Striking the French Match: Jean Bodin, Queen Elizabeth, and the Occultation of Sovereign Marriage," in *Political Theology and Early Modernity*, ed. Graham Hammill and Julia Reinhard Lupton (Chicago: University of Chicago Press, 2012), 240–63, Drew Daniel revisits Elizabeth I's failed marriage negotiation with the Duke of Alençon, emphasizing the politico-theological significance of the queen's protracted unwillingness or inability to decide on marriage. Daniel reminds us that Jean Bodin was present at these 1581 negotiations as Alençon's secretary. Bodin encountered a female sovereign's protracted indecision, in a form that should have made quite visible some of the qualifications regarding absolutist rule made explicit in *Six livres de la République*. Daniel considers the importance of Elizabeth's indecision for understanding the way Carl Schmitt would come to rely on Bodin to construct his ideas about the sovereign decision. Irresolvable questions about why Elizabeth would or could not marry belie Schmitt's presentation of the sovereign decision as a core political truth that bridges modernity with early modernity.

38. King, *Spenser's Poetry*, 150. See also John N. King, "Queen Elizabeth I: Representations of the Virgin Queen," *Renaissance Quarterly* 43, no. 1 (Spring 1990): 30–74. This essay reconsiders William Camden's frequently quoted report that in 1559, the young Queen Elizabeth had declared before the House of Commons, "I am already bound unto an Husband which is the Kingdome of England." King questions the accuracy of Camden's reporting and the likelihood that the queen would have cultivated a myth of perpetual celibacy at such an early date. Yet King traces how the "complicated symbolic matrix" of the cult of Elizabeth's virginity did arise decades later (53).

39. Marie Axton, *The Queen's Two Bodies: Drama and the Elizabethan Succession* (London: Royal Historical Society, 1977), 38–39.

40. Ibid, 75. For a very different engagement with Kantorowicz's theory, see David Lee Miller, *The Poem's Two Bodies: The Poetics of the 1590 Faerie Queene* (Princeton, NJ: Princeton University Press, 1988). Miller reads Spenser poem as being "organized with reference to the anticipated-but-deferred wholeness of an ideal body" (3). The wholeness that Miller discerns is not necessarily the unity of Spenser's poem but rather the unity of historicist and formalist modes of reading.

41. The Palmer's teaching echoes a lesson that Ariosto advances through the story of Orlando's errant desires. "Yet all shall finde," as John Harington's translation puts it, "loue's a thing of naught, / For sure, it is an open signe of madnes" (189; 24.1.6–7). Guyon's status as the Spenserian hero with no conjugal destiny

plays a key role in A. S. P. Woodhouse's argument, in "Nature and Grace in the *Faerie Queene*," *ELH* 16, no. 3 (September 1949): 194–228, that Guyon operates in the order of nature rather than of Christian grace. Anthea Hume, in *Edmund Spenser: Protestant Poet* (Cambridge: Cambridge University Press, 1984), 59–71, argues that Guyon's awareness of God cannot be explained by a natural understanding of deity, as he professes an avowedly Christian identity after he first emerges in the poem.

42. On the pattern of similarities and differences relating Medina's feast to Dido's, see John Watkins, *The Specter of Dido: Spenser and Virgilian Epic* (New Haven, CT: Yale University Press, 1995), 127–30.

43. Virgil, *Virgil: Eclogues, Georgics, Aeneid, Appendix Vergiliana*, trans. H. R. Fairclough, rev. G. P. Goold, 2 vols., (Cambridge, MA: Harvard UP, 1999–2000), 1:316; 2.3.

44. Paul Alpers, *The Poetry of* The Faerie Queene (Princeton, NJ: Princeton University Press, 1967), 256.

45. Judith H. Anderson, in *The Growth of a Personal Voice:* Piers Plowman *and* The Faerie Queene (New Haven, CT: Yale University Press, 1976), 64, notes that Mammon's status as a "Guyler" associates him specifically with Langland's Lucifer. Anderson offers an insightful account of *Piers Plowman* as a precedent for the episode of Mammon's Cave, and for the way that the Protestant poet relates to Guyon's partially Christlike form of heroism.

46. Virgil's underworld traveler is curious to learn more about the punishments that the damned suffer. The Sibyl briefly refers to "him over whom hangs a black crag that seems ready to slip and fall at any moment"—namely, Tantalus (Virgil, *Virgil* [Fairclough], 1:575; 6.602–03). Aeneas is not called upon to interact with the damned but only to learn a lesson: "'discite iustitiam moniti et non temnere divos" (1:575; 6.620).

47. These matters come to a head in book 5, when Talus punishes Munera. As David Landreth argues, in *The Face of Mammon: The Matter of Money in English Renaissance Literature* (Oxford: Oxford University Press, 2012), 94–101, Talus and Munera are surprisingly alike. Both are mere instruments that nonetheless express human forms of agency. Munera's wickedness in particular engenders a "commutative transumption of cause and effect," whereby the people around her become "indifferently guilty" (99). As a result, transferred guilt persists among the people even after Talus metes out harsh justice upon Munera. Talus does try to turn justice into a public display. After he chops off Munera's hands and silver feet, he nails them "on high, that all might them behold" (Spenser, *Faerie Queene*, 5.2.26.9) As an inferior version of Christ's crucifixion, the spectacle of Munera's dismemberment still raises questions about why guilt should be transferrable and capable of being displaced onto the innocent.

48. On the relationship between Spenser's Bower of Bliss and Armida's palace in *Gerusalemme liberata*, see Robert M. Durling, "The Bower of Bliss and

Armida's Palace," *Comparative Literature* 6, no. 4 (Autumn 1954): 335–47. More recent discussions have focused the political energies at play in Guyon's destruction of the Bower. Stephen Greenblatt's claim, in *Renaissance Self-Fashioning: From More to Shakespeare* (1980), updated ed. (Chicago: University of Chicago Press, 2005), 157–92, that colonialist impulses lie behind Guyon's destructiveness has been influential. For a reconsideration that likens Guyon to the biblical Josiah, see Anthony Esolen, "Spenser's 'Alma Venus': Energy and Economics in The Bower of Bliss," *English Literary Renaissance* 23, no. 2 (March 1993): 267–86.

49. Torquato Tasso, *Gerusalemme liberata, poema eroico*, ed. Angelo Solerti (Firenze: G. Barbera, 1895), 3:134; 14.66.8.

50. Ibid., 3:183; 16.21.7–8.

51. As Ayesha Ramachandran reminds us, in "Tasso's Petrarch: The Lyric Means to Epic Ends," *MLN* 122, no. 1 (January 2007): 202, Tasso's *Rime d'amore* revises the Petrarchan trope of mirrors and Narcissus-like frustration by suggesting that mirrors could "symbolize both narcissism and a desire for mutuality." By experiencing something like two-way narcissism, the speaker of Tasso's *Rime* is more successful than Rinaldo in his crude attempt to hang a literal crystal from his neck. Spenser's own organization of lyric and epic parallels Tasso's, but with the poet claiming an even greater triumph in love. For a relevant discussion of Platonism in the *Amoretti* and Tasso's *Rime*, see Reed Way Dasenbrock, "The Petrarchan Context of Spenser's *Amoretti*," *PMLA* 100, no. 1 (January 1985): 38–50.

52. On the ambiguities surrounding Armida's possible recuperation through conversion and marriage to Rinaldo (and on Tasso's inability to decide on the matter), see Jo Ann Cavallo, *The Romance Epics of Boiardo, Ariosto, and Tasso: From Public Duty to Private Pleasure* (Toronto: University of Toronto Press, 2004), 199–218.

CHAPTER 2

1. Alan Stewart, *The Cradle King: A Life of James VI and I* (New York: Random House, 2011), 111.

2. Ibid., 158.

3. Regina M. Schwartz, *The Curse of Cain: The Violent Legacy of Monotheism* (Chicago: University of Chicago Press, 1997), 140.

4. Carl Schmitt, *Hamlet or Hecuba: The Intrusion of the Time into the Play*, trans. David Pan and Jennifer R. Rust (New York: Telos Press, 2009), 45.

5. This chapter relies on scholarship detailing how *Othello* has been a site of thinking about Blackness. This is not to deny the complexity of the play's presentation of Moorishness as a diffuse construction involving an unstable combination of ethnic and religious difference. Scholars have refused to allow that complexity to function as an alibi for ignoring the racial thinking that has operated and still operates in and through *Othello*. See, for example, Michael Neill, "'Mulattos,'

'Blacks,' and 'Indian Moors': *Othello* and Early Modern Constructions of Human Difference," *Shakespeare Quarterly* 49, no. 4 (Winter 1998): 361–74; Ania Loomba, *Shakespeare, Race, and Colonialism* (Oxford: Oxford University Press, 2002), 91–111; Kim F. Hall, *Othello* and the Problem of Blackness, in *A Companion to Shakespeare's Works*, vol. 1, *The Tragedies*, ed. Richard Dutton and Jean E. Howard (Malden, MA: Blackwell, 2003), 357–74; Joyce Green Macdonald, "Black Ram, White Ewe," in *A Feminist Companion to Shakespeare*, ed. Dympna Callaghan, 2nd ed. (Malden, MA: Blackwell, 2016), 206–25; and Ayanna Thompson, "Introduction," in *Othello*, rev. ed. (London: Arden Shakespeare, 2016) 1–116.

6. Hammill and Lupton, "Introduction," 1.

7. The editors of the *Riverside Shakespeare* place "Indian" in brackets in the main text to signal the textual variation; see Shakespeare, *Othello*, 1296n347.

8. See Arthur Freeman, "'Base Indian': V.ii.347," *Shakespeare Quarterly* 13 (1962): 256–57; Richard Levin, "The Indian/Iudean Crux in *Othello*," *Shakespeare Quarterly* 33 (1982), 60–67; and Julia Reinhard Lupton, *Citizen-Saints: Shakespeare and Political Theology (Chicago: University of Chicago Press, 2005)*, 118–20.

9. See William Shakespeare, *A New Variorum Edition of Shakespeare*, vol. 6, *Othello*, ed. Horace Howard Furness (Philadelphia: Lippincott 1886), 327–31n421.

10. Benedict Robinson, *Islam and Early Modern English Literature: The Politics of Romance from Spenser to Milton* (New York: Palgrave Macmillan, 2007), 74.

11. Dennis Austin Britton, *Becoming Christian: Race, Reformation, and Early Modern English Romance* (New York: Fordham, 2014), 138.

12. Stanley Cavell, *Disavowing Knowledge in Six Plays of Shakespeare*, updated ed. (Cambridge: Cambridge University Press, 2003), 126.

13. Ibid., 129.

14. Gasparo Contarini, *The Commonwealth and Government of Venice*, trans. Lewes Lewkenor (London, 1599), 197. All quotations from this text will be cited parenthetically by page number.

15. Lupton, *Citizen-Saints*, 107–9.

16. Andrew Hadfield, *Shakespeare and Republicanism* (Cambridge: Cambridge University Press, 2005), 216.

17. Ibid., 219.

18. Andrew Sisson, "Othello and the Unweaponed City," *Shakespeare Quarterly* 66, no. 2 (Summer 2015): 139.

19. See A. C. Bradley, *Shakespearean Tragedy: Lectures on* Hamlet, Othello, King Lear, Macbeth, ed. Robert Shaughnessy, 4th ed. (London: Palgrave Macmillan 2006), 158.

20. Lupton, *Citizen-Saints*, 121.

21. Urvashi Chakravarty, "Race, Natality, and the Biopolitics of Early Modern Political Theology," *Journal for Early Modern Cultural Studies* 18, no. 2 (Spring 2018): 140–66.

22. See Christopher Pye, *The Storm at Sea: Political Aesthetics in the Time of Shakespeare* (New York: Fordham University Press, 1995), 105–24.

23. The motif of hazardous sea crossings that sunder familial bonds (which then need to be renewed) connects Shakespeare's earlier comedies to the late romances. Among the romances, *Pericles* provides an obsessively repetitive meditation on the sea, familial love, and politics. Each time that Pericles crosses the sea, he gains only to lose some aspect of his royal identity and family. The play ends with a restoration of his family and with a reconciliation between the goddess Diana and marriage. This reconciliation takes place in Ephesus; as in the earlier *Comedy of Errors*, the Ephesian setting is connected to a plot of marriage in a way that might suggest the relevance of the Epistle to the Ephesians. As Patricia A. Parker reminds us, in *Shakespeare from the Margins: Language, Culture, Context* (Chicago: University of Chicago Press, 1996), 56–82, *The Comedy of Errors* points to the deeper meaning of its plot's antics through a wide array of biblical echoes, including Paul's redefinition of marriage. At the end of *Pericles*, the sacrifice that Diana demands underwrites a new marriage and also seems politically cathartic, allowing the people to overlook the wickedness of Cleon and Dionyza. Yet Gower's prologue informs us that the threatened honor of Pericles's family sparks the people of Tharsus to exact popular justice. In this case, the conservative streak of romance coexists with the legitimacy of insurrection.

24. When Othello first appears in the play, he declares that he fetches his "life and being / From men of royal siege" (1.2.21–

22). The *OED* quotes Othello's remark as an example of the use of "siege" to mean "seat," but sets it apart as a unique instance of figurative usage; see *OED*, s.v. "siege" n.1, def. 1. The military senses of "siege" (and the entirely masculine makeup of his claimed ancestry) suggests that Othello's merit as a soldier is already overshadowing this fleeting claim to royal descent. Later in the play, Othello does articulate anxieties about how Desdemona's unfaithfulness would sully the purity of any future progeny. Yet even those moments tend to suggest that the birth or rebirth that matters most in Othello's jealous imagination is his own.

25. Shakespeare, *New Variorum Edition*, 6:34n31. The line from *Othello* in question is 1.2.31 in Furness's variorum edition.

26. Edward Muir, *Civic Ritual in Renaissance Venice* (Princeton, NJ: Princeton University Press, 1981), 121.

27. Ibid., 127.

28. Ibid.

29. Contarini, *Commonwealth*, 47.

30. Steve Mentz, *At the Bottom of Shakespeare's Ocean* (New York: Continuum, 2009), 26.

31. Lewkenor's own dedication likens Venice to a beautiful virgin and hopes that his dedicatee, Lady Anne, Countess of Warwick, might be her patroness

(Contarini, *Commonwealth*, 3). Lewkenor is presenting virginal Venice as a kind of metaphorical surrogate daughter for Lady Anne, whose marriage to Ambrose Dudley had produced no offspring. In this case, the implied relationship between literal and metaphorical marriage functions to affirm not Venice's maritime power but instead the transmission of Venetian knowledge to England.

32. Schmitt, *Hamlet*, 25.

33. Kahn, *Illusion*, 45. Kahn goes on to offer a brilliant reading that shows how the very speech Schmitt refers to in his title undercuts his claims about history and aesthetic experience.

34. Walter Benjamin, *The Origin of German Tragic Drama*, trans. John Osborn (London, 1985), 158.

35. See Schmitt, *Hamlet*, 26n15.

36. See ibid., 65.

37. Carl Schmitt, *The Nomos of the Earth in the International Law of the Jus Publicum Europaeum*, trans. G. L. Ulmen (New York: Telos Press, 2003), 42. For a discussion of Schmitt's selective and even distorted presentation of *nomos* as originating from the settlement of land, see Feisal G. Mohamed, *Sovereignty: Seventeenth-Century England and the Making of the Modern Political Imaginary* (Oxford: Oxford University Press, 2020), 81–90.

38. Andreas Höfele, *No Hamlets: German Shakespeare from Nietzsche to Carl Schmitt* (Oxford: Oxford University Press, 2016), 161.

39. Schmitt's earlier thinking appeals to the Roman Catholic Church as an institution that adjudicated the friend/enemy distinction in a way superior to liberalism, capitalism, and communism. See *Roman Catholicism and Political Form* (1927), trans. G. L. Ulmen (Westport, CT: Greenwood, 1996).

40. Qtd. from Höfele, *No Hamlets*, 168.

41. Höfele, *No Hamlets*, 188.

42. Qtd. from Höfele, *No Hamlets*, 178.

43. Ibid., 169.

44. Ibid.

45. See also Wojciech Engelking, "Shakespeare as a Method: Carl Schmitt's Reading of *Othello* and *Hamlet*," *History of European Ideas* 45, no. 7 (October 2019): 1058–71. Building on Höfele's explorations of Schmitt's diaries, Engelking proposes that Schmitt's engagement with *Othello* takes the place of his earlier application of Freudian thinking in the 1910s.

46. The *Othello* myth—to use the term that Celia Daileader elaborates in *Racism, Misogyny, and the Othello Myth: Interracial Couples from Shakespeare to Spike Lee* (New York: Cambridge University Press, 2005)—continues to be a form in which these anxieties are negotiated. For examples of scholarship that details *Othello*'s role in race relations in the United States, past and present, see Ayanna Thompson, *Passing Strange: Shakespeare, Race, and Contemporary America* (Oxford: Oxford University Press, 2011); Miles P. Grier, "Staging the Cherokee

Othello: An Imperial Economy of Indian Watching," *William and Mary Quarterly* 73, no. 1 (January 2016): 73–106; and Brigitte Fielder, "Blackface Desdemona: Theorizing Race on the Nineteenth-Century American Stage," *Theatre Annual* 70 (2017): 39–59. The paradigm set by *Othello* can help us understand the recent reemergence of cuckoldry as a political slur in the United States. The shorthand *cuck* (or *cuckservative*) has been deployed by racist nationalists to mock conservatives deemed to be insufficiently vigilant against perceived threats, including demographic shifts, immigration, and global finance (still aligned with Jews in the antisemitic imagination), as well as the presence of Muslim Americans. Cuckoldry is mocked as an emasculating acceptance of national and racial impurity. For a discussion of this slur, see Geoffrey Lokke, "Cuckolds, Cucks, and Their Transgressions," *Porn Studies* 6, no. 2 (2019): 212–27. As Lokke observes, the political and racial anxiety about metaphorical cuckoldry coexists with the popularity of cuckoldry as a genre of pornography. This is a racialized genre in which, typically, a White man watches as a Black man has sex with his wife or other White family member. As Ariane Cruz observes, in *The Color of Kink: Black Women, BDSM, and Pornography* (New York: New York University Press, 2016), 136–50, this genre can forge queer identifications between the humiliated but also fascinated White cuckold and the Black man or men he witnesses. It should be clear that this potential for queer identification is bound up with racist forms of fascination.

47. See Pye, *Storm at Sea*, 125–41.

48. James Knapp, in "Visual and Ethical Truth in *The Winter's Tale*," *Shakespeare Quarterly* 55, no. 3 (Autumn 2004): 259, describes how this opening exchange "introduces what will be the play's epistemological dilemma—the relationship of the seen to the true." In Knapp's account, Leontes must move past the dichotomy between certainty and seeming and toward more genuinely ethical response to the demand of an other, in the mode of a face-to-face encounter that Emnanuel Levinas has theorized.

49. For a different reading of this speech, see Virginia Lee Strain, "*The Winter's Tale* and the Oracle of Law," *ELH* 78, no. 3 (Fall 2011): 557–84, esp. 565. Strain argues that Camillo reasons in a deliberative manner, but in a way that partially anticipates the function of oracular knowledge in the play.

50. Santner, *Royal Remains*, xxi.

51. Sarah Beckwith, *Shakespeare and the Grammar of Forgiveness* (Ithaca, NY: Cornell University Press, 2011), 128.

52. Ibid., 131.

53. For an insightful discussion of the relationship between Paulina's husband, Antigonus, and Camillo, see David Schalkwyk, *Shakespeare, Love and Language* (Cambridge: Cambridge University Press, 2008), 263–98.

54. Stephen Orgel, "Introduction," *The Winter's Tale* (Oxford: Oxford University Press, 1998), 10.

CHAPTER 3

1. John Aubrey, *'Brief Lives,' Chiefly of Contemporaries*, vol. 1, ed. Andrew Clark (Oxford: Clarendon, 1898), 204.

2. Ibid.; see 204nh on how Aubrey initially wrote that Davenant was making his mother out to be a "whore" but crossed the phrase out. For a discussion of Aubrey's report, as well as the claim that Shakespeare was Davenant's godfather, within the broader history of attempts to reconstruct Shakespeare's sexual life, see Michael Keevak, *Sexual Shakespeare: Forgery, Authorship, Portraiture* (Detroit: Wayne State University Press, 2001), 41–66.

3. William Davenant, *Sir William Davenant's Gondibert*, ed. David F. Gladish (Oxford: Clarendon Press, 1971), 16. All quotations from *Gondibert* are taken from this volume and will be cited parenthetically by book, canto, stanza, and line numbers.

4. *The King's Cabinet Opened* (London, 1645), 8. For a discussion of this publication and the project to emasculate Charles I while portraying Henrietta Maria as a menace, see Diane Purkiss, *Literature, Gender, and Politics during the English Civil War* (Cambridge: Cambridge University Press, 2005), 71–97.

5. See, for example, the work of the royalist soldier and poet Martin Lluelyn, published as *A Satyr Occasioned by The Author's Survey of a Scandalous Pamphlet Intituled, The King's Cabanet Opened* (London, 1645). In defending the queen's active role in state affairs, Lluelyn denies the relevance of gender difference: "*Reason* and *Judgment* are not things of *Sexe*" (4). Even more controversially, Lluelyn downplays Henrietta Maria's Roman Catholicism by appealing to a kind of sectarian relativism: "'Tis Her *Religion's Care*: She tryes Her Powr's, / To keep that still. Doe not we so for Ours?" (6). This appeal was far likelier to stoke rather than to quell the antimonarchical sentiments that *The King's Cabinet Opened* was designed to inflame.

6. See Kevin Sharpe, *Criticism and Compliment: The Politics of Literature in the England of Charles I* (Cambridge: Cambridge University Press, 1987), 63–70.

7. Ibid., 80–81.

8. *To the Honourable Knights, Citizens, and Burgesses of the House of Commons Assembled in Parliament: The Humble Remonstrance of William Davenant* (London, 1641).

9. Sir William Davenant, "To the Queen," in *The Shorter Poems, and Songs from the Plays and Masques*, ed. A. M. Gibbs (Oxford: Clarendon, 1972), 140; line 46. All quotations from Davenant's poems, with the exception of *Gondibert*, are taken from this volume and will be cited parenthetically by line numbers.

10. William Davenant, *Salmacida Spolia: A Masque* (London, 1639 [1640]), C4^r, D1^v. Quotations from this text will be cited parenthetically by page number.

11. As Lois Potter observes, in *Secret Rites and Secret Writing: Royalist Literature, 1641–1660* (Cambridge: Cambridge University Press, 1989), 94–95, when critics

have tried to decode *Gondibert* as a straightforward political allegory, their readings have run into incoherence. Potter reminds us that narrowly topical readings conflict with Davenant's stated design in setting his poem in a distant past. On the hints within the poem that the narrative takes place around the year 750, see Gladish, "Introduction," xii–xiii. Davenant consulted Paulus Diaconus's *De origine et gestis regum Langobardorum* for Lombardian history, but the plot of *Gondibert* (and many of its characters) are wholesale fabrications.

12. Davenant, *Gondibert*, 14–15.

13. This device is not a Shakespearean invention but a romance motif that affiliates *Much Ado about Nothing* with *The Faerie Queene*—specifically, the episode in book 2, canto 4, in which Phedon is tricked into believing that his future bride Claribell is unfaithful. Behind both Spenser's and Shakespeare's versions of this motif lies the story of Ariodante and Ginevra in *Orlando furioso*. For the case that Shakespeare borrowed the story directly from Spenser, see Alwin Thaler, "Spenser and *Much Ado about Nothing*," *Studies in Philology* 37, no. 2 (April 1940): 225–35. For a discussion of Ariosto's, Spenser's, and Shakespeare's iterations of this ruse of female infidelity, see Melinda J. Gough, "'Her Filthy Feature Showne' in Ariosto, Spenser, and *Much Ado about Nothing*," *SEL: Studies in English Literature, 1500–1900* 39, no. 1 (Winter 1999): 41–67.

14. Davenant, *Gondibert*, 50.

15. Ibid.

16. Kahn, *Wayward Contracts*, 136.

17. Ibid., 143.

18. Ibid., 142–43.

19. Ibid, 143. For other accounts of the importance of Hobbes's response to Davenant, see Quentin Skinner, *Reason and Rhetoric in the Philosophy of Hobbes* (Cambridge: Cambridge University Press, 1996), 332–34 and 430–31; and Timothy Raylor, *Reason, Rhetoric, and Thomas Hobbes* (Oxford: Oxford University Press, 2018), 271–74. Skinner takes Hobbes's correspondence with Davenant as evidence of a growing receptiveness to rhetorical eloquence and poetry; Raylor argues that Hobbes is more consistent in subordinating the role of rhetoric in his political philosophy.

20. Thomas Hobbes, *Leviathan: With Selected Variants from the Latin Edition of 1668*, ed. Edwin Curley (Indianapolis: Hackett, 1994), 222–23.

21. Ibid., 223.

22. Ibid.

23. Potter, *Secret Rites*, 95.

24. Davenant, *Gondibert*, 4.

25. Ibid., 303n28.

26. Ibid., 304n33.

27. Insofar as this emerald is reminiscent of Desdemona's handkerchief in *Othello*, Davenant's talisman is designed to sort out the gender confusion involved

in the earlier expression of jealousy. Othello tells Desdemona that the handkerchief had belonged to his mother, who used it to maintain her father's affections. Yet Othello is in the odd position of giving to Desdemona a magical token of a woman's supposedly secret sway over her husband. Othello's story of the handkerchief turns out to be a fabrication. In the final act, Othello admits that the handkerchief was "an antique token / My father gave my mother" (5.2.216–17). Precisely as a confused fantasy, the story of the handkerchief expresses Othello's true anxiety over his own fixed place in Desdemona's eyes affect. Davenant's emerald works in an opposite direction, with Gondibert positioning himself as the object of jealous curiosity. By offering a magical form of ocular proof of his fidelity, he keeps Birtha in a state of emotional thrall even when he is absent from her.

28. Davenant, *Gondibert*, 28.

29. Ibid., 29

30. Qtd. from the translation of the Latin original available on the website of the Royal Society: https://royalsociety.org/-/media/Royal_Society_Content/about-us/history/Charter1_English.pdf.

31. Thomas Sprat, "To the King," in *The History of the Royal-Society of London* (London, 1667).

32. Ibid.

33. Ibid.

34. Sprat's motives have been the object of open skepticism stretching back at least to Samuel Johnson's *The Lives of the Poets*. For a defense of Sprat's *History* as authoritative, see Margery Purver, *The Royal Society: Concept and Creation* (1967), reprint ed. (Abingdon: Routledge, 2009), esp. 1–19; see also J. R. Jacob, "Restoration Ideologies and the Royal Society," *History of Science* 18, no. 1 (March 1980): 25–38. For a critical view, see Paul B. Wood, "Methodology and Apologetics: Thomas Sprat's *History of the Royal Society*," *British Journal for the History of Science 13, no. 1* (March 1980): 1–26.

35. Giorgio Agamben, *Homo Sacer: Sovereign Power and Bare Life*, trans. Daniel Heller-Roazen (Stanford: Stanford University Press, 1998), 8.

36. *Ibid.*, 6.

37. Ibid., 83.

38. Ibid., 8. For a meditation on the curious fact of Agamben's appeal to an obscure ancient Roman concept forming the basis of a highly influential account of sovereignty in premodern and modern forms, see Peter Fitzpatrick, "Bare Sovereignty, "*Homo Sacer* and the Insistence of Law," in *Politics, Metaphysics, and Death: Essays on Giorgio Agamben's* Homo Sacer, ed. Andrew Norris (Durham, NC: Duke University Press, 2005), 49–73.

39. Agamben, *Homo Sacer*, 5.

40. Heather Latimer, "Bio-reproductive Futurism: Bare Life and the Pregnant Refugee in Alfonso Cuarón's *Children of Men*," *Social Text* 108, no. 3 (Fall 2011):

53. See also Heather Latimer, *Reproductive Acts: Sexual Politics in North American Fiction and Film* (Montreal: McGill-Queen's University Press, 2013), 134–59.

41. Karen Weingarten, *Abortion in the American Imagination: Before Life and Choice, 1880–1940* (New Brunswick, NJ: Rutgers University Press, 2014), 19.

42. Agamben seeks to address Foucault's failure to connect biopolitics with an understanding of twentieth-century totalitarianism in part through a dialogue with Hannah Arendt (see Agamben, *Homo Sacer*, 3–5, 126–35). Yet Agamben ends up replicating, in altered form, Arendt's valorization of a classical past that relegates women and reproduction to the *oikos*, entirely outside of the political sphere. This becomes apparent when, for example, Agamben immediately follows a discussion (alongside Arendt) of natural life being "wholly included in the *polis*" in modernity with an account of how, "Since the First World War, the birth-nation link has no longer been capable of performing its legitimate function" (*Homo Sacer*, 131). Although Agamben refers to the link between nativity and nation as "the original fiction of modern sovereignty," he is less interested in its fictive status than in its perceived legitimacy being upended by influxes of immigrants across Europe (*Homo Sacer*, 131).

43. Ibid., 87.

44. Ibid., 101.

45. In *The Use of Bodies*, trans. Adam Kotsko (Stanford: Stanford University Press, 2016), Agamben elaborates upon his earlier genealogical account. "The two terms *bios* and *zoè*, on the opposition of which Aristotelian politics were founded, now contract into one another in a peremptory gesture that . . . points toward an unheard-of-politicization of life as such," and in this modern-facing form of political subjectivity, natural and civic life contract into a single "*form-of-life*" (*Uses*, 219). Agamben touches on the ways that sexual preferences can become the basis of self-defining lifestyle choice. Yet here, too, he has very little concern for reproduction as the literal generation of *bios* or for the political project to regulate women's reproductive bodies. Bracketing off the linked matters of physical reproduction and the politico-theological function of marriage is not an accidental but instead a constitutive feature of Agamben's theory. In *The Highest Form of Poverty: Monastic Rules and Form-of-Life*, trans. Adam Kotsko (Stanford: Stanford University Press, 2013), Agamben theorizes the constitution of the form-of-life by returning to the history of monastic life. In this work, he attends to the paradoxical formations of monasticism, which blur the lines between voluntary acceptance and involuntary obligations in a way that eludes a Roman understanding of law while establishing a form of a self-referential vow that can bind individual and communal lives together in a rule-based organization. The basic fact that monasticism is supposed to be based on celibacy remains an implicit and largely untheorized premise of his investigation.

46. Agamben, *Homo Sacer*, 149.

47. See Achille Mbembe, "Necropolitics," *Public Culture* 15, no. 1 (Winter 2003): 11–40; and *Necropolitics* (Durham, NC: Duke University Press, 2019). See also Alexander G. Weheliye, *Habeas Viscus: Racializing Assemblages, Biopolitics, and Black Feminist Theories of the Human* (Durham, NC: Duke University Press, 2014), esp. 33–45 and 53–73.

48. Davenant, *Gondibert*, 31.

49. For an account of this episode, see Alfred Harbage's biography, *Sir William Davenant: Poet Adventurer, 1606–1668* (Philadelphia: University of Pennsylvania Press, 1935), 111–19.

50. Ibid., 32.

51. On Davenant communicating with Cromwell's secretary of state James Thurloe and receiving endorsement for the play *The Cruelty of the Spaniards in Peru*, see Janet Clare, *Drama of the English Republic, 1649–60* (Manchester: Manchester University Press, 2002), 236–38. As Clare notes, the first performance of *Cruelty* seems to have been delayed by the embarrassing failure of Cromwell's Western Design. During this delay, Davenant composed other works, such as his successful 1656 operatic drama *The Siege of Rhodes*. For a reading of *The Siege of Rhodes* as offering "a curious justification for European imperialism, not as a good in itself, but as preferable to Ottoman hegemony," see Judy H. Park, "The Limits of Empire in Davenant's *The Siege of Rhodes*," *Mediterranean Studies* 24, no. 1 (2016): 47–76.

52. For Restoration poets, awareness of Charles II's decadence posed an obstacle to affirming the monarchy's renewed affective claims over English subjects. For a reading of *Astraea Redux* as offering "optative praise" to Charles II (rather than straightforward affirmation of virtues) in a way that allows Dryden to advise the king in matters including relations with the Dutch over maritime trade, see G. M. MacLean, "Poetry as History: The Argumentative Design of Dryden's *Astraea Redux*," *Restoration: Studies in English Literary Culture, 1660–1700* 4, no. 2 (Fall 1980): 54–64. On the way Dryden would later, against the backdrop of the Exclusion Crisis, accommodate Charles II's sexual license in the 1681 *Absalom and Achitophel*, see Steven N. Zwicker, *Lines of Authority: Politics and English Literary Culture, 1649–1689* (Ithaca, NY: Cornell University Press, 1993), 132–45.

53. This sequence is clearly reminiscent of the opening of *The Tempest*, which Davenant would adapt in collaboration with Dryden for a 1667 performance. The echo is revealing insofar as *The Tempest* opens with a boatswain declaring that the roaring sea is utterly indifferent to the authority a king.

CHAPTER 4

1. As Anthony Low observes, in *The Reinvention of Love: Poetry, Politics, and Culture from Sidney to Milton* (Cambridge: Cambridge University Press, 1993), 165–66, the 1641 pamphlet *Animadversions* contains what may be the only instance

in all of Milton's writings in which the metaphor of Christ's marriage is deployed in a positive fashion.

2. John Milton, *The Complete Prose Works of John Milton*, ed. Don Wolfe et al., 8 vols. (New Haven, CT: Yale University Press, 1953–82), 2:732. All quotations from Milton's prose writings are taken from this edition and will be quoted parenthetically by volume and page number with the abbreviation *CPW*.

3. Milton may have taken steps to secure a replacement for his first wife. According to Milton's nephew Edward Phillips, Milton had some plans to enter into an adulterous second marriage with a woman identified only as one of Dr. Davis's daughters. We have not been able to confirm this family gossip. Phillips tells us, at any rate, that Dr. Davis's daughter was "averse . . . to this motion." See Helen Darbishire, ed., *The Early Lives of Milton* (London: Constable, 1932), 66–67.

4. John Milton, *Paradise Lost*, ed. Alastair Fowler, 2nd ed. (Harlow: Longman, 1998), 180; book 3, line 212. All quotations from *Paradise Lost* are taken from this volume and will be cited parenthetically by book and line numbers.

5. Sharon Achinstein, "*De Doctrina Christiana*: Milton's Last Divorce Tract?" *Milton Quarterly* 51, no. 3 (October 2017): 154.

6. For some examples, see Mary Ann Radzinowicz, *Toward* Samson Agonistes: *The Growth of Milton's Mind* (Princeton, NJ: Princeton University Press, 1978), esp. 83–108; Fredric Jameson, "Religion and Ideology: A Political Reading of *Paradise Lost*," in *Literary Politics and Theory (*1986), ed. Francis Barker et al., reprint ed. (Abingdon: Routledge, 2003), 35–56.

7. For examples, see Stevie Davies, *Images of Kingship in* Paradise Lost: *Milton's Politics and Christian Liberty* (Columbia: University of Missouri Press, 1983); and Christopher Hill, *Milton and the English Revolution*, and *The Experience of Defeat: Milton and Some Contemporaries* (1984), paperback ed. (London: Verso, 2017).

8. The matter remains uncertain because James Thurloe provides the only firsthand account that Oliver Cromwell verbally nominated his son. For considerations of the evidence, see E. Malcolm Hause, "The Nomination of Richard Cromwell," *The Historian* 27, no. 2 (February 1965): 185–209; and A. B. Nourse, "The Nomination of Richard Cromwell," *Cromwelliana* (1979): 25–31. For a skeptical view of Thurloe's report, see Jonathan Fitzgibbons, "'Not in Any Doubtfull Dispute?' Reassessing the Nomination of Richard Cromwell," *Historical Research* 83, no. 220 (2010): 281–300. Milton's views about *Cromwell* and the Protectorate have been the subject of disagreement. For claims for Milton's mounting unhappiness, see Austin Woolrych, "Milton and Cromwell: 'A Short but Scandalous Night of Interruption?'" in *Achievements of the Left Hand: Essays on Milton's Prose*, ed. Michael Lieb and John T. Shawcross (Amherst: University of Massachusetts Press, 1974), 185–218; Blair Worden, *Literature and Politics in Cromwellian England: John Milton, Andrew Marvell, Marchamont Nedham* (Oxford: Oxford University Press, 2007), 241–325; David Armitage, "John Milton: Poet against Empire," in *Milton*

and Republicanism, ed. David Armitage et al. (Cambridge: Cambridge University Press, 2009), 206–26; and Martin Dzelzainis, "Milton and the Protectorate in 1658," *Milton and Republicanism*, 181–205. For a survey of the debate concerning Milton's views, see Tobias Gregory, "Milton and Cromwell: Another Look at the Evidence," *Journal of British Studies* 54, no. 1 (January 2015): 44–62. For a broader discussion of the political significance of Oliver Cromwell's fatherhood, and the way it developed at odds with republican ideals, see Su Fang Ng, *Literature and the Politics of Family in Seventeenth-Century England* (Cambridge: Cambridge University Press, 2007), 103–29.

9. Qtd. from Nigel Smith, ed., *A Collection of Ranter Writings: Spiritual Liberty and Sexual Freedom in the English Revolution* (London: Pluto Press, 2014), 45–46.

10. Ibid., 98.

11. Gerrard Winstanley, *The Complete Works of Gerrard Winstanley*, ed. Thomas N. Corns et. al, 2 vols. (Oxford: Oxford University Press, 2009), 1:507.

12. See *Tempest*, 2.1.147–67.

13. Winstanley, *Complete Works*, 2:236–37.

14. Qtd. from Smith, *Collection of Ranter Writings*, 56.

15. As Christopher Hill remarks, in *Milton and the English Revolution*, "Milton himself was not an extreme radical, Leveller, Digger, or Ranter. . . . But if we look for analogies with Milton's ideas among the radicals we shall easily find them" (99). When it comes to Edenic communalism, Milton is like Winstanley insofar as he identifies marriage as the key exception. Yet Milton is not necessarily in agreement with the Diggers; his views about Eden do not translate directly to his beliefs about property in a fallen world. David Williams, in *Milton's Leveller God* (Montreal: McGill-Queen's University Press, 2017), makes the case that *Paradise Lost* is saturated with the ideals and principles of the Levellers, even though Milton's explicit engagement with Leveller writings remains minimal.

16. As John Rogers argues, in "Transported Touch: The Fruit of Marriage in *Paradise Lost*," in *Milton and Gender*, ed. Catherine Gimelli Martin (Cambridge: Cambridge University Press, 2005), 115–32, the anomaly of Edenic marriage helps to explain the Fall because it embeds an "inflexible aristocratic hierarchy" that proves incompatible with an egalitarian paradise.

17. David Quint, *Inside* Paradise Lost: *Reading the Designs of Milton's Epic* (Princeton, NJ: Princeton University Press, 2014), 1.

18. See 10.180–81, 11.116, 11.155, 12.327.

19. John Milton, "Sonnet XIX," in *The Complete Shorter Poems*, ed. John Carey, 2nd ed. (Harlow: Longman, 1997), 348; line 1. All quotations from Milton's poetry apart from *Paradise Lost* are taken from this volume and will be cited parenthetically by line number.

20. See Milton, *Shorter Poems*, 347, for citations of scholarly discussions surrounding this uncertainty.

21. *Epitathium Damonis*, Milton's Latin elegy mourning his close friend Charles Diodati, offers an example of Milton imagining sex in the afterlife. The poem ends with a description of how Diodati (imagined as Damon) will experience an orgy in a classical version of heaven as a reward for his chaste life on earth.

22. Targoff, in *Posthumous Love*, 207–9, reminds us that the myth of Orpheus and Eurydice lie behind both the Miltonic sonnet and the Virgilian narrative. Targoff concludes that Milton's sonnet "is the closest that Renaissance English poetry comes to inhabiting the Orpheus myth" (208).

23. Virgil, *Eclogues, Georgics, Aeneid, Appendix Vergiliana*, trans. H. R. Fairclough, rev. G. P. Goold, 2 vols. (Cambridge, MA: Harvard University Press, 1999–2000), 1:369; book 2, lines 790–91.

24. See Quint, *Inside*, 218–23, for a discussion of the differences between Aeneas and Milton's Adam.

25. I discuss the significance of this echo in *Dominion Undeserved: Milton and the Perils of Creation* (Ithaca, NY: Cornell University Press, 2013), 107–10, and in "*Paradise Lost* and the Poetics of Delay: Virgil, Vida, Milton," *Milton Quarterly* 50, no. 3 (October 2016): 137–56.

26. Virgil, *Aeneid*, 363; 2.701.

27. Quint, *Inside*, 223.

28. C. A. Patrides, "Milton and the Protestant Theory of Atonement," *PMLA* 74 (1959): 9.

29. For a discussion of this, see Martin Dzelzainis, "Milton and Antitrinitarianism," in *Milton and Toleration*, ed. Sharon Achinstein and Elizabeth Sauer (Oxford: Oxford University Press, 2007), 171–85.

30. Gregory Chaplin, "Beyond Sacrifice: Milton and the Atonement," *PMLA* 125, no. 2 (March 2010): 364

31. Milton published "On the Death of a Fair Infant" with the claim that he had composed it when at the age of seventeen; scholars have pointed out that if the poem really were about his niece, then he would have been nineteen at the time. Milton may have lied to make the poem seem even more of a juvenile effort than it was.

32. Raphael's lesson has been a focal point of debates concerning Milton's views about the Trinity. The temporal specificity of God's declaration (on a certain day) would seem to reflect Milton's heterodox understanding of the Son of God. In *De doctrina Christiana*, Milton concludes that the Son was begotten according to the will of the Father and within time rather than in the eternal past. As John Rumrich observes, in "Milton's Arianism: Why It Matters," in *Milton and Heresy*, ed. Stephen B. Dobranski and John P. Rumrich (Cambridge: Cambridge University Press, 1998), 75–93, some of Milton's early readers (who did not have access to the unpublished manuscript of *De Doctrina*) recognized his theology as anti-Trinitarian and his Christology as dangerously Arian. I agree with Rumrich that twentieth-century attempts to align Milton with more orthodox views distort

the content of his writings. Yet my claims about the affective pressure that Milton puts on substitution do not require the belief that *Paradise* Lost is anti-Trinitarian. For other discussions of Milton espousing or accommodating anti-Trinitarian views, see Barbara K. Lewalski, *Milton's Brief Epic: The Genre, Meaning, and Art of Paradise Regained* (Providence: Brown University Press, 1966), esp. 138–48; and Michael Lieb, "Milton and the Socinian Heresy," in *Milton and the Grounds of Contention*, ed. Mark Kelley et al. (Pittsburgh: Duquesne University Press, 2003), 234–83.

33. David Norbrook, in *Writing the English Republic: Poetry, Rhetoric, and Politics, 1627–1660* (Cambridge: Cambridge University Press, 1999), 478, remarks that the political import of Raphael's lesson is directed toward the reader rather than toward Adam, the latter having "no political experience whatsoever." Norbrook, 478, then observes that in the poem's final book Adam's responses to the revealed future indicate that "his mentality is naturally republican." My speculations about Adam's and Eve's feelings propose how Raphael's instruction might embed some kernel of republican sentiment even in their early, limited understanding.

34. Regarding this moment, Norbrook, *Writing the English Republic*, 454, observes that "Satan is being praised in this monarchical way for a pre-eminently republican virtue." Milton makes it difficult for readers to make a sharp distinction between Satan's ersatz republican rhetoric and his tyrannical aims. This difficulty reflects Milton's conflicted views of the English Protectorate and his engagement with narratives of the corruption of the Roman Empire.

35. Mary Nyquist, in *Arbitrary Rule: Slavery, Tyranny, and the Power of Life and Death* (Chicago: University of Chicago Press, 2013), 43, observes that it might be "helpful to refer not to a single doctrine of natural slavery but rather to Aristotle's dual doctrines of natural slavery, since both chattel and political slavery are represented as endemic to non-Greek, Asiatic populations." This distinction, in turn, "enables us to grasp the interplay between discursive registers, together with the invidious slippage between the household and *polis* as discursive contexts" (43). Nyquist makes these points within an important account of how the distinctions between chattel slavery and political slavery—and between abolitionist and antityrannical discourses of freedom—developed and were maintained in the early modern period.

36. For a reading of Milton's translation as a clever adaptation designed "to establish a kind of Greek/English dialectic which previews important arguments" developed in the text, see David Davies and Paul Dowling, "'Shrewd Books, with Dangerous Frontispieces': *Areopagitica*'s Motto," *Milton Quarterly* 20, no. 2 (May 1986): 33–37. For a rebuttal that argues that Milton's translation is straightforward, see John K. Hale, "*Areopagitica*'s Euripidean Motto," *Milton Quarterly* 25, no. 1 (March 1991): 25–27.

37. Nyquist, in *Arbitrary Rule*, 166–68, observes that whereas Milton's earlier divorce tracts had appealed to an analogy between the household and political

rule, the *Tenure* heavily restricts that analogy. This is necessary because the link between patriarchal and sovereign forms of power tends to affirm the absolutist theories that Milton needs to contest. Nyquist's discussion clarifies the seeming paradoxes at play when Bodin, a key theorist of absolutism, denounces chattel slavery as inimical to political well-being, whereas thinkers such as Milton appeal passionately to liberty while ignoring the reality of chattel slavery.

38. Adriel M. Trott, *Aristotle on the Nature of Community* (Cambridge: Cambridge University Press, 2013), 119. Trott discusses how Aristotelian freedom should be compatible with nature insofar as the freedom to pursue ends rationally allows people to express their nature outwardly. Yet Trott also considers how rationality itself can mark a break from nature and the natural. "*Logos*," Trott observes, "which makes us human, also makes it possible for us to fail to achieve our ends through our own efforts or lack of them" (120). Milton relies on some of the paradoxes of Christianity to describe how God turns his Son's self-defeating choice into the proper (and beneficial) one. See also Moira M. Walsh, "Aristotle's Conception of Freedom," *Journal of the History of Philosophy* 35, no. 4 (October 1997): 495–507.

39. We can contrast Milton's myth of Satan and Sin with an important strand of thinking in Roman Catholic theology. In the thirteenth century, Duns Scotus broke from Aquinas's Aristotelianism by shifting the locus of freedom from reason to the will. Scotus's focus on the will allows him to explain how Lucifer and the rebel angels could have fallen when they were incapable of intellectual error. An illogical but voluntary choice had been difficult to explain under a notion of freedom premised on the ability to make choices conforming to reason. "What is unique about Scotus's explanation of Lucifer's desire for equality with God," Tobias Hoffman observes, in "Freedom beyond Practical Reason: Duns Scotus on Will-Dependent Relations," *British Journal for the History of Philosophy* 21, no. 6 (December 2013): 1083, "is that the intellect need not have conceived beforehand the precise objected desired by the will. . . . Lucifer could not have remained unaware *that* he was wishing for something, for, according to Scotus, one has immediate awareness of one's acts." Milton (whose dim view of scholasticism is well known) turns the question of satanic choice into a myth of consummated narcissism.

40. Milton, *Paradise Lost*, 164.

41. The Son's remark anticipates Adam's mortalist conclusion after the Fall:

> what dies but what had life
> And sin? The body properly hath neither.
> All of me then shall die. (10.790–92)

For discussions of Milton and mortalism, see George Williamson, "Milton and the Mortalist Heresy," *Studies in Philology* 32, no. 4 (October 1935): 553–79; Norman T. Burns, *Christian Mortalism from Tyndale to Milton* (Cambridge, MA:

Harvard University Press, 1972) 148–91; Gordon Campbell, "The Mortalist Heresy in *Paradise Lost*," *Milton Quarterly* 13, no. 2 (May 1979): 33–36; Nicholas McDowell, "Dead Souls and Modern Minds? Mortalism and the Early Modern Imagination from Marlowe to Milton," *JMEMS* 40, no. 3 (Fall 2010): 559–92; and Rachel Trubowitz, "Reading Milton and Newton in the Radical Reformation," *ELH* 84, no. 1 (Spring 2017): 33–62.

42. For discussions of this episode, see Diane Kelsey McColley, *Milton's Eve* (Urbana: University of Illinois Press, 1983), 74–85; Richard J. DuRocher, *Milton and Ovid: Paradise Lost and the Metamorphoses* (Ithaca, NY: Cornell University Press, 1985), 85–93; William Kerrigan and Gordon Braden, *The Idea of the Renaissance* (Baltimore: Johns Hopkins University Press, 1989), 191–218; Mandy Green, *Milton's Ovidian Eve* (Farnham: Ashgate, 2009), 23–51; and Maggie Kilgour, *Milton and the Metamorphosis of Ovid* (Oxford: Oxford University Press, 2012), 165–228.

43. In the long history of the Narcissus myth, Neoplatonic readings had taken Narcissus to be an allegory of the soul unable to leave behind the physical register to reach spiritual truths. Marsilio Ficino provides an influential Neoplatonic interpretation of the Narcissus myth; see *Commentary on Plato's Symposium on Love*, trans. Sears Jayne, 2nd ed. (Dallas: Spring Publications, 1985), 140–41.

44. Alison A. Chapman, *The Legal Epic: Paradise Lost and the Early Modern Law* (Chicago: University of Chicago Press, 2017), 135.

45. Ibid., 136.

46. On Milton's hypocrisy when it comes to marriage as a metaphor for political contract, see David Aers and Bob Hodge, "'Rational Burning': Milton on Sex and Marriage," *Milton Studies* 13 (1979): 3–33.

47. See Milton, *CPW* 2:448, 2:589.

48. Mary Astell, *Some Reflections upon Marriage*, in *Astell: Political Writings*, ed. Patricia Springborg (Cambridge: Cambridge University Press, 1996), 46–47. For discussions of Milton and Astell, see Nyquist, "Gendered Subjectivity"; Shannon Miller, *Engendering the Fall: John Milton and Seventeenth-Century Women Writers* (Philadelphia: University of Pennsylvania Press, 2008), 217–30; and Sharon Achinstein, "Early Modern Marriage in a Secular Age: Beyond the Sexual Contract," in *Milton and the Long Restoration*, ed. Blair Hoxby and Ann Baynes Coiro (Oxford: Oxford University Press, 2016), 363–78.

49. Virgil, *Aeneid*, 144; 9.427–28.

50. Chaplin, "Beyond Sacrifice," 362.

51. Leah Whittington, "Vergil's Nisus and the Language of Self-Sacrifice in *Paradise Lost*," *Modern Philology* 107, no. 4 (May 2010): 604.

52. Ibid., 606.

53. Barbara K. Lewalski has, in *Milton's Brief Epic*, esp. 133–63, detailed how the true locus of meaning lies not in action but in the poem's "identity motif"— the interpretive challenge surrounding the Son's nature and being.

54. Richard Strier, "Milton against Humility," in *Religion and Culture in Renaissance England*, ed. Claire McEachern and Debora Shuger (Cambridge: Cambridge University Press, 1997), 275.

55. Lee Edelman, *No Future: Queer Theory and the Death Drive* (Durham, NC: Duke University Press, 2004), 14.

56. There have been many critical responses to Edelman and to the alignment of queerness with antisociality. For a range of brief discussions with a response from Edelman, see Robert L. Caserio et al., "The Antisocial Thesis in Queer Theory," *PMLA* 121, no. 3 (May 2006): 819–28. Katherine Bond Stockton, in *The Queer Child, or Growing Sideways in the Twentieth Century* (Durham, NC: Duke University Press, 2009), turns to queer childhood to present a complex understanding of reproductive futurity and queer antihistoricity. For a proposal of a reparative understanding of queer sociality informed by the later work of Eve Sedgwick and by disability theory, see Ellis Hanson, "The Future's Eve: Reparative Reading after Sedgwick," *South Atlantic Quarterly* 110, no. 1 (Winter 2011): 101–19.

57. See Lee Edelman, "Against Survival: Queerness in a Time That's Out of Joint," *Shakespeare Quarterly* 62, no. 2 (Summer 2011): 148–69.

58. Jacques Derrida, *Archive Fever: A Freudian Impression*, trans. Eric Prenowitz (Chicago: University of Chicago Press, 1996), 79.

59. See ibid., 38–39, 60–62.

60. See Song, *Dominion Undeserved*, 111–51.

61. See Conti, "Apocalyptic Virginity," for an insightful discussion of the way Jerome's vision of virginity in particular lingers in Milton's later imagination.

62. The presence of Ganymede and Hylas plays a key role in Gregory Bredbeck's discussion, in *Sodomy and Interpretation: Marlowe to Milton* (Ithaca, NY: Cornell University Press, 1991), 189–231, of the strategies Milton deploys to deflect homoeroticism within classical, biblical, and other poetic traditions. Despite Bredbeck's pioneering work, Milton scholarship had largely failed to engage meaningfully with queer theory until recently. See "Queer Milton," ed. Will Stockton and David L. Orvis, special issue, *Early Modern Culture* 10 (2014); this issue formed the basis of *Queer Milton*, ed. David L. Orvis (London: Palgrave Macmillan, 2018).

63. For work in the nascent field of asexuality studies, see Benjamin Kahan, *Celibacies: American Modernism and Sexual Life* (Durham, NC: Duke University Press, 2013), esp. 142–54; Ela Przybylo and Danielle Cooper, "Asexual Resonances: Tracing a Queerly Asexual Archive," *GLQ* 20, no. 3 (2014): 297–318; Kristina Gupta, "Compulsory Sexuality: Evaluating an Emerging Concept," *Signs: Journal of Women in Culture and Society* 41, no. 1 (Autumn 2015): 131–54, and "'And Now I'm Just Different, but There's Nothing Wrong with Me': Asexual Marginalization and Resistance," *Journal of Homosexuality* 64, no. 8 (2017): 991–1013; and Ela Przybylo, *Asexual Erotics: Intimate Readings of Compulsory Sexuality* (Columbus: Ohio State University, 2019).

64. Ian Watt offers a formulation of Milton's influence on the future of the novel when he refers, in *The Rise of the Novel: Studies in Defoe, Richardson, and Fielding* (1957), 2nd American ed. (Berkeley: University of California Press, 2001), 137, to *Paradise Lost* as "the greatest and indeed only epic of married life"—a poem that gives influential expression to a "Puritan conception of marriage and sexual relations [that] generally became the accepted code of Anglo-Saxon society."

CHAPTER 5

1. For a different reading of the *Memoirs* alongside *Order and Disorder*, see Katharine Gillespie, *Women Writing the English Republic, 1625–1681* (Cambridge: Cambridge University Press, 2017), 282–331. Focusing on Hutchinson's engagement with materialist philosophy and hermeticism, Gillespie concludes that in *Order and Disorder*, Christ is not the exemplar of a godly politics. Instead, Hutchinson "selects Eve and her 'daughters' as her anti-epic heroines" (288). I go on to consider how Hutchinson promotes an unstable identification between Christian wives and Eve (one that strains the temporality of typology) in an attempt to reaffirm Pauline marriage as well as the desirability of reproduction.

2. Lucy Hutchinson, *Memoirs of the Life of Colonel Hutchinson*, ed. James Sutherland (London: Oxford University Press, 1973), 229. Unless otherwise noted, quotations from the *Memoirs* are taken from this edition and will be cited parenthetically by page number.

3. N. H. Keeble, "The Colonel's Shadow: Lucy Hutchinson, Women's Writing, and the Civil War," in *Literature and the English Civil War*, ed. Thomas Healy and Jonathan Sawday (Cambridge: Cambridge University Press, 1990), 240.

4. Derek Hirst, "Remembering a Hero: Lucy Hutchinson's Memoirs of Her Husband," *English Historical Review* 119, no. 482 (June 2004): 682–91.

5. David Norbrook, "Memoirs and Oblivion: Lucy Hutchinson and the Restoration," *Huntington Library Quarterly* 75, no. 2 (Summer 2012): 233–82.

6. Hirst, "Remembering a Hero," 685.

7. Norbrook, "Oblivion," 244.

8. Hirst, "Remembering a Hero," 689.

9. Erin Murphy, "'I Remain, an Airy Phantasm': Lucy Hutchinson's Civil War Ghost Writing," *ELH* 82, no. 1 (Spring 2015): 107.

10. We eventually learn of the greater importance of White's shameful marriage. White is among the conspirators who travel to London to try to discredit John Hutchinson's authority before the Committee of Nottingham; the conspirators gain favor with MP Gilbert Millington. Lucy Hutchinson expands on the earlier account of White's lust to attack Millington's character. Together, the two of them frequented "Taverns and Brothells" until they were so "ensnar'd that they married a couple of Alehouse wenches, to their open shame and the conviction of the whole country of the vaine lives they led, and some reflection upon the Parliament itself" (146).

11. In "'Words More Than Civil': Republican Civility in Lucy Hutchinson's *The Life of John Hutchinson*," in *Early Modern Civil Discourses*, ed. Jennifer Richards (Houndmills: Palgrave Macmillan, 2003), 68–84, David Norbrook observes that Chadwick and Plumtree shuttle the problem of fractiousness out of the realm of practical politics and toward the realm of religious myth. Norbrook points out that Chadwick and Plumtree function as Machiavels, but the plots they participate in do not merely resemble satire or city comedy but are reminiscent instead of the narratives of good and evil found in *Paradise Lost* and *Order and Disorder*.

12. Regarding Lucy Hutchinson's motivations in undertaking this project as well as its exact dating, see Reid Barbour, "Between Atoms and the Spirit: Lucy Hutchinson's Translation of Lucretius," *Renaissance Papers* (1994): 1–16. Barbour describes how Hutchinson seems to have been motivated by the desire to test both the compatibility between Christian teaching and scientific knowledge and the underpinnings of her political allegiances during the Civil War period. For a subsequent reconsideration of how thoroughly Hutchinson repudiated Lucretius's atheistical tendencies, see Barbour, "Lucy Hutchinson, Atomism and the Atheist Dog," in *Women, Science and Medicine 1500–1700*, ed. Lynette Hunter and Sarah Hutton (Phoenix Mill: Sutton, 1997), 122–37.

13. See Lucretius, *On the Nature of Things*, trans. W. H. D. Rouse, rev. Martin F. Smith, rev. reprint ed. (Cambridge, MA: Harvard University Press, 1992), 78–79 (book 1, lines 935–43); 276–77 (book 4, lines 10–18).

14. Lucy Hutchinson, *Order and Disorder*, ed. David Norbrook (Oxford: Blackwell, 2001), 4. All quotations of *Order and Disorder* are from this edition and will be cited parenthetically by canto and line numbers.

15. In the autobiographical sketch added to the *Memoirs*, we have seen, Hutchinson claims that intermarriage between Normans and Saxons had given rise to her own family alongside Britain's mixed form of governance. Yet intermarriage with Catholics only produces corruption. Near the opening of the *Memoirs*, Hutchinson recalls how, under King James's reign, "the mix'd marriages of Papist and protestant famelies" served as a source of the abominations—including murder, incest, and adultery—that spread in England (42). With Charles I and Henrietta Maria in mind, Hutchinson declares that "wherever male princes are so effeminate to suffer weomen of forreigne birth and differents religion to entermeddle with the affairs of State, it is always found to produce sad desolations" (48).

16. For a reconsideration of Anne Fairfax (née Vere) against the negative reputation she acquired, see Jaqueline Eales, "Anne and Thomas Fairfax, and the Vere Connection," in *England's Fortress: New Perspectives on Thomas, 3rd Lord Fairfax*, ed. Andrew Hopper and Philip Major (London: Routledge, 2016), 145–68.

17. By appealing to her husband's preference for retired domesticity, Lucy Hutchinson downplays the significance of his decision to join Colonel Francis Hacker in plotting against Colonel Lambert—and his eventual decision to

support George Monck as the figure most likely to preserve the Republic. As John Hutchinson is off to meet with Hacker, a revealing episode takes place. Before departing, Hutchinson "caus'd his wife to write a letter to [Charles] Fleetewood, to complain of the affronts had bene offer'd him" (231). Fleetwood offers assistance, but this offer turns out to be a ruse, and three hundred troops are dispatched to Owthorpe. John Hutchinson flees, leaving his wife behind. This episode threatens to become a farcical repetition of his early abandonment of his wife. Yet when Major Grove arrives at Owthorpe, he meets with Lucy Hutchinson in her husband's stead: "With whom Mrs. Hutchinson so easily dealt that, after she had represented the state of things to him, he began to apologize" (221). Lucy Hutchinson claims to have convinced Major Grove of what she is now trying to convince the reader: that her husband had sincerely desired to avoid the troubles of public life and to retreat to domesticity. As a result, this episode looks ahead to Lucy Hutchinson's later act of life-preserving forgery. John Hutchinson may have planted the seeds for this forgery by asking his wife to write in his name. Lucy Hutchinson's narrative completes the arc between this earlier letter and her later act of forgery. When she recalls how, in 1660, she used the forged letter to sway Parliament into sparing her husband's life, she also recounts how "poore Mrs. Hacker, thinking to save her husband, had brought up the warrant for [Charles I's] execution with all their hands and seales" (230). Isabella Hacker's honest but misguided attempt to exonerate her husband ends up facilitating his conviction. By contrast, Lucy Hutchinson emerges as the wife who saves her husband's life through pious disobedience.

18. Oliver Cromwell's younger son Henry did have extensive military experience although he was not necessarily successful or popular as a leader. As Su Fang Ng, in *Literature and the Politics of the Family*, 105, observes, it is possible—although not certain—that Oliver Cromwell actively prepared to have his oldest surviving son succeed him by keeping the younger Henry stationed in Ireland.

19. The split role that John Hutchinson plays—immersed in a world of economic interests and yet supposedly apart from it—is revealed in an episode detailed at length (see Hutchinson, *Memoirs*, 195–200). Before the Restoration, John Hutchinson had persuaded Parliament to allow the Roman Catholic Anne Somerset, Countess of Worcester, to sell a piece of her inheritance. When the countess begs Hutchinson to buy the manor in Leicestershire himself, he eventually relents. Major-General Harrison advises Hutchinson against the purchase, pointing out that it would put money in the hands of Roman Catholics, but Hutchinson remains resolute. Lucy Hutchinson can only justify her husband's decision by attacking the major-general as a class-climbing hypocrite. Yet she also explains that the countess's true motivation was to broker a marriage with Henry Pierrepont, Marquess of Dorchester. John Hutchinson tries but fails to broker this deal (which would have violated Lucy Hutchinson's belief that Catholics and

Protestants should never intermarry). Later, Lady Somerset marries the Roman Catholic Henry Howard, and the couple attempt underhanded means to regain the Leicestershire manor. After the Restoration, Howard tries to persuade Lucy Hutchinson to sell the estate at a heavily discounted price, while promising assistance in preserving John Hutchinson's safety. When Lucy Hutchinson refuses to make such a deal, he threatens to have the estate returned to him without any remuneration. The Hutchinsons eventually emerge as rightful owners of this contested real estate. Yet this episode reveals the different ways they strain their political and sectarian allegiances to arrive at some balance of moral rectitude and economic self-interest.

20. David Norbrook, "Lucy Hutchinson's 'Elegies' and the Situation of the Republican Woman Writer," *English Literary Renaissance* 27, no. 3 (Autumn 1997): 471.

21. See Jonathan Goldberg, *The Seeds of Things: Theorizing Sexuality and Materiality in Renaissance Representations* (New York: Fordham University Press, 2009), 158–78.

22. Hugh de Quehen, ed., *Lucy Hutchinson's Translation of Lucretius, 'De rerum natura'* (Ann Arbor: Michigan University Press, 1996), 139.

23. See Lucretius, *On the Nature of Things*, 358; book 4, lines 1058–60.

24. Ibid., 359; book 4, lines 1061–67.

25. Ibid., 136; book 2, lines 541–43.

26. Ibid., 17; book 1, line 169. Lucretius promotes this general understanding of speciation as it applies not only to animals and humans but also to vegetal life and (what we might refer to as) inorganic materials. Goldberg observes that *De rerum natura* thereby suggests that "[h]eterosexual intercourse . . . is not privileged as an explanatory principle" (170).

27. For a discussion of Lucretius's critical view of love and its relevance for Renaissance thought, especially by way of Ficino, see Marion Wells, *The Secret Wound: Love-Melancholy and Early Modern Romance* (Stanford: Stanford University Press, 2007), 61–74.

28. Hutchinson defines time (which in itself is "insubstantial") as nothing but "Motion's measure, as a twin / Born with it" (1.154–56). This echoes Lucretius's teaching that nobody "has a sense of time by itself [per se] separated from the movement of things" (see Lucretius, 39; book 1, lines 462–63). Unlike Lucretius, however, Hutchinson believes that the material world is finite in duration:

> When Motion ceasing, Time shall be no more,
> But with the visible heavens shall expire
> While they consume in the world's funeral fire. (1.168–70)

29. Guillame du Bartas, *Bartas His Divine Weekes and Workes*, trans. Iosuah [Joshua] Sylvester (London, 1605), 12.

30. Ibid., 251.

31. In canto 6, Hutchinson states her belief that frustrated Petrarchan desire is a ruse not only of "lustful devils" but also of "female empire" (6.476, 6.491). The *Memoirs* had offered guarded praise of Elizabeth I's Protestantism while describing the unmarried queen as an exception who proves the patriarchal rule. In *Order and Disorder*, Hutchinson criticizes the manipulation of male desire as a ruse of female power. Hutchinson redirects Lucretius's lessons about the benefits of eros and the vanity of frustrated desire to different kinds of political and religious ends.

32. Hutchinson amplifies this problem by ventriloquizing Christ's words to his bride: "'My spouse, my sister,' said he, 'thou art mine; / I and my death, I and my life are thine'" (3.477–78). Hutchinson suddenly has Christ echo Solomon, who sings, "Thou hast ravished my heart, my sister, my spouse" (Song 4:9). In "Saints or Citizens? Ideas of Marriage in Seventeenth-Century English Republicanism," *Seventeenth Century* 25, no. 2 (October 2010): 240–64, Sharon Achinstein considers this invocation of the Song of Songs as part of a broader republican effort to reconceptualize marriage as a vehicle of mystical incorporation. In my own reading of Hutchinson's poem, the unanticipated celebration of a love for a sister is jarring, and it reminds us of the temporal disorientation that Hutchinson attempts in order to render Christian typology compatible with her understanding of married love.

33. Hutchinson's treatment of suicide similarly echoes but also diverges from Milton's in *Paradise Lost*. In canto 5, Hutchinson affirms that death provides a decisive resolution to mortal suffering. In the latter half of the canto, Hutchinson's Eve proposes suicide as a response to the Fall. In *Paradise Lost*, Milton's Eve also proposes suicide—but only if abstaining from sex proves too difficult. Suicide, in other words, is an extreme birth control measure. Milton's Adam reminds Eve of the prophecy about the woman's seed, which redeems sex and reproduction. In Hutchinson's narrative, Adam does echo the language of the *protoevangelium*, but only as he imagines sexual pleasure as the consolation to fallen existence:

> There on Love's sweet refreshing green banks roll,
> Where, ecstasied with joy, we shall not feel
> The serpent's little nibblings at our heel. (5.552–54)

Hutchinson's Adam is focused on delight and remains blithely indifferent to the realities of postlapsarian reproduction.

34. Goldberg, *Seeds of Things*, 174.

35. Earlier, in canto 4, Hutchinson had described how the devils could exhibit a debased version of republican cooperation. Even if they unite to "promote their common interest," they are not "linked . . . by faith and love" but rather by "hate of God and goodness" and the avoidance of "civil wars" that might "make their empire fall" (4.90–94). The devils are, in other words, royalists at heart who cooperate for all the wrong reasons under their "black prince" (4.88). In the form of

political and patriarchal reproduction that Cain practices, the devils find a human manifestation of their own wicked ambitions.

36. Hutchinson, *Order and Disorder*, 136n256.
37. Miller, *Engendering the Fall*, 131.
38. Norbrook, in Hutchinson, *Order and Disorder*, reminds us that Lucy Hutchinson had, at one point in the *Memoirs*, "compared her husband's enemies at the time of his arrest in 1663 to Laban and Esau" (258n473). Norbrook suggests a compatibility between Jacob and John Hutchinson in Lucy Hutchinson's imagination. My own reading makes the case that the importance of John Hutchinson's status as the older brother who deserves more of his father's inheritance makes this kind of identification unstable and, ultimately, untenable.
39. When Esau marries Canaanite Aholibamah, Hutchinson explains that he exhibits an ersatz form of freedom. Esau "[c]ontended not for freedom but to have / The base ends which his flagrant lust did crave" (17.475–76). When Isaac disapproves of this marriage, Esau argues for its political utility: "Is't not a princess that inflames my love?" (17.489). Esau subsequently pursues and marries "Adah, Duke Eber's daughter" (17.513). Yet Esau learns that Jacob has been sent to find a wife from within his own circle of kin. Esau responds by marrying Ishmael's daughter—a descendant of Abraham, but not from Sarah's chosen lineage. Hutchinson criticizes Esau not only for having committed polygamy but also for having adopted the idolatry of his Canaanite wives.
40. For a reading of this dream as reminiscent both of the *descensus* episode in the *Aeneid* and of Jacob's dream in Genesis 28, see Gillespie, *Women Writing*, 329–31. Gillespie acknowledges that, "To be sure, Hutchinson is reluctant to credit her husband's dream as entirely 'inspired.'" Yet Gillespie nonetheless sees the dream as emphatically placing John Hutchinson within in a biblical framework. My reading emphasizes Lucy Hutchinson's explicit self-consciousness about the possible fictiveness of her own interpretation which, in turn, signals her awareness of the unresolved typological tensions involved in her particular promotion of Christian marriage.
41. Qtd. from Norbrook, "Elegies," 513; lines 13–14.
42. Ibid., 515; line 1. As Susan Wiseman observes, in *Conspiracy and Virtue: Women, Writing, and Politics in Seventeenth-Century England* (Oxford: Oxford University Press, 2006), 222–23, in this elegy, a "tendentious revaluation of Restoration political language coexists with what seems to be an attempt to integrate her earlier philosophical and political interests into the writing of mourning." Questions remain about how, exactly, the duration of mourning—bound to be temporary even if protracted—can establish a viable political position. In Wiseman's account, Hutchinson offers the dynamic relationship between the mourning subject and the lost, beloved object as a poetic answer to that question.
43. Qtd. from Norbrook, "Elegies," 515; line 17.
44. Ibid., lines 23–24.
45. Ibid., 487; Elegy 1, lines 1–2.

CHAPTER 6

1. Janet Todd, *The Secret Life of Aphra Behn* (New Brunswick, NJ: Rutgers University Press, 1997), 71.

2. As Derek Hughes observes, in *The Theatre of Aphra Behn* (Houndmills, Basingstoke: Palgrave Macmillan, 2001), 30–31, *The Forc'd Marriage* is reminiscent of a number of Shakespearean and Restoration plays. In addition to the direct influence of *Othello*, Hughes mentions the relevance of *Much Ado about Nothing*—like *The Winter's Tale*, a Shakespearean precedent for the mock resurrection of a wronged wife providing a comic reconciliation. Hughes also describes the influence John Dryden and Sir Robert Howard's *The Indian Queen* (1664) and the Earl of Orrery's *The Generall* (1661) may have had for Behn's debut play.

3. Readings of *The Forc'd Marriage* are marked by split impulses toward narrowly topical and very broad registers of political concern. For the suggestion that Behn may have been thinking of James's marriage to Anne Hyde, see Maureen Duffy, *The Passionate Shepherdess: Aphra Behn 1640–89* (London: Cape, 1977), 103; and Todd, *Secret Life*, 140–41. Judy A. Hayden, in *Of Love and War: The Political Voice in the Early Plays of Aphra Behn* (Amsterdam: Rodopi, 2010), 60–88, proposes a number of identifications, including Orgulius with George Monck, while also acknowledging that such identifications are imprecise. Anita Pacheco, in "'Where Lies This Power Divine?': The Representation in Kingship in Aphra Behn's Early Tragicomedies," *Journal for Eighteenth-Century Studies* 38, no. 3 (September 2015): 317–34, describes Orgulius as a dramatic version of the Earl of Clarendon—one whose reputation can be recuperated. This claim is part of a broader consideration of how Behn's earliest plays test the limits of a commitment to the monarch's absolute power. Alvin Snider, in "Aphra Behn's *The Forc'd Marriage* at Lincoln's Inn Fields," *Studies in Philology* 115, no. 1 (Winter 2018): 193–217, focuses on the site of the play's first performance and considers the relevance of James, Duke of Monmouth, having taken part in a drunken brawl (and having possibly killed a beadle) in nearby Whetstone Park.

4. After noting that two of the Restoration plays that influenced Behn in the composition of *The Forc'd Marriage* (*The Indian Queen* and *The Generall*) were more overt celebrations of Charles II's return to the throne, Hughes notes, "In *The Forc'd Marriage*, however, justice requires change: a determined female challenge to a status quo in which sexual and political power are indivisibly invested in men" (*Theatre* 32).

5. Laura Brown, *Ends of Empire: Women and Ideology in the Early-Eighteenth Century* (Ithaca, NY: Cornell University Press, 1993), 25.

6. Ibid., 47–48.

7. Virginia Woolf, *A Room of One's Own*, annot. Susan Gubar, ed. Mark Hussey (London: Harcourt, 2005), 65.

8. Ibid., 64.

9. Aphra Behn, *The Forc'd Marriage, or The Jealous Bridegroom*, in *The Works of Aphra Behn*, vol. 5, *Plays, 1671–1677*, ed. Janet Todd (Columbus: Ohio State University Press, 1996), 10; act 1, scene 1, line 49. All quotations of *The Forc'd Marriage* are taken from this edition and will be cited parenthetically by act, scene, and line numbers.

10. Todd, *Secret Life*, 139.

11. The viability of a secret marital contract is a familiar plot device. For a discussion of the legal basis of this dramatic trope, see Subha Mukherji, *Law and Representation in Early Modern Drama* (Cambridge: Cambridge University Press, 2006), 17–54.

12. Stanley Cavell, *Pursuits of Happiness: The Hollywood Comedy of Remarriage* (Cambridge, MA: Harvard University Press, 1981), 20.

13. See ibid., 58, 87–88, 146, and 150–52. Cavell does not emphasize how Milton's claims for the spiritual benefits of marriage—and thus the benefits of divorce and remarriage—are explicitly grounded on the needs of the husband. This is true even when Cavell specifically relates the difficulty of imagining the heroines of these Hollywood romantic comedies as future mothers to Milton's claims about the spiritual rather than physical basis of marriage. Cavell mentions in an aside that Bergman's *Smiles of a Summer Night* is the only comedy from the period that he can recall in which "a child is justified apart from marriage, even apart from any stable relationship with a man, merely on the ground that you bore it" (58).

14. As the titles of *The Lady Eve* (1941) and *Adam's Rib* (1949) suggest, the Genesis story continues to operate as a familiar ur-myth of a husband and wife who must deem each other to be irreplaceable.

15. See Cavell, *Pursuits*, 73–109.

16. Behn, *Works*, 5:63.

17. We also recognize Alcippus as an unhappy version of Pygmalion. Hughes, *Theatre*, 36, reminds us that Galatea was the name of Pygmalion's statue, and in Alcippus's story, Galatea is the future wife who will offer him redemption. Hughes notes that Behn's twist on the Pygmalion story affiliates her drama of the mock-resurrected wife with *The Winter's Tale*.

18. Behn, *Works*, 5:69.

19. Ibid., 5:70

20. Todd, *Secret Life*, 140.

21. Ibid., 229. For a detailed study of the conditional rather than absolute royalism of Behn's early plays, see Jessica Kate Bentley Pirie, *Princes, Power, and Politics in the Early Plays of Aphra Behn* (PhD diss., University of Birmingham, 2019).

22. Richard Kroll, "'Tales of Love and Gallantry': The Politics of Oroonoko," *Huntington Library Quarterly* 67, no. 4 (December 2004): 574.

23. Ibid., 578.

24. Ibid.

25. Aphra Behn, *Oroonoko*, ed. Joanna Lipking (New York: Norton, 1997), 56. All quotations from *Oroonoko* are from this edition and will be cited parenthetically by page number.

26. Aphra Behn, "Pindarick Poem on the Happy Coronation of His Most Sacred Majesty James II," in *The Works of Aphra Behn*, vol. 1, *Poetry*, ed. Janet Todd (Columbus: University of Ohio Press, 1992), 202; line 84. All quotations of Behn's poetry are taken from this volume and will be cited parenthetically by line number.

27. For the importance of Behn's treatment of honor, see Anita Pacheco, "Royalism and Honor in Aphra Behn's Oroonoko," *SEL: Studies in English Literature, 1500–1900* 34, no. 3 (Summer 1994): 491–506. Pacheco's reading relies partly on George Guffey's earlier discussion in *Two English Novelists: Aphra Behn and Anthony Trollope* (Los Angeles: University of California Press, 1975), 3–41.

28. Near the end of *Oroonoko*, Behn revisits the motif of the arrow to describe an unhappier configuration of substitution, sacrifice, and conjugal love (or its ignoble variant). During the failed slave revolt in Surinam, Imoinda takes up weapons and wounds the corrupt deputy governor Byam with an arrow. Behn tells us that this wound have killed Byam except that "his Indian Mistress heal'd" him "by Sucking the Wound" (58). In this case, the Indian mistress undoes the effects of Imoinda's heroic violence in support of her husband.

29. For a detailed account of these events, see Larry Gragg, *Englishmen Transplanted: The English Colonization of Barbados, 1627–1660* (Oxford: Oxford University Press, 2003), 29–57.

30. William Pettigrew, *Freedom's Debt: The Royal African Company and the Politics of the Atlantic Slave Trade, 1672–1752* (Chapel Hill: University of North Carolina Press, 2013), 31. Pettigrew, 179–209, discusses how *Oroonoko*—especially through its many adaptations and retellings—would shape eighteenth-century debates about slavery and abolition in general, and in particular the perceived capacity of the Royal African Company to curb moral corruption, both in Africa and among slave traders.

31. See Todd, *Secret Life*, 69.

32. Richard Kroll, *Restoration Drama and "The Circle of Commerce": Tragicomedy, Politics, and Trade in the Seventeenth Century* (Cambridge: Cambridge University Press, 2007).

33. Charlotte Sussman, in "The Other Problem with Women: Reproduction and Slave Culture in Aphra Behn's *Oroonoko*," in *Rereading Aphra Behn: History, Theory, and Criticism*, ed. Heidi Hutner (Charlottesville: University of Virginia Press, 1993), 216–17, describes Imoinda's body as the victim of two forces: a "crisis in property relations" that would make her royal offspring chattel and her potency as a virtuous and alluring romance heroine.

34. Stephanie Athey and Daniel Cooper Alarcón, "*Oroonoko*'s Gendered Economies of Honor/Horror: Reframing Colonial Discourse Studies in the Americas," in *Subjects and Citizens: Race and Gender from* Oroonoko *to Anita Hill*, ed. Cathy N. Davidson (Durham, NC: Duke University Press, 1995), 37–38.

35. John Maxwell, in *Sacro-Sancta Regum Majestas, or The Sacred and Royal Prerogative of Christian Kings* (London, 1680), 257, includes the story of Gibeah among examples of how "Religion is defaced, Justice is abused, Honesty and Civil moral Conversation is shaken off; Dishonesty, Impiety, Uncleanness are avowed" in the absence of kingly authority. Nath.[aniel] Bisbie, in *Two Sermons: The First Shewing the Mischiefs of Anarchie; The Second, the Mischiefs of Sedition* (London, 1684), 4, cites Judges 19 as a warning and goes on to enumerate the consequences of anarchy: "Sacriledge and Theft . . . then marches Whoredom, Rape, Adultery; after these Murder, Bloodshed, Civil War." Bisbie would later refuse the oath of allegiance to William and Mary. By contrast, William Denton, who had previously served as court physician to Charles I and dedicated a treatise to Charles II, appeals to the story of the Levite in Judges to argue for the propriety of the 1688 revolution. In *Jus Regiminis: Being a Justification of Defensive Arms in General and Consequently of Our Late Revolutions* (London, 1689), 50, Denton remembers that God sanctions Israel to expiate "on a *whole Tribe,* which had so offended," which sets a precedent for "Christian Men, to maintain and defend the true Christian Religion in it's [*sic*] purity against all opposers." For Denton, the installation of Protestant monarchs is a version of reform that is analogous (but also preferable) to the retribution that Israel exacts on the tribe of Benjamin for its sins.

36. Elliott Visconsi, in "A Degenerate Race: English Barbarism in Aphra Behn's 'Oroonoko' and 'The Widow Ranter,'" *ELH* 69, no. 3 (Fall 2002): 673–701, discusses Behn's concern for a domestic rather than foreign threat of barbarism—one that results from cultural debasement.

37. Margaret Ferguson, "Juggling the Categories of Race, Class, and Gender: Aphra Behn's *Oroonoko*," in *Women, "Race," and Writing in the Early Modern Period*, ed. Margo Hendricks and Patricia A. Parker (London: Routledge, 1994), 222.

38. See Joyce Green MacDonald, *Women and Race in Early Modern England* (Cambridge: Cambridge University Press, 2002), 108–23, on stage adaptations of *Oroonoko*, beginning with Thomas Southerne's in 1696, that recast Imoinda as a White character. MacDonald interrogates the sentiment, circulated in modern criticism, that women are commodified in a way analogous to slaves in Southerne's play. She shows how Southerne's adaptation fosters this kind of misleading conflation by removing the presence of the Black heroine as well as the affectively incongruous scene of Oroonoko killing Imoinda and their unborn heir as a supposedly lovely expression of noble honor.

39. Behn did compose a Pindaric ode for William's supporter Gilbert Burnet. See Todd, *Secret Life*, 424–28, for a discussion of the politically ambiguous message of this ode.

Epilogue

1. Mary Shelley, *Frankenstein*, ed. J. Paul Hunter (New York: Norton, 1996), 32. All quotations of *Frankenstein* are taken from this edition, which is based on the 1818 text, and will be cited parenthetically by page number.

2. I consider the daemon's claim to have read *Paradise Lost* through an unidentified French translation in "*Frankenstein, Paradise Lost,* and the Fiction of Translation," forthcoming in *Modern Philology*. In *The Madwoman in the Attic: The Woman Writer and the Nineteenth-Century Literary Imagination* (1979), Veritas paperback ed. (New Haven, CT: Yale University Press, 2020), 187–202, Sandra M. Gilbert and Susan Gubar provide an influential account of Milton as a restrictive, patriarchal precedent for Shelley. For notable qualifications or challenges to that account, see John B. Lamb, "Mary Shelley's *Frankenstein* and Milton's Monstrous Myth," *Nineteenth-Century Literature* 47, no. 3 (December 1992): 303–19; Lauren Shohet, "Reading Milton in Mary Shelley's *Frankenstein*," *Milton Studies* 60, nos. 1–2 (2018): 157–82.

3. George Eliot, *Daniel Deronda*, ed. Graham Handley (Oxford: Oxford University Press, 2014), 211. All quotations of *Daniel Deronda* are taken from this edition and will be cited parenthetically by page number.

4. For a discussion of *Daniel Deronda* and Milton, see Anna K. Nardo, *George Eliot's Dialogue with John Milton* (Columbia: University of Missouri Press, 2003), 216–46. Nardo focuses on the relevance of *Paradise Regained* for Eliot's presentation of Deronda as a messianic figure.

5. For discussions of *Daniel Deronda* and Shakespeare, see Marianne Novy, *Engaging with Shakespeare: Responses of George Eliot and Other Women Novelists* (Athens: University of Georgia Press, 1994), 117–37; John Lyon, "Shakespearean Margins in George Eliot's 'Working-Day World,'" *Shakespeare Survey* 53 (2000): 114–26; and John Rignall, "George Eliot," in *Scott, Dickens, Eliot, Hardy, Great Shakespeareans*, ed. Adrian Poole (London: Bloomsbury, 2011), 5:95–138.

6. Eliot engages with *Paradise Lost* much more extensively in *Middlemarch* (1871–72); for discussions of this, see Nardo, *George Eliot's Dialogue*, 111–34; Dayton Haskin, "George Eliot as 'Miltonist': Marriage and Milton," in *Middlemarch, Milton and Gender*, ed. Catherine Gimelli Martin (Cambridge: Cambridge University Press, 2005), 207–22; and Erik Gray, *Milton and the Victorians* (Ithaca, NY: Cornell University Press, 2011), 130–51.

7. Nancy Armstrong, *Desire and Domestic Fiction: A Political History of the Novel* (Oxford: Oxford University Press, 1987), 252.

8. For various discussions concerning the divided political sentiments of *Frankenstein*, see Lee Sterrenburg, "Mary Shelley's Monster: Politics and Psyche," in *The Endurance of Frankenstein: Essays on Mary Shelley's Novel*, ed. George Levine and U. C. Knoepflmacher (Berkeley: University of California Press, 1979), 143–71; Gayatri Spivak, "Three Women's Texts and a Critique of Imperialism," *Critical*

Inquiry 12, no. 1 (Autumn 1985): 243–61; H. L. Malchow, "Frankenstein's Monster and Images of Race in Nineteenth-Century Britain," *Past and Present* 139 (May 1993): 90–130; Diana Reese, "A Troubled Legacy: Mary Shelley's *Frankenstein* and the Inheritance of Human Rights," *Representations* 96, no. 1 (Fall 2006): 48–72; and Marie Mulvey-Roberts, *Dangerous Bodies Historicizing the Gothic Corporeal* (Manchester: Manchester University Press, 2016), 52–91.

9. See, for example, Edward Said, "Zionism from the Standpoint of its Victims," *Social Text* 1, no. 1 (Winter 1979): 7–58; Deirdre David, *Fictions of Resolution in Three Victorian Novels* (New York: Columbia University Press, 1980), 135–79; Susan Meyer, "'Safely to Their Own Borders': Proto-Zionism, Feminism, and Nationalism in Daniel Deronda," *ELH* 60, no. 3 (Autumn 1993): 733–58; and Mikhal Dekel, *The Universal Jew: Masculinity, Modernity, and the Zionist Movement* (Evanston, IL: Northwestern University Press, 2010), esp. 39–94.

10. On ancient deployments of the idea of Noah's curse, see David M. Goldenberg, *The Curse of Ham: Race and Slavery in Early Judaism, Christianity, and Islam* (Princeton, NJ: Princeton University Press, 2009); on the relevance of the myth of Noah cursing Ham for the early modern transatlantic slave trade and for anti-Black racism, see Stephen R. Haynes, *Noah's Curse: The Biblical Justification of American Slavery* (Oxford: Oxford University Press, 2002); and Sylvester A. Johnson, *The Myth of Ham in Nineteenth-Century American Christianity: Race, Heathens, and the People of God* (Houndmills, Basingstoke: Palgrave Macmillan, 2004).

Index

Achinstein, Sharon, 137, 302n32
Actaeon, 33, 35–36, 38, 48, 58, 276n14, 277n19
Adam and Eve: as Christ and the church, 202; creation of, 149–50; *felix culpa* paradox, 144, 153–54, 164; and free choice, 162–66, 168; gender hierarchy, 146, 160–62, 166, 168, 257; and narcissism, 159–60; and pride, 114–16; reconciliation of marital love, 144, 146, 167–70; rejection of remarriage, 136–37, 142–44; in relation to the second Adam and second Eve, 30, 44, 144, 171–72; and Satan, 148–49, 160, 163
Adam's Rib (film), 305n14
Admetus and Alcestis, 91, 144–45
aesthetic subjectivity, 72–75, 82
affective individualism, 270n25
affect theory, 17
Agamben, Giorgio, 124–27, 289n42, 289n45
agape vs. erotic love, 31–32, 105
Alarcón, Daniel Cooper, 251
Alcestis and Admetus, 91, 144–45
Alpers, Paul, 51
Amoretti (Spenser): asymmetric reciprocal desire, 35–37, 59; erotic love as reflection of Christ's agape love, 31–32; freedom and fate, 40, 41; husbandly merit, 30–31; narcissistic desire, 33–35, 37, 51, 54, 57; and ransom theory of atonement, 38–40
Anderson, Judith H., 280n45
angels, 145, 149–50, 156–58, 164, 165, 257, 262
anger and wrath, just, 47, 49, 53
Anna of Denmark, 61–62
Anne, Countess of Warwick, 283–84n31
Anselm of Canterbury, *Why God Became Man*, 5–6, 268n12
antisemitism, 15–16, 80, 274n46
Arendt, Hannah, 289n42
Ariosto, Ludovico, *Orlando furioso*, 8–9, 27–28, 66, 287n13
Aristotle: *Nicomachean Ethics*, 155; *Politics*, 154
asexuality studies, 176
Astell, Mary, 165
atheism, 190–91, 199
Athey, Stephanie, 251
atonement: Anselm of Canterbury on, 5–6, 147, 268n12; artistic representation, 115; and free choice, 151–53, 154, 155–59; and friendship, 166–67; and imputed righteousness, 31, 43–44, 48; penal theory of, 6, 40, 137, 147–48, 268n12; ransom theory of, 31–32, 38–40, 158–59, 278n27; Socinian theory of, 148; spot and wrinkle language, 95; and transferability of guilt, 52–53, 280n47

Aubrey, John, 97
Augustine, 241
authority. *See* sovereignty and kingship
awe, 104, 118, 133–34
Axton, Marie, 45

Barbour, Reid, 299n12
Barkan, Leonard, 38
Beckwith, Sarah, 89
beguilement, 35–36, 39, 43, 47, 50, 51–53, 55–57, 60
Behn, Aphra: "A Congratulatory Poem to Her Sacred Majesty," 254–55; *The Luckey Chance*, 220; "Pindarick Poem on the Coronation," 239–41, 254–55. See also *The Forc'd Marriage*; *Oroonoko*
Bendersky, Joseph W., 273n45
Benjamin, Walter, 78
Berlant, Lauren, 274n50
Berry, Helen, 270n25
biopolitics, 124–27, 289n42, 289n45
Bisbie, Nathaniel, *Two Sermons*, 307n35
Bissenbakker, Mons, 271–72n31
Bodin, Jean, 279n37, 295n37
Boyle, Elizabeth, 30, 37, 40, 278n31
Bradley, A. C., 66, 70
Britton, Dennis, 66
brotherly merit, 188, 189, 190, 212–13, 303n38
Brown, Laura, 222
burial, proper, 121–23
Burnet, Gilbert, 307n39

Calvin, John, 8, 31, 276n12
Camden, William, 279n38
Catherine of Braganza, 132
Catholicism, 61, 100, 132, 136, 155, 205, 239–41, 284n39, 286n5, 295n39, 299n15

Cavell, Stanley, 66, 228, 305n13
celibacy and virginity, 45, 174, 279n38, 289n45
Chadwick, James, 188–89, 299n11
Chakravarty, Urvashi, 72
chance, 84, 90
Chaplin, Gregory, 148, 166
Chapman, Alison, 161
Charles I, King of England: execution of, 10, 14, 104, 106, 180, 239, 245–46; marriage of, 100, 102–4, 132–33, 140–41, 182; and patriarchal piety, 130–31
Charles II, King of England, 103, 121, 130–35, 244
Charlottesville, VA, Unite the Right Rally (2017), 15–16, 274n46
childbirth and motherhood, 19, 22–23, 30, 88–89, 125, 140, 160, 171–72, 202–3, 305n13
Childe, Maccabaeus, 60
choice, freedom of, 40, 41, 42–43, 49, 56, 84–85, 151–59, 162–66, 168, 295n39
Christ: as Actaeon, 38; as begotten, 293n32; as child of reproductive futurity, 172–74, 176; enthroned, 118; Gethsemane allusion, 56; indifference to sex and reproduction, 174–76; marriage with the church, 1–2, 202; merit *vs.* birthright of, 150–52, 157–58, 169, 170–71. See also atonement
church, Christ and, 1–2, 5–6, 202
circumcision, 72–73, 173
Clare, Janet, 290n51
class prejudice, 195, 197, 204–5
colonialism and imperialism, 127–29, 238, 243–46, 252–53
comedy, 8, 98, 104–5, 110, 228–29, 269n23, 305n13. See also tragicomedy

commerce and trade, 131–35
commodification and fungibility, 12, 238, 243, 248, 251, 272n32
Contarini, Gasparo, *Commonwealth and Government of Venice*, 67, 69, 76, 77
Coppe, Abiezer, *Some Sweet Sips, of Spirituall Wine*, 139–40
COVID-19 pandemic, 275n59
Cressy, David, 270n25
Cromwell, Henry, 300n18
Cromwell, Oliver, 129, 139, 193, 194–95, 291n8, 300n18
Cromwell, Richard, 194–95
crowns, 117, 118
Cruz, Ariane, 285n46
cuckoldry, and race, 285n46
Cupid, 58

Daileader, Celia, 284n46
Daniel, Drew, 279n37
Davenant, William: artistic lineage, 97; and Behn, 220; *The Cruelty of the Spaniards in Peru*, 129, 290n51; *The History of Sir Francis Drake*, 129; *Humble Remonstrance*, 101; "Poem to the Kings Most Sacred Majesty," 131–35; "Poem upon His Sacred Majestie's Most Happy Return to His Dominions," 130; *Salmacida Spolia*, 101–2; *The Siege of Rhodes*, 290n51; *The Tempest* (with Dryden), 290n53; *The Temple to Love* (with Jones), 101; "To the King on New-Yeares Day 1630," 102–3, 104; "To the Queen," 101, 103, 132–33. See also *Gondibert*
Denton, William, *Jus Regiminis*, 307n35
Derrida, Jacques, 172–73

Diggers, 140, 292n15
divine justice, 147–49. See also atonement
divorce, 136, 139, 143, 165, 228–29
Dolan, Frances, 9
Donne, John, 3, 268n7; *Holy Sonnet 18*, 1–2, 3, 7, 8, 63, 267n1, 267n5
drunkenness, 207
Dryden, John: *Astraea Redux*, 130; *The Indian Queen* (with Howard), 304n2; *The Tempest* (with Davenant), 290n53
Du Bartas, Guillaume, *Divine Weeks*, 200
Dudley, Ambrose, 284n31
Duns Scotus, 295n39

Edelman, Lee, 172–73, 176
Edenic marriage. See Adam and Eve
Edwards, Calvin, 34
Eliot, George, *Daniel Deronda*, 256, 258–66
Elizabeth I, Queen of England: execution of Mary, Queen of Scots, 78; and Harington, 28; protracted marriage negotiations, 279n37; and two bodies theory, 45–46; as unmarried and heirless, 10, 302n31; as Virgin Queen, 45, 279n38
Engelking, Wojciech, 284n45
epic: artistic lineage, 97; comic subversions, 110; and the novel, 176, 298n64; redefined around love, 143, 146, 179, 298n64; *vs.* romance, 246; Virgilian, 54, 146
Erasmus, Desiderius, 276n12
erotic *vs.* agape love, 31–32, 105
Este, Ippolito d', 27–28
ethnicity. See race
Eucharist, 247
Euripides, *Alcestis*, 144–45

314   *Index*

Eve. *See* Adam and Eve
Everard, William, 140

The Faerie Queene (Spenser): overview, 28; beguilement, 43, 47, 50, 51–53, 55–57, 60; and *Gondibert*, 110; goodwill and freedom, 42–43, 49, 56; heroism and identity of Arthur, 28, 43–44, 45, 278–79n35; heroism limited to justice *vs.* love, 46–50, 54; heroism of redeemer wife, 54–57, 59–60; husbandly merit, 43–44, 48, 57; and *Much Ado about Nothing*, 287n13; narcissistic and reciprocal desire, 58–59, 276–77n17; and *Piers Plowman*, 38; sovereignty's compatibility with Christian truth, 42, 43; two bodies theory, 45–46
Fairfax, Anne, 192–93
Fairfax, Thomas, 100, 192–93
Fall, the. *See* Adam and Eve
familial honor, 85–89
fascism, 15–16, 24–25, 273n39, 274n46
fate, 40, 41
Ferguson, Margaret, 254
Ficino, Marsilio, 296n43
filial piety, 130–31, 196
flattery and praise, 119–21
Fleetewood, Charles, 300n17
The Forc'd Marriage (Behn): overview, 221; authority, 223–24, 226–27, 236; gender hierarchy, 235, 236–37; and *The Generall*, 304n2; heroic merit disconnected from desire, 224–25; husbandly merit, 232–33, 235; and *The Indian Queen*, 304n2; jealousy, 225–26, 229; mock resurrection, 230–32, 234; and *Much Ado about Nothing*, 234, 304n2; and *Oroonoko*, 247–49; and *Othello*, 221, 224–25, 248–49; political context, 221, 304n3; promiscuity reformed into monogamy, 233–35; remarriage as solution, 227–28, 229; and *The Winter's Tale*, 221, 229–30, 231, 236, 305n17
forgiveness, 89, 232, 237
Foucault, Michel, 15, 124, 125
Foyster, Elizabeth, 270n25
fraud, 183–85, 186–87, 212, 215, 300n17
Fraunce, Abraham, 38
Freccero, John, 276n9
freedom: bodily, 160–62; of choice, 40, 41, 42–43, 49, 56, 84–85, 151–59, 162–66, 168, 295n39; and limits of sovereign power, 40–41
Freud, Sigmund, 21, 22–25, 176, 275n57
friendship: of Christ, 166–67; *vs.* competition among men, 81, 83–84, 93
Frye, Northrop, 269n23
fungibility, 12, 53, 133, 238, 243, 248, 251, 272n32
Furness, Horace Howard, 75

Gardner, Helen, 267n1
Gell, John, 188
gender in relation to self/other dichotomy, 22–23, 34–35, 37
gender hierarchy: and divorce, 165; parity attempts, 236–37; superiority of husbands, 116–19, 160–62, 256–57, 287–88n27; superiority of wives, 146, 166, 168, 235; unstable Pauline definition of marriage, 2, 6–7, 23, 116, 267–68n5; and uxoriousness, 141, 143, 169, 182, 192–94. *See also* husbands/men; wives/women
Gilbert, Sandra M., 308n2
Gillespie, Katharine, 298n1, 303n40
Gladish, David, 114
Gless, Darryl, 43

God: divine justice, 147–49 (*see also* atonement); obedience to, 148, 153, 155, 163, 164; replacement of fallen angels, 149–50; will of, 183, 185
Goldberg, Jonathan, 197, 205, 301n26
Gondibert (Davenant): overview, 97–100; and biopolitics, 124–27; burial of the dead, 121–23; erotic *vs.* agape love, 105; and *The Faerie Queene*, 110; Hobbes on, 110, 111, 287n19; husbandly merit, 106–9, 116; husbandly superiority, 116–19, 287–88n27; imperial ambitions, 127–28; pride, 114–16; religious belief and poetry *vs.* scientific knowledge, 112–14, 119–21; subversion of comedy formula, 104–5, 110; vengeance, 107, 108–10, 123
goodwill, 37, 40, 42–43, 49
Gouge, William, *Of Domesticall Duties*, 7
greed, 50–51
Greenblatt, Stephen, 281n48
Gregerson, Linda, 277n12
Gregory of Nazianzus, 39–40
Grotius, Hugo, *De satisfactioni Christi*, 148
Gubar, Susan, 308n2
guilt: inducements to feel, 230–31, 234–35; and innocence of Christ, 32, 52–53, 137, 148; and remarriage, 136, 144–45; transferability of, 52–53, 280n47

Hacker, Francis, 299–300n17
Hacker, Isabella, 300n17
Hadfield, Andrew, 69
Hamilton, A. C., 43–44, 279n36
Hammill, Graham, 15, 64
Harington, John, *Orlando furioso*, 27–28, 54, 279n41
Hayden, Judy A., 304n3
Henrietta Anne of England, 131
Henrietta Maria, Queen consort of England, 100–102, 103–4, 130–31, 286n5
hereditary succession: divine, merit *vs.* birthright, 150–52, 157–58, 169, 170–71; legitimacy concerns, 81–82; liberation of personal love from, 74–75, 94; monarchical crises of, 10, 139, 240; monogamy in conflict with intergenerational demands, 208–11, 215, 303n39; and mortality, 81–82, 83, 103–4; mythic foundations of, 204–8, 212–14, 302–3n35; primogeniture *vs.* republicanism, 194–97; and reproductive futurity, 174; and slavery, 248, 306n33; tenuous restoration of, 91–92, 94–95; women's role in royal, 18–20, 104, 131
heroism: of Christ's triumph in hell, 38–40, 44; disconnected from desire, 224–25; in epic *vs.* romance genre, 246; fraudulent, 43; *vs.* husbandly merit, 65–67, 69–70, 106–8, 283n22; limited to justice *vs.* love, 46–50; self-sacrifice, 48, 55–57, 59, 65, 107, 123, 167–68, 242, 250–51; of wives, 54–57, 59–60, 116, 117, 306n28
heteronormativity, 2–3, 256
heterosexual subject formation, 22–24
Hill, Christopher, 10, 270n25, 292n15
Hirst, Derek, 184, 185
historical objectivity, 63–64, 77–79, 81
Hobbes, Thomas, 287n19; *Leviathan*, 110–12
Höfele, Andreas, 79, 80
Hoffman, Tobias, 295n39
Holy Spirit, as turtledove, 199–200

homosexuality, 22, 24, 34–35, 175–76, 271n28, 275n57
honor: familial, 85–89; of monogamy, 241–42
hounds, 35–36, 47–48, 276n14
Howard, Henry, 301n19
Howard, Robert, *The Indian Queen* (with Dryden), 304n2
Hughes, Derek, 304n2, 304n4, 305n17
Hume, Anthea, 280n41
hunting, 35–37, 106
husbandly merit: *vs.* heroic worth, 65–67, 69–70, 106–8, 283n24; imputed, 30–31, 43–44, 48, 232–33, 235; *vs.* political corruption, 188–89; reflected in wife, 182–83
husbands/men: Christlike, 2, 7, 44, 65, 67, 96, 104, 118, 132, 178, 204; friendship *vs.* competition among, 81, 83–84, 93; superiority of, 116–19, 160–62, 256–57, 287–88n27. *See also* gender hierarchy; wives/women
Hutchinson, George, 183, 188, 189, 190, 196
Hutchinson, John. See *The Memoirs of the Life of Colonel Hutchinson*
Hutchinson, Lucy: *Elegies*, 197, 218–19; translation of Lucretius's *De rerum natura*, 191, 197–98. *See also The Memoirs of the Life of Colonel Hutchinson*; *Order and Disorder*
Hutchinson, Thomas, 195–96
Hyde, Anne, 221, 236, 239

immigration and naturalization, 11–12, 271–72n31
immortality, 103–4
imperialism and colonialism, 127–29, 238, 243–46, 252–53
imputed merit, 30–31, 43–44, 48, 232–33, 235

innocence *vs.* guilt, 32, 52–53, 137, 148
intermarriage, 181–82, 205–6, 260–62, 264–65, 299n15. *See also Othello*
Irenaeus, 39
It Happened One Night (film), 228–29

James I, King of England, 10, 14, 61–62, 63, 78
James II, King of England, 10, 221, 236, 237, 239–41, 244
jealousy: and dishonor, 89; divine, 8, 62–63; and husbandly merit, 66–67, 69–70, 283n24, 288n27; and husbandly superiority, 116–18, 287–88n27; as irrational passion *vs.* ennobling love, 71, 229, 231, 249–50; loving, 259–61, 262; and remarriage, 142, 143; sexual, 70–71, 80, 82–83, 92, 225; and skepticism, 66, 68–69; as solution to forced marriage, 225–26; as solution to promiscuity, 233–34; sovereign, 111–12; stalemate with love, 109–10; as tyrant, 227
Jesus. *See* Christ
Jews: and antisemitism, 15–16, 80, 274n46; biblical interpretation, 216–17; in Christian typology, 129; cultural identity, 260–61, 262, 264–66
Johnson, Samuel, 75
Jones, Inigo, *The Temple to Love* (with Davenant), 100
Jordan, Constance, 272n36
justification. *See* atonement

Kahn, Victoria, 25, 78, 110–11, 271n27, 284n33
Kantorowicz, Ernst, 14–15, 17–18, 20–21, 45, 125–26, 273n39
Keeble, N. H., 183

King, John, 45, 46, 279n38
The King's Cabinet Opened, 100, 141
kingship. *See* sovereignty and kingship
king's two bodies. *See* two bodies theory
Knapp, James, 285n48
Kroll, Richard, 237–38, 247

The Lady Eve (film), 305n14
Landreth, David, 280n47
Langland, William, *Piers Plowman*, 38–39, 43–44, 280n45
Latimer, Heather, 125
Leo, Russ, 276n12
Levellers, 197, 292n15
Levinas, Emmanuel, 285n48
Lewalski, Barbara K., 296n53
Lewis, C. S., 269n22, 278n32
Lewkenor, Lewes, 67, 76, 77, 283–84n31
Lieu, Judith, 5
Lluelyn, Martin, 286n5
Lokke, Geoffrey, 285n46
Low, Anthony, 290–91n1
Lucretius, *De rerum natura*, 191, 197–99, 301n26, 301n28
Lupton, Julia Reinhard, 15, 64, 71–72
Luther, Martin, 4, 31, 268n12, 276n12

MacDonald, Joyce Green, 307n38
Machiavelli, Niccolò, 69
MacKinnon, Catherine, 277n20
Maitland, Lord, 241
Marcion, 5
marriage contracts, 270–71n27
Mary, Virgin, 30, 240
Mary, Queen of Scots, 63, 78
Mary II, Queen of England, 254–55
Mary of Modena, 239–41, 255
Maxwell, John, *Sacro-Sancta Regum Majestas*, 307n35

Mbembé, Achille, 127
medical knowledge, 113, 190–91
The Memoirs of the Life of Colonel Hutchinson (Hutchinson): overview, 178–79; brotherly merit, 188, 189, 190, 212–13, 303n38; disavowal of romance genre, 185–86; dream allegory, 217–18, 303n40; husbandly merit, 183, 188–89; intermarriage, 181–82, 299n15; justifiable fraud, 183–85, 186–87, 300n17; and *Order and Disorder*, 204, 205, 208, 209, 212–13; political martyrdom, 180–81, 184; property rights, 195–97, 300–301n19; republican values, 194–95, 196–97; uxoriousness *vs.* moderate love, 182–83, 192–94; wifely disobedience and preservation of life, 180, 184–85, 190–92, 300n17
men. *See* husbandly merit; husbands/men
Mentz, Steve, 76
merit: brotherly, 188, 189, 190, 212–13, 303n38; divine, 150–52, 157–58, 169, 170–71; imputed, 30–31, 43–44, 48, 232–33, 235. *See also* husbandly merit
Miller, David Lee, 279n40
Miller, Shannon, 208
Millington, Gilbert, 298n10
Milton, John: and celibacy, 5, 174; and heterodoxy, 148, 293–94n32; marriages, 136, 144–45, 291n3; political views, 138, 140–41, 150–52, 153, 155, 292n15, 294n34, 295n37; *Animadversions*, 290–91n1; *Areopagitica*, 154, 261; *Colasterion*, 136; *The Doctrine and Discipline of Divorce*, 141–42, 165; *Eikonoklastes*, 141, 182; *Epitathium Damonis*, 293n21;

Milton, John (*continued*)
  Judgment of Martin Bucer, 165; "Methought I saw my late espoused saint," 136, 144–45; "On the Death of a Fair Infant," 150, 293n31; *Paradise Regained*, 170–72, 173–74, 175–76; *The Passion*, 137; *The Ready and Easy Way*, 155; *Samson Agonistes*, 173–74, 258; *Some Reflections upon Marriage*, 165; *The Tenure of Kings and Magistrates*, 155, 294–95n37; *Tetrachordon*, 146–47, 165. See also *Paradise Lost*
mirrors/mirroring: and narcissism, 21, 33–34, 53–54, 77, 156, 276–77n17, 281n51; and two bodies theory, 45; wives as, 182–83, 197
monarchy. *See* sovereignty and kingship
monasticism, 289n45
Monck, George, 300n17
Montrose, Louis Adrian, 275n6
More, Anne, 3
mortality, 81–82, 83, 103–4, 159, 295n41
motherhood and childbirth, 19, 22–23, 30, 88–89, 125, 140, 160, 171–72, 202–3, 305n13
Mouffe, Chantal, 273n45
Muir, Edward, 76
Murphy, Erin, 185–86
Murphy, Sharon Ann, 272n32

narcissism: and chaste love, 57, 58, 159–60; and greed, 50–51; and mirrors, 21, 33–34, 53–54, 77, 156, 276–77n17, 281n51; and nationalism, 24–25; remedies for, 53–54; and reproduction, 24, 160; satanic, 156, 160; self/other dichotomy, 22–23, 34–35, 37; wounded, 21–22

Narcissus, 21–22, 33–35, 47, 50, 58, 276n14, 277n19, 296n43
natality, 72
nationalism, 15–16, 24–25, 273n39, 274n46
naturalization and immigration, 11–12, 271–72n31
Nazism, 126
necropower, 127
Ng, Su Fang, 300n18
Ngai, Sianne, 17
Nohrnberg, James, 278–79n35
Norbrook, David, 184, 197, 207, 273n39, 294n33–34, 299n11, 303n38
novel, 176, 238, 256, 298n64
Nyquist, Mary, 294n35, 294–95n37

obedience: to God, 148, 153, 155, 163, 164; to sovereign, 85–88, 111, 118; of wives, 19, 118, 180, 184–85, 300n17
objective historical reality, 63–64, 77–79, 81
Order and Disorder (Hutchinson): overview, 179–80; Christian *vs.* Jewish biblical interpretation, 216–17; frustrated desire, 201, 212, 302n31; medical knowledge, 191; and *The Memoirs of the Life of Colonel Hutchinson*, 204, 205, 208, 209, 212–13; monogamy in conflict with intergenerational demands, 208–11, 215, 303n39; mythic foundations of hereditary succession, 204–8, 212–14, 302–3n35; political ambition, 214–15; reason, love, and chastity in alliance, 211–12; reproductive rationale for marriage, 201–4, 302n33; temporality, 301n28; turtledoves as exemplars of love, 199–201
Orgel, Stephen, 92

Oroonoko (Behn): overview, 221–23; colonialism and disruption in chain of authority, 238, 243–46, 252–53; and *The Forc'd Marriage*, 247–49; fungibility and commodification, 12, 238, 243, 248, 251; generic shifts, 246–47; heroism, 242, 246, 250–51, 306n28; jealous violence, 249–50; literary mediation, 253–54; monogamy as honorable, 241–42; and *Othello*, 13, 248–49; political context and commentary, 237–39; religious *vs.* secular significance, 241, 247, 251–52; stage adaptations, 307n38

Orrey, Earl of, *The Generall*, 304n2

Othello (Shakespeare): overview, 62–64; aesthetic subjectivity, 72–74, 75; and *Daniel Deronda*, 259–60; and *The Forc'd Marriage*, 221, 224–25, 248–49; husbandly *vs.* heroic merit, 65–67, 69–70, 283n22, 288n27; and *Oroonoko*, 13, 248–49; personal *vs.* state affairs, 67–68, 69, 71, 75, 81; presentation of the sea, 73, 75, 76–77, 94; racial and religious difference, 64–65, 71–72, 80, 272n34, 281n5; Schmitt on, 79–80; sexual jealousy, 70–71, 80; skepticism, 66, 68–69

Ovid, *Metamorphoses*, 33, 35, 38, 40, 58, 277n19

Pacheco, Anita, 304n3

Paradise Lost (Milton): overview, 136–37; and *Daniel Deronda*, 261–62; divine justice, 147–49; divine succession by merit *vs.* birthright, 150–52, 157–58, 169; *felix culpa* paradox, 144, 153–54, 164; and *Frankenstein*, 257; free choice, 151–54, 155–59, 162–66, 168; friendship, 166–67; gender hierarchy, 146, 160–62, 166, 168; humanity as replacement, 149–50; narcissistic desire, 156, 159–60; necessity rhetoric, 143, 163; reconciliation of marital love, 144, 146, 167–70, 228; rejection of remarriage, 142–44; reproductive rationale for marriage, 141, 142, 169–70, 172, 201, 302n33; Spirit imagery, 200

Parker, Patricia A., 283n23

Patrides, C. A., 147

Pauline theology: inclusion *vs.* exclusion, 7–8; remarriage, 267n4; reproductive rationale for marriage, 4, 141; spiritual and sacrificial rationale for marriage, 1–2, 4–5, 70, 107–8, 123, 137, 141; unstable simile of marriage, 2, 6–7, 23, 116, 267–68n5

peculiarity, 101, 105, 132–33

Pelikan, Jaroslav, 268n12

penal (substitutionary) theory of atonement, 6, 40, 137, 147–48, 268n12

Petrarch, *Canzoniere*, 30, 33–34, 35, 36, 239–40, 276n14

Petrarchan sonnet, 28–29, 30, 32–37

Pettigrew, William, 244, 306n30

Philippe, Duke of Orleans, 131

Phillips, Edward, 291n3

Pierrepont, Henry, 300n19

Plumtre, Huntingdon, 188, 190–91, 299n11

poetry: myth of husbandly superiority, 116–18, 287–88n27; *vs.* scientific knowledge, 113–14, 120

political authority. *See* sovereignty and kingship

political theology, 14–17
Pope, Alexander, 65
Potter, Lois, 112, 286–87n11
Powell, Mary, 144, 145
praise and flattery, 119–21
Presbyterians, 193
pride, 114–16
primogeniture, 194–97, 204
property rights, 195–97, 204, 300–301n19
Pye, Christopher, 72, 82
Pye, Henry James, 75

queer studies/theory, 34–35, 172–73, 175, 267–68n5, 271n28, 275n57, 285n46, 297n62
Quint, David, 143, 146

Rabkin, Norman, 66
race: and nationalism, 15–16, 274n46; and religious difference, 64–65, 71–72, 80, 272n34, 281n5; and sexual anxieties, 80, 285n46; and stage adaptations of *Oroonoko*, 307n38. See also slavery
Racovian Catechism, 148
Raleigh, Walter, 42
Ramachandran, Ayesha, 281n51
ransom theory of atonement, 31–32, 38–40, 158–59, 278n27
Ranters, 140, 292n15
Raylor, Timothy, 287n19
reciprocity, 35–37, 59, 108, 224–25, 226, 277n17
redeemer, wife as, 54–57, 59–60, 116, 117
redemption. See atonement
religious and racial difference, 64–65, 71–72, 80, 272n34, 281n5
religious belief *vs.* scientific knowledge, 112–13, 119–21

remarriage: after death, 136, 143, 144–45, 260; after divorce, 136, 143, 144, 228–29; after forced marriage, 227–28, 229; after resurrection, 219; as economic necessity, 209
reproduction: and biopolitics, 125–26, 289n45; Christ's indifference to, 174–76; future-oriented, 144, 169–70, 172–74, 176–77; gender disparity in, 140, 203, 302n33; and narcissism, 24, 160; as rationale for marriage, 4, 141–42, 169–70, 172, 201–4; and surrogacy, 60. See also hereditary succession
republicanism, 69, 138, 150–52, 153, 155, 194–95, 196–97, 294n33–34
resurrection, 89, 104, 131–32, 145, 219, 230–32, 234
revenge. See vengeance
righteousness, imputed, 31, 43–44, 48
Robinson, Benedict, 66
Rogers, John, 292n16
Roman Catholicism, 61, 100, 132, 136, 155, 205, 239–41, 284n39, 286n5, 295n39, 299n15
romance (genre): comic subversions, 104–5, 110; dilations, 246–47; *vs.* epic, 246; Hobbes's rejection of, 110–11; precedent, 8–9; royalist, 185–86, 242
Royal Society, 121
Rumrich, John, 293–94n32

sacrifice: political martyrdom, 180–81; rationale for marriage, 1–2, 4–5, 70, 107–8, 123, 137, 141; of self, 48, 55–57, 59, 65, 107, 123, 167–68, 242, 250–51
same-sex marriage, 271n28
Sanchez, Melissa, 2, 267–68n5, 277n20
Santner, Eric, 16, 87

Satan, 39, 148–49, 151, 152, 156–57, 170, 171, 175, 295n39
Schmitt, Carl, 15–16, 63–64, 77–81, 273n45, 279n37, 284n39, 284n45
Schwartz, Regina, 62–63
scientific knowledge: and atheism, 190–91; *vs.* religious belief and poetry, 112–14, 119–21
sea/sea voyage, 73, 75–77, 78–79, 93–94, 243–45, 283n23
Sedgwick, Eve Kosofsky, 268n6
self-sacrifice, 48, 55–57, 59, 65, 107, 123, 167–68, 242, 250–51
sex: chaste reflections of divine love, 58; and frustrated desire, 198, 199, 201, 211–12, 302n31; and jealousy, 70–71, 80, 82–83, 92, 225; and promiscuity, 233–34; and temptation, 48, 53–54
Shakespeare, William: and Davenant, 97; *Comedy of Errors*, 283n23; *Cymbeline*, 74–75, 94, 109; *Hamlet*, 63–64, 77–79, 81, 172–73, 176; *Henry IV*, 214; *Henry V*, 214; *Much Ado about Nothing*, 109, 234, 287n13, 304n2; *Pericles*, 283n23; *Richard II*, 18–22, 86–88; *The Tempest*, 140. See also *Othello*; *The Winter's Tale*
Sharpe, Kevin, 100, 101
Shelley, Mary, *Frankenstein*, 256–58, 263, 264
Singh, Devin, 277–78n27
Sisson, Andrew, 69
skepticism, 66, 68–69
Skinner, Quentin, 287n19
slavery: and disruption in English colonial authority, 238, 243–44, 252–53; fungibility and commodification, 12, 238, 243, 248, 251, 272n32; as metaphor for marriage, 235, 248–49; natural, chattel, and political, 154, 155, 294n35, 295n37; racist myth of, 265
Smiles of a Summer Night (film), 305n13
Snider, Alvin, 304n3
Socinian theory of atonement, 148
Somerset, Anne, 300–301n19
sonnet, Petrarchan, 28–29, 30, 32–37
Southerne, Thomas, 307n38
sovereignty and kingship: authority of, challenges to, 85–89, 118–19, 223–24, 226–27; authority of, disruption in chain of, 238, 243–46, 252–53; authority of, renewed, 90–91, 94, 221, 236; and awe, 104, 118, 133–34; chaos in absence of, 252, 307n35; Christlike, 14, 18, 87–88, 104, 131–32; compatibility with Christian truth, 42, 43; economy of praise, 119–21; imperial ambitions, 127–29; involvement in personal affairs, 40–41; limited power of, 40–41, 113, 119, 127; political cohesion through marriage, 100–102, 133; political cohesion through trade and commerce, 131–35; subject-ruler relationship, 111–12; two bodies theory, 16, 18, 20–21, 45–46, 86, 87–88, 125–26. See also hereditary succession; state power
Speght, Rachel, *Muzzle for Melastomus*, 6–7
Spenser, Edmund, 97. See also *Amoretti*; *The Faerie Queene*
Spinoza, Baruch, 265
Spirit, as turtledove, 199–200
Sposalizio del Mare, 75–77
Sprat, Thomas, *History of the Royal Society*, 121

state power: and biopolitics, 124–27, 289n42, 289n45; involvement in personal affairs, 63, 67–68, 69, 71, 75, 81, 125; and Sposalizio del Mare, 75–77; teleological narrative of, 63–64, 77–79. *See also* sovereignty and kingship
Stewart, Alan, 61
Stockton, Will, 2, 267–68n5
Stone, Lawrence, 270n25
Strain, Virginia Lee, 285n48
Strier, Richard, 170–71
subject/object reversals, 35–37, 47, 59
substitutionary (penal) theory of atonement, 6, 40, 137, 147–48, 268n12
succession. *See* hereditary succession
suicide, 65, 72, 79, 146, 226, 250, 302n33
sun, woman clothed with, 240–41, 255
surrogacy, 60
Sussman, Charlotte, 306n33
Sylvester, Joshua, 200

taboo, 63, 78, 79, 80
Targoff, Ramie, 293n22
Tasso, Torquato: *Gersualemme liberata*, 53–54, 55; *Rime d'amore*, 281n51
Taubes, Jacob, 273n45
Theobald, Lewis, 65
Thurloe, James, 291n8
Todd, Janet, 220, 225, 236
trade and commerce, 131–35
tragedy, 18, 20–21, 64, 77–81, 246–47
tragicomedy, 18, 20, 89, 91, 126, 228–32, 236–37, 247
transferability of guilt, 52–53, 280n47
Trinity, 38, 156, 199, 241, 293n32
Trott, Adriel, 155, 295n38
Trump, Donald, 15, 275n59
turtledoves, 199–201, 209–10

two bodies theory, 16, 18, 20–21, 45–46, 86, 87–88, 125–26

uxoriousness, 141, 143, 169, 182, 192–94

Venetian Sposalizio del Mare, 75–77
vengeance: and desire, 59; displaced, 32, 39, 53, 71, 149, 163, 167, 183; jealous, 70–71, 108–10, 123, 234; just, 48–49, 53; unobtained, 250
violence: acceptable *vs.* unacceptable, 121–24; jealous, 71, 225, 231, 249–50. *See also* heroism
Virgil, *Aeneid*, 27, 49–50, 106, 146, 166–67, 280n46
virginity and celibacy, 45, 174, 279n38, 289n45
Virgin Mary, 30, 240
Visconsi, Elliott, 307n36
Vitkus, Daniel, 272n34

Walton, Izaak, 3, 268n7
Warner, Michael, 34–35, 275n57
Watt, Ian, 298n64
Weingarten, Karen, 125
White, Charles, 188, 298n10
White nationalism, 15–16, 125, 266, 274n46, 285n46
Whittington, Leah, 167, 168–69
will, of God, 183, 185
William III, King of England, 254
Willoughby, Francis, 243–45
Winstanley, Gerrard, 175; *The New Law of Righteousness*, 140; *A Vindication*, 140
The Winter's Tale (Shakespeare): overview, 62–64; aesthetic subjectivity, 82; and *Daniel Deronda*, 258–59, 261; and *The Forc'd Marriage*, 221, 229–30, 231, 236, 305n17; intergenerational replacement and

renewed authority, 89–92, 93–94; kingly prerogative *vs.* familial honor, 84–86, 88–89; legitimate reproduction concerns, 81–82; male friendship *vs.* competition, 81, 83–84, 93; presentation of the sea, 93–94; sexual jealousy, 82–83, 92; tenuous restoration of succession and marriage, 91–92, 94–96, 228

Wiseman, Susan, 303n42

wives/women: Christlike, 57, 71, 116; instrumental view of, 70–71; as mirrors, 182–83, 197; motherhood and childbirth, 19, 22–23, 30, 88–89, 125, 140, 160, 171–72, 202–3, 305n13; obedience/disobedience of, 19, 118, 180, 184–85, 300n17; as redeemer, 54–57, 59–60, 116, 117; and reproduction, gender disparity in, 140, 203, 302n33; role of royal, in hereditary succession, 18–20, 104, 131; superiority of, 146, 166, 168, 235. *See also* gender hierarchy; husbands/men

woman clothed with the sun, 240–41, 255

women. *See* wives/women

Woodcock, Katherine, 145

Woodhouse, A. S. P., 280n41

Woolf, Virginia, 223

worth. *See* merit

wrath and anger, just, 47, 49, 53

wrinkles, 95–96

Wyatt, Thomas, "Whoso list to hount," 35, 36, 40–41

Cultural Memory in the Present

Niklaus Largier, *Figures of Possibility: Aesthetic Experience, Mysticism, and the Play of the Senses*

Mihaela Mihai, *Political Memory and the Aesthetics of Care: The Art of Complicity and Resistance*

Ethan Kleinberg, *Emmanuel Levinas's Talmudic Turn: Philosophy and Jewish Thought*

Willemien Otten, *Thinking Nature and the Nature of Thinking: From Eriugena to Emerson*

Michael Rothberg, *The Implicated Subject: Beyond Victims and Perpetrators*

Hans Ruin, *Being with the Dead: Burial, Ancestral Politics, and the Roots of Historical Consciousness*

Eric Oberle, *Theodor Adorno and the Century of Negative Identity*

David Marriott, *Whither Fanon? Studies in the Blackness of Being*

Reinhart Koselleck, *Sediments of Time: On Possible Histories*, translated and edited by Sean Franzel and Stefan-Ludwig Hoffmann

Devin Singh, *Divine Currency: The Theological Power of Money in the West*

Stefanos Geroulanos, *Transparency in Postwar France: A Critical History of the Present*

Sari Nusseibeh, *The Story of Reason in Islam*

Olivia C. Harrison, *Transcolonial Maghreb: Imagining Palestine in the Era of Decolonialization*

Barbara Vinken, *Flaubert Postsecular: Modernity Crossed Out*

Aishwary Kumar, *Radical Equality: Ambedkar, Gandhi, and the Problem of Democracy*

Simona Forti, *New Demons: Rethinking Power and Evil Today*

Joseph Vogl, *The Specter of Capital*

Hans Joas, *Faith as an Option*

Michael Gubser, *The Far Reaches: Ethics, Phenomenology, and the Call for Social Renewal in Twentieth-Century Central Europe*

Françoise Davoine, *Mother Folly: A Tale*

Knox Peden, *Spinoza Contra Phenomenology: French Rationalism from Cavaillès to Deleuze*

Elizabeth A. Pritchard, *Locke's Political Theology: Public Religion and Sacred Rights*

Ankhi Mukherjee, *What Is a Classic? Postcolonial Rewriting and Invention of the Canon*
Jean-Pierre Dupuy, *The Mark of the Sacred*
Henri Atlan, *Fraud: The World of Ona'ah*
Niklas Luhmann, *Theory of Society, Volume 2*
Ilit Ferber, *Philosophy and Melancholy: Benjamin's Early Reflections on Theater and Language*
Alexandre Lefebvre, *Human Rights as a Way of Life: On Bergson's Political Philosophy*
Theodore W. Jennings, Jr., *Outlaw Justice: The Messianic Politics of Paul*
Alexander Etkind, *Warped Mourning: Stories of the Undead in the Land of the Unburied*
Denis Guénoun, *About Europe: Philosophical Hypotheses*
Maria Boletsi, *Barbarism and Its Discontents*
Sigrid Weigel, *Walter Benjamin: Images, the Creaturely, and the Holy*
Roberto Esposito, *Living Thought: The Origins and Actuality of Italian Philosophy*
Henri Atlan, *The Sparks of Randomness, Volume 2: The Atheism of Scripture*
Rüdiger Campe, *The Game of Probability: Literature and Calculation from Pascal to Kleist*
Niklas Luhmann, *A Systems Theory of Religion*
Jean-Luc Marion, *In the Self's Place: The Approach of Saint Augustine*
Rodolphe Gasché, *Georges Bataille: Phenomenology and Phantasmatology*
Niklas Luhmann, *Theory of Society, Volume 1*
Alessia Ricciardi, *After* La Dolce Vita: *A Cultural Prehistory of Berlusconi's Italy*
Daniel Innerarity, *The Future and Its Enemies: In Defense of Political Hope*
Patricia Pisters, *The Neuro-Image: A Deleuzian Film-Philosophy of Digital Screen Culture*
François-David Sebbah, *Testing the Limit: Derrida, Henry, Levinas, and the Phenomenological Tradition*
Erik Peterson, *Theological Tractates*, edited by Michael J. Hollerich
Feisal G. Mohamed, *Milton and the Post-Secular Present: Ethics, Politics, Terrorism*
Pierre Hadot, *The Present Alone Is Our Happiness, Second Edition: Conversations with Jeannie Carlier and Arnold I. Davidson*
Yasco Horsman, *Theaters of Justice: Judging, Staging, and Working Through in Arendt, Brecht, and Delbo*
Jacques Derrida, *Parages*, edited by John P. Leavey
Henri Atlan, *The Sparks of Randomness, Volume 1: Spermatic Knowledge*
Rebecca Comay, *Mourning Sickness: Hegel and the French Revolution*
Djelal Kadir, *Memos from the Besieged City: Lifelines for Cultural Sustainability*

The authorized representative in the EU for product safety and compliance is:
Mare Nostrum Group
B.V Doelen 72
4831 GR Breda
The Netherlands

www.ingramcontent.com/pod-product-compliance
Lightning Source LLC
Chambersburg PA
CBHW032055230426
43662CB00035B/423